Well…How Did I Get Here?

(Survival Tales of Growing Up Black, Queer and Finding Recovery)

By Juan T Salter

Author Name: Juan T Salter

ISBN: 9798890750730

Dedication

I dedicate this to; Corene Virginia, Ida Louise, Mary Elizabeth, Deborah Kaye and Lurishia Shibre: the women who nurtured all that I am and passed before me.

Contents

Dedication 5

Acknowledgments 9

Introduction 11

Kool (1981) 14

SupercalaFragilistic (1981) 17

Loss, Lost (1981) 23

A Virgin's Valentine (1982) 26

Born Again (1982) 28

A Word; For Nothing Left to Lose (1982) 37

Queeny (1983) 48

Burning Bridges (1984) 54

"Owner of a Lonely Heart/ What's Love Got to Do with It" 58

28 Days (1984) 66

Just Say No (1984) 71

Cream Filled, Bear Clawed (1984) 77

Seasoned (1985) 82

Suckers and Lollipops (1985) 87

Blasted (1986) 92

Loose Ends (1987) 100

Red, Delicious (1987) 106

Place Like Home (1987) 113

Not Good, Bad and Ugly (1988) 117

The Breath Taken in Between (1989) 123

Have Pipe, Will Travel (1989) 128

Fountainology (1989) 131

Rock-N-Roll (1989) 142

Billy Wayne (1991) 149

C-Notes: Calling the Kettle Black (1991) 158

Streets of San Francisco (1991) 168

Behind the Golden Gates (1991) 172

"Bruno" (1991) 179

Right-N- Wrong (1992) 187

Sleeping Dogs Lie (1992) 193

Olive- Branches (1992) 201

The Gig Was Up (1994) 209

Hollyweird (1994) 216

Silly freak Tweek'n for Kids (1994) 225

When Stars Fall (1994) 233

Up...Must Come Down (1995) 257

Fall Down Seven times, Stand up Eight (1995) 262

July 8, 96: Forward 266

They Like Me! Really Like Me! (1997) 269

2K (1999) 276

Erotic Neurotic (2001) 287

911/ It's Not the End (2001) 294

About the Author 299

Acknowledgments

Eddie Coleman of Excel Publishing, Olive Burke Giovanetti for always encouragement, My sponsors, Chistopher, Chad, Tony and Shannon. Loved friends and family

Introduction

Why this book, memoir? I'll tell you. The writing of and finishing these tales is in essence my 'baby'. Particularly, since I'm queer and didn't have children. I simply could not rest or go to my rest, so to speak, until this was accomplished.

Years ago, when I first saw the documentary film "Tongues Untied", I had the sense, knowing then, there was scant if any evidence of stories about Black queer men, told from their own viewpoint. I wanted to someday make that fact untrue. Here is my attempt to add to that cannon.

Most of my life as an adult I carried a desire that I needed to document, somewhere, what was happening to me. All the places and people I'd found myself encountering. Much of the time I just couldn't believe what was experiencing, either for good or not. As I survived and came out the 'other side', I've yet to have a fabulous career, own a home, graduate degree. Maybe those are yet to come, but now I have this. A triumph. So, here's the adventure that happened in the life of a boy, now, man named Juan T. Salter.

First off it was the 70's. I mean this is when I first have memories of something going on. The first news story I recall was a big one; Watergate. It played all over the television in the summer. Probably, I was mad that that was all that was to watch on the three channels. No cartoons, no "As the World Turns", no, nothing but boring Watergate.

Absolutely a child of television. My favorites: Sonny & Cher then, it was just Cher and "Wonder…Wo..maaan", I'm still singing the theme song. If I got to stay up late on Friday nights, I got to see the "Midnight Special", where I might get a peek at wonderfully wild and freakishly loud David Bowie as Ziggy Stardust, maybe wearing a dress, and most certainly a lot of fabulous makeup. I found myself filled with utter delight whenever the original 'Diva'; Diana Ross, appeared anywhere on the TV screen.

Hailing from the Rust Belt and of the working class, all the adults I knew of worked a job somewhere in a factory. This in the 70's before most factories shut down and moved away in the 80's, leaving behind vast sites of deteriorating plants gathering rust and no jobs.

Despite manual labor and working class backgrounds my parents had the wherewithal to realize that us kids needed a better education than the neighborhood public school could give. The bulk of my mother's brood got shipped off to a nearly all-White Lutheran elementary school. That's where my family attended church services, baptisms and the like. As a child I never recognized my family feeling uncomfortable there until hearing about it, much later.

At the tender formative age of seven my family moved into public housing; the 'Projects'. What does a kid know about it? Our actual living quarters, there, I saw as a step up from the house my mom had inherited from my grandmother. No mice, no holes in the floor, no basement that smelled like funky feet. By the time we moved to public housing such locales began to have notorious reputations. I never knew it, even when another one of the five Black students in my class at school would throw it in my face, "At least…we don't live…in the 'Projects!" She'd yell at me during a session of the 'dozens' at recess (White people and others, if you don't know what the 'dozens' is, go ask your one Black friend). I'd be like, "What!.." I had no clue that where I lived was bad. I was expecting her to say, "Yo momma fat…Black and ugly!" And then the fight was 'on'.

When I turned eleven, me, my next eldest brother and my mom moved from the hood to the suburbs. Talk about culture shock. So lost and out of place I was, that at the end of the first week after our move, it being summer right before school started, I hopped on my new Sears, 10-speed and rode it all the way back to my old neighborhood in the 'jets'. At about 10miles total, there and back, I never did that again. For the first time in my life, I attended public school. In the sixth grade, my school was Whiter, than the Lutheran parochial one I'd been at since kindergarten.

Thinking back on it, I probably carried intentions of going back to my old neighborhood to see Gary, the White boy, whose family had recently moved to projects. Sure, I'd been around plenty of White kids at school. Still, Gary was something different. In a way he was 'hood' cause he was from the hood like us. Intrigued I was. I can state, now, that that had been my first crush. My first 'feelings' for another boy. I didn't even know it, then.

As much as part of me missed my old friends, a growing, different part of myself remembered being bullied and teased. In my new neighborhood no one knew me. More importantly no one knew my past. I could kinda start all over. A new me. I dropped using my middle name. Of course, at home family wasn't having it, I was, still, Todd. Yet, from there on out, new friends and people knew of me as Juan. I experienced my first 'geographic' and I liked experiencing its magic. Even if the feeling was temporary. Kinda similar like the effects drugs would give me, much later, the feeling also temporary.

Other more important changes surfaced too. As much as I would have loved to remain an elusive impeccable boy. Nature and life had other plans. Puberty with all its raging and twisting hormones arrived on the scene with a vengeance. All roads led to having sex on the brain. I went to the movies to see, "Dressed to Kill", an R -rated movie about a transvestite slasher murderer. I stayed at the cinema through at least two showings. Stayed cause the film contained two near pornographic sex scenes with the actress Angie Dickenson. I just had to see it again. The ecstatic thrill of masturbation was the vehicle in which I discovered my homosexual; gay, inclination.

The mold that shaped me turned out a pretty queer bird, even before I actually was sexually queer. I remember times helping my sister pick out her clothes when I'd go over to visit. No sport rougher than kickball could I be enticed to play and participate. Even and the risk of being teased by other boys. I made and played with paper dolls, when my mother refused to buy me real dolls and not the GI Joe kind. See a pattern here.

One solitary effort my mom took to help mold me into a normally socialized boy. At about 10years old I was made to join an all-Black, kid's bowling league. Each Saturday I had to traipse off to the bowling alley on Lake Avenue. For nearly two whole years I attended and never made any new friends. I did what I had to do, just waiting for the break period to go to the snack area, then, till the next week. Momma wanted me to be integrated into the Black community and be 'normal'. Only, by then it was too late. I was my own person, and I knew and felt the sense of being forced to do something. "I hated it!" Oh my God, I was so elated when finally, she told me I could quit going. Turns out, that last Saturday that I bowled a 200. Nobody said, "Wow...way to go!" Nothing. So much for that forced shit. Parents do what they think they must do.

The 80's. Reagan got shot, Jheri curls were greasing up pillows everywhere and 'Funkytown' blasted out boombox radios. Life saw fit to have me doing my best, and failing, to fit my queer square peg into the round hole that was high school. At some point I really just kinda gave up. I definitely hated hanging with boys, and the girls too. Both sexes either acted ignorant and or silly. "Ain't nobody...got time fo dat!"

All that felt miniscule to the year my mother got sick and eventually died. Leaving me behind heartbroken and confused, mad at God. The tale of this twisted hopefully inspired journey begins there.

Kool (1981)

The afternoon sun always beamed through the windows during my therapy sessions on West Wayne Street. That meant, as I remember it, the sessions took place after my mother got off work to drive me there. Aunt Deborah connected my mom with this therapist. I have a foggy notion of how and why they got the idea I needed outside professional help. We, my mother and I, had already been to another family counseling center, and for whatever reason, it didn't seem to work out there. I did feel more comfortable with the one on here, more private. The therapist was a middle-aged, white woman who knitted as I talked. It seemed odd at first, but I got used to it.

Then, on one particular afternoon, "I'm gay, and there's nothing you can do about it." I forcefully stated, unsure of what to expect.

"Ok, would you like to talk about it?" She calmly responded to me while continuing to knit. There it was. I'd just exposed my most urgent fear right there in that room. That therapist was the first time, the first person to whom I had said who I was, out loud. No one in my family, not even my mother, knew about me. That's what I thought at the time.

Summer passed by. Fall of that year, I would be a sophomore. I became close friends with a girl I'd met from school who lived two streets away from our apartment complex. The one out in the suburbs, where I lived with my mother and next oldest brother. Cathy, a diminutive White girl, a year older than me, with frizzy blond hair. We bonded, sharing the poetry we wrote. She and her brothers sometimes took advantage of using the pool at my apartment complex.

Cathy probably was the next person whom I told I was gay. She took it in stride, often times teasing me, but in good fun, it seemed.

During the previous freshman year, I became infatuated with my biology lab partner, Mark Shyder. He was tall, lean, white, and dark blond with glasses, unassumingly quiet. Cathy knew of my longings and would teasingly egg me on. She thought it was so cute, my first crush on a guy.

Glenbrook Square Mall on the north side proved a good place to spy out attractive young guys, adding to the shopping experience. Getting to the mall, from where we lived, meant taking two busses with a transfer downtown. This the early '80s, the city's downtown lay declining with very few if any stores. This was also when our part of the Midwest began to evidence the title of the 'Rust Belt.'

On Saturdays, the buses only ran once an hour. On this particular Saturday that summer, with me distracted, probably scoping out guys, I'd gotten on the last bus from the mall missing the transfer to go home. No problem, I felt, Aunt Deborah lived close to downtown in the West Central. Later on, I'd come to know that that area of the town happened to be where many gays and gay-friendly folks chose to live in the city.

I felt especially close to my Aunt Deborah. We were like soul mates, both of us being the youngest sibling in our families. I could walk from the bus transfer to her apartment and call my mother to come to pick me up there.

Her apartment building was more similar to what you see in a large city like Chicago or New York. The multi-storied building of red brick looked more like a row house. As the stiff, hardwood door opened up, "Todd, I'm glad you're here. Sit down a minute," She greeted me. "I have something I want to ask you." Everything seemed normal yet, I was curious. "You want something to drink?" She prompted me.

"Yeah, you got any pop?" I shot back.

Seated and refreshed, she asked me finally. "Todd (family refers to me by my middle name), are you gay?"

Stunned, frozen, and taken aback. I waited a few seconds to take in what I'd been asked. "Ye…ye…yeah." Slowly, but surely the affirmative response passed from my lips.

"You know it's ok." She confirmed but then added. "I want you to know I have gay friends, but you need to understand that being gay can be a lonely life."

At that moment, that day, all I heard or grasped was the fact that I'd admitted to someone in my family that I was gay, a faggot, a punk, and that that family member said it was ok. Later in my life journey, what my Aunt Deborah mentioned, after that being gay was ok, would grow to haunt the reality I lived.

When my mother arrived to pick me up, nothing else was mentioned to the fact of my 'coming out' at the ripe, horny pubescent age of 15 years old.

That summer, fates worked overtime. Mom became ill, so severely she needed to be hospitalized. At first, she had passed a kidney stone. The pain of such so torturously horrible to my mother that, at the hospital, my normally emotionally macho brothers nearly threatened violence over having to witness our mother in such mortal pain. Despite our mother's pain, I would have paid money to have been witness to my brothers' display such emotions.

Up until that time in my 15 years on this earth, I'd barely ever recalled my mother having any serious health issue, let alone being in the hospital.

One afternoon, while she was still in the hospital, I wandered into my mother's empty bedroom for what specific reason I still have no clue. Her bedroom had the smaller portable television that actually had been a Christmas gift for me that got relocated to her room because my brother Craig had purchased a full-sized Sony TV to go in our shared bedroom.

Sunlight cast an orangish glow outside my mother's bedroom window. On the television that day presented the pageantry of the British royal wedding of Prince Charles and Princess Diana. As in a Disney storybook fantasy tale, the primary red of Prince Charles's uniform blazer alongside the pure white of Princess Diana's wedding gown, full of yards long trailing train, played in real-time on the screen. I watched, transfixed, the scene taking me momentarily away from my reality.

Next, I turned to stare at a pack of Kool Filter Kings cigarettes that lay in the space of a missing drawer of what had been my grandmother's, previously grand, dresser chest. The thought came as quickly as the action; I fingered the pack, pulled out a cigarette, and lit it. Different than times before sneaking a cigarette, that time I inhaled it. I drew it in past my lips, down my throat, and into my lungs. No cough, no feeling nauseous. What I did feel seemed to give me calm, less anxiety. Astonished by this bodily reaction, I slowly finished smoking the cigarette.

There was it, my first drug. My first experience of having an outside chemical seemingly soothe my inner anxiety, fear. Today, I am much more familiar with that feeling. The reality I sought escape from that day was the acknowledgment that the person I loved dearly, who loved me without conditions, was an actual mortal human being. Like all things mortal, they will die.

SupercalaFragilistic (1981)

Neither the high school nor puberty arrived on the scene with ease for me. Gender role expectations alongside my ever-changing emotions and body turned my once seemingly safe little world inside out. As if that was not more than enough to handle, add to that mix realizing that I was gay, and also my beloved momma becoming ill. Everything got heated up to boiling over, leaving me to cope with the overflow of myself and this world.

Being gay, I later read Essex Hemphill, a black gay writer, described as "the love that dares speak its name." Yet at 15, I'd never heard of him or anything such. What I had heard were the derogatory rumors about the friend of Aunt Deborah and the friend of my sister Sandra. My sister's friend happened to also organize bus excursion trips to Chicago. A taste of cosmopolitan life in the big city. I once traveled along to see the Broadway play "A Chorus Line." That I'd later recall it having a gay character, that trip, we ate dinner at a rather fancy restaurant where I tasted a quiche for the first time.

Both of those men were gay, my sister's friend being Black as well. Nothing of those men, from the way my family background judged them, reflected or inspired anything that I wanted to be, to follow, nor be known as. All indications pointed me to be anything other than punk, fag, gay!

Lacking any valid, seemingly respectable role models, I turned inward. I sought outside myself what I feared to acknowledge within me—a method of escape and a defense. One path to vent my raging hormones was via the release of masturbating. Stealing pornographic material from my older brother actually confirmed my homosexuality. Gradually, viewing straight porn, only the pictures including a male, led me to reach ejaculation. Such releases did prove detrimental, though. The more I practiced, the more I craved for more.

We lived out in the southwestern suburbs apartment complex in which I was perhaps the only Black kid my age. At school, other Black kids were bussed from neighborhoods in town. About this time, I started going to Friday night dances at the YMCA. The Y in the heart of the Black neighborhood. Still, frustration at having to fake 'getting at' girls would lead me further away from that social scene. I just wanted to dance, hear the music and be a part of it. It was at the Y that I first heard the song, "Rapper's Delight." I thought, "that DJ needs to shut the hell up!"

At school later that week, I found out that the 'rapping' was the song. I didn't attend the dances to fake being some junior womanizer. I never 'graduated' or got the notion of seeing females as 'bitches'. Moreover, the girls that were my friends started to become weirder too, acting all silly, fake, bashful. Never mind that some of them were the smartest in class, twice at intelligent as the dudes. I gave up with it all.

Soon, I became close friends with Cathy, a girl from my neighborhood; We'd seen one another around the neighborhood and on the school bus. Many times I hung out with her, her brother Chris and some other neighborhood kids, all of them White, at the Pizza King joint, within walking distance of where we lived. Cathy's mother waited tables at that restaurant, part-time. The Pac-Man video game was all the rage at that time. Some of them spent hours playing; I never got the knack, hand, and eye coordination, of video games either.

Cathy officially became the first friend I told that I was gay. Rumors of that fact surely were not a surprise. After telling her, nothing seemed to change between us. Even when she also told her brother, revealing that truth, I faced no real ostracism other than the occasional joking remark. I felt inside that I could trust her. I was right, instinctually. Desperately, I wanted the truth to get out to find someone to bond with and release that fact. Possibly, from that friendship, I trusted and confided more in my white friends. That pattern was formed in my friendships. When drowning, one grabs for the nearest lifeboat.

Before my family moved out to the suburbs, we had lived in town, in public housing; 'the projects. I remember that last summer living there, a white family moved into the same courtyard where we lived. The children in that family were mostly boys around my age. One boy, in particular, Gary, seemed to fall right into the surroundings. Looking back now, for whatever reason, whenever I would hear him playing outside in the courtyard, I wanted to go out to play too and be on his team. Probably kickball. In any other sports, I'd get embarrassed cause of my lack of skill and get picked last to play. It seemed I had forgotten all my other friends in the neighborhood. Maybe, it was because he was new, different. Now, improbable as it sounds, I think Gary may have been the first boy, male, I had a physical attraction to. Who knows, maybe it was love, infatuation? Crazy, I was only 11.

Along that same theme, in ninth-grade biology, we needed to have lab partners; I picked this tall, sandy-blond, unassuming White boy with glasses like mine. Again, I was infatuated.

Over time eventually, and I'm not so proud of this now, I locked on to that young boy, literally stalked him. Whether hormones, gay yearnings, or no role models for the direction, it all seemed to lead me to be out of control. He wasn't giving off any signs that he was gay or that he shared my yearnings.

I shared with Cathy my crush for that boy, Mark. She accepted and took my crush as just a part of who I was. Her acceptance allowed me further indulgence into fantasy.

Cathy and I wrote what we considered poetry. We'd spend hours sharing our poems over the phone or at the Pizza King. Many of my poems were dedicated to Mark.

Finally, so wound up, I made up my mind that would finally tell that boy how I really felt about him. Cathy had encouraged almost enabled my delusional yearnings by passing anonymously written love letters to him in classes she had with him.

I remember it being a Tuesday in the school library where I went to the brink. Cathy or I presented Mark with a confessional love letter signed with my name. What I was expecting, I have no clue, now or then, all pumped up on adolescent emotions.

When he obviously rejected my desires, my fantasy, my dream bubble burst. In that particular moment, like a high voltage jolt, reality knocked me back down to an innermost core of loneliness and deep depression. I had made a complete fool of myself. I felt like an unwanted, unlovable freak. Such feelings were not completely unknown to me, although; finally, I had had enough. It felt too much to bear.

After school, departing the bus that day, a feather could have dropped me. The emptiness felt unbearable. Certain emptiness always just below the surface became more evident through teenage peer pressures pushed me toward being coupled, mated. That afternoon I sought to escape feelings, the heart-wrenching wounds.

Home alone, entering my mother's bedroom reminiscent of when, in that same room, I inhaled my first cigarette. I knew of my mother having a prescription for Tylenol 3's, hydrocodone. "I'd just fall asleep... never wake up." I told myself, "nothing painful." Opening the pill bottle, it contained less than about 15 pills. I added handfuls of aspirin as an extra boost. This required patience in spite of my need to rush, never before swallowing so many pills. Slight crocodile tears fell upon my cheeks. "This is really it." Whispered, my thoughts mixed in with fear and somewhat twisted joy.

Next, sleep came.

As I turned over, I could hear the TV in the living room and the sound of my mother's movements. Coupled with an indescribable urge to scratch, I tried to lift my head. I fell back, dizzy. "Aww shit!" Came out of my mouth, simultaneously, I realized my not being dead. Were my immediate first thoughts. Desperately I uncontrollably scratched my whole body, "Fuck it!" I concluded. My grand plan was not going as I'd intended. I staggered up from the bed and out into the living room where my mom was.

Looking at me with concern noticing my incoherent state, "What's wrong!" she asked, gathering all her maternal strength to seize the situation. Somehow, I could not summon the ability to speak. I rushed back to the bedroom to hold up the empty Tylenol 3 pill bottle in my hand. "You took those pills?" She calmly questioned me, still, no words. I shook my head in confirmation. I continued uncontrolled scratching, nearly tearing open my skin. Momma gathered me up to drive me to the emergency room. Without panic, she seemed to do simply what needed to be done. On the way to the car, "Do you want to go get Deborah?" She asked to comfort me. My aunt had taken on the role of confidant since my coming out gay. Again, I was only able to move some movement to signal my agreement.

In what appeared to be a reversal of roles upon picking up my Aunt Deborah. She did panic in reaction to my near suicide attempt. I would have expected her to be the calmer and understanding one assessing the circumstance. Her voice grew shrill, asking me, "Why did you do this, Todd!" She didn't comprehend that in my state of near-death, I was without the ability to cognitively or emotionally reply to why I had taken an overdose of drugs.

Rolled in a fetal position, in the back seat, I just continued scratching at myself.

Doctors at Lutheran Hospital Emergency Room accessed that I did not need to have my stomach pumped. Instead, I was given syrup of Ipecac in order to puke out the drugs, gagging, throwing up violently, and making guttural noises as if from hell. Actions to save my life proceeded as my mother looked on nearby. In her eyes, I sensed clearly the heartache she tried and meant to conceal watching me convulse on that gurney.

Later, beyond puking my guts, wiser powers counseled my mother to have me admitted to the hospital psychiatric ward. "No! Please don't, mamma. No!" I begged, pleading not to place with the crazies. Selfishly, I ignored the torment such pleading caused my mother, now evident, her full with tears. I continued begging, almost screaming, really.

On the ward, I pouted in an effort not to reveal my true reasonings for the actions I had taken. I figured, just the same, my attitude helped play on my mother's guilt just enough so I'd get out of the ward sooner. I came around to conversing with some of the other teenagers there also. One evening later in the week, when my mother and Aunt Deborah came to visit, I made such a scene I could have been given an Oscar for the performance I put on. Clueless, I was to how such actions only proved more evidence of my needing to be in psychiatric care.

One visit became one of the most peculiar memories in my life. My brother James, who had the most macho demeanor of all my brothers, came up to the ward to see me unannounced. Taken by complete surprise, I would have expected him to be the last one to have come to see me there. What I do remember was him earnestly telling me, in a whispered but audible tone, "people say shit about you being gay?... Fuck um!.. Don't try to kill yourself!" Of all my family, I never believe I'd heard him say something like that. Especially after the way I had heard him make such derogatory remarks about other rumored gay folks. But there he was before me with tears streaming from his eyes. Was this, in his own way, him saying that my being gay was ok? For sure, the intensity of his emotions did show that he cared. Still, I was left with how to square the contradiction of his previous actions and previous comments? I fail to recall my response to my brother that evening. I must have been in somewhat of emotional shock.

I returned back home within two weeks. For the most part, things went back to the way they had been before, even at school. I did mention my attempt at suicide, so neither did anyone else. Silence as a method of coping was a family tradition, so I figured. The feelings between my mother and me grew closer. One evening while watching a TV show that showed a young couple making out, I remember she asked me how I felt about seeing such displayed. My response was that I wished I could do the same, with the same acceptability.

That November was my mother's 48th birthday. Oddly, I requested some money to go to the mall to get her a gift. At Spencer's Gifts, I came across a poster with the saying:

Where there is faith, there is love

Where there is love, there is peace

Where there is peace, there is God

Where there is God, there is no need:

Anon.

On returning home with that poster as my gift, my mother asked me to sit down because she had something to tell me. Not realizing this to be anything out of the ordinary, more recently, we had been sharing with one another, more so like as adults. What I remember more was the intent and meaning of that conversation than exactly what was said.

Mom began by informing me that she had been the initiator in getting me to come out as being gay. It had been her idea to have my Aunt Deborah be the first to ask. Believing I would be more likely to be upfront and truthful with confiding in my aunt. As well, she told me the exact day and time when she informed my dad that I was gay.

I recalled that day, too, during her hospitalization, when I had to go over to my dad's home to pick up a child support check. Hearing the information, she told me, reflecting on my memory of that day, I remembered how my father said absolutely nothing in response to what he learned about me. Nothing, either negative or positive, about learning that his son was gay. Upon hearing this, right then, I drew a proverbial thumbs down on my dad's lack of emotional support. Sure, it may have been too much to handle. Still, he was the adult.

The bombshell of the conversation that day was hearing my mother tell me of how she had felt shame over having had us six children out of wedlock. That fact shook my sense of what had been normal. A child has no sense to judge whether or not his family is out of the ordinary; you are used to what you experience. In fact, I told my mother how I saw it as a sign of strength that I had grown up with one parent. How at school, when other kids' families went through a divorce, I felt like, "Get over it! I've always had one parent, and I'm no less than." My counter-argument to society standards probably made little difference to a life-long indignity my mother had carried. I felt heartened, though, that she had chosen to share such deep concerns. Still, it puzzled me as to why then.

Later that same month, my mother had another bout of illness that required her, again, to be hospitalized. Coinciding that, we had discussed considering that my being gay, I may have easier acceptance in a larger city. My sister Sandra had since moved to Houston, Texas. We'd, momma and I had gone to visit her there for Christmas the previous year. Always desiring to seek wider horizons, I was elated with the idea of going to a big city. I carried no doubts about being away from my mother, especially since recently we'd had become so much closer.

`The Saturday before I set was to leave for Houston, my brother Craig took me up the hospital to see my mother. Looking back on it now, I can only speculate on that last time I saw, touched, my mother. Maybe, it was the whole idea that her gravely ill was just too much for me to cope with. To this day all, I seem to remember is some dreamy image of my momma clothed in white in a hospital bed.

As if steam from a pressure cooker, my world had just boiled over. I was off and away while fate would make other plans.

Loss, Lost (1981)

It was after 10 pm on that chilly December night. Even as it never snowed in Houston, it could get below freezing. Sandra and I left her apartment and headed to a payphone due to her phone being cut off. She had awakened, saying something prompted her to call back home to Indiana and check on the status of our mother, who'd been hospitalized again.

Sandra talked on the phone to Aunt Mimi. "Todd...momma died!" (family uses my middle name). She announced the grave news to me with tears beginning to form in her eyes.

"What...we're orphans!" were the first words that came out of my mouth upon first learning that my mother was dead. I wanted to cry, felt like crying. Still no real tears came. I must have been in emotional shock, stupor. This just could not be happening. No way could make the one person on the planet who loved me unconditionally, gayness, sissyness and all, be gone. "How could I be left here all alone!" Those sentiments would have described my feelings and state of mind, If I could have articulated them, then.

My nephew Stacey was waiting on us when we walked back to the apartment. He was upstairs in Sandra's bedroom waiting for news. "Graandmaaaw!" He began to cry as we told him of her dying. Sandra really sobbing now herself, consoled him. Still, there was I, eyes only moist, as they sobbed. I appeared outwardly emotionless. There. I felt numb in every sense of that term.

All that previous month had been spent whining my days away. Weather gloomy as can be. It had rained at least two days of every week I been in Houston. The whole idea of me coming there seemed to have fallen flat, having me living in a bigger city, an environment more accepting of me being gay. Sandra had failed to get me enrolled in school, albeit due to her not being my legal guardian. I did venture out on a city bus taking it all the way downtown to the central library. I'd not met one single new friend the whole time living there.

Sandra flew back to Fort Wayne the very next day. Stacey and I were to follow on a flight departing Christmas Day. My sister's boyfriend, Dean; from Inkster, was to get us off safely to the airport.

Christmas morning arrived as it would despite our gloom. Looking forlorn, Stacey carried on and moved about, unable to hide his grief. On the other hand, I kept on a certain feeling of numbness, as if everything going on really was not happening, but just somehow a very bad dream. At our layover at Chicago's O'Hare I took to writing a poem for my mother. (A poem I've since lost the original) Words spoke to how mom now had peace from the body and an inside peace within. Finally, we boarded a small propeller engine plane for the last leg flight to Fort Wayne. The chill of snow and ice outside seemed to be felt along with almost every minor turbulence. Such a precarious flight in a small flimsy airplane could have frightened one, but again, I felt numb to it all.

Back home in Indiana, all the family gathered at what had been my mother's apartment on Woodhaven Drive. Amongst the hugging and intermittent crying, I clung on to keeping to myself. All the more ironic, as the world celebrated Christmas festivities my family lived and felt deep emotional pain. My friend Cathy called to comfort me. It being a humorous joke of the family seeing this diminutive White girl as my close friend.

I desperately needed to have my hair styled at the funeral scheduled that Monday. My hair relaxer straightened and dyed to a not so mild shade of auburn. A high school girlfriend of my sister's offered to touch up my 'wig', as it were, at no charge as condolence. I recall my mother's own long-time hairdresser, Irene, insisting on styling my dead mother's hair for the funeral.

The wake on Sunday at Micheax Funeral Home, a local Black institution, gathered many a family friend I had not seen in years. The Black funeral carries legend about the dead person's character and respect. I had heard mentioned such folk legends, around many a kitchen, as a kid eavesdropping on 'grown' folks' conversations. Ida Louise Salter's character in 'this' world witnessed much respect by the multitudes of people who paid their respects at the wake. Many I had been introduced I had no clue who they were. I remember my mother's other sister; Aunt Mary Louise, having performed a loving service of greeting folks and helping to be there for our family.

All the displays of respect to my mom's lived character belied the inner shame she had carried. Shame shared in conversation with me merely a month prior.

Pent-up grief burst to surface as all my mother's children, the tribe, gathered together around the casket bearing my momma's body. Sandra, in a diagonally green striped dress I clearly remember, buckled to her knees in cathartic transcendence, letting go of the human pain of living, as we the dark-suited brothers, crying ourselves, held her aloft. My Blackness, our Blackness, stood clear if not painfully proud in that utter agony with mixed emotion.

Monday morning under a light snow and Arctic wind chills the family gathered first at my Uncle Don's home. Quiet withheld feelings permeated amongst all of us. As Steve, my middle brother, passed through the doorway Aunt Mary broke the quiet, burst into tears. I recalled, then, never having seen Aunt Mimi cry. Clearly, not all was well.

Funeral services were held in the chapel of Concordia Lutheran. The congregation where all except for my sister had attended the school, where all of my mother's tribe of illegitimate children had been baptized. Where we were members of probably 20 black families out of a couple of hundred white.

Something rose up in me on that frigid December morn. Momma laying out stiff, lifeless, in that casket meant finality to the reality I didn't want to feel. What felt like an ocean of tears let loose. My body, my feelings, no longer able to deny the fact my unconditionally loving mother was no more. Not a word of the eulogy did I hear. Pent-up grief blotted out everything else. Outside of crying, I can barely recall being there. I cried loud tears, caring not who or if anybody heard me. That was my mom we were all there for!

Riding in the back of a big Cadillac limo holding on tight to my Aunt Mimi, tears continued rolling. My 6' 2", 165-pound Black maleness be damned. I cared less. Not until after the closed casket at Lindenwood Cemetery and the repast at Uncle Don's did my surface emotions calm. Though inside, numbness remained; even grew comfortable. Part of my own soul lowered into that frozen Indiana soil. What was left wobbled above, on shaky ground.

A Virgin's Valentine (1982)

I found out about and went out to a Valentine's party and dance on a school night held at the gay men's shelter. Eager and excited to have the possible opportunity to meet someone to finally explore what was sex. What was 'real sex' like for gays? I'd grown accustomed to sex with a man only recently, outside of my masturbatory fantasies.

The crowd there was mostly white, same as most who lived at the shelter. Basically, the shelter was a house that a gay minister had opened for other gay men who had been kicked out and rejected by their families. The gay 'community' as it was all mixed together; black, white, rich, poor, educated and trash. One of the guys knew and sometimes hung out with was the son of the president of Lincoln National Life Insurance, the company that basically ran the city. Others I'd come to know probably it would've been better not to have met.

At the party, I flirted all night long with this one cute guy, Jerry. In attendance were some other e Black gays closer to my age I'd never seen before. One of them I found attractive, a cute small, cocoa butter colored hottie. We both were curious. I later discovered through the grapevine that that guy, Jeffery, had been locked up. Somehow, I could not jive the fact that he could have been in prison. Probably, it was juvenile detention. Even as cute as he was, such reputation struck me as too dangerous and not what I wanted to be involved with.

I ended up exchanging phone numbers with Jerry. Talking to him that night, he told me about other guys he knew to be gay at my school. I did my best to turn our conversation sexual, anything in order to get into his pants. Nothing ever materialized that evening but me and my hand, later.

That particular spring there was a freezing rain storm one morning. School got cancelled. Still sexually frustrated, I got it into my head to go out and walk over to Jerry's house that same day. We had since been talking somewhat over the phone. His house located not far from where I lived, yet it was 'on the other side of the tracks' in all senses of that term. He lived where I had heard 'grown folks' call the 'po White' side of town when I was growing up. Undaunted, determined, horny, I slipped and slid my way toward his address. I would have done about anything for a piece of ass.

All to no luck, he wasn't home. I can remember the person who answered the door giving me that look that said, "Who the fuck is this nigger? and a sissy one at that." Nonetheless, young and horny, nothing could stop me.

Later that day, guess who knocks on the door at my house, but Jerry? I let him in, my aunt not being home; we sat down on the couch in the living room as he tried to play coy. Soon began kissing and making out, my insides racing, with an erection so hard it hurt. Off to the bedroom, we went next. Jerry insisted on wanting to fuck me. Willing and eager, I tried to please. It felt as if I was being ripped apart, along with the fact that I didn't know what the hell I was supposed to be doing. We fumbled through. I don't remember whether I had an orgasm and got off. More significant to me was that I was no longer a virgin.

He later denied to friends having sex with me that freezing rainy afternoon. I come to figure, the clash of us being from the wrong side of the tracks. That White boy could not admit that he had fucked somebody who was Black. So it was.

Born Again (1982)

Similar to how a caterpillar spins a cocoon changing into a butterfly. Less than a year after my mother's death, my life transformed beyond anything I had ever imagined into the beginnings of a journey beyond any I could have conceived. I felt confident of my purpose alongside a willingness to try whatever was needed to reach my yet unnamed goal.

Nightmares crowded my sleep many a night. Those nights I'd awaken exhausted, terrified of the places my mind had journeyed to in unconsciousness. Always it was the same dream, the same theme, familiar characters. My mother was still alive in all those dreams that turned into nightmares upon my awakening to actual reality. My eyes would open, me nearly screaming with tears rolling down my cheeks. The dreams were so real, there really were no words to describe the emotional pain that greeted me when the dreams ended, jolting me into real-time. I'd awaken so emotionally exhausted my body ached.

I remember Aunt Debra just holding me close in her arms on one of those mornings. No explanation needed or necessary for my pain. All the family harbored grief. As a mama's boy I may have been grieving more deeply. I disbelieved reality. How could my friend, confidant, and protector be gone and leave me still here. My aunt had also lost her mother, my grandmother, when she had only been 17 herself. She in particular surely could have understood my unspoken, inner pain. Intuitively, that led to the decision to ask to live with her after my mother's funeral.

I began a fight or flight reaction in responding to my reality and the emotions that haunted me. I began keeping to staying out late hours on school nights. Becoming even more, less interested in school altogether. Meeting other gay friends around my age led up to losing my virginity. All such added spark to life. *Grieving, what grief?* I was spinning out of control; an emotional outburst, upheaval, was sure to come.

$200 turned out to be my portion of my mother's life insurance policy (after other bills were paid, which I was not told about). I was all about the clothes, such as being a typical gay teenager. My aunt felt I deserved consequences per my recent behaviors on that sunny spring afternoon. "Todd… I'm not gonna give this money now! She told me in holding back giving me' my' money. I was having none of it. I threatened to upturn the whole apartment in a foolish teenage rage until I found where the money was hidden. Fearing the threat of physical harm, cause in that moment, out of my mind, I was probably capable of causing harm. Saying nothing of the emotional harm I was inflicting to our relationship, the one whom agreed to take me in, simply upon my asking. She relented over the money along with telling me I could no longer live there. So be it I huffed.

Where was I to live? In the moment I didn't care. Meeting up with one of my recent gay friends, we took off to the mall. In 82', $200 brought a lot of outfits. If anything, I was gonna be the most fashionable queer/queen teen. I do particularly recall being well waited on by sales staff that day.

On the return to 1102 Rockhill Street, Apartment C, with my gay friend Kriss gone elsewhere, walking up the steps, I recognized my brother's chocolate brown Buick 225 parked out front. He and I the only siblings still residing at home at the time of my mother's death. Approaching the door hearing voices, I assumed he and my aunt had been discussing the terms of my circumstance while I'd been out spending the last financial remaining of my mother.

As I turned my key to enter, Craig met and stopped me on the front porch of the apartment building. With a stern, earnest face, he looked me in the eye and said emphatically, "I know that you're gay. That's up to you." What he stated what was, by now, a known fact. "I'm not!" he went on. "If you keep your things in your room," guessing meaning my 'gay' things. "I'm ok with you coming to live with me."

"All right…," was my dazed but humble response. Every now and then I 'could' come around to compromise. What other real options did I have considering the consequences of my actions I'd taken that day? Maybe, I could have gone to the gay shelter. My friend Chris had been living there since his fundamentalist Christian family had thrown him out for his 'gay' ways. I sensed my brother had thrown me a metaphorical lifeline. I grabbed ahold.

Within the previous 6 months, I lived in 4 different households: my mom's, my sister's, my aunt's, and now my next oldest brother's. In some sense, by trial and much error, I'd auditioned roles for a replacement parent. Inside, often, I still felt left out and orphaned.

The agreement between Craig and I; a somewhat acknowledgment of my gayness, provided me an outlet to continue, even expand, my exploration of what being gay was going to be. That meant me taking in more of the scene to be found hanging out late into the night. As long as I attended school, my brother in the role as my parent/ guardian, let me do pretty much as I pleased. Perhaps, he felt he didn't need or even want to know the details of what I did or whom I was doing it with while I was away from the house. How was he to know or have the wherewithal to guide a heathy path for a gay teenager in his defense. He is only 6 years older and has not been an academic star during his high school years.

Too young to enter the one gay bar. But, I got 'sneak in' privileges to the adult bookstore located next door, providing me an outlet for sexual release, either by myself or my growing range of sexual experiences with the same sex. Most the gay guys were older by at least 5 or more years. Still, I did meet a few other gay teenagers. Many of them also in various stages of being 'out' at the schools they attended.

Hanging down around Pearl Street neat the bar and bookstore signaled a freedom as gay youth we did not have much of anywhere else, so it seemed. In the daylight, we had to return back to our assigned roles in the hetero world. I'd mostly given up caring how other people felt about my being gay, a faggot, or whatever term they'd chosen to call me.

The only human opinion that mattered about me being gay, had been my mom. She left 'this' world accepting me just as I was. So, to me, no one else had a 'right' to an opinion about whom or what I was. *"Did they bring me into this world? Well then, fuck'um!"* I bluntly reasoned.

Going out nights put me among a motley assortment of characters. A year older than I, Kriss lived at the men's shelter while he tried to finish high school. Kriss only attracted to Black men, me notwithstanding. Rebelling against his family background, he appeared as the most outrageous, loudest person I knew. I come off as modest in contrast to him. There was also Gino (Gene)Black, tan-skinned, short and a body built to the point where he could pass as straight to most folks. One time, Gino showed up at my brother's house to meet me and proceeded to smoke a joint along with me and my brother Craig. Nothing ever was said, although my brother had to wonder if Gino was actually gay. Tony Platter (using his real name in memorial), a skinny White kid who attended the same high school as me and lived just a block away from my aunt's place, in his own 'apartment', in his parent's basement. Then there was Michael, tall with bleached hair hailing from the 'hillbilly' part of town, as did also Jerry, to whom I lost my virginity.

Gino was close buddies with Mark, who had lived for some time in Los Angeles. Mark's was 'hillbilly' extraction too despite him carrying heirs as if Fort Wayne and its gay scene in particular being so passé. Often, I encountered him as a staggering, slurring drunk.

I received news that my Aunt Mary, in Michigan, was going out to visit my cousin Rhoda. Who had moved and now lived in LA. More important, there happened to be an extra ticket and she wanted to inquire if I wanted to go along? *"Like Duh! You have to ask?"* Hearing various tales of gay life in Los Angeles from Mark I grew so excited I hardly contain myself. It seemed I literally breathed going to Los Angeles that summer.

Ricky, a senior at my high school, also Black, but in the closet in and around school. Ricky was not so much 'in the closet' at school. Most everyone knew him to be gay or suspected at much, but as long as he never outwardly acknowledged it, he seemed to get a pass and less teased and ridiculed. At school, we never saw much of one another, he felt I was too obviously gay. If only closeted folks knew what people actually said behind their backs. We hung out exclusively under the dark shadows of the Pearl Street strip.

I mention Ricky because he ended up bedding(fucking) a guy who, I thought, I was dating; Michael, a slim, handsome guy from out in the county. Just so I happened to find out this betrayal, knife in the back, on the very night of our city's Block Party for gay pride, a big deal in itself our little gay world. The big 'event' of the year, and I had a date. We arrived, me with my chest puffed out, in my finest threads, for sure. After some time, I noticed Michael seemed to have disappeared. Next thing, I recall along with everyone else, especially folks that saw me arriving arm in arm with Michael, view him driving off in the passengers' seat of Ricky's green Nova. Feeling humiliated, my breath was proverbially taken away. Not sure whom I was supposed to be madder at, Ricky or Michael. I felt as if I wanted to hang my head. More likely, I ended up taking a stronger toke on the nearest, hidden, but offered joint of weed or gulped down a Budweiser, it was illegal for me to have anyway.

The very next day scheduled off on the trip to California. New adventures beyond 'that' small gay world, I consoled myself, off beyond the hurt I had just experienced in that same community. To my good fortune were to touchdown in LA the last weeks of June, the historical anniversary of the Stonewall Riots, which became the beginning of Gay Rights, when celebrations took place. I studied up on such facts and information about the gay areas in LA.

The first leg of the vacation journey traveled me, via the Greyhound bus, on through to Toledo, Ohio and Detroit and finally on to Flint, Michigan where my cousins lived. I traveled the same exact same route before with my mother going on earlier visits to my cousins. It was the first time I'd been on a bus all by myself. In the not too distant future, travelling on a bus, alone, sort of become part of a way of life. In those moments, all I cared about was adventuring out in the world. What a change life had now brought.

Aunt Mimi assigned her ex-husband, my Uncle Bobby, to be my travel chaperone to look out for me when I arrived at the big, possibly dangerous, bus terminal in Detroit.

I carried a seemingly vague to no remembrance of my uncle. Yet, he, or the reputation of him, I'd heard to be this outsized, dangerous legend that my aunt had married right out of high school and moved away to the big city of 'De'troit' (Ebonic pronunciation), way back in the 50's. They had since been divorced most of my life, due to his being a wife batterer, a probable side-effect of his possible post-traumatic stress, Korean War affliction, back long before PTSD was acceptably diagnosed.

Departing the bus, slowly I entered the large waiting area, scanning the place with my eyes, I see him there sitting next to my Cousin Damion, his son. There he, a small man somewhat shriveled with age, looking nothing like the infamous, bad-assed nigga, legend I'd heard so many tales about. That day was actually the first time we'd ever met and spoken to one another, nothing of anything which I remember. I had been anxious. Anxious about the fact of me not being the most masculine of relatives. Inside myself, I felt ready for confrontation. This man needed to answer, I felt, for beating the shit out of my beloved aunt. Yet, what was right there before my very eyes, in the flesh, sat this little old dude. My uncle's outward appearance seemed to outwardly reflect what could have been a description of my insides: a battle-weary survivor. Empathy came over me despite what I had known to have taken place, by his hands and his rage. The dynamic duo of Unk and Damian spared me facing any big city demons, them notwithstanding. I safely made it to my aunt in Flint.

Days later had me seated in the 747, TWA jet, still disbelieving really the fact that I actually was headed to California, to Hollywood, the West Coast. A genuine small city kid raised on television going to the place where the fantasies beamed out of that box in my living room took shape. Carried alongside my 'secret' knowledge of LA's gay life and the sense of freedom that I imagined entailed there.

I remained unimpressed on those first few days in LA. Cousin Rhoda exceeded my expectations, fascinated was I by her having gone to college then on to pursue her dreams out in the wider world, particularly outside of the Midwest. At the time, I didn't register that I had already had another cousin who had moved out to California years before. My not remembering being a flaw that ruled out positive recognition of any of my male relatives, besides, his move had happened when I was younger and less aware. That relative had crossed family boundaries more similar to the taboos I would cross; he married outside of the color line, yet memories of his pioneering spirit I'd left out.

As a family we took in the usual tourist itinerary; movie studios, Chinatown, Farmers Market, Hollywood Boulevard. We were in a taping audience of the Family Feud game show (the Richard Dawson version, not Steve Harvey).

On the evening of dinner in Chinatown, the entourage: Aunt Mary, Cousin Gloria, her son's and Rhoda's ex-husband, Terry and myself left the restaurant, fortune cookies and all, to pursue a route out to the beach, via Santa Monica Boulevard. Traveling along the path of that thoroughfare, Terry made sure to point out the male prostitutes, posed, plying their wares as our fully-loaded car passed by. I in that moment, felt as if I needed to be as nonchalant as possible, staring through the glass of our car window. Quietly inside suffering. 'Freaks'! I remembered hearing someone in the car describe them. I knew of them as like myself, 'my' people.

Reaching the evening's final destination, the beach, I took off my shoes and strove rigidly through the sand in bare feet. I entered the warm foaming waves, the dark star-speckled sky overhead. "It smells like fish!" I blurted out, simultaneously realizing how stupid I sounded. My words, just my senses actually conveying the total surprise of someone who had never been to the ocean. I had only seen images of the ocean through pictures, in the movies and television, none of which, as of yet, can convey smell.

Terry planned us a trip to the renowned San Diego Zoo, including an excursion across the Mexican border to Tijuana. I thought of all the traveling and experiences in different places more in such a short period than I'd ever before in my life.

San Diego, as I remember it then fit as the perfect place. Perfect weather. Mountainous geography alongside with beautiful bayside parks and of course, the ocean. The city looked similar relation to LA only much greener, less crowded, feeling less rushed. I'd only discover, much later, how generally conservative the city was. The zoo should have been enough to have worn anyone out yet, still, we had Tijuana within in our sights and intentions.

I have never been to another country I don't really know what I had expected. Taking in what I was seeing the desperate surroundings filled me with anxiety and tension. Passing along a rundown street this Mexican man walked up to our group and began propositioning Terry. He pointed to a big-eyed little girl through broken English and hand gestures, what we assumed to be his daughter. He asked if Terry wanted to buy his young daughter. Terry motioned and pointed to his own daughter, two-year-old Tierney, in somewhat horror and disbelief. Signaling, the intention, that he already had one. Among such out and out destitution and poverty shocked my sense of what was right in my own little world. Whatever else there was left to see and explore in TJ, I knew I was more than ready to leave?

Later as the bright Baja sun was setting lined up at the border, idling in our car, the wait to enter back into the United States took over and hour or more. Dread filled within me as I observed the bewildering sights taking place, surrounding the waiting vehicles. Poor, desperate people and begging children weaved in and out and between the cars amongst the blazing heat and exhaust fumes. Some of them sold cheap by American standards, handmade wares. My Aunt Mary (Mimi) gestured and engaged this little Mexican woman selling a rug for $10. Mimi leaned out the car window in effort to haggle over the price of the rug. Seemingly appalled, I'd had all I could take and exploded, "Give her the money, Mimi!" Cousin Gloria chimed in, as well, on my aunt's appearance of ethical lapse. I loved my aunt but," really, what was a lousy $10 to her?" For what must have been the first time in my young life I felt grateful to be an American, grateful for the ability to get back on the other side of that border.

Cruising along Interstate 5, in destination heading back to my cousin's in LA, the radio played the tune "Designer Music", by Lipps Inc of "Funkytown" fame. At the time it was the baddest, hippest song I'd ever heard. The funky, post-disco sound with the crazy camp of new wave symbolized the theme of my free, open-eyed wonder at being young gay and out in California. I, amazed that such music actually was being played on the radio.

After that first week I was set to make my bold move. I borrowed Terry's bike to go riding around to go up to Santa Monica Boulevard and West Hollywood. My cousin's house was less than just a mile or two from where I had been told to find the gay district. Once I'd rode up to Santa Monica Boulevard, I turned and headed west, after which I locked up the bike. Walking, I saw what appeared to me a few recognizably gay folks. The further I went the more gay people happened to appear as the sidewalks became more crowded. Finally, I came upon the Pacific Design Center, the site of Gay Pride Festival. Surely my eyeballs must have been about to pop out of my horny little head. In front of me stood all these boys, guys, and men, all of them appeared to be gay. For sure, there were lesbians too, just that my eyes skipped right over that aspect of the scenery. 'Man, o man', literally, all such colors, shapes, sizes and flavors. In LA's contained substantial Latino population as well as Asian, mixed racial Black and White and everything in between. Before then, I could have never imagined such sights, but it was all right there, in real time.

I paid the fee to enter the festival area. Gravitating toward the dance tent, surely, I must've bumped into folks, my eyeballs locked in on each wondrous beautiful male creature. Soon, I found myself standing near a dark-skinned Black guy about near my age; he dressed to the nines with his hair slicked back. We introduced one another, maybe I think even danced together. He soon after introduced me to his brother. Donnie, fixed in my memory, a tall, lean, medium-skinned Black brother with bright green eyes and short reddish fro. They told me that they were of Cuban descent, the first Cuban people I'd ever met. Alongside, it just blew me away that Cubans were Black. I never knew. Certainly, I could have never imagined such Black people back home in Indiana. My body, my senses, seemed about ready to burst. Handsome, gorgeous males all around me, eager and willing. I'd died and gone to heaven. If this was all real, I had to have more!

Right before sunset, I arrived back to my cousin's home. I remember the family barbequing that evening. I knew I had to tell my cousin Rhoda, at least, where I had been all that day, assuming somehow, she, with her education and living in California, would likely be the most receptive and accepting. Sitting alone with her in the kitchen as she prepared a dish, I blurted out, "Well, I found something to do today."

"Yeah, what?" she inquired, curious.

"I rode up to West Hollywood...and the Gay Pride Festival." I said with no special emphasis. As if it was no big deal that I was confirming the suspicions about me being gay, also, that I meant to pursue, here in LA, whatever being gay meant. Rhoda registered a slight double-take trying her best to be unsurprised.

"Well, I'm glad you found 'something' to do.' That moment there in the kitchen summed it up, I was out to the whole family, and at least, from my cousin's response, nothing seemed to be amiss.

Leading up to the vacation, I did a cram course in reading up all I could get my hands on about gay life in LA. Back then, the one national gay news magazine was the Advocate. I borrowed someone's Damron Gay Guide; the best nationwide info on gay bars and clubs but, most of all, the cruisy areas and gay bookstores.

I can recall reading something that took my notice, it had to do with a certain illness. It was called, at that time, 'gay cancer'. Gay men, particularly those in the large cities, reported becoming sick with unexplained ailments and rare diseases. The only definite link among all those becoming ill was that they were gay men. Even at 16 years of age, average intelligence told me such a diagnosis made no sense. Cancer was biological, while homosexuality was something psychological. What occurred to me reading that knowledge, even then, was the idea that being gay could be dangerous to my health, even to my life. Still, something didn't fit, didn't add up. As with most gay folks in that era we couldn't connect the dots of what actually was going on.

Somewhere, somehow meeting folks among all the festivities of gay pride I found out about a gay dance club for underage folks like me, it didn't serve alcohol. The Odyssey was a 'juice bar' where they played the new wave type music like I had heard on the radio coming back on the trip to Tijuana. I asked Rhoda go with me to the Odyssey. She if not reluctantly, agreed to take me.

That night we both dressed all decked out to the club. Rhoda seemed a little taken aback that the crowd being mostly White. Having gotten somewhat used to the 'gay' world, the crowd's complexion didn't surprise me. When we got up to dance, she muddled her way through on the dance floor. More than likely, the music was not to her taste either.

Anyway, looking back on it my cousin attempted to do her best to help me feel accepted and not a freak, even as I still felt that way inside.

California, LA, turned me out. I'd seen and been to the Promised Land, and there was no turning back. Even my humiliation at my first effort at dating faded from the memory banks.

Back home friends on Pearl Street just didn't get 'it'. I consoled myself, "they had no idea" of the sights I'd experienced. Looking back on it, neither had I really.

A Word; For Nothing Left to Lose (1982)

We settled into a rhythm with my brother as guardian while I lived life as an adolescent, gay and otherwise. School grades were average, leaving out algebra, of course. Always included the nightly excursions to hang out downtown. Drinking alcohol, smoking weed, and screwing at any chance I got. Yes, the cork on any sexual chastity had completely been popped. I'd unwrapped the seal on my body, my inhibitions, and my judgment. I indulged. The beginnings of existence; no holds barred.

Witnessing weed smoked in my presence at home, not much fazing me, never much to my liking, though. The circle of folks I started gravitating toward as friends smoked. I desired to be a part and included, so I snuck a little from my brother's stash. I could show up and hang with folks as like I had been smoking the stuff all along.

With sex, all bets were off. Too much seemed never enough. Add to the mix I being 'new meat,' fresh kid on the block. Like a kid in a candy store, I ate enough to get a toothache. What more could a young, hormone-horny teenager ask for? All flesh, no substance. Little did I know how unquenched I'd become.

California that summer opened me and my eyes to a life I could envision myself living. A life I could not have imagined before when I believed that my being gay was a curse. A life that was not worth living. Now, I came to believe that whatever had saved me from dying (through a suicide attempt) must have meant for me to live in order to see that maybe I was not a freak and I did have a purpose for being. Maybe, I just needed to suffer through till I could escape my silent, if not close-minded, siblings along with the backward environs of Fort Wayne, Indiana.

We now lived in the converted first-floor apartment of a house that the landlord kept her beauty shop in the front part. I had my own bedroom and needed to do chores. I requested the responsibility of doing laundry. A gay queen had to be in charge of my threads; such could not be left to just anyone. Mopping and vacuuming are my duty as well.

Vacuuming one lazy afternoon in August, I went to move the sectional couch, the rust-patterned one my mother had originally purchased. Looking down, I spotted a blue plastic bank deposit pouch. Ever curious, I unzipped it to find somewhere around $500 in cash. I knew of my brother to be the treasurer of the social club he formed with some of his buddies.

With no explanation, even to this day, the idea flashed to my mind almost instantly, similarly, like that day when Aunt Deborah refused to hand over the money from my share of my mother's death policy. Nearly panting, transfixed, I possessed a single-minded thought process. A blinded insight, if you will. "I could buy a ticket and go back to LA." I clearly heard a voice tell me.

Unbelievably, within less than a half-hour after discovering that bank pouch, I'd packed a bag of clothes, called to check Greyhound's price of a one-way ticket to Los Angeles, and called for a cab to drive me to the bus station.

That was all it took. I was on my way back to LA. True, in doing this, I would be an underage runaway. Did I have an exact destination? No. Could I be heading for danger? Very possibly. When abandoning all care, there is a certain, if somewhat foolish, freedom. I had no real parent, really. So, I assumed, "Why couldn't I just take off?"

Selfishly, I probably figured since my brother received my Social Security survivor's benefits, I rationalized; I was just taking in effect my own money anyway.

Waiting nervously at the Greyhound bus station, now just a converted gas station, for a bus first bound for Indianapolis. I looked around at other waiting passengers, and to my complete surprise, I spotted my father among the small assemblage. Rather cunningly, looking back on it, I walked over and made small talk, learning he was there to see off my stepmother going on another bus.

My father; basically, I knew who he was and where he was. He and my mother never married; in fact, he was already married when they got together and ended up birthing three sons. Complicated ain't the half of it. Really, I only saw my father on weekends. And as I remember it, almost every visit, he could be found drunk or well within in the process of becoming so. It is his 'right,' a working man, "he went to work each day," paid his bills. Child support is never late.

Physically maturing and starting to act as what my mother would say, "as if I could smell myself," she'd threaten to call my dad when my behavior had gone too far. Probably necessary but deeply resented by me. "A little late for him to get involved. How did he, now, have a right?" I'd mumble in anger under my breath.

But right there, that day, at that moment, I had to come up with some excuse, a lie to continue on in my escape. Clearly, I recall telling him that I was going to see an aunt in Indianapolis. He not knowing whether or not I had any relatives in that city spoke volumes to how much we were involved in each other's lives. Anyway, my lie, it worked.

Note: My first instance of applying survival skills. Doing what I needed to do to get what I wanted.

Not until that bus reached Indianapolis did the reality sink in that I really was off to LA, own my own and on my own terms. I was free! Psychically unbound and making it on to the next bus, I headed for Saint Louis. I popped in a cassette into my Walkman. The song was "Waiting for Tomorrow all of My Life" by the band "The The." lyrically that tune fit exactly my feelings right at that moment; it was tomorrow, riding off on that bus with not a care in the world as my 'new wave' soundtrack set the scene:

"All my childhood dreams are bursting at the seams

and dangling around my knees.

I've been deformed my emotional scars

and the cancer of love has eaten out my heart.

I've been stripped bare, and nobody cares

and all the people I've looked up to are no longer there.

All my desires have been denied to put me in this state of mind

another year older, and what have I done

my aspirations have shriveled in the sun.

Crippled by guild

blinded by science

I've been waiting for tomorrow all of my life."

- Song lyrics from "The The"

Shortly before midnight, our bus made the approach, on interstate70/55, to St. Louis. The sleek design of Eero Saarinen's Gateway Arch shimmered in the night up ahead. Down below the roadway, the mighty Mississippi River came into view gleamingly reflecting the night lights. Having heard so much about that storied body of water, now, I was actually there above it. The adventure real, no books, no movies, except me living it. In retrospect, I worked more on my survival skills, a young, naïve kid all alone in a big city bus station at night. Game face on; I kept to myself all the while appearing to know what the hell I was doing.

Early the next morning, I boarded another bus, destination reading: Albuquerque. Waking up on and off, a landscape of gentle hills and rocky outcrops appeared outside my bus window. I'd never known southern central Missouri had hills. How would I have known? In fact, Interstate 44 going out of St. Louis traverses' part of the Ozarks. All places I'd only seen on maps. Recollections of the next day took in Tulsa and Oklahoma City. Remembered most for the red dirt and dust. There I was traveling on the route of U.S. 66 made famously sung in tune; about getting one's kicks. Surely, I was getting my kicks. Past Oklahoma City through to Amarillo, a plain, flat dusty nothingness passed by my window, straight and as far as the eye could see. The bus rolled into Albuquerque late that night. Someone, I recall in the rear of the bus, most likely older, stated that when they had first traveled to Albuquerque, some thirty years prior, the town basically consisted of a motel, gas stations, and desert dust.

Exaggerated as such a claim may have been, talk like that came from the folks in the rear of the bus; the smoking section (this was the early 80's). Oh, yes, by then, I was a smoker. Smoking Kools cigarettes, the same brand my mother had smoked. Smokers seemed less uptight. Therefore, I figured, less tuned in to my visibly gay ways. More likely, they could have cared less.

A dusty desolation rang true to what my eyes saw upon waking the next morning, day three, out in Gallup, New Mexico. At a stop right before the Arizona state line where there seemed to be not much more to look at than a red dirt landscape, nearly treeless, with what appeared to be a few isolated trailer homes and far afield blank dry mountains. Everything was covered with an overcast of dusty red clay.

Leaving Flagstaff, our bus then headed down toward Phoenix. Some friends from back home had told of tales of gay life living in that city. Mostly, their stories spoke of comparisons of how dead Fort Wayne was to life in Phoenix. Never having been there myself, I took what they told to be as fact. The route south along Interstate 17 traveled across some majestically high mountain ranges. Nothing like anything I'd ever seen before my eyes glued to the window as simultaneously my ears popped from the steep elevation heights.

Strolling outside at the rather small Greyhound station in Phoenix, my eyes witnessed nothing, to which impressed me. Coming in on the bus, the city spread out in its entirety dull, identical suburban sprawl sameness.

Finally, the bus heading destination read: Los Angeles! Seemed so excitingly unreal. What I was doing, what was happening, where I was? I could have just pinched myself. All of real now, with no looking back at that point. An aspect of tension entered my being in acknowledgment of the fact that the 'trip' portion of the journey was soon to be at its end. Such tension coincided with witnessing a rougher, blacker group of fellow passengers on board the bus out of Phoenix. Assuring myself this all was to be an expected part of big city life. About a half-hour or so, I detected the smell of weed. Talking voices grew louder. I steeled myself in preparation for when some asshole would make some remark about fags. Would I respond back? I wondered. Most likely, I'd just put on my headphones and listen to The The's "Perfect Day."

If I'd thought the New Mexico desert looked bleak, the wastescape (made up that word) desert entering into California was like from central casting; dry, sagebrush with an occasional cactus passing us by here and there. Picturing movies scenes where people die thirsty out in the desert heat fit exactly what I looked at, mile after blank dry mile.

Our bus stopped in Palm Springs as a couple of passengers boarded. The coach now was completely full. The only seats open were in the 'hood' that was the rear smoking section. Just then, I noticed two humongous, buffed-out guys make it past my seat on their way to the rear. It clicked in my mind that these guys were together, a couple. The one appearing darker-skinned, maybe Latino, then asked one of the, heretofore badasses, if he would mind moving to another seat, so the other buffed dude could sit with him. In near silence, as compared to the prior raucousness, Mr. Badass got up and moved his seat like a scared little puppy. The gay 'couple' sat down. Not one word of protest or disgust could have been heard, except for the wide-assed smirk on my face that I made known by facing toward the rear. Taking in that incident, I believed and took it as a sign that I, clearly, was headed to the right place to be, among people 'like' me.

LA's vast suburbs and its vast urban sprawl sprung into view along the I-10 San Bernardino Freeway and continued for an hour or more before the bus exited and pulled into the station downtown. As the soles of my shoes hit the ground on Los Angeles soil the real adventure began. I, me, was now a part of that huge multi-racial, multi-sexual, multicultural metropolis. Eager-eyed, horny, free, and gay I had to put my ideas into action. Reality.

I caught an RTD city bus out on Olympic Boulevard. Headed straight to my Cousin Rhoda's house, nervously anxious of how I'd be received. Fact was, I was a minor and a runaway and had been missing for the last three and a half days. Arriving, Rhoda answered the door looked right through me with a stern chastising. "Boy! Where yo ass been? You know people been worried sick about you?" Her words scolded, informing me that family had been concerned, especially Aunt Mimi, who had brought me to LA in the first place. Rhoda said that she assured them that I was probably headed for LA.

My divorced, single-mother cousin in no way had asked for a flaming, unruly teenager on her hands to care for along with raising a two-year-old. After a day or so passed with me there at her home, I was given the ultimatum of returning home to Indiana or finding other living arrangements. I could not live with her. Really, such meant to put a fire under my young ass to return home as opposed to really coldly putting me out on the streets.

Those few days of rest at my cousin's had allowed me to have some, probably foolish, backbone. In my way of thinking I had been too far, took such risks, so much so that I felt, now, unbound. The home was wherever I was. I felt empowered to make my own decisions, own my own terms, delusional, so I thought." No!" I was not giving that up. The adventure exhilarated me, freed me.

Out of somewhere, I made contact to resources for runaway youth. Within the week, I had a bed at a youth shelter on Beachwood Drive, up in the hills just below that famous, white gleaming 'Hollywood' sign. I snagged one of only 15 or so beds available for minor-aged runaways in the whole of Los Angeles County. Rhoda dropped me off at the shelter, staring at me with a look of disbelief regarding my prospects, yet I could still feel her love for me. Even then, I sensed she vicariously admired me but couldn't allow me to know that she felt that way.

Being 16, legally, I could work, so my plan of living at the shelter entailed me getting a job. As I can vaguely remember, my shelter mates were me and a short, rather butch looking Black girl, a thin, red-haired, White girl, another White girl who came across to me as being gay. Two days after my arrival, John; a brooding, gorgeous white boy, moved in too.

One evening when all of us were to be asleep in bed, I guess we must have decided to play some kind of truth or dare. The black girl and I french kissed on a dare. I remember my amazement at how much the kiss seemed similar to kissing a guy. Maybe, that was because she was so butch anyway. I got turned on by that kiss, not the same heat I felt with another guy, but not a horrible feeling either.

To my luck, a local businessman had seen a television news segment reporting on the plight of runaway youth out in Hollywood. His company offered a job to a willing youth in order that the runaway had no need to turn to the streets. The job was offered to me, and I took it. The job put a wrench in my family's hopes of having me return back to Indiana. I'd be an entry-level helper apprentice at a company which built studio sets for television commercials. Boldly, I had struck out for California, snagged a full-time job in the somewhat entertainment industry. I was making five dollars an hour, way over the minimum wage of 1982. When I informed my cousin of my fortunes, she relented and allowed me to come back and live at her home.

Two brothers owned the company. They both drove Saab sedans, the very European-looking, bubble-shaped models. I thought to myself working one day, "When I 'make' it, I'm getting me a Saab."

My duties were to clean up and haul out the lumber scraps leftover after building the set facades. One of the carpenters, Jack; a stocky built, blond guy with a mustache, always wore shorts that seemed to reveal more than he intended. I recall making an effort not to stare in the direction of his sexy muscular thighs and calves covered in bleach-blond fur. I kept my stares hidden, discreet.

Another of my duties included me tagging along, taking scrap lumber, and disassembled set pieces in the truck out to the landfill. The landfill lay up in the hills above Eagle Rock. With the amazed eyes of kid, I sensed the adventure never having been inside a landfill and one way up with expansive views of the LA plain landscape. Oddly, the smell happened not to be as offensive as I had imagined. Seagulls and buzzards flew, circling overhead. The older assistant and driver, a long-haired white guy, I've long since forgotten his name, who gave off the impression he'd been smoking weed for decades too long. He'd blared his Frank Zappa music on the stereo as I sat looking out the window of the company truck plying up and down the freeways.

Being unbound to me meant that my main objective for living centered around getting out to experience all the gay life that I was able. Weekends would find me traipsing all about West Hollywood. I had my own money, meaning, I needed someplace to display and show off my latest fashions I'd purchased with that said money. The Odyssey, the juice bar, often found me in attendance many a night. Through going there meeting folks, I discovered where the hip, coolest, new wavers gathered after the club closed for the night. Oki Dogs; a rather run down looking joint that served hot dogs served over chili. Naïve, it appeared that just about everyone there just happened to be funky, wild and gruff. I just figured it was all just part of the scene. Only later did I get a clue about the street element of drugs, the selling of sex, and young runaways alongside sexual predators also present there. All I cared about, and could see, was hanging with other 'cool' kids my age, just like the song "Cool Places" played and danced to at the Odyssey. All of us unbound and just free-living. Rhoda naturally grew concerned of my night-living ways with the ensuing neglect of my obligations at home.

That gay scene was White cultured nearly exclusively. I glossed over such aspects feeling it still being better than my hidden, if not sexually repressed, family environment. I have become more disconnected from my family environment. If it was ok for me to be gay, that required me to become a part of that culture. My physical attractions had always leaned toward White guys anyway.

Los Angeles being the multi-racial mecca it was meant that out in the gay world, I meet much more than just Blacks and whites. Tommy, a Latino kid, caught my eyes one evening while strolling by up on Santa Monica Boulevard. I'd never been with someone Latino. Tommy being long and lean possessing a sharp Aztecan nose and jet-black hair. We started up talking to one another, saying nothing important while walking together a few blocks. Before long we found ourselves making out, slinging tongues back and forth, getting all hot and much bothered. Neither of us having our own place for further exploration of our heated passions. Right on the corner of Santa Monica and La Brea Boulevards stood a Carl's Jr. Hamburger joint. "Let's go in there...in the restroom!" Tommy egged on.

"Won't we get caught in there?" I quizzed him all the while with a look in my eyes that said, "Yes, of course." We did almost get caught, aborting our sexual tryst. Just the same, I needed to get home early enough to get sleep, in time to be up for work. Begrudgingly, that night I did the responsible thing, leaving hot and sexy Tommy at the bus stop to go home. Being responsible felt like such a drag amongst all the exciting happenings going on; all the men and boys left yet to explore and try to screw.

Many of those mornings, I barely made it to work on time, a pattern that continued later on. I discovered the necessary benefits of consuming coffee. I recall times at work when I'd be nearly half asleep running the table saw cutting down pieces of wood from the lumber yard. God must've been watching out; that's the only explanation of why I didn't cut a finger or something.

Not long afterward, my cousin had had enough of my stubborn, unruly- assed ways coming home at all hours of the night. Once again, she told me I needed to leave her house. One time I didn't arrive back home until the next afternoon, after having been at the beach with this girl and two guys who lived in their car. Further denizens I'd met up hanging on Santa Monica Boulevard.

After getting put out, I tried to continue to work for a few days. Finally, I just didn't go back to work either. All those nights hanging out and around those wilding runaways, hustlers and another assorted riff raff, now, I was right there alongside them. In a sense, somehow, I felt belonged in such an atmosphere. Fucking up my home situation and relations with family, my job, now, I literally was on the streets. It was my home. Only by this point, did I begin to realize what made this whole scene all fit together; the drugs, the type more treacherous than anything like the weed I messed around with.

On one of those what I called the lost days, in found myself hanging around with this hot-looking, White hustler I'd met up at the Gay and Lesbian Center on Highland Avenue. He had me go accompany him just after sunset one night, to a parking lot behind a 7-11 store. More or less I was to be the lookout, an extra set of eyes. I looked on as he took out an orange pill and he dropped it into a little brown glass bottle. The kind of bottle I'd seen gay guys from the bars sniffing from, reeking from that nasty smell. Next, he added water then took out a lighter to heat the bottom of the bottle. Still watching, quickly the water boiled, and the pill dissolved. Nervous as I was, I paid close attention. He then took a tiny cotton ball and put it in the bottle which then had an orange paste floating on the top of the water. With a hypodermic needle he drew into it a clear liquid. Not at first did I realize he meant to stick the needle in his arm. So naive. God, I was so queasy about needles. I put my back to him, blurting out some holier than thou speech about the dangers of drugs and needles. I'd just witnessed someone, a junky, shoot up the drug Preludin. Much later, I'd come to know that that drug was a powerful amphetamine. Luckily for me, I had no desire to partake in that activity, at least not in that period of my life. Knowing what I know now, with my later drug habits, I believe if I had used what he had that night I possibly would not be alive, here today. All that happened before folks knew much about HIV/AIDS, sharing needles, and the like.

I hooked up with two guys out on the Boulevard; Joe and Brett. We were young and out living on the streets for our own various reasons. We made a pact meaning we were to stick together and share resources. Yet, I still had money from the last check from my job. Often, I ended up footing the bill. Down at Oki Dogs where all the street folks seemed to frequent, serving as a central point to find somewhere to crash for the night or maybe find someone you knew to buy or share something to eat. Also, you could run into the latest newly arrived runaway, all cute and fresh. Men looking to have sex with the underaged, especially young boys for sex congregated around Oki Dogs as well. Still mesmerized with wild abandon and the sense of freedom, I got all the excitement I craved.

When my funds ran out, so to ended the Three Musketeers group of Joe, Brett, and myself, I met and mingled with all sorts of folks. I got welcomed to sleep on the floor of a gay couple; Steve and Farah. Farah White, rail thin skinny maybe 30yrs old , but looked way older. Steve; skinny too, Native Indian with long jet back hair. Their relationship bond was liquor that they drank by the fifth a gallon. Somehow, they took a liking to me as long as I could stand their constant arguing and fighting. They wanted nothing more from me but a bottle of booze. I figured, for a warm place to sleep it seemed a cheap and fair trade.

Eventually, the excitement of night living wore off. I felt abandoned. The real emotions of processing the deep grief I didn't want to feel and had no clue how to deal with. An inner sense of hopelessness and depression set in and took over me. With the little money I had left, I made the desperate decision to take myself out, suicide, by an overdose of drugs.

It was a Friday night I remember I ran into Steve, this tall hustler I had been lusting for. Telling him my plans, he agreed to help hook me up to buy some dope. More than likely, I left out my suicidal intentions.

Next thing I recall, had us in the front living room of a small bungalow off Santa Monica Boulevard. A heavy-set Black dude bolted the door with a 2by4 after he let us in. At threatening as the scene appeared, I figured Steve must've have known the dude. As I sat on the couch, scared as hell, I made certain not to sit too close to Steve, even as I wanted to grab ahold on his big long arm and hold on for dear life. With my eyeballs about to pop out my head, I clearly remember staring at a pyramid pile of white powder, four or five inches tall, laid out on a mirror on the coffee table. Surely, that was cocaine. I was certain of that fact even as I'd never ever seen such before. I think Steve purchased some pill from the big dude.

My next memory, of that same night, Steve and I were inside the Sizzler steak house on Highland. By then, we'd copped the pills, some kind of downers for sure. I swallowed a small handful. We were getting food at the salad bar, then, all of a sudden my legs gave out and I fell to the floor. Immediately, we left the restaurant. I recall feeling sick to my stomach and staggering, not being able to walk without Steve doing his best to hold me up and not make a scene.

Next, I remember coming to the entrance way of the Gay a Lesbian Center, just a block away from the Sizzler. A concerned someone, in the meantime, had called 911, and Steve, I noticed, was nowhere around. When the paramedics arrived, I just coherent enough to refuse to be taken to the emergency room. Incredibly, they allowed to go free despite my obvious deluded, drugged, condition.

For a day or so, I was in a black out, after that night, I have no memory of what I did. Whatever happened, I ended up arrested and getting hauled into the West Los Angeles police station. My cousin and family were contacted. They offered to fly me to Houston to where my sister was living at the time. My Cousin Tisa, Rhoda's sister, came to find and pick me up someplace on the Boulevard with just the clothes on my back. Immediately, off to LAX she took me. DeBarge's "All This Love" played on the soul station, on the drive. Feeling as much as if I'd failed as just plain lost and alone. My grand adventure turned out to be a mess. Houston, a new change of scenery seemed an improvement to the dismal situation of which I had made things.

Even Houston proved no solution to my deep depression and the feeling I was at a loss to express. I ended up growing a beard caring less about how I looked.

Chaos reigned it seemed in the home that was my sister's. My brother James and his family of four moved in alongside me, my sister Sandra and my nephew. With three floors, three bedrooms, there was nowhere to hide. All I felt was miserable.

Such the Chaos; our electricity got turned off for two weeks, then sis got arrested for bouncing a check. One night she and I got into an argument, after which I stormed off and proceeded to walk, in cowboy boots, the style at the time, all the way to Westheimer, the gay district. The gay district I came upon that night looked nothing to what I experienced back in LA and on the Boulevard. Dejected, frustrated, no visible runaway youths, I turned myself around and walked back to the apartment, a trip of 10 maybe 15 miles round trip. The pain in my limbs lingered for days afterward

Finally beaten, I become humble enough to beg my brother Craig to allow me to come back to live with him in Fort Wayne. Somewhere in there's maybe. Hopefully, I apologized. In the end, I failed making the 'great' escape. Inside, although I did not know it, I'd just built up a callus. My cravings for such excitement lingered on.

Queeny (1983)

"No one can make you feel inferior without your permission." Eleanor Roosevelt.

No doubt about it, I was a mama's boy. All the things I idolized were feminine; toys, female characters on television, and in the movies. I had to escape being something other than a fey, Black boy who was no go at and hated sports, all the same, possessing overly feminine behaviors. A 'sissy' is what they called me.

Already hiding behind my mother's skirts, so to speak, why shouldn't I just go ahead and wear them as well? By the time I started school, I also began to play dress-up when I was by myself. Usually, it evolved me putting on makeup foundation and lipstick as I was parading in front of a mirror in high heel shoes, pretending to be my favorite female characters; Lynda Carter as Wonder Woman or Tina Turner playing the Acid Queen in the movie version of "Tommy"(ironic note: the same movie starring a real sissy icon; Elton John) All of its thrills and excitement until I'd get caught, hopefully by my mother. If caught in women's clothes by brothers, surely, I'd be in for beat down, sissy shaming included.

Over time, my little mind figured if I was going to be called a sissy, I might as well be one. The toys I got as gifts included a G.I. Joe with his manly camping vehicle. The male 'action figures', I believe thinking back on it, were intended to satiate my desire to play with dolls, except male dolls did not have hair to be styled or fashionable changes of clothes. One Christmas, the girls up the street, daughters of my mom's best friend, got the gift of a Barbie Styling Salon. Often, I couldn't wait for the chance to go up to the girl's house to play and style the hair of the almost life-sized Barbie head.

Creative and subversive, if I could not have female dolls I wanted to play with, I'd make my own paper dolls. I'd color and cut out each one and design matching color-coordinated outfits and accessories for each. The adult folk just had to bear it and hope I'd grow out of it.

I got my fashion sense from perusing my sister's fashion magazines. My eyes would just light up when I'd get taken along clothes shopping at the mall, in contrast to my nephew's exasperation at being dragged along also when my sister shopped for clothes. Later on, she would seek my fashion sense advice on what outfits to wear. Even later as a teenager, when I lived with my brother Craig, he too sought out my advice of fashion sense. He'd come to awaken me in the mornings, seeking my counsel on which tie coordinated best with which shirt or suit.

Growing up, I overheard many opinions rebuking men who lived lives as dressed as women. Ironically, those men (trans women) who did such seemed to be widely known in the community, even if notoriously so.

As an adolescent, my nightly excursions into our town's gay scene put me in close interaction with a spectrum of gay men, lesbians, butch dykes, and drag queens(transgender). Hung out and partied with them all.

It was then that I met Clancy, aka Miss Nicki. She was loud, obnoxious, but always fun and to be found the center of any party. Later on, I could be found spending a day or two at her apartment cause it was not unusual for the best party happenings to be found there. Hanging out there, I discovered my taste for 'new wave' music. It was there I first heard and danced to Madonna and The B52's.

I remember as well her warning me against wanting to date 'White boys.' "Honey, it's alright to fuck them, for fun. But chu need to be with a Black man!" she reprimanded. I neither confirmed nor gave any sign that I opposed such advice she gave me.

I knew Miss Toni; tall, big-boned, and dark-skinned with a fierce reputation for taking no shit from anyone. She treated me well. There was Tominika Starr' a White queen who was only into Black men. She performed shows at the one lesbian bar. Another, Miss Erica, was rumored to have had a complete sex change. I could not verify that knowledge, even if, at times, she did try to come on to me sexually. Years later, Miss Erica and I smoked crack together. More than a few nights, we were 'sing'n' as we humorously referred to such activities.

The finest of all the 'queens' being Zena. In her non-drag life, he/she danced for a professional ballet company. Zena; petite with smooth light cocoa-colored skin, always dressed impeccably, in and out of drag. She was not known for being notorious.

On Halloween, the year that I was 17, I got the idea into my head that I was going to go out dressed up in drag. As a kid loving dressing up in women's clothes, now, I had the chance to do so in 'real-life.' That's considering going downtown in the dark of night to gay bar real life.

As Halloween neared, my perfect opportunity appeared. Aunt Deborah was scheduled to be in the hospital for a hysterectomy. She'd given me the key to her apartment while she was to be away. I was there; I'd be able to wear some of her clothes and have use of her place to get myself dressed, no chance of me being caught in a dress by my brother Craig.

Ever since puberty hit, I grew hair everywhere; my legs, arms, and chest. Too much hair to shave off with a razor, so I applied Magic depilatory, to get my body smooth. I'd since gotten used to that awful smelling mixture from removing my facial hair, yet, removing hair from my whole body proved quite an endeavor. Added to the fact the process needed to be clandestine.

My aunt wore wigs anyway, so that essential element was taken care of. One day I arrived at her apartment to go through her clothes, looking for something glamorous that could fit me. Finally, I picked out a blue-green shift gown, a house dress really, but when I hiked it up and bloused it over a belt, it came out as a baggy mini-dress. I'd put out the word to all the drag queens that I needed a pair of shoes. I received a pair of bright vintage plaid, open-toed pumps. Timmy Todd, an acquaintance, who was quite the character at nearly 7ft tall and more than 300 pounds and as devious as anyone I ever knew, luckily got me the shoes. The heels were too tight, so I cut the back seams and made do. I gave my female self the name of Christine. Folks told me that night I looked like a sweet school teacher type out for a night on the town.

Halloween, 'Christine' got me into the bar without ID. Whoever carded the door that night obviously did not recognize me. Being only 17. I brought myself a drink and found a seat to watch the queens perform. Zena performed a number that evening in an outfit made of glitter and sequins, as I remember. None of the other performers could top her.

Zena and I got up on the stage and danced to the song "Addicted to the Night" by the group Lipps Inc. I felt as fabulous as she looked, shaking my ass in my mini-dress and heels.

After Halloween night was over, in Cinderella fashion, I returned all my 'borrowed' items to exactly where they were before I used them. I had the returning process down to a science from my childhood clandestine dressing-up days. Later at school, I know folks thought I might have had crabs from all the scratching and itching, the effects from my body hair regrowth.

That night turned out to be the first and last time I dressed in public as a female. Astonishingly, I no longer had that desire after all my yearnings when I was a boy. Maybe it had all been a phase, and I did just grow out of it. Still, in no way did I lose the desire to express my feminine essence.

Speaking of queenliness, another incident, the same year, further describes my eventual gender expression panned out.

A group of us young gay gays was fit to travel for a night out dancing, to be seen, and of course for possible new sexual trysts, at a recently opened gay club, Bretz, in Toledo, Ohio. About a two-hour drive away, Ohio allowed beer drinking at 18. Being the youngest in the entourage, I could definitely pass for 18. I had looked the part since my facial hair first arrived at 14.

Friday night. Brian, my caffeine pill connection, and his boyfriend, myself, my running buddy John, Ed; also known as Edwina, and one other guy all loaded into a roomy, black, 79' Oldsmobile Toronado.

Pointed-toe shoes were in fashion. My pair, with a slight heel matching with pleated pegged pants, set me off as the sharpest dressed of the crowd. The rest dressed in the latest styles; designer jeans and colognes, hairspray, and shoulder pads to top off the final look. Only the least unaware could not have spotted and picked us out as gay. We would have easily fit right into any major city 'gay ghetto' despite hailing from small Fort Wayne.

Our driver steeled himself not to drink or toke on any of the copious weed smoked. Allowing him to be safe enough to drive and plus; not to injure his big pretty Olds. Our ride took off with music blastin while passing the latest gossip, mostly about who was screwing whom or who.

Darkened corn and soybeans fields of Indiana, Ohio, whizzed by at 60 plus miles per hour below a sky of a bright moon. Somewhere near the town of Napoleon, one of us queens either had to pee, make sure his mascara hadn't smeared, or check if the hair needed a touch-up spray.

The city-fancy, big black Oldsmobile pulled into a truck stop with a stereotypical greasy spoon diner inside. Upon entering, we all bolted for the restrooms, each of us smelling of way too much cologne for any man to be emanating in such a locale. Set against the surroundings of the truck stop, we appeared as if we were aliens from the planet Urgaynus. "What the fuck are they staring at?" one of us whispered under his breath, careful not to make too much more of a scene than we were already making.

My face had a look that said, *"fuck off!"* while I remained silent, believing my distasteful attitude toward the gathered patrons needed no words.

All reconfigured and recoiffed, it was, now, time to reboard the gay batmobile. Someone needed an item out of the trunk. I may have been that someone. All in the rush, confusion, anxiety amongst all the rude looks we were getting, I happened to close the trunk with the keys inside. Recognizing my mistake, the General Motors car, similar to my brother's

Buick, it did not need the key to open the trunk. There was a switch in the glove box. Just so, this model did indeed need the key to release the trunk.

Now, there we were, a car full of flaming, obviously gay guys, excited, ready to taste the gay nightlife, stuck and stranded at some hick truck stop in tiny Napoleon, Ohio.

Justifiably, I got reamed out for being so damned careless. We concluded that in such a place, one of the 'real' men present knew how to get into the trunk of that car. The irony. Now, we needed the help of the disdained patrons. I fail to recall which one of us gay 'dandies' braved himself/herself to ask for help.

The men who did come to rescue us from our predicament pulled out the rear seat to access the trunk. To no avail, it was still blocked by a metal panel. Next, they popped out the trunk lock, nothing.

Meanwhile, Ed; Edwina came to life, lightening the scene with classic campy humor. "Honey...one of them hunks could work on my vehicle anytime." He blurted out as the men worked one solution after another. Edwina's humor helped ease the guilt I felt as our driver's beautiful car got racked apart.

Finally, the only way to get access to those keys was to pry open the steel trunk cover with sheer brute force.

As a group of about 3 or 4 guys sweated and heaved apart the trunk, Edwina clowned even more, "Oooh yes chile... just like that. That's right, put them muscles into it!" I was busting up laughing. The crowd gathered around our vehicle made Ed's campy, cutting up all the more hilarious. I felt terrible to have been the cause of that lovely car being mangled.

Nonetheless, Ed had tears coming to my eyes from riotous laughter. "Yeah, baby... you can work on me like that." He carried on, oblivious to our dire circumstances. The keys got retrieved.

Having come all that way with only an hour or so left before the club would be closed, we pressed on the mangled limousine, mascara, and all.

Brian's car had been fully insured.

As a sweet young queer of 17, I lived out what I had always meant to be, even when 'this' queen put aside the need for dresses and heels.

Burning Bridges (1984)

Passing my last year of high school, I paid little attention to the choices and action I made. I attended school regularly. Classes I enjoyed, I excelled. Others, like math, I failed miserably, general math even. Hanging out nightly with folks older than me, adults, aping the things they did may have affected my academic endeavors. Out drink and smoking weed with the best of them as I tried to perform at in the daytime.

To my thinking, I just needed to graduate and escape Fort Wayne and go live the 'real' life. As a senior, I took a full schedule, including a night adult education math class. All in order to graduate with my class and be done with what I considered high school cluelessness.

At home, living with my brother reflected the choices I was making. Hanging out one evening, before going downtown with my friend Kurt who attended another school, we were at my house to sneak watching a gay porn video while my brother was not home. No idea how I obtained the material being underage. Anyway, I put the tape into the VCR. With the lights out or on low, we started watching, engrossed, pretending as we were as experienced as what we were viewing displayed on the TV screen. Just then, I could hear noises; you had to enter our apartment through a back porch, so you could not see the television until coming around the corner in the kitchen. My brother Craig came in. In some freak accident, just exactly as he would have been able to see the TV, the videotape just so happened to switch to some taped-over basketball game. That was a close call, more so a discussion I didn't want to have. Living with him, I'd agreed that I would keep my 'gay' stuff in my room. So, I was not keeping up my end of the bargain. This after I'd been forgiven for taking his money and running away to California the previous summer.

I now had my driver's license and my own car; my mother's 1976, by then rusted, orange Camaro. Again, I was clueless, careless, as a wild teenager testing having adult responsibilities. The car's title and insurance were all in my brother's name. I had since gotten some tickets and subsequently failed to mention them to him until he got tickets notices in the mail. The same evening as the tickets arrived, Craig sat me down in the living room to scold me on how 'my' actions while driving affected his record. I recall having a semi-nonchalant attitude as he was being serious. "What, you think I'm supposed to take the fall for what you do because you're my little brother?" incredulously, he questioned me. In my head, I wanted to use the fallback as the irresponsible little brother. Yet, as I heard him say those words, my more mature self knew he was right. It would not be fair to him. Thinking back on that moment, now, I know I matured a few years. Matured in my sense of fairness and matured in how I reasoned what was just. I would use whatever 'lesson' learned, that evening having that conversation, as a reference point for how I dealt with associates out on the streets. I'd be telling them, "If my brother, my own flesh and blood, wouldn't take a rap for me, I'll be damned if I take somebody's!"

The choices made regarding sex had lasting effects that I didn't realize or couldn't even comprehend at the time. There was Kent, a sexy Latin boy, the cousin of another friend, who gave me the pleasure of losing myself in sensual passion, albeit without emotional commitment. What I most desired was more than just the heat of flesh on flesh. We just so happened to cross paths downtown on the gay stroll. I practically felt him strip me naked, leering at me with his luscious brown eyes. Vulnerable, and horny, what was I to do when such an attractive young male specimen was singularly focused, on just me? I did think better of the notion of trying to take him back to my house even with the chance of my brother awaking and discovering us. He told me of his family having a summer cabin at a lake, about thirty miles outside the city. "The door is always left unlocked," he said. Off we drive, in the dark at two in the morning, to the lake in my rusted but sturdy Camaro. I believe it may have been about March or April, definitely not quite summer cabin weather for Indiana. The memory of being snuggled up tight, skin to skin, with Kent, even now, is a heavenly sensuous thought. Our bodies needed to make enough heat to keep us warm in that unheated cabin. Even then, I knew within me, that no matter how hot and sexy Kent was, I longed for, needed, more than what took place there in that cabin. In the early hours the next morning, we rushed back to town, probably driving over the speed limit. No matter the inadequate sleep that night, I had to attend school. Amazingly, how was I supposed to concentrate on learning after what I'd experienced just hours before.

My choices of running buddies, John and Jeffery, much influenced the world and environs which I roamed. Both were already out of school without any serious-minded career plans. Jeffery, the whole time hanging together, never had a job at all. More important. Still, they always seemed to be where the party was and didn't mind my coming along, so I went wherever.

This just so happens to be when I first turned a trick (had sex) for money. Jeffery kept on pestering me about some older White man who wanted to have sex with me and would pay me to do so. The idea somewhat grossed me out, and it wasn't he wasn't paying high dollar. John, the only one of us gainfully employed, often made sure I knew my contribution to the party funds was sorely lacking. So, I got convinced. I can still hear, in my head, Jeffery saying, "You broke bitch… Twenty dollars is twenty dollars!" Add to the real fact that my sexual promiscuity, in all honesty, was meaningless.

"Why not get paid for something that was as well, meaningless," I thought. With that, rationalized, I fucked the old man; Bob was his name, I remember. Just like that, I now was a hooker, hustler, a 'hoe.' Not a high school grad, but a hoe.

I found myself participating in other shady events that I had no business in being involved in. One Friday night, my buddy Kurt and I ran into John and Jeffrey downtown. Jeffery clandestinely informed me John was out with some older man, who thought he was going to get to screw John. Turns out that the man was staggering drunk with a wallet full of cash, having cashed his paycheck earlier that day. John intended to lead him on, just enough to roll(rob) him for his money. My involvement, cause, I was the only other one with a valid drivers' license, I needed to drive John's truck which was actually John's grandfather's. I needed to drive in case the old dude discovered his missing wallet and money and decided to come looking for John. And just like that, I'm the getaway driver, accessory to a strong-arm robbery. I drove the pickup until I felt sure I had lost the guy. Me driving all up on the curbs, never having driven anything as big as an F-150. We, after we assumed all was clear, later retrieved John hiding in some bushes on Superior Street. Kurt, meanwhile, followed behind in my car.

There's more. Since John had done the real 'dirty' work that night and had all the cash, he got to determine where and how we were going to party for the evening. John, ever with his taste for 'rough trade' (straight men), the Blacker and rougher, the better. So, it got decided we were off to an illegal bootleg joint. The spot was smack dab in the heart of the Black part of town, the 'hood' really, on Hanna Street. Kurt, although being White, he came along with us too. So, there we were, four gay gays, some of us obviously so, two of us underage and one being White, going to hang out and drink in this sleazy bootleg club, all in the name of fun and partying.

My nerves were so on edge, thinking someone would try to start something when they figured we were gay. To ease my tension, I ended up getting drunk. Nothing did happen, though. And no, I did not, in the least, enjoy myself. At the end of the night, I had to drive Kurt home. Never believed in drinking and driving, especially not to that state of intoxication, but figured I had to. Kurt got driven home safely. But as I was coming around the corner to my own house, I got pulled over by a cop. I figured certain I was getting arrested. Just the kind of circumstances my brother had warned me about. When the cop saw my driver's license and my address, he allowed me to go on with only a warning. I, too, made it safely home that night.

Just ever so much so, I pushed out to the edge, always seemingly just short of getting burned…singed maybe.

"Owner of a Lonely Heart/ What's Love Got to Do with It"

This section does not follow the regular format of this memoir. These stories are based on one theme, my romantic, sex relations in the time period from 1984 to 1986

Since my arrival in the fabulous world of LA, I carried a longing for love, to have a companion to call my own, someone to who I belonged to and to me as well. Such longings belied the sexual virility of my 18 years. Unable to deny myself tasting all the many flavors of men available. West Hollywood, LA, never let me down in my pursuing the tasting. Finding something anyways near bouts love, consistent, and meaningful proved hit and miss and negligible.

When with Art, my first lover, we did love one another and I stayed faithful, except for one infidelity near the end of our coupleship. I felt obligated to him; that meant staying faithful for what felt to me, then, like an eternity was only actually four months. We eventually grew apart from one another, at least I did. The guy I cheated on him looked a real-life version of Piccoli, the character played by Sean Penn in "Fast Times at Ridgemont High." A blond-haired surfer type whom you could tell smoked way too much weed while living in his van. We just so happened to get hot and heavy in the back of that van one evening. Like a dog in heat, hormones betrayed me, the only time I enjoyed swallowing. No illusions, there, nothing more than anything other than a one-night stand encounter.

As an inmate in the Los Angeles County jail at HOJJ (Hall of Justice Jail), in the fall of 84', found me in close quarters with a guy I hoped something more to become of us. Typically, anyway, there is much cruising taking place in such all-male settings; both of us noticed the other showing an interest in one another. Odd note as well, we both read the daily newspaper. No small feat to get a copy in jail. I felt that particular commonality made him even more special. He had the looks and something more, I thought. Most of our other fellow inmates carried no outward intellectual curiosity. Many if not most of the inmates seemed interested only in lies of high living they carried on, on the outside, readily omitting how dumb or stupid that such living ended up resulting in having one's freedom taken away.

Mark was a tall, lanky dude having long dark blond curls, receding a bit, with prominent bug eyes. His manner noticeably didn't give off that he was gay. My ego swelled that such a handsome masculine guy found me attractive.

One afternoon, as both of our tiers arrived back from the eating hall, the deputies not paying close attention, I made a beeline and snuck onto his tier. "What you doing here?" Mark quizzed me.

"I came by to see you," I responded, being proud of my cunning.

He smiled at me while showing concern, "Don't get in trouble," he wisely admonished me. He showed no sign that he was disappointed I took the risk to be with him. The rest of that stay in jail, we continued flirting with one another and sharing the daily newspaper.

Months later, I'm out along the Boulevard in West Hollywood, I spot Mark passing through riding in a car. He hollered, calling out my name. Standing on Fairfax waiting, I had just crossed the street in order to catch the # 1 Hollywood Boulevard bus. He happened to be riding in a somewhat beat-up older van with a Black guy doing the driving. They pulled over, as I recall, he may have offered me a ride, with my destination being all the way to downtown LA as way too far. By then, I'd felt a little frustrated. *"What was he about?"* the thought floated in my mind. That day he gave me his phone number telling me to call him sometime. Then, Mark, the black man driving, took off in the beat-up van to wherever it was they were headed.

I about jumped out of my skin with nervous anticipation. There was this masculine, handsome, slightly mysterious dude whom I, by this point, now harbored somewhat like romantic feelings. Now, was the feelings about to become real? I felt there was something to look forward to; I'd get to quench my longings via something with more potential than just fucking and quickie sex encounters.

Not too long after that day, I called. We agreed to meet up in which I would come over to his apartment. *"Oh my God! This man's inviting me to a 'date' at his home"*, I told myself. I'd never before been on a date. Truly, a romantic, this is what I had always hoped for. LA, finally, appeared to be fulfilling my dreams. When the day arrived for me to go over to Mark's apartment, I tried my best to contain my anxious desperation when I called him for directions. His place was located out on West Third Street, past La Brea, almost by the tar pits and the LA County Museum. I'd only ever passed through that neighborhood, known to be a Jewish enclave. The day was bright and comfortably warm as LA is known to be. Departing the bus, I took close notice walking around the area, looking at his building, before I came up to knock on the door. Pretty nice digs for a guy I had met in jail and along the hustler stroll. Mark greeted me, after letting into the gate and said that he needed to go grocery shopping for ingredients for our dinner. Walking with him to the Ralph's Supermarket nearby, I felt deliciously proud to be out in public accompanied by this tall attractive guy.

When we returned back to Mark's simple but clean apartment, I just froze up. Words of what to say just would not fall from my lips. Social skills failed me. It seemed to be one of those situations when one should have been careful of what you ask for due to it actually becoming true. Up until that moment, in such instances of being with someone I was attracted to and vice versa, I'd have been naked and about to have sex by then. The words of what to say would not fall from my lips. I felt afraid to mention how nervous I was. *"Was I too gay?"* I thought he was thinking of me. So, I determined it best to let him take the lead that evening. All of the previous chemistry between Mark and me seemed to misfire that night. I seem to remember Mark having cooked spaghetti, which back then I carried an irrational, almost phobic, distaste for due to its usual pairing with garlic bread. I may have declined to eat much, if any, more misfiring.

We did not get intimate physically. We made no further plans to get together. Maybe we kissed one as we parted. Never again did I cross paths with Mark. To this very day, I've been left wondering what or how did it go so wrong. I soon clouded out that letdown, though I never forgot about him.

Of all the men I bedded personally, with romantic sexual intention, nearly all were white, a few were Latinos. That's who I desired, what I was attracted to. Inside myself this troubled me, being Black with my upbringing. Was I betraying who I was, where I came from? Does one carry his family into the bedroom when the lights are dim?

One guy I met, Ruben, light-skinned Black with brown or maybe even green eyes. Nothing lasting resulted between us. I believe Reuben picked me up twice, from where else, but, along Santa Monica Boulevard. Our lovemaking (sex) was so passionate that I was left breathless, panting. He kissed marvelously, always a plus, in my opinion. Maybe somewhere inside of me, I felt our coupling would have been more acceptable with my rearing. Very clean-cut Rueben was. He worked a legitimate job, more than what could be said for me. After Rueben, my tastes returned back to the usual vanilla.

Another guy I met, I've long since forgotten to recall his name. The mark on my memory again was due to our encounter having felt like more than just a screw. He was small, built like a swimmer, with very blond hair, almost nearly albino. I met along the boulevard. He picked me up in his sports car convertible. I remember him saying he was a student at UCLA out in Westwood, a year or two older than me. We went out to the movies twice. Absolutely, I remember the movie, "The Breakfast Club." We both felt so moved by the film, the reason we saw it twice. Like in the film, we ourselves were not too far beyond being in high school. The movie characters played out my own sense of having been a misfit in my school days. Afterward, we intently discussed the movie. Later, our sex held such intensity as he as well another passionate kisser. I felt my mind was left panting, as were my loins. Our trysts confirmed I could and needed to connect to on a deeper level than mere physicality. *Who knew?*

Out among the environment of Hollywood, would it not be uncommon for fame if not notoriety, to cross my path? On more than one occasion, I met and fucked around with Scott Thorson; he being the kept younger lover of the world- famous pianist, Liberace. I had heard mention of Scott by talk of other hustlers. Scot though not unattractive, I can say I was more impressed of his 'status.' Not much to mention in our couplings except that Scot was very much strung out, snorting coke. I myself, a budding addict, that detail awed me as well. During our intimacies, he seemed to be as clouded out as the coke lines going up his nose. Somehow, I could relate. Not having a clue of anything else more important I could have been doing, I always went when he came by and summoned me.

Around that summer of 85' another Scott entered into my realm. Actually, he rode past my spot, the bus bench at the corner of Santa Monica and Holloway Boulevards. My spot was hidden, at night, amongst tropical foliage surrounding the entrance of an office building. A non-descript locale to the average passing driver and, more importantly, to passing cop cruisers. The bench was a good distance away from where other hustlers regularly chose to sling their wares to catch a trick.

Looking like a real live grown- up version of the character Christopher Robin, from my childhood of reading Winnie The Pooh. That's in my mind how Scott appeared to look; tall, thin and wiry with big- toothed smile and laughing eyes. Almost instantly, when I first met him, I fantasized him as being my ideal vision of what I wanted my boyfriend to look like.

On occasion, as we'd met, Scott ended up telling me his boyfriend was also Black. Intently, I hated the fact that another brother had snagged Scott before I could. This knowledge further solidified my fantasy of Scott as could have been 'my' boyfriend.

At first, all Scott and I did was to carry on some heavy making out, preceded by a ride on his moped to a secluded spot. Neither of us had anywhere to go to engage in anything more. One night, lo and behold, I happened to find Scott in a private room at the Hollywood Spa bathhouse, located one block from the famous corner of Hollywood and Vine streets. I had begun to frequent the establishment, particularly after taking a hit of acid or snorting speed. Going to the bathhouse served as a shortcut to finding someone for sex, opposed to finding it out on the Boulevard. As in most gay bathhouses, I suppose, every other guy went there for one main purpose; to fuck.

That night lying there under dim lights, was my dream guy. Scott invited me in. He locked the door and then shortly took out some powered coke to snort, we then indulged. It surprised me he did drugs other than weed he had smoked with me. Next, for what seemed like hours, I screwed every part of his beautiful smooth, slender body. I devoured him, licking, sucking, stroking till it almost hurt. Hooked I was, on the dope and him.

When Scott and I finally ended our fuck marathon, I composed myself wrapped my nakedness in my towel to further cruise around. No one else did I desire. I only longed for more of him, cringing at the idea of Scott screwing someone else right there that night. My ideal fantasy or not, he did not belong to me, and there was nothing I could do about it. He did his best to comfort my unrequited longings. I could sense him holding back cruising another black man when I'd pass by again, and we'd end up conversing.

That morning and into the day happened to be when the "Live Aid" concert was taking place in London, to aid the famine crisis in Ethiopia. I watched Tina Turner perform her hit song "What's Love Got to Do with It" up on the big screen in the cinema room. The usual movie fare on the big screen would have been showing hardcore gay porn.

I sold weed that summer. I passed on such information to Scott that long evening only to be informed that it was also his birthday. As I slipped Scott a $10 bag, he plastered me with a lip-smacking kiss right there in front of Michael, one of my regular street running partners.

"You fell for that it's my birthday shit?" Michael questioned my gullibility after the transaction.

"Well yeah!" I responded, beginning to sense his implication.

"Hell! He came back, "As cute he is, I'da done it too." Michael's confirmation of my taste in men allowed a slight swagger the rest of that stay at the spa.

Over time my longings for Scott faded. Every so often I'd see him when he cruised by my bench, flashing his killer smile. Each successive visit, Scott seemed to appear thinner and thinner. His bones never carried much weight, to begin with; now, even his gorgeous face took on the look of skin taut over bones. Later, I wondered if he had contracted HIV. That same summer, the public shockingly learned actor Rock Hudson's death from AIDS. What we hustler types started to phrase as 'the disease' showed its ugly morbidity out along the Boulevard. I wondered, *"Could my not snagging Scott, as my dream boyfriend, save me from exposure?"* 'Safe sex' regimens had yet to arrive. I would never know for sure about Scott.

Love and romance crossed my path, just not with who I wanted or desired. Around that time, a small thin, Puerto Rican guy with big eyes and an overbite relentlessly pursued me despite my lack of interest. Paul was his name. He always wore this dark overcoat. He was from back on the east coast somewhere, New York maybe. Often nights, I would be scoping out for a customer to buy weed or out looking for a trick; Paul would suddenly appear like a lost puppy dog. He did become one of my regular weed patrons, an incentive for him to be in my presence. Looking back on it, he may have been the companionship I was searching for. Paul certainly was persistent, if anything. Admittedly, he was not my 'type.' Was that because he was not White, maybe?

By the close of summer, I got out of selling weed and had found a legitimate job (more detailed in another story). That job panned out after only a few months. Then, I entered a job skills training program, all in effort keeping with me being legit.

Around about springtime, my usual loneliness resurfaced. I evermore yearned to be with someone. Such loathing of my life led me emotionally to feel, *"What's this all for?"*

The exact memory is blurry on the time and details but, walking alone one sunny LA afternoon what but, this attractive, sandy blond hustler caught my gaze. "What's up?" I may have coolly commented in passing.

"Nutt' in, you know. Whatchu do'in?" He likely responded to me. We started up a conversation. It was Devin. He mentioned that he had noticed me before going up and down the Boulevard, "like as if I had some purpose," he said. In other words, what I heard, not just some average everyday street hustler. My fragile self-esteem honed in on his acknowledgment, straight to my gut. That's all I recall of that first encounter.

Other night, Devon, I, and someone else, I've forgotten who, ended up getting drunk, out on the Boulevard, swigging a bottle of Mad Dog 20/20 cheap wine. Just us broke young hustlers escaping the reality of the street, by the cheapest means available.

Next time we encountered each other out on a fine Hollywood night hustling. Reeling in desperation, I asked Devon if he knew where to cop some speed. By then, that night, I'd decided to blow off completing the job skills training program. Feeling hopeless inside, why not just fuck it all off, really do some drugs? At least I'd be in Devon's presence as I abandoned my cares and responsibility. He gave me a look as to check whether I knew what I was about to do. Reassuring him, I knew what I was doing off we went to cop dope. Somewhere in the back of my thoughts, I knew the dope would eventually run out.

Then what, suicide maybe? I didn't want to consider or even think about the end results. The dope would help me escape. In the meantime, there, I was spending time in the company of this beautifully handsome guy, who saw me as something more than the average.

Finally, we scored speed then got some cheap motel room on Sunset Boulevard, up near where Hollywood's female hookers strutted their wares for sale. Shortly after getting the room, Devon proceeded with a syringe to inject that sweet poison into my veins. As it panned out, hours flew by, we spent the rest of the night, well into the morning, jabbering non-stop with some other tweekers that somehow ended up getting invited up to our motel room.

On into the next day, we got separated. I still had money to keep the escape going. Cashing out my monthly welfare allotment, how I got the funds for the dope, which also meant when the dope ran out, I'd be homeless too. I spotted Devon out on Highland Avenue as the afternoon sun beamed down. Yelling out his name across the six-lane roadway, hoping he wouldn't ignore me, now that that first high had worn off. He responded, and I took this as a sign that everything is still good between us; still reluctant to state what my emotions, my loins wanted from him, instead, more speed another cheap hotel room. Somewhere within that last session of getting high with Devon, I sensed the close of my delusions was near. At the same time, I was out of money. I told him I wanted to also score some downers, get the suicide thing going. I believe he did his best to dissuade my intentions. Adding to my emotional downfall were the effects of withdrawal from two days of speed. He took me with him to help me score valium, about a handful, we parted and that turned out to be the last I ever saw Devon..

When darkness fell that next night, I caught the #4 bus and rode all the way to the end, the beach in Santa Monica. A block or so from the actual beach, I stopped into a corner store to buy a tall can of Budweiser, which I hated the taste of. Minutes later, I'd walked to the beach, myself plopped down in the sand, swallowed the valiums and proceeded to quickly gulp down the nasty tasting 'tall one'. Warm, white foam waves came up over my feet as I stared out into the vast blackened sky above the Pacific. *"Juan, get up! Walk out into the water!"* an inner heard voice encouraged. Woozy, feeling the effects of beer and barbiturates come over me, I staggered to stand. *"Go ahead...Go on, if you want to die!"* that voice again echoed. I stood still...

Next, I must have backed out due to the fact I wound up in jail at the West Los Angeles substation. I remembered nothing of what happened, except what the police told me afterward, of my causing a ruckus out in the streets of Santa Monica, enough so to get me arrested.

Not too long after my beach blackout, homeless with only the clothes on by back, among limited choices, I decided to take myself and my emotional wounded soul b1ack towards home to Indiana. I called it quits. *"LA, Uncle...You win"!*

28 Days (1984)

"A hard head makes a soft ass!" I'd oft heard that old proverb my elders speak, a warning, in the household I grew up. The phrase about describes my early efforts at prostituting in LA. The first time out on Santa Monica Boulevard found me propped up in front a strip mall where there was a 7 Eleven, just a block or two west of Oki Dogs. All went smoothly. Most likely someone got a headjob. Not sure whether I was giving or I got. What I was sure of, I had not set out intending to turn a trick that evening. My young, dumb self and full of it thinking afterward; *"Hey, I made $30 for about ten, maybe fifteen minutes of my time...not too bad."* I should have been out of the house that day looking for a 'legitimate' job Having not put in much real effort to that end, I wasn't rushing to return home to be nagged over my joblessness by Art; my now former lover, and our roommate Ty.

A week later, I found myself trying again to sell my ass for money, same locale in front of that 7Eleven. Bam! That time the trick turned out to be an undercover vice cop. I got busted for prostitution. The second time trying this out in LA and my dumb ass ends up getting arrested for the first time in my life.

Being transported by police in handcuffs, all seemed so surreal, having never been arrested. Initially taken to the Los Angeles County Sheriff's Station in West Hollywood. I remember, at the time, thinking how sleek and fashionable I looked with hair weave extensions, a look I copied from early Tom Bailey of the Thompson Twins band. A cowl lick bang in front and a straight fall in the back. This other queeny-looking Latino guy also in the holding cell took to bluntly informing me, "Girl, you better get that out your head, or it'll be ripped out downtown," referring to my fake straightened hair extensions.

My first thought was, *"Who the hell is this, she don't know me?"* But, as the gravity of reality set in, I realized and figured he knew more about what would be expected than I did, even if it was a blunt way to help me. With his help, we then proceeded, with my head held between his knees, to unbind my weave. I recall a feeling of somewhat kinship. There we were two gay 'children' of color helping take care of one another's needs in spite of us both ensnared within the dehumanizing Los Angeles County system of correction.

Finally, reaching downtown, I shuffled to and through the massive Los Angeles, Main Men's Jail. LA is and was so big almost unbelievably it had its own gay wing in jail. Known to its frequent visitors as HOJJ (Hall of Justice Jail). The building was built as an early skyscraper in the 1920s in the Civic Center area. HOJJ was the old jail located on the top floors. Whenever I did get close enough to the windows, at the edges of the cell tiers, I was privy to a high above view of the Hollywood Freeway and downtown LA through iron-barred windows.

I spent two or three days there in a cell with an older, Black trans queen (now more appropriately called transgender). No problems arose between us. What I will never forget was when she revealed to me where, on her body, the silicone injected into her thighs had since fallen. What remained, right there before my amazed eyes, were drippy folds of skin and flesh. Almost as if she had side gills.

I appeared my first time in a court room, before a judge and pleaded no contest to the charges as recommended by the, just then, appointed public defender. Seeing myself walking away from that gate at the main jail, I consoled myself that I'd gained a new experience and, now, had a criminal record. What would be my first, but not the last, in a career of misdemeanors.

After getting arrested and going to jail my roommates definitely decided it was time for me to leave the house. The whole ordeal proved to them evidence of my lack of seriousness about getting a job and being responsible. So with that, I headed back out the Boulevard to make the best of the situation I put myself into. With no viable prospects, I turned back to the notion of hooking.

"Fuck!" Talk about no luck, on my third try, I got popped again. That time when I appeared in court for my second prostitution offense, the judge sentenced me to serve 28 to 45 days in jail. I was headed for a return visit to HOJJ.

The transfer classification process in the main jail that time around lasted about ten hours. I had been there before, still, all I was going through bewildered me. While waiting in one of the many holding cells, I just so happened to look over to the next cell to notice this young Black, kid in a red jumpsuit. Ear hustling the conversations, I found out that the red jail clothing meant that he was a juvenile inmate. The adult general population wore orange jumpsuits, while the gay unit, HOJJ, inmate's jumpsuit color was blue almost grey. That kid was in the cell hog-tied, shackled with both hands cuffed behind his back attached to his cuffed ankles. I watched him, there in the next cell, as he was rolling around grunting and growling like some trapped wild animal. I had not been a witness to what had happened prior, to why had the deputies put him in such restraints. All the same, what I saw shocked me to my very core. *"How could this be happening?"* I was thinking.This was no Hollywood movie scene taking place no more than a few feet from where I stood. He could not have been any older than 13 or 14. I was only 18 myself. Deputies were shouting at him to do as they commanded. That very young, Black, man-boy resisted their pleas rolling around on the cold hard, concrete floor grunting. Right then, I sensed the feeling that up until that point, my life had been sheltered. I imagined, maybe, in different circumstances, I myself could have been that feral, Black juvenile, right there in that red jumpsuit.

Days passed in jail depression set in. For only the second time in my life, I let my facial hair grow out into a beard. What the hell did I care? I wasn't going anywhere and had nowhere to go. I settled into my cell, not really speaking to anyone, and I only recognized one or two people I'd seen from out in the streets in Hollywood. Sam, Black in his thirties, I'd seen before. I'd heard him brag about supposedly having connections at Motown Records. Despite such 'connections,' he usually could be found hanging at Oki Dogs chasing after the latest arrived White, boy hustler.

Awhile into my 28 day stay, I was to meet Keith; skinny, dark, and tall. He seemed to know everyone and took a liking to me, and oddly enough, nothing sexual. Keith never pressured me in that way. Looking back on it, he may have set out to try and fuck me but just gave up when I showed no interest. I sorta became protégé to his mentorship. He was the one on my tier that had 'juice' or with enough influence to work around what you wanted or needed in jail. Eventually, I desperately needed a haircut and a clipper shave. The single-bladed, jail-issued razors caused the skin on my face to break out severely. Keith either paid for my cut or more importantly, got it done to get me a clipper shave. I still relish good memories of Keith. In a way, I forgot the fact that we were locked up when I was around him. The actual reality of being in jail made forgetting a good thing.

At breakfast chow one morning, which usually consisted of powdered eggs, I got up to go get the salt from another table, something to add some taste. A queeny-looking, big Black, gay "Miss Thing" did the best to give me 'grief' and attitude overtaking the salt shaker. I'd taken notice of getting the looks of death coming from his direction. *"It was like who did I think I was?"* Me being Black and Gay, how come I wasn't t a known associate of the same crew as that big queen? *"Whatever!"* I thought. That morning, in particular, I was not the one to be taking shit from "Miss Thang" In the process, a loud 'cuss out' ensued. Breakfast ended as we were ordered back to our own separate tiers. *"Bitch, I'a...fuck you up!"* I woofed out on my way back to my tier, making a dramatic scene.

Just so next morning, as I usually walked up the several flights of concrete stairs, bounded by thick iron railings, on the way to chow hall, up ahead of me on the next flight of stairs, I looked to see standing, maybe four or five big, built, scary, hardcore street queens. Miss Thing, the one from the scuffle the day before, right in the middle of the pack. I stopped, shocked, terrified really, and at a loss of what to do next. Obviously, this pack of Black queens before me seemed to be my payback for 'messing' with one of theirs. Their plan entailed taking care of me even if in the end, it meant throwing my 'lone' ass over those metal railings, tossing me down the middle of the stair corridor, from ten or eleven storeys up. Exactly, not a moment too soon, Keith appeared and intervened; as mentioned before, he had 'juice.' No doubt, I could have taken out that one big, old queen, who started the whole mess, but no I was not 'bad' enough to take on the whole bunch of them. Either way, I definitely was grateful for Keith helping me as much as I was stunned at how the whole situation unfolded.

Oftentimes, after chow, I made my way back to my tier quickly. My intent was to be able to take a shit in semi-privacy. Having no privacy while on the crapper remained one of the aspects of being in jail I never grew accustomed to. There was another important aspect of jail life, also not to my liking, I later discovered.

Somehow, I usually managed to scrounge up a newspaper to read on most of those days in HOJJ. On one particular afternoon, as Keith set out to drum up players for a game of Spades. I declined on playing on account of my wanting to read the newspaper.

Later, I looked up to notice Keith standing near the bars of my cell. "Childe what chu read'n that White newspaper fo?" Keith stated dejectedly. That exact particular moment sticks out in my memory. I laid there on my stomach, in my bunk, facing Keith and the cell bars, my mouth hanging open. Speechless! No explanation is needed to his question. I knew exactly, without explanation, the meaning he conveyed. True, as he just said, nearly every item or news story in that day's paper detailed things about White people and their lives. Yet, as sure as I understood that, how could I convey to him the fact that the paper's title did not read "The White Los Angeles Times." To me, it seemed almost just as clear, as well, that unless or until Keith realized such facts, he would indeed keep coming back and forth and be in and out of jail cells. Never understanding, seemingly clueless as to why. I remember just remaining silent, not having enough words to answer Keith's question that day. Not wanting or intending to be 'above' his understanding.

In the cell next door held this kid around my age, yet he was more immature in nature. I've since forgotten his name, so I'll refer to remember him as BD, which stands for Big Dick. For certain, I'd recalled seeing him around in the same Hollywood environment as I did my own dirty work. BD would be classified as gay-for-pay or just gay while behind jail bars. A rusted-out hole had developed in the steel wall in between our cells. One of those nights, BD entertained me and my cellmate, a beaten-down, older White guy, with his art of pleasuring himself. His size reputation was real, no joke.

Keith got it into his mind that it was his 'mission' to have sex with BD. They both seemed game. It was only a matter of timing. The amorous moment duly arrived one evening as a group of us played a game of Spades in front of BD's cell. Up went the jail-issued blanket tied to the cell bars, the only shield of any privacy.

"There it is, big joker baby!" one of us players roared.

"Ooh, mmmh," we could hear the noises in the background.

"Like that dick, huh?" came out slightly whispered from beyond blanketed cell.

I just couldn't get over that there they were fucking, with the sounds and smells obstructed only by a blanket, less than a mere few feet away from us and our card game. In fact, we were the 'lookouts' for their illegal sex tryst.

BD gave off hints that he'd welcome me taking advantage of similar opportunities with him if I wanted to do so. Well, being that there was not much else to occupy oneself in jail and he was willing and eager. So, a few evenings later, I pushed him into his cell and groped his crotch. Up went the blanket on the bars. Note: the unofficial rules in such situations are that the one who is not 'gay' is acted upon. I got down to sucking that rather large dick. Then, I stopped a few minutes into the action. *"Fuck! I wanted to be pleasured as well"*, I was thinking to myself. Besides, everyone else was right there, just a few feet from us on the other side of the sheet. It almost felt as if they were part of the sex too.

I got the realization that there was another aspect of jail life, I would never get used to; plenty available sex but no privacy.

I survived HOJJ. I knew, even back then, the 28day experience proved clear to me I didn't have intentions to make the jailhouse my long long-term, recurring residence. From then on, I had to keep in mind how my activities on the outside could lead me back to jail or even worse; prison.

Just Say No (1984)

You'd not be wrong in describing me as curious. My curiosity, for better or worse, made me who I am. Never to be the one who followed the crowd, usually because I never really felt I fit in anywhere. Therefore I reasoned, why should I subject myself to the rules and demands of people and places where I didn't feel welcome?

By 16, gay and out, I just assumed to make the best of my life; I needed to escape to California. Still, I sustained three and a half years of high school; after knowing this fact about myself, finally, I left without graduating. In spite of that minor, not so minor detail, I didn't let that deter me. 18 and growing, particularly in Black working-class terms, "I's grownn!" Meaning I could do exactly as I pleased. So, I'm thinking, I'm off, headed to join 'my' crowd.

Art, my first lover, and I had broken up by the end of the summer. In truth, I realized, then, that I may never have been in love with him, yet, I did love him much. He'd rescued me from the street and provided me, love. The love I couldn't understand. We were an eclectic, if not odd match. I recall seeing him one afternoon, a tall, soft-built, blond White guy in the living room, with the stereo on, singing along loud and deeply to Patti Labelle, at her most black diva voice. And then there was me; this, then, skinny queer black, White acculturated, boy- man intently into jamming to the likes of The B52's and Devo. My hair was made up in the style of one of the Thompson Twins, a cowl lick weave bang over my forehead.

With my limited experience in matters of love and romance, I figured that just maybe love was not always meant to be mutually reciprocal. Oftentimes, I thought, maybe the whole idea of being in love was overrated anyway. I'd never been in love.

18, gay, and free. As 'free' as I imagined how to be. More so, being just as well consistently horny and ready to get and be laid. Love overrated or not, I never turned down the sex. It was the delirious distraction I enjoyed never getting enough of.

Even after all my experience 'performing on my back,' so to speak, Art was probably the loudest person I ever had sex with. In those moments, he could get on my last nerve. At the time, it seemed to me like he felt he needed, literally, inform the whole fucking neighborhood that we were fucking and that he was gettin' some.

Once while lovemaking, I fucked him with him, as usual, being extra noisy. I had gotten off and laid there beside him, caressing. Calm, relaxed, and before I'd realized what was actually happening, he'd entered and was inside me. Suddenly, I could not believe that the sensation of getting fucked was not being as excruciatingly painful as it had always previously been. Art wrapped his arms around tightly and held me. Our mouths were deeply locked as he moved gently, lovingly. I trusted him. That night I, actually, may have been the loud one. I enjoyed that fuck. That pleasure of getting fucked never again happened to me.

The job I worked on felt meaningless. David Orgel's; is located in the Farmer's Market on 3rd Street and Fairfax. I did stock for a store that sold silverware and other wedding gifts. Most days, I remember being completely bored out of my mind. Any job was bound to feel meaningless and boring cause I had sex, 'on the brain' as I always seemed to have back then. In fact, it was not uncommon for me to provide myself some relief sexually on a restroom break. I just couldn't get enough.

I got stimulation within the interaction of diversity of my coworkers. My boss, a Black woman, an immigrant from Beliz. I'll forever remember her lilting accent I'd actually never heard from an actual person before. Two other co-workers were women who'd immigrated from the Philippines. Until that time, I'd certainly never been in any setting among people of such backgrounds, with multiple accents to boot. I could have never imagined, even six months prior, my workplace so international, cosmopolitan even. I recall my Pilipino coworkers telling me of a native delicacy in which one of the ingredients involved the blood of a fertilized egg. Such became a hotly discussed topic for a few days. Especially by my other coworker, a hefty, down-home Black sister who insisted that the Pilipino dish was "nasty" This despite her having no qualms about proudly touting Black American folk's eating chitlins, pig's feet, and various other hog innards. Which I, for one, often considered as "nasty."

The anticipation of nightlife sustained me. Rarely a night did I miss going out, hanging on and around spots along Santa Monica Boulevard in West Hollywood. Still, my favorite stop being The Odyssey, down on Beverly at La Cienega. The venue I'd once brought my cousin to, back when I'd first come out to her. They didn't serve alcohol; thus, you only had to be over 16 to get in. Totally into the New Wave music scene that LA radio stations like KROQ pumped out the sound of. It thrilled me to no end to have found in LA a hip dance club playing this new funky music. 'New wave' fit my niche; not disco, which was officially dead then anyway yet, it retained that beat toward the dancefloor with a lot of synths and spacey sounds. And it was not rapping that I felt was too Black for me and that particularly rejected any sensibility toward gayness. Inside that club, I felt as I had arrived. The Odyssey was the shit, where all the freshest hip kids hung out. Guys danced with other guys, and not all who did so were gay. No one really cared there at The Odyssey.

Being with Art, he basically paid all the bills, so the money I earned got to use and wasted as much as I wanted. Sharp and dressing to the nines. "Thank you very much!" Off I'd go on weekends shopping down to the Garment District, downtown along Los Angeles Street. I could find the latest styles at less than retail prices. Sometimes, I haggled for an even cheaper cost, as I once witnessed my Cousin Rhoda do. I was in heaven.

"Music!" I'd almost literally go wild buying albums to add to my growing prized music collection. I can see that now, looking back on it, I spent money compulsively buying music, the way I would later have the compulsion to buy drugs. Just similar to my dope days, whenever I'd be in the record store, my bladder felt like releasing. I had an advantage being on the West Coast, the place where bands came to make it; I'd find the latest music by unknown and upcoming bands and get them cheap, allowing me the first to find the latest in the hip, club music. "That was important, you know."

I learned to drive a stick shift, manual car. I have loved the thrill of a manual ever since. Art taught me on his little white Mazda GLC. That better facilitated me to take the car out alone. From the first of me getting a driver's license, I've been a safe driver. I never viewed getting being behind the steering wheel or gripping that stick shift as an extension of my dick size, a display of my manhood. Probably, cause of too many experiences, high school days, riding along with my mostly White male friends driving recklessly at high speeds, having visions of my like flashing by, like they had something to prove.

Safe driver aside, I did wind end up getting that little GLC towed away one night, parked at Vaseline Alley. Had to call and tell Art the news of such at like 2:30 in the morning. An hour or so later, low and behold, he shows up in this huge black Cadillac limo. Art later informed me that the limo service just happened to be the only one willing to come out to City Terrace- East LA past 2 in the morning. We lived in a heavily Latino neighborhood in East LA with a known reputation for gang activity. Both I and the car were rescued that night.

Vaseline Alley; a cruising spot easy casual sex, oftentimes where I'd ended up when out on the town, particularly due to being underage for the bars. That site's where I'd come to know many of my later friends and associates. Many who'd come to play major roles along the LA journey. One such Michael Chaffin, a wiry and loud-mouthed lush who somehow always ended up appearing and making himself known to the folks I was hanging and me. At first, just the sight of him, usually drunk and obnoxious, filled me with loathing. Whatever he was on, I wanted no part of. Michael seemed to be proof evidence of a seamy, low-life slice of West Hollywood and gay fabulousness. Yet, as would come to pass, more and more 'that' nightlife; Vaseline Alley, the hustlers, sex predators, the drunks, and speed heads made up the world in which I chose and found myself roaming.

Work grew more and more dreary, taxing. Often than not, I found it hard to keep myself from falling asleep while on the job, all due to my happenings from the night before. Assuring myself, I had things under control. *'I'm only smoking a little weed here and there... had a few (illegal) drinks here and there, all harmless young, gay adult fun.*

In the alley one evening, my gaze beamed on two very blond, very White, surfer-looking guys sitting together on the wall next to the parking lot. For sure, I figured they were together. Still, oddly enough, I thought, *there they are a couple sitting in the cruisiest spot for sex in all of West Hollywood.* Up I walked and spoke, not really sure if I thought I had the chance to fuck one of them. "What the worst that could happen?" The 'most butch' one was Larry and younger, more soft-looking guy; John. Yes, they did happen to be a couple. John (Beerman) would later tell me how my forwardness that night made him partial to me. Starting that night, John became one of my close buddies and 'street dogs' out on the Boulevard. John's beach blond, good looks gave me a thrill. The thrill of being closely linked to someone whom everybody else wanted, desired. I think John, being so sought after sexually, enjoyed having a friend who did not just want to ultimately screw him.

Later hanging in the scene, I encountered Junior Boy. Like something, someone I had never ever actually seen before in real life. Junior; the definition of a 'pretty boy,' eternally natural- tanned skin, the color of cream in the coffee, thin, with a sharp, Romanesque nose and with straight, brown-highlighted hair that covered just above his shoulders. We both noticed one another around and about those streets. To me, at first, I felt he was just way too good-looking to be interested in me. Yet, he always returned my attentions, at least in a cruisy kinda way. My so brief romantic experience taught me the belief that good-looking, White guys, the ones particularly attracted to black men, tended and seemed to be lose sluts. The kind that aimed to see how many black men they could fuck, a numbers game. Junior Boy, a mixed-raced Latino, maybe he fits that category too. So, overwhelmed by his beauty and his being attracted to me, I felt unsure whether he just wanted me for another sex trick.

There I was, another night out on the town, escaping from my dreary work and home life. Walking my regular stomping grounds, Santa Monica Boulevard, the block or two right around the Circus of Books. That night, I happened onto Junior Boy looking gorgeous and tasty as ever, flashing his pretty, brown eyes and wide overbite smile. In spite of my 18 years, I reverted back to puberty and middle school awkwardness. He was just that beautiful. Leaving me near about babbling nonsense. Sometimes within our encounter and awkwardness, Junior happened to ask me, "You wanna get...some acid...and split it with me?" Deeply desiring to be close to him, be in his presence. Until then, any ambivalence I had about doing 'hard' drugs faded to nothingness. I responded, "A...a...Ok." He could have just well said, *"Juan...let's get a gun...and go rob a store."* I would have said yes to whatever he'd asked me. *"Here will you drink this arsenic with me...you go first?"* Since it was only half a hit and he'd promised to stay with me. *It was a reasonable offer.* Before then, I'd never taken any drug harder than a joint of weed.

Yes, I ended up buying the hit of acid. Junior Boy, then, tore a tiny dark piece of what looked like blue cellophane or plastic, no bigger than a breath mint. "Leave it on your tongue and... suck on it!" he instructed, staring straight intently into my eyes as he made the sexually suggestive pun.

Without fear of what might happen, I put my trust in him and did as he told me. Soon after, we were close together, holding hands tightly, wrapping our arms around each other. After a short while, it all of a sudden came on. Immediately, euphoric rush sensations exploded in my brain. Seemingly like fireworks, my body tingled like a million times over, from the tip of my toenails to hair follicles atop my head. I pulled him even closer, tighter. Our lips touched, tongues met, lost ever so completely in that moment right then, right there. Nothing else in the world mattered!

Everything seemed to meld together. The sensual sensation of feeling, all over, the most beautiful man(boy) I have ever seen, held in my arms, with lips locked tightly. Like as if no one else existed!

Junior and I began to laugh our heads off, between caresses, at the stupidest things. Simply just the way someone would look at us would send us cackling. Only us two were in on the joke. Eventually, I realized the time, although; minutes passed like hours. I needed to catch my #4 bus back downtown and make the transfer to another bus back home to East LA. Junior as well, needed to catch a bus home to somewhere else in the vastness that was, is, LA, far beyond the queer fabulousness of West Hollywood, beyond that 'one night' in Boystown. I nearly spilled the change for the bus fare on the floor because he and I were laughing so hard. *Acid peaking!*

Even then, amongst all the sensual, sexual and euphoric excitement, I knew I felt hooked. As if I'd waited for this all of my life. My world, the world, was right. My experience, my feelings, right then, I never wanted it to end.

"If I could feel like this, I wouldn't give a fuck about nothing!" I thought.

My next thought drew me back to childhood, where I carried a memory of seeing a 'wino' passed out alongside a curb near the neighborhood liquor store, Angelo's. Where my daddy could not often be found hanging out there also, especially weekends. Just a kid, I remembered being completely dumbfounded, staring out the car window at the condition of that passed-out wino. *Now!* That night on that #4 bus, with Junior Boy, I understood.

"He musta been feeling… like I feel now!" Said the voice said in my head, "I don't give a fuuck!"

Junior Boy and I continued our laughing among heavy kissing, right there on the bus, as if we dared anyone to say something. Truly, I felt I had lived all my life for what was happening at that moment.

We got off the bus at the corner of Hill and Temple Streets, across from HOJJ (Hall of Justice Jail). Then crossed the street to wait for our transfer busses. The bus stop stood directly in front of Los Angeles City Hall, the iconic art deco tower that stood the city's tallest for decades and was made famous in the logo of the 50's cop show "Dragnet." We waited there intertwined, legs, crotches, limbs, chests, lips, hands, fingers, tongues right on top of a large steam grate. Steam intermittently rose up, increasing the heat we were already generating, blowing loose Junior Boy's shirt and exposing his smooth bare skin underneath my dark fingers. When our bus finally came, we made one last, lovingly long kiss and parted ways.

I seem to recall arriving for work, late again, the next morning and getting fired. If not, then I got fired not too long after that night. The first firing from a job that would not be the last. *What did I care*? I had been to 'heaven's the highest mountain peak.

Sometime later, I did have a more formal date with Junior Boy, taking him out in my ex-lover's GLC. Somewhere or somehow, we fizzled out; I think I paid for everything that evening also. *My momma didn't raise no fool!* Never actually did we fully consummate our passions; fucked.

For certain, now, the monkey gripped on my back. I ever so craved that feeling again, that blissful moment. Heaven or hell, I had to have it. No way could I just say no.

Cream Filled, Bear Clawed (1984)

As winter came around, wherein LA temperatures dropped from balmy 75 to like 55, and it rained, I ended up out on the streets of Boystown. LA winter translates into the wet season.

More and more, I learned the ropes of how to be a wild and carefree denizen of the streets, out among the beautiful people. In plainer terms, I was young, broke, and hustling the sidewalks-

"La da di, la dada, la, da di, la dada."

Drugs seemed a natural aspect of the atmosphere which I roamed. I'd had my taste of the forbidden poison that would eventually be my drug of choice; crystal meth. Still, being broke most of the time meant that smoking weed and drinking usually served as my most common pastimes.

Down at Okidogs, the scene had become a little too rough for my tastes to be hanging out there on a regular basis. It was more just the place where young newbie runaways showed up, the same as I did when I was 16. The perv types who preyed on young and naive often flocked there as well, along with all the old burned-out hustlers who'd serve as go-betweens and procurers to the chicken hawks.

I wanted to be less associated among that gritty side of the Boulevard. So, I gravitated further west along with Santa Monica. There it seemed the Boulevard still had at least the illusion of being the place of beautiful gays, without any blemishes.

The Dunkin Donuts, by the corner of Crescent Heights Avenue, a block away from Vaseline Alley, became the new stomping grounds. There I'd cruise for sex, cop dope, and hang out and talk shit with my fellow affiliates.

Considering myself less than a full-time prostitute hustler, I still had the lost hope of getting picked up, any night now, by some handsome guy who would sweep me off my feet and take me away from the degraded environment I had succumbed. Dream on.

Not all was in my dreams. Every now and then, the slight glitter of Hollywood did rain down along the Boulevard.

On such a random nameless night I sat, hanging out on the parking lot wall outside Dunkin Donuts, sitting there shooting the shit with Skyler, who claimed to be the son of the actor who played Barnabus in the television series "Dark Shadows." I'd never even heard of that show, so I just figured him as some street queen trying to be more than actually were. Skyler, loud-mouthed and lanky, made up for in reputation what he lacked in the looks category. He made sure everyone he met knew of his Hollywood 'pedigree'.

"Bieatch! It's Chaka Khan in here!" He shouted out toward me, standing next to a long, black Mercedes sedan with dark-tinted windows.

"Shut the hell up! You always ly'in." I responded to his outburst.

"I ain't ly'in, come look!" he shrieked, pointing into the open sunroof of the Mercedes. I got up and walked over to the car just to prove him wrong. Sure, enough, as I looked in, it was her in the flesh, famed R&B funk, singer Chaka Khan. Her solo hit, "I Feel for U," burned up the airwaves that year. She sat in the driver's seat, behind the steering wheel. Some older white guy and a passed out, real butch looking, a Black female was there laid across the backseat.

Skyler kept on talking much shit, as was his usual. I proceeded to reach in to shake Chaka's hand, doing my best at being polite when I ran into someone famous. She took down our names for free passes to her upcoming concert at the Greek Theater. Then, just as suddenly as she had appeared, she was gone. Yes, we did meet a famous singer just hanging out as usual on our hustler/how-to spot.

My luck, within that same week, I ended up getting busted for prostitution, again, so I happened to be locked up in county jail the night of that concert.

I had melted into my environment. LA's wet season had arrived just as I had worn out my tourist visa, the one I'd proverbially carried since I first arrived at 16. I was LA; LA was now me. As an adult, a series of decisions put me where I was, in that condition.

Art, my former lover, and partner, came out to the Boulevard to meet me one last time. He intended to say goodbye before he left town to join the Navy. "Don't you have to be straight to be in the service?" I queried Art as we sat down someplace on Santa Monica, maybe even grabbing a bite to eat. Avoiding my question, Art instead said to me, "I'm not going to tell you not to do what you feel you need to do. (meaning selling my ass for money) Just don't get busted!"

"I won't," I assured him as we hugged tightly for the last time. His honest assessment of me demonstrated how much he loved me.

Yet, he jinxed me. Less than a week after our meeting, I was arrested, again, for hooking. That time I was determined not to get sentenced for my prior record, knowing I could end up getting 6months in jail. Right away in the West Hollywood sheriff's substation, I started biting and chewing on my fingertips. I meant to botch up being fingerprinted. As well, I also gave an alias, David Rogers. Luck turning my way, it worked. I got released after 3days with time served. *Another lesson in street life; cops and jail come with the territory-you work the system as best you can.*

Later back out working the Boulevard sidewalk, on an unusually breezy and chilly evening, a big stocky, thick-necked guy in a BMW happened along my way. He stopped. I got in and told him to drive down round towards Melrose.

The alleys behind the businesses there had carports in the rear, where you could inconspicuously turn a trick in a car without any notice. The dude is not more than 30 or so and really muscle-bound. Unlike most gay guys, I found myself not too impressed.

Small talking prior to getting down to the sex, he mentioned that he either was with or trying out for the Raider's NFL Team. The Raiders team had recently relocated the franchise from Oakland down to Los Angeles. His massive body made what he told me to sound believable.

Giving him a head job, only afterward, it occurred to me when I wiped my lips off his cum; I had made a mistake. So overtaken with his body and masculinity, I neglected to negotiate a price for services; beforehand.

He passed me $15, saying, "That's all I have...on me."

"Really," I thought, burning him with my stare. *"You're a pro football player or whatever, and that's all you got!"* What could I do, take a swing at him? He could've knocked me out with one tap. So, I rolled up my meager earnings in my pocket as I stepped back out on the sidewalk, in the exact spot where he had picked me up. It since was even colder since then. Now, with the wind blowing, no sympathy was given as I shivered there, closing the door of his BMW.

That lesson cut deep in my brain. In the course of hooking, *never, ever, go with a trick I could not physically overtake*, in case things got off course and turned out like they did that breezy, chilly, broke evening.

LA is paradise, nearly 68 degrees or so all year long. So rarely does it ever get cold that when it occurs, it's something you remember. That night my balls, literally, felt the chill of being out there with nowhere to crash for the night.

Santa Monica Boulevard looked bare. Hustlers that did get lucky had since gone. No luck was I having. The later it got my balls, and the rest of me got no warmer. It occurred to me, the longer I stood out there, how obvious what I was doing appeared to the cops.

Midnight or so, I popped into the Dunkin Donuts to warm up and get my face off the Boulevard for a while.

Inside, I noticed as this pasty-looking, skinny, White dude no older than about 30 pulled up into the parking lot outside. He drove an old long, Lincoln Continental, the kind in which Kennedy rode in when assassinated. He came in, and since we were the only customers, we made some small talk. He looked too young to be picking up hustlers. Not really that attractive to be looking for a freebie. In a real sense, the guy appeared kinda unhealthy looking.

Time passed. He inquired where I was headed at such an hour. I told him the truth. "Nowhere." He then offers me to crash at his place. Instincts, maybe street smarts, told me the dude was not out to pull a fast one on me. In my desperation, I could have just wanted to believe he was on the up and up.

We hopped into his big Lincoln and took off from Dunkin Donuts. As we drove, the Boulevard seemed so eerie that night with barely a hustler nor street person to be seen.

His place was out in the 'Valley,' North Hollywood. In my snobbish opinion, the San Fernando Valley section of Los Angeles wasn't the 'real' LA to me. It had only been about a year or so since the song "Valley Girl" by Moon Zappa had made that hot, suburban expanse nationally infamous.

He lived in one of those apartment buildings with two floors with parking underneath. Each apartment had its own outside door, like a motel. LA appeared as if it had millions of apartments just such as his, especially out in the Valley.

Once inside, he passed me a clean pillow and blanket. He may have even made me a sandwich. Then, turning on the stereo, he put on Depeche Mode, the "Puppets" album. I loved that group; it stunned me this guy liked the new wave as well. It was at that moment I really felt comfortable, and he seemed ok, kinda cool even.

True to his word, he allowed me to get sleep without pushing me to have sex or anything like the sort. I got a well-needed night's rest, sleeping well into the next day. Not knowing when or where I'd be able to lay my head down next, I knew I needed to take the best advantage of what rest I could get.

The next day, the night really, when both of us were up, I took a shower as he got dressed to drive me back, through the Cahuenga Pass by the Hollywood Bowl to the other side of the hill, back to Hollywood.

He pulled the car over, and I got out on Highland, right by Hollywood High School. Then, unassumingly, his big vintage Lincoln Continental drove off.

I never saw that guy again. I think I remember his name being Tim. Whatever his name was, I never forgot him or lost sight of his kindness to me that night.

Looking back, many years later, his pasty emaciated appearance may have signaled him as an early sufferer of HIV/AIDS, well before it was a commonly named diagnosis.

Another lesson learned: no matter the harshness of the street life I found myself in, there were moments when I had been taken care of, just when I needed it. Unaware at the time, such genuine grace would shape who I became.

Seasoned (1985)

A year, in LA, on my own, proved I had what it took to live the city life. LA was my home, even if sometimes 'home' meant wherever I laid my head at the end of the night or home being a trashy room down amongst the expanse of Los Angeles' skid row. Still, I envisioned my sojourn to the balmy paradise as a success. Within that vision, I still believed I would meet the love of my life. Surely a possibility among such quantity and variety available here. Failing to encounter him here, to me, meant he was not to be found.

My more than humble abode, a single-room-occupancy hotel on the east side of downtown LA, at Sixth and San Pedro Streets. Public assistance (welfare) meant for able-bodied males provided me with such accommodations.

My associates out in West Hollywood, along the Boulevard, were terrified of the type of area I was living in. At first, I too felt myself to be above such environs. Sleeping at night or two on the pavements of Hollywood coupled with harassment from the county sheriffs or the LAPD induced a change in my sentiments, a change in what I could tolerate. Looking back on it, my White associates shunned their noses at public assistance lodgings. I suppose had I the fortune to be picked up every night; I could have looked askance at such options.

On the Boulevard, my constant compatriots were Michael and John. Michael a drunk coping with enough street smarts to make do. John, on the other hand, possessed California surfer, blond looks that got him picked up with such frequency and easy street smarts were not a necessary prerequisite to get along. They contrasted the highs and lows of hustlers living along Santa Monica Boulevard.

In time, Michael schooled me in ways and skills of survival. For example; If a trick gets to acting funny, like he doesn't want to pay, after the fact, break something of their property like kicking his car. He instructed me. "Go off...make a scene!" The reasoning being; that john, married and established, would be more worried about the police showing up and possibly getting arrested. In short, a hustler in such circumstances had almost nothing to lose by the cops showing up, i.e., going for a night in jail would not scare them. Michael's training helped me be less fearful working those hard-edged streets. Like the more you do something, the more it becomes what you are used to. What would frighten most people started not to faze me.

Just like one day, Michael and I were out sitting on a bus bench, a typical sunny afternoon in paradise right across the street from the Pussycat Adult Theater. Sitting out there not even really hustling, still, as hustlers, we were always on the ready if we became so lucky. We were just passing the time before more lucrative happenings come evening time.

Out of nowhere, all of a sudden, cop cars, marked and unmarked, appeared at the stoplight, less than 10feet or so in front of our bus bench. "Shiit...What the fuck!" One of us surely said out, shocked, at the same time assessing the situation and our need to take cover. Shotguns and large rifles appeared just as instantly. I could hear the cocking of triggers, like in some fucking cop action movie. All the guns pointed, aimed at this small compact car, stopped at the light. Thinking of that moment, now, the realization that any mishap and we could have been hit in the crossfire of stray bullets.

I seem to recall the suspects having been quickly removed, snapped in handcuffs, as simultaneously Michael and I discreetly, as two streetwise characters could be, sure to make no sudden moves in all the confusion, slipped away from that bench. One second, we were sitting, talking shit, and then, in the next, it was Dirty Harry times 10, right before our eyes. For sure, we both had some tale to tell for the rest of that day.

Contrastingly, hanging with John provided ease, a sort of seamlessness to being out on the street. John's looks being in high demand meant he always had a place to crash away from the actual streets. He may have intended to even out the score of my catch as you can fortunes. Often, he'd buy me something to eat and share his drugs, all the while never making me feel I was less than or that owed him.

The atmosphere of West Hollywood's gay ghetto felt like a sexual supermarket, open 24/7. It was nothing to make some quickly needed money or partake in a desired fuck with some hot attractive guy. If one fits the accepted standard of 'beautiful,' folks often seem to feel they had the prerogative to taste. John endured experiences from such attitudes. After all, we were out there smack dab in the middle of the supermarket, sitting on the shelf, so to speak.

John, then, was dating Curtis, who was nearly ten years older, 30 maybe. Curtis was crazy over him. I believed I knew it was not going to work out between them. John could never really respect or take seriously any guy too infatuated with him.

Curtis knew people in West Hollywood's world: bar owners, high up drug dealers, some folks in the gay porn; the sleazy producers and some performers

For a week or two that summer, we had the use of a house in the hills above Hollywood Boulevard just off of Highland, by way of one of Curtis' connections. John, Michael and I got the idea to have a party at the house. It really turned out to be a series of parties.

I made up a flyer as an advertisement for the party and had it printed at some shop on the Boulevard. This would be one time when we enjoyed ourselves without fear of harassment by the cops, plus we'd be in control of with who we partied. I grew so excited over having these parties, stemming from my idyllic expectations of life in LA, gay, free, taking pleasures in the delights of the city.

The night of the first party just kinda blurred by. We all ended up in like one room of the house. All through that night, just in that one room, it seemed like every few minutes or so, someone pulled out something to snort, smoke, or toot. I vividly remember memories of myself blowing someone weed shotguns, almost like we were simulating kissing. The hazy room was full of hustlers, gay and straight, a female or two maybe, a couple of guys I knew who had been in gay porn and, I recall, a particularly older man; likely that old guy produced porn. We all blended together that night, in some 'Hollyweird' way.

Drugs got consumed and began taking on full effect as outside daylight arose, giving a signal to the end of that first party. Ergo the blur.

Not remembering exactly whether it was the next night or a week later, party number two took place. At this one, we advertised it as costing $5 with all the beer you could drink. We passed out the flyers all along the Boulevard. To Curtis's amazement, that fest turned into a real hustler's ball.

Michael arrived with Brent, who was even worse drunk than Michael. Brent already blitzed when they arrived, happened to fall down the back steps, and passed out. That was the last we saw or heard of him, "Fuck it! Just leave him there; he won't remember any of it tomorrow anyway, said Michael, as we heard the thump Brent's body made as he hit the ground. He was left there on the ground where he passed out. We saw him days later on the Boulevard; we reminded him of how he'd ended up in the back of that strange house.

I bartended that night. Never favoring much drinking, myself, I witnessed folks in the process of becoming way too drunk. Seeing such results further cemented my poor opinion of alcohol. It surprised us having all the 'straight' trade having no qualms eagerly partying with us for 'real gay' hustlers.

The alcohol we ran, and Michael and I threatened to leave if Curtis did not go buy more. That would have left him there with all the rough, straight trade, who had paid a cover charge and knew his address. The threat worked. Curtis sacrificed making money as opposed to having property destroyed, but that ended our stints as the Hollywood party hosts with the most.

In the real everyday world, beyond escaping it, drinking, and getting high, sustenance provided, I make use of public assistance. In so navigating such, I became familiar with the down and out scene in downtown LA. It was not that I was opposed to legitimate work. It's just that my living a Boulevard lifestyle presented problems that conflicted with following the disciplines of getting a real job. Supposed freedom, youth, and living gay came first and foremost.

Public assistance entailed its own restrictions and disciplines that also had to be met. I panicked when I had failed to meet some requirements demanded by my social worker. Which could mean I would be given a 60day, no-service penalty. I simply could not see how I was to survive, even feed myself for 60 or more days.

Waiting outside the Department of Social Services office for that decision, I just so happened to notice this fellow sitting parked in a late model Volkswagen Jetta making a none too subtle cue my way. Having nothing but time, I walked over to see what he wanted; a Black man in his forties, maybe. *"Was he trying to pick me up?"* I was thinking, *"Here, at the welfare office?* Pleease!" I muttered.

Turned out he 'was' gay, or at least 'family' as some of us have been known to claim. He; retired from the military. Clearly, he made known his interest in me. Yet, I didn't bite. I sensed him having a view of me as young and green, which was true. If anybody was 'desperate,' it was not going to be me. As we sat there in his car conversing, he advised me that I should find work such as a night watchman, security maybe. That way, I could make good use of downtime to study and go back to school. We parted to no avail. His sage advice, I recall, more or less went in one ear and directly out the other.

Surely, I did get the penalty with my welfare case. I actually would be out on the street for the next 60 days, at the least. At a loss of what to do, I remembered Art had sent for and obtained my brother's birth certificate as well when he got mine. I recall the reasoning having something to do with the IRS. So, right at that moment, I figured out to use my brother's name to reapply for assistance. "Just.... till I can use my own name again." I rationalized to myself.

In furtherance of this plan of minor fraud, I was to make the 'new' application at another DSS (Department of Social Services) office, the one in West Los Angeles on Pico Boulevard. Sitting there in that office, my new name, Craig Salter, came out over the PA system. I got up and entered the door where I was instructed to go.

Once inside that room, all of a sudden, I saw two tall, wide-shouldered men, one white and one Black, who told me to sit down. They stated to me that they were fraud investigators. FBI, they could have said because I don't remember exactly starting to feel nervous. Definitely, the men fit the image of what I imagined FBI agents should look like. I began feeling a sorta cold sweat come over my body. *"Was I going to jail ...and not some puny county stint but federal, felony time?"* Such fears ran through my head.

For the next few minutes, I failed to listen or comprehend what they were saying to me or what they were accusing me of doing. Some wherein, the question of whether I had any family they could contact came up. In a panic, I gave them my father's 'real' phone number, known by heart, since I was a kid. One of the agents left the room. I prayed foxhole prayers, believing somehow, I was headed on my way to a prison term.

The agent returned; the Black one, if I remember it right, with my outcome. "I called the number and talked to a... Mr. W. Bailey." The agent said in a most serious tone. "He said: Sir, my son got himself into this. He'll have to get himself out of it," the agent quoted.

For sure, I knew those sounded like the exact words my daddy would say a; straight up, Black working man's rebuke to my not taking my own responsibility. In my gut, I knew he was right, too, even if I didn't want to accept its truth to my reality.

The agents finally informed me that if I did such actions again, I'd be prosecuted. Furthermore, that incident would be kept on file. I had been given an out.

So relieved I was that I think I may have walked back the whole 3 or 4 miles to West Hollywood, back 'home" to Santa Monica Boulevard.

I found Michael, my reliable road buddy, sitting out on a bus bench. I relayed to him what I believed to be my narrow escape from the FBI. Most likely, Michael said something condemning toward my using welfare in the first place; it was easy for him to have that opinion.

We continued sitting there talking shit, scanning the scene for the next get high. I felt safe, if uncertain, at peace with my chosen chaotic surroundings. As my father's admonishment circled around my head, I may have been a loser, but I was there holding my own, under my own wings.

Suckers and Lollipops (1985)

"Anybody can be a millionaire, so everybody's gotta try."

Lyric from song by "The The" (Matt Johnson)

I was drawing unemployment payments that summer due to the crazy method of how benefits are structured. The claim had been for the last job I'd been fired from, an answering service owned by a middle-aged gay man and his sister. I found that job from a posting up at the Gay and Lesbian Center on Highland Avenue. The claim that paid my benefits actually stemmed from another position in which I sold subscriptions to the Los Angeles Times over the phone. The phone bank site was located way out east of LA, requiring me to take two busses with a transfer in El Monte, taking me nearly two hours to get there. I stayed there less than a week cause one evening after work, I ended up getting myself busted for prostitution. In an odd fate of luck, unemployment ruled that the job was too difficult to get to for the amount payable. Therefore, I got collect payments. However, little it was it worked for me.

My memory is hazy, recalling exactly where I picked up the idea of selling weed. But I think I remember hanging out with somebody out on the Boulevard who hooked me up to how and where you could buy a quarter ounce wholesale. Never had I been a big-time marijuana smoker; I thought it good mostly for listening to my music loudly, on my headphones while dancing in my room. A little bit would go a long way for my own personal use. Somehow, somewhere, I realized an opportunity to make some money to go along with funds from my unemployment check.

$40 bought a quarter ounce. I made my first 'wholesale' purchase up where we on Santa Monica used to call 'Little Mexico,' off De Longpre Street just east of Highland. I purchased there till I became aware that the spot was too hot for cops.

Eventually, I migrated my purchases to a pot wholesale distribution area, down around Alvarado and Pico, just south of Koreatown. I'd ride down to get my quarter ounces on the bus. Eventually, I'd stop off and buy some miniature Ziploc baggies, then; I'd go back to wherever I was staying and split it up into $10 bags. Depending on the size of the quarter, I'd get about six to eight weed bags retail. Eight or more bags on a 'real good' quarter. I was making $30-40 profit off the top each day.

What mattered more to me was that I was making money, not needing to have to suck, not one single dick. Not that I was opposed to sucking dick, except this way only if I wanted to. If I chose to sell my ass, the money I made could be added to what I'd already made-the icing to the cake sorta speak.

Selling weed required certain effort and labor. After I had bagged up my product, I'd go to a corner store and buy some 5, 10, and 25¢ candies and get a small, brown paper sack. I'd drop the weed baggies and the candy into the sack. Out on Santa Monica Boulevard, I'd walk up and down the street selling. Typically, I'd walk during the course of 'work,' from LaCienega to Vine Streets and then back again. All that added up to anywhere between six to about eight miles a day. If I ran into a customer, I'd scan the scene for cops, and then we would walk together start talking or at least make sure we looked like we were talking. That customer would be handed the brown sack. He'd look in, put his $10 in and take out the weed along with a piece of candy. I'd encourage them to eat the candy right then and there as cover.

Priding myself knowing a little something about economics and the American ideal of the businessman earning his own. There, I was doing exactly that. Never mind what 'business." Each day I got up off my ass, purchased and priced a commodity, found a way to improve its retail distribution, to earn my own keep; the American Way.

That period was the first and probably and the last time in my life in which I had and had to have at the least $40 in my pocket twenty-four hours, seven days a week. I had to have that amount to make a new purchase- 're-up.' This required me to be conscious of how much I spent each day, having only $20-30 to work with. Typically, I ate at Slice 'O' Pizza, I recall, two slices of green olives and anchovy pizza for $4 plus tax. As well, I'd buy my pack of cigs which were about $2.50 back then(there nearly 3times that now)

My customers were usually hustlers out on the Boulevard during the daylight hours. At night I'd park myself around 'Vaseline Alley.' It was behind (pun intended) the porn bookstore and down the block from the porn peepshows. The Yellow Submarine, a sandwich shop that had pool tables and a jukebox, was just across the street. Hustlers and assorted street milieu could be found hanging out in the Submarine. Finally, there was the Dunkin Donuts down the block going the other way, a late-night refuge for all comers.

One of my regular customers that kept me in business was who I called the Pasadena Kids. The group of young guys would come over to West Hollywood, usually five or so all in one car. That would mean that whatever happened that night or who got fucked, all one of them had to return back to the alley in order to get their ride back to Pasadena. Albert; big and loud, and Black served as their ring leader. Albert, in his full-on drunk, would call out to me, "What's up guurl! Got some...you know?" to me. Luckily, I might sell two or more bags just to them. Then I'd scamper off. Always, there was the possibility that Albert would get loud and no need to be at the scene of the crime when and if the cops happened to show up.

At that same time period, I roomed in an apartment directly above the porn bookstore with Tom, a kinda ogre looking, heavy guy from Massachusetts. Tom worked as a chef at the Hard Rock Café down in the Beverly Center. He tried to carry a certain air about himself. Yet still, look at the locale he chose to live. I had an excuse; I was a dope-dealing hustle/prostitute. Really, the main reason he agreed to share his apartment with me was to have a steady weed connection. Tom first prodded me to drink something called espresso. He described consuming such as one of the 'finer 'things in life. I just thought it tasted like mud water (tastes change; I enjoy espresso now in the age of Starbucks).

Just before that year's Gay Pride Festival, the annual gay holiday, I'd spent too much, probably on dropping acid. So, the times found me without the funds for my re-up. Being broke, a fellow street associate of mine, a 15year old, rankly skinny, White kid named Quinn, made bank (a well-paying trick) the day before the parade. He paid for both of us to get into the festival area on the grounds of the Pacific Design Center. Also, as Quinn would likely do, he had possession of a hit of acid for both of us. There we were, our broke street urchin asses, high, and off to the party.

Once inside the festival, we just so happened to stumble into my old roommate Ty. We'd lived together back in East LA. Back when I had first arrived in Los Angeles and had met my former lover, Art. Ty, diminutive in size and more flamingly gay than I was, most likely instigated, and with good reason, me ending up out on the streets after I had been arrested for prostitution.

Yet, seeing him that day, I was in no mood. I felt like, "You dirty little bitch!" Ty happened to be there with his best friend, Fredrick. I suspected, too, that Fredrick had gotten all my record albums. I remembered him coveting my INXS records. The story relayed to me when I ventured back there to retrieve my tax refund check was that all the albums had been thrown out in the trash. "Fat fucking chance!"

But there I was, high, thinking I looked good, hanging off some attractive guy and dancing my fucking ass off. Surely, I must have felt like I had the last laugh concerning Ty, literally, since being high on acid, Quinn and I were probably more than likely laughing like fucking banshees; tripping. I lost track of Quinn amongst the day's festival activities, all the beautiful men and the bodies.

Later, deep into that night, I started coming down from the acid high at about the same time as it would be the last call at the bars. By then, Michael, my street ways partner in crime mentor, happened upon the scene. "I got two dollars, just enough to get a beer...

I'm gonna come outta there with a trick, bitch!" I informed him with sure confidence, standing outside one of the bars in downtown West Hollywood. The bar both of us went into was my favorite, low-key, somewhat a dive, where most of all, usually I wasn't carded.

Sure enough, by 2:30 am, I found myself getting into a cab with this guy on our way riding up to his hotel off Hollywood Boulevard. Once there, we fucked. Apparently, the fuck was so good he needed to go the bathroom to repair himself.

My usual modus operandi was not to rob, but I was broke, so I rationalized the next actions I took. Looking and scanning around the room, I found his luggage. Jackpot. Right there in the first side pocket, I put my hand into; I reached and pulled out four twenty-dollar bills. Only needing forty to re-up so, I took sixty dollars. Leaving one twenty, just in case, to appease the gods of Karma.

Upon this guy exiting the bathroom, I told him, "My roommate is having a party for the parade tomorrow...you know? I need to get home and help clean things up." For certain, I recall him with a satisfied grin on his face as I left. I made sure to take side streets returning to the Boulevard.

Sunday, the next morning, the queers, fags, gay boys, dykes, drag queens, lipstick lesbians, faghags, leather freaks, and all else anyone wanted to find streets packed the streets of West Hollywood. I knew, or least figured, many of those throngs needing to get high. A perfect opportunity to increase my finances. I sought to make it happen.

By two that afternoon, I had sold out and prepared to go get more supply. My only problem was how to get out of West Hollywood amongst all the traffic and the crowds. With a will, I figured a way, so by the time it got dark, I had sold out again.

With all my hard-earned effort, I felt I deserved to reward myself. Christine, my usual acid connection, who looked like a strung-out Lisa Bon'et with a large mole on the left cheekbone, was nowhere to be found. Desperate, I ended up copping from some sketchy, greasy-haired hustler. During our transaction, I heard him make a sexual pass at a drag queen walking past. "That's what I wanna get with tonight," he announced to my disbelief. With raised eyebrows, I listened as he explained his authoritative definition of bisexuality. "When I'm with a woman, I'm the man. When I have sex with a man (trans woman), I'm the woman," He matter of factly informed.

This kept to my memory because, in some ways, it made sense, or at least I discovered a viewpoint that I'd never thought of before. I also remembered that the little fucker sold me bunk acid too.

Beyond the pride festival, I still carried on selling from my 'candy' sack. Police were much more on the prowl than usual the weekend following. So paranoid I became about getting busted, I decided on letting one of my less than reliable 'alley' associates take hold of my weed stash.

First mistake; Arnie, a rather air-headed, queeny guy with long hair, rumored to have an extra-large dick, lacked the appropriate demeanor to sell weed. Smoke, not doubt but not sell. Warned by me to keep and play it cool, he ignored my direction and ended up getting popped by the cops.

Mistake two; With Arnie's arrest and my loss of money, I should have closed shop cause of all the extra heat. Yet, on the same night, I continued on, needing the money. I cruised by and into the Yellow Submarine just to hang out there and play the jukebox until some customers might drop in needing weed. While there, some cops came in and cased the place real slow-like but eventually left.

Mistake three; I waited about one minute, with my heart pumping nervously, I walked out being the first to leave. Those same cops were at the corner waiting to see who would come out. They frisked and busted me. Strikeout!

That particular arrest in the Beverly Hills substation holding tank, I was sweat'n it. I had never ever been busted for any drug charges and didn't want any. The times were Reagan-Bush Era war on drugs. I carried the knowledge of not getting caught up being a statistic in it. By Monday, all charges had been dropped. Cops took the weed, of course, and my cash, the crooked muthafuckers!

With just the same quickness as I had come up with the notion to become a drug dealer/ entrepreneur, I knew with enough sense that this was the end. It ended as I was released from the Beverly Hills jail. I made my way discreetly up to Santa Monica Boulevard and then started a running jog eastward to get back within the limits of West Hollywood. My logic being, *get the hell outta Beverly Hills before the cops and courts realized they'd made some mistake and rearrest my dumb ass.* The theme for that whole epoch to me, 'easy come easy go.'

Blasted (1986)

Having all the answers I needed. I was different. My answer; a dusty powder that also could appear as clear liquid. With it, I felt stronger, invincible even. Zipping faster than a speeding bullet leaving no time to see evidence of destruction left in the wake; my life.

Right after the New Year, I was laid off from my job at Chanin's; a hip, LA-based clothing store. I happened to be pleased that I'd been laid off and not outright fired; either way meant I was jobless without an income. The notion of just picking myself up to start again and simply find another position, did not come to mind. I detested looking for work. Having to be evaluated with the possibility of being rejected.

I sought comfort, familiarity, something I felt had some practice in. My best thinking took me back to the streets and on welfare. I did get a 'bright' idea upon receiving that last paycheck. I had only used crystal meth by snorting it. Still, in the milieu I surrounded myself, I heard about all the thrills of taking speed intravenously. Street folk, hardened hustlers, and just plain old speed freaks raved about the 'real' high of shooting methamphetamine.

Coping and admitting getting laid off was the same as being fired wounded self-esteem. I walked wounded. I'd failed again. Yet, the people I emulated seemed to escape from failure, from reality. With split-second reasoning, I decided I needed to take that plunge to the 'other side', take a hit directly to the bloodstream. Finally, I would experience that ecstasy I'd only heard about.

In the same week of that fateful decision, the space shuttle Challenger disintegrated on lift-off Cape Kennedy in Florida. Its whole crew perished in the explosion, seen by millions on television screens that repeated that death scene continuously on video. That scene gave off a sense of disbelief, knowing you just saw 7 people die in real time.

Having made up my mind to get high using a needle, I thought back to when I was 16, remembering being in a parking lot with some hot-looking hustler as he shot up Preludin into his veins. At that time, I had been so adamant to the dangers of doing hard drugs and especially using needles. Time and addiction eventually came to overrule all previous caution, sanity.

I considered it a good idea to find someone I trusted, someone who knew at the least what the hell he was doing. Matthew, otherwise sometimes known as Yukmouth, because of his mouthful of gold-capped front teeth that had since begun to rot. He happened to be one of slickest hustler, dopeheads I knew. We both possess a lustful infatuation for the same pretty young guy, Junior Boy. Many a time, Matthew had come to me telling of his unrequited love for 'the boy.' This being the same 'boy' I have taken that first hit of acid with that got me hooked.

The previous summer, when I was selling weed, Matthew had been one of my best customers. He'd mentioned how he admired my work ethic and my drive to make my quota.

"Let's go get some crystal! And some rigs too." I fatefully announced as I ran into him that night.

As I handed him the cash, he questioned me surprised. "Juan...you know what chu do'in!"

In truth, I had no clue what I was doing nor why, but in no ways did I say that. Instead, I blurted, "Hell yeah!... Come on now." I responded, trying to act as if this was nothing special.

We caught the #1 bus up to Hollywood Boulevard, getting off at Ivar Street by the Hollywood Spa bathhouse. Matthew had me wait as he went to a phone booth. I'd made sure to give him enough money to get both of us to get high, so I didn't feel the need to worry he would take off without me. Plus, I was relatively new to the dope game, so therefore I just trusted him.

He copped the dope, and then we made our way back to the Boulevard. Upon our return we found an anonymous-looking apartment building with a carport for parking underneath, so common in LA. Getting water from the end of a garden hose he fixed up the speed in the needles. I recall it clearly being 15cc units in the syringe. Matthew softly told me, "That's as much as you should do... on your first time." I squeezed my right arm with my left hand while he searched and tried to find my vein.

"Pump your fist and be still!" Matthew ordered me. Trying my best not to look or faint as the needle poked the skin of my vein and went in. Split seconds later, the dope pushed in and the needle point came out. I stood there somewhat stiff somehow knowing I'd just crossed some dangerous threshold, there in that carport. In mere seconds endorphins blasted my brain like lightning bolts; I remained almost motionless. "Juan, Juan...you alright!" Matthew yelled under his breath, but not loud enough to get us noticed.

"Yeaaah." I finally got out my mouth in response "It's just so fucking…" I trailed off actually failing finding the words to describe the feeling I felt. Matthew gave me a look confirming that he exactly understood my speechlessness. My mind made the analogy of my brain blasting off the same as did the shuttle that week. The difference, I was alive while just a little dead inside too.

Quietly, but as expected, Matthew finished off the 2/3 rest of the dope. He'd done almost exactly as I requested him to do, so I figured he deserved that majority of it.

Walking back up to Santa Monica Boulevard, we had the look as if we had just done something we shouldn't have. So self-conscious I was and probably looked so too. My brain, nervous system was doing backflips. Raging with abundant energy, somehow, we ended up at West Hollywood Park, on San Vicente by the Pacific Design Center, more than two miles away, within minutes. It has a reputation known as a late-night pick-up spot for sex.

Suddenly it seemed I just could not stop talking, babbling a mile a minute. Barely, I paid any attention to whether guys were scoping me out. I remember some other guys our age hanging out also. Maybe they were high on speed as well because it seemed all of us were talking as if seeing who could speak the fastest.

Matthew, later, took off to go market his wares, maybe for the next hit. I started to feel as if I was coming down from that initial blast rush. Later on, in my speed sojourn, I'd learn that the faster you go up, taking speed, the quicker the comedown. Just the same I had tasted the poison that stung, and there was no looking back.

By then, I had moved from the hotel on Sixth and San Pedro Streets, deeper into skid row on Sanford Street, to another welfare hotel. In spite of my developing street sense exterior, I still kept the belief of being down and out as temporary.

I got up one morning having a bright idea. To me, it appeared all the Latinos I saw seemed to have jobs. Maybe, just maybe, I needed to search for work in the same places as they did. Folks I associated up in Hollywood, mostly White, didn't seem interested in legitimate jobs. I failed to connect all the drug use to be the result of the lack of such a work ethic.

That morning I got up bright and early and planned to go to the employment office in predominantly Latino, East LA. My trek would be a walking one. I had no money for bus fare, even lacking enough funds to eat breakfast.

Walking straight east from downtown, I crossed over the concrete bottomed LA River, passed the vast rail yards, nearly close to two or more miles. Leaving at around 6:30 am, I intended to be the one of if not the first in line. With the sun rising above the morning skies, I passed among a world somewhat strange to me. I lacked the habit of finding myself up and out at such hours, mixing with the hordes aimfully making their way to work.

The further east I walked, the more my darker, African featured presence stood out in the heart of LA's barrio. I got a few stares, maybe double-take here and there along my way.

Exhaustion from the distance, all on an empty stomach, began to take toll on my body. Needing to rest and regroup, I sat down on the curb near a bus stop. Not paying attention to my surroundings this young, maybe high school-aged, Latino kid started up a conversation. He told me he was waiting there for his school bus. Some older guy making a fool of himself at the stop, most likely drunk, also happened to be that kid's uncle, he said. The youngster offered to buy me something to drink and a little smack. Maybe he had noticed my somewhat haggard condition. I thanked him as he boarded and caught his bus to school.

I continued my trek onward on pondering. *"Was that kid gay?"* Whatever reason he has noticed me, it was a generous gesture. That young boy was an angel. I was almost close to the point of passing out when he appeared.

My luck, when I did arrive at the Employment Development Department office, they had stopped taking walk-ins for that day. I used the change the kid had given me to catch the bus back to my room, mission incomplete. Always I remembered him.

Living rough ones builds scar tissue. Chances made me deal with whatever might come my way, for better or worse. Dire circumstances make way for survival. Scarred emotional insides even dope, could not totally heal. By chance hanging out with varied hustlers, dopeheads and just general street folk, we, from time to time, opened up to one another. Sharing some of what really had happened to us, that had made us turn to trading out our bodies as a lifestyle and living. Pumping ourselves full of dope, a poisoned strategy, whereas the soul remained wounded beyond the leasing of our bodies.

As far back I could remember, I carried a terrible nightmare of having had sex with my two next oldest brothers. That dream was so vivid I could recall the angle of the sun outside the window of the room where this dream had taken place. I swore, however unbelievable, I could remember the sensation of tasting my brother's penis in my mouth. In my childhood, I had awoken many a night scared from having dreamt that same horrific vision. *Was I just some sick, sexual freak?* I would think. Fear of even thinking such a thing, never ever would I speak of this to a single soul.

Dope could be responsible for moments that loosened inhibitions. I began to hear stories of similar sexual abuse, incest, most specifically from other hustlers. Putting two and two together, I noticed a pattern. *How could it just be mere coincidence that many of us had shared similar sexual deprivation histories?*

Almost unconsciously, my lifelong nightmare I began to accept as reality. I began to accept that no kid could have come up with such a wicked vision, all own his own. That emotional scarring gnawed at my most inner self. Dope nor illusions of fabulous, wild, carefree living ever completely covered up those wounds.

Doing dope and living aimlessly all mixed with my obsessive mind that would not allow me to hold my terrible memories, nightmares. Somewhere, somehow it had to be let out.

I had since lost contact with my Cousin Rhoda for more than a year. Since I had been homeless, been to jail, and now had a budding addiction to crystal meth. We reconnected. I phoned her one night from up on the Boulevard. I told her that I needed to come over.

On the bus ride to her house, I carried intentions of being rescued. Rescued from my detrimental choices along with the pain I felt inside. Sitting in the living room of where I had once, with tears called home, tears streaming down my cheeks, I told her the details of my childhood sexual abuse. Never before had I shared this with anyone in the family.

Rhoda told me she understood. She said that all my trials, the death of my mother, being gay, running away from home, and now the sexual abuse of it made me a survivor. "You're strong! A survivor... that's right!" She told me emphatically. I had hoped she would have taken me in her arms, like a hurt, wounded child, to tell me that she would take care of everything.

She said she loved me and that I should go home and that everything was going to be alright. That night, my interpretation of being told to go back home I viewed as rejection. A sign of family not wanting to be involved with my problems, I felt turned away, my emotions realistic or not.

Life seemed as if it was falling apart, clueless that the effects of using speed would take me to experience deep lows, just exactly the opposite of the drug-created manic highs.

Out of the blue, so it seemed, coming home one morning, after a late-night out, I felt desperately I needed to call my daddy. Feeling that I had to let him know, even if he had not been around to comfort me as I would have wanted, still, he never had taken off and that he helped my mother support us. I made the call from a phone booth outside the Greyhound station, downtown on 6th Street. Probably I babbled on, nothing I really remember exactly, just that I thanked him. He took the call and received my words appreciatively, if not taken aback, strong and silent as was his manner. This from a man I had only spoken to two or more times in as many years. I believed it important to let him know my appreciation. When my feelings, my emotions, surfaced, it felt like there was no stopping them.

The day of my 20th birthday, I listened over the radio, in my hotel room, to news of the nuclear explosion happening in Chernobyl, USSR. Coverage of the worst nuclear disaster in history ran all over the newspapers and on television. My grip on living, on reality, seemed as well to be in the mold of a meltdown.

The same evening, I met an incredibly handsome, blond dude up on the Boulevard. He had the looks of actor Chris Atkins in the movie "The Blue Lagoon." Cruising by in a pickup truck he takes with him to his place in Camarillo, far out of LA along the Ventura Freeway.

I loved the idea of a road trip as he promised to bring me back to Hollywood. Driving the freeway, he started giving me a head job. I grabbed hold of the steering wheel simultaneously as he grabbed and sucked. The long and short of what took place had us fucking out in what appeared to be wilderness in a wooden shack, in a sleeping bag. It seemed as if we carried on fucking all that night and into the next morning. Sex always served as a distraction and uplift to my emotions. I got very distracted by him.

I still carried the feeling of being all alone. Telling my cousin of my past abuse changed nothing. So, I turned to my reliable refuge; the streets. Sanity out the door, I sought a hoped-for love interest that was dope-fueled it, which ended with me attempting suicide, again (detailed in "What's Love Got to do With it")

Out aimlessly one night, I go along for a ride with this lanky, dirty blond hustler. The one I'd since had told my friend Michael my lust for. He had finished up a trick and was driving the john's car. Looking for someone to party he spotted me on the Boulevard. We drove and parked somewhere off the strip. We lit up and got wasted. Passing the joint back and forth among one another, he dropped somewhere between his legs on the car floor. He just left it there for me to look for. The scene seemed his way to set up for me to slyly reach for his dick. I turned the offer down, recalling Michael telling me, "When you're with one of those 'straight' guys, let him make the first move."

After smoking the weed, he drove cruising Santa Monica Boulevard. Just as it would happen, we saw lights flashing in the rear window. Police pulled us over. What a scene, as the smell of marijuana wafted out the window when the cop walked up. The sexy hustler happened to be, of course, driving without a license. My luck, the cops let him go, but I just so had a bench warrant for not paying a jaywalking ticket. Out came the silver cuffs, into the back seat of the squad car, and off to jail, I go.

This arrest, I got sent to traffic court and then released with time served. Leaving jail days later I was unshaven, smelling rank and with nowhere to go, having previously spent the rent on love, drugs and foolishness... I started walking toward Hollywood, from downtown LA nearly six or more miles. By the time I made it the Western Avenue, with afternoon sun beaming, my mind had said, *"Fuck this!"* I jumped on a bus through the crowd departing the rear door.

With luck, I got picked up not too long after I'd started strolling the Boulevard, a White guy in his thirties. Roger, he told me his name while adding that his lover was a Black professional dancer out on tour. Back at Roger's place I shower up and finish my 'business.' Beyond us having sex, I end up telling Roger the story of my woes. Listening, he suggests and agrees to purchase me a bus ticket back to Indiana.

LA the city of dreams and illusions had, now, kicked my ass, twice. At that point, I accepted that fact as real. Time to call it quits, tap out, I had had enough.

I may not remember his face yet never have forgotten Roger's generous spirit as I waved him goodbye with dejected sadness, that morning at the Greyhound station, that is no longer there on 6th and Los Angeles Streets.

This Greyhound trip, my first cross-county going the other direction. The bus pulled into Las Vegas around midnight. A neon sign flashed the temperature as 99degrees. With an extended layover I took in a casino. I played $5 in a slot machine, winning nothing. That would be my first and last attempt at casino gambling, for decades.

I thought I still appeared fresh looking, *why not try my luck at finding the hustler's strip.* The money Roger had given me surely would not last the whole trip, I figured. *And it's legal here! Isn't it?* Vegas' taxis kept spooking me, painted black and white, they looked the same as the patrol cars in LA. Eventually, I gave up the idea of turning a trick.

Back waiting in the bus terminal, I struck up a conversation with this older, White couple. Somehow, we spoke about family. I recall them saying how, over time, you would forgive your siblings over things you had fallen out over years earlier. Listening, I had my doubts.

That long sobering bus ride took us crossing the Rocky Mountains in Colorado. I recall how the sun was out and shining at the base of a mountain, then, as the bus climbed thousands of feet in elevation, it snowed a blizzard like up near the peaks.

LA seasoned me, in my two years, to the ways of those streets. I'd given it my all. With the proverbial tail between my legs, I returned home to Indiana, nothing to show for my travails. Except, I carried a knowledge that I had to be responsible for myself. Coming 'home' along with me was the opened wound of my inner turmoil and a way to cope with it: addiction.

Loose Ends (1987)

10:30, Friday night I put on my brown shirt and hat. The hat read; Arby's. I worked the overnight shift to 6am. I'd caught a new bug, a new habit. Just recently I returned back from a weekend visit to New York City. Hooked, I was on travel. Therefore, I needed to increase my income to make that happen, hence Arby's. The restaurant, just a few blocks walk from my downtown apartment and just one block away from my main job; answering the phone as a switchboard operator at the Hilton Hotel.

A single guy with no dependents, I made reasonable money. For the first time in my young adult life I hoped to be able to purchase Christmas presents for my family that year.

The city of Fort Wayne had invested funds to enliven the central city. The Hilton and Convention Center where I worked had been all part of that revitalization effort. A few nightclubs recently opened and were popular. The gay bars which numbered two were in the downtown area as well. In the state of Indiana bars stopped serving alcohol at 2am. Fortunately, for my income, it just so happened that the only places to grab a bite to eat, after the bars closed, were the Arby's and a McDonalds, located right next door to us in the same parking lot.

Working the register, taking customer's orders, it was not uncommon for me to see and serve just about anyone. Particularly young club goers and some folks I'd gone to high school with. A number of those former classmates happened, also, to be the same ones who had teased, bullied and socially terrorized me for not being able or willing to keep my 'gayness' hidden. Yet, I too experienced my own adolescent rebellion. The more it seemed I got teased, the more I flaunted and fought against, what I'd come to know as homophobia. Foolish for sure, but it felt like the only way I knew how to vent out my aggression at the unfairness of what I endured.

"A Big Beef and Cheddar…small fries and large… Jamocha shake." A tall, soft- spoken White guy ordered.

"That's all…$3.90" I responded, taking his order, sensing somehow I'd seen this guy somewhere before.

In the process of filling and completing that order I turn back around and see Tom. His bright red hair I'd notice anywhere. "I did know that guy I'd waited on!" It was Mark Shyder. Tom was his best friend in high school. Just then, anxious, I started to sweat a little, almost forgetting what I was supposed to be doing. Now, seeing him standing at the counter, Mark looked even more handsome than I had remembered. Back at the counter I did best to remain composed and do what I was paid to do, my job. That attractive man standing right in front of me, was now the adult, who as a straight high school student, I became infatuated and obsessed over. In a real sense I'd stalked when we were sophomores, back in the 10th grade.

Overcome by his presence. Embarrassed really. All I could do, now, was hope that he had healed from the strife I'd caused in his life back then. For those few fleeting moments, at that fast-food counter, I felt the feeling I'd felt back then years ago. A lonely -hearted, selfish and confused young queer kid.

Now, as an adult hopefully I'd grown and moved onto better environs. In celebration of my 21st birthday, I had given myself the gift of a trip excursion to New York City. Symbolic of the grown man I'd become. Having 'tasted' the finer things this world had to offer I wanted and desired more. I planned my next vacation in LA, coming up next year. Going out shopping and buying presents for the family was another symbol of my budding adulthood.

With luck and good fortune, my boss at the Hilton hotel was gay too. I could take some comfort in possessing a somewhat gay- integrated world. Most all of my friends and associates happened to gay or tolerant and, now, I could also include my place of employment. Now, getting to my family and where I came from, well, it's best to label my non-heterosexuality as being an open secret. Something known yet never really discussed in conversation.

Just in the course of hanging out and partying with a few of my queer associates I stumbled into discovering another family's secret. In the time of my absence, out on the West Coast, Fort Wayne gained a gay restaurant downtown, on East Wayne Street. Eventually, I ended up living right across the street from where the restaurant was once located. According to my associates the place had held good reviews on its food and atmosphere. My Midwestern hometown surprisingly ventured into having some cosmopolitan tastes. I knew more than one person who had worked there at one time or another. When one of them recognized my last name, he asked me if I knew James Salter. I responded that I did know him, in fact he was my brother.

Taken aback and more than curious on how these White gay men had come to know my brother. Come to find out, James, my brother, had once been employed as a cook at said 'gay' restaurant. Hearing what these guys told me, apparently, he'd been well liked and got along with folks there. I thought, "they must be mistaken!" Certainly, they were not referring to my Black, more macho than any man brother. Not the same brother I'd heard so many a time making disparaging comments as to "punk ass… faggots!" Not him. Still incredulous, I described his physical features to them, yes, they said that he had been the one they'd worked alongside.

Knowledge of my brother's former employment at a 'gay' establishment I just kept to myself. I somehow, still, couldn't believe or comprehend such a fact. Was he keeping some kinda secret associations? Maybe it just happened to be where he worked, at one time. Given the history of growing up in the same family with him, none of this made sense. Maybe that's why I never brought it up or said anything about what I'd heard. Now, I was one assisting in keeping a family secret.

Despite having cosmopolitan travels, I creeped too, among and along the low underside just as well. A none to discreet hospitality professional by day transformed into a slithery, fiendish crackhead in the hours of moonlight. My dichotomous lifestyle signaled all was under control. Fooling others by the fact that I'd not completely slipped yet, to the point of no return. Being the biggest fool of them all, I believed it too.

Such was the times in the late 80's. Many 'normal' folks I associated eventually grew curious enough to also want to take their own late-night ride up into the clouds of crack smoke. Usually, convened at my place of residence. I remained ever so ready to be their deliciously fiendish tour guide into crack rock stardom.

Most all of those friends being White, meant I'd be required to go cop the crack cocaine for them, alongside an implicit understanding I'd help them consume it. With irony, even in the 'hood', my large Black manhood seemed to trump my gay element. Possibly, it was the overarching darkness of night or the fact of having enough cash helped to make strange bedfellows.

Speaking of bedfellows, I came to be associated with a family of brothers; the Gillmans. I'd met them hanging out drinking and smoking up at Hippie Dave's place. The three brothers; James, Tim and Mark all considered themselves to be straight, although, they each carried no qualms about selling their bodies for gay sex to men when the need arose.

On some dark twisted night, I don't even remember how Mark, the youngest brother, underage even, and I, again the strange bedfellows thing, ended up buying and getting some crack together. I never trusted him and in fact, bringing him to my place to smoke up, nothing good was sure to befall. Anyhow, there alone, doors locked, in my high-ceilinged studio apartment. Glass pipes and crack cocaine rocks out and ready for action. We ended up smoking like nobody's business. Eventually, I believe I had intended to finagle some of the cocaine rocks and stash it away, for myself only and put Mark the hell out of my apartment. As I remember that night, I'd taken a big hit on the glass pipe and either I fell out on the carpet or looked away for a few minutes, from Mark. Coming to and back to consciousness, I smelled funk. Looking toward him, I spotted that he'd taken off his shirt. Exposing his scrawny pale, hairless chest. Reeling at the same time my senses took in his rank odor. Suspicious of Mark trying to entice me with his nakedness. Aiming to bait me to come out of pocket for more dope. "Not happn'ing!" Within short order his ass was up and gone. White male skin or not, this faggot did have some taste in my selection.

"Thank you for choosing the Fort Wayne Hilton…How may I connect your call?" I spoke in my most professionally White voice.

"Hey Juan...can we get together after...you get off? I… got some money!" The voice on the other end asked and answered. It happened to be James. The oldest of the Gillman brothers. James, the more mature acting and quiet one. He'd caught me off guard. Surely, he knew I'd get the gist of the meaning of his coded language, 'get together'. Translation: "Let's cop and smoke some crack rocks."

I agreed to meeting up, later, with him. James, the most attractive of the brothers too, had straight blond hair and the absolute sexiest deep brown eyes. He'd surprised me that he'd want to be alone crack'n out with me. I'd made no bones of how all he had to do was give a signal and I'd be all over him. He'd always kept to his, "I'm not gay demeanor", nothing obnoxious but more silent and unspoken though.

This had to have been the deepest of winter, January or February maybe. I remember walking the few blocks from work that night, feeling the Arctic-tinged winds blowing right through me. Cold enough for it to feel like my balls were freezing. Entering the lobby of my apartment building, startled, I discover to find James there outside waiting, shivering and teeth chattering. Talk about being a dope fiend. If he'd been waiting for much more than a half hour or so, he'd have nearly froze to death.

I don't recall whether I walked or drove my car to go cop crack. Either way I know I copped everything in one fell swoop. Probably, I talked some shit about how I hated when 'crackheads' went to the dope house to just buy one or maybe two rocks. Knowing, in the end that they was gonna continue to smoke crack until all the money was gone. 'Real' crack fiends, meaning me, were wise enough, I reasoned, to go and spend it all the first time. Besides, one could haggle a better price for spending more money, wholesale like.

Once back at and inside my apartment, the outside north pole temperatures be dammed, the door got locked tight. On the wall, stood a poster-sized photo of a Times Square street I took while in New York City. It hung just above my homemade DIY sectional couch, constructed of materials from Home Depot and Jo-Ann Fabrics. James and I proceed to huff and puff through layers upon layers of cocaine smoke. Glass pipes, brillo and 151 proof Bacardi Rum lay splayed out across my geometric angled, mirrored coffee table. The one I designed and constructed myself as well. The drug cocaine; a stimulant, stimulated more that my brain cells late in that night. "Hey...you wanna fool around?" I slyly asked James in a forward off-handed way, my inhibitions shed. Looking back at me with his pretty brown eyes he replied gently.

"I don't...a...think of you...know...like that." With that he turned me down. Disheartened, I let it go. Still, we continued on smoking till all was gone. Gone! Without too much searching the carpet for phantom, missed, crack rock pieces, James and I parted each other that night on good terms. Later, I heard from my buddy Jonny, how James had told others that I had made sexual advances to him. I thought it unusual for a 'straight' guy to even gossip about such things, but there it was.

The 80's other scourge, the HIV/AIDS epidemic, entered the bounds of my hometown since I'd been away in LA. (real names mentioned here are in memoriam) Soon after I'd returned to town , I remember the night of the benefit show at the Old Forge, the lesbian and drag show bar. The queens performed a show in tribute to Bobby Camus, who'd often had performed in drag. Bobby had just recently succumbed to AIDS and died.

A not too old memory flashed in my mind. It was a memory of the spring prior to my leaving for LA. Bobby and I and one another guy were out sitting on a porch across the street from the cruising parking lot off the Pearl Street strip. What I had remembered was Bobby that night, literally, bragging as if he was proud of the fact that the Indiana State Board of Health contacted him to be able to track down all his sex partners. This had been due to his having contracted some rare and untreatable venereal disease.

So, just my first week back in town and he'd passed. Bobby being the first person I actually knew died from HIV/AIDS. Ironically, while I discussed with a number a gay folks my having lived in Los Angeles, one of the things I'd hear them say, "Ooo...they got all that disease there chile." I'd not even known of anyone with AIDS there, but yet here in 'safe' Fort Wayne people I knew had the disease and were actually dying.

Not too long after there'd be the deaths of Zena. The African American professional ballet dancer and female impersonator. Barron Johnson, who also was a drag performer. Barron and I had both attended Wayne High School together. And then, Bobby Tigner, who had been a boyfriend of my buddy Johnny. All this death and dying happening while the disease seemed to remain an unspoken topic. Foolishly, folks denied the existence of HIV and carried on doing what they always did, despite not realizing the circle of sex partners to be much smaller than say out in LA. Fear and helplessness caused peculiar coping reactions.

As per my hopes that year, I was able to buy Christmas presents for all my nieces and nephews. Having five brothers and sisters, I had many. Paying special attention, I sought to get each one a present just for them. The family gathered at my sister Sandra's on that Christmas Eve. I settled in among the frivolity, drinking and the smoking of weed. I contented myself that I'd done my part for my nieces and nephews to make them feel some of the season's cheer.

Michael Jackson's video of "The Way You Make Me Feel" showed across the television screen. Excitement mixed with a sense of Black pride filled the living room space as his style and his musical talents thrilled us gathered watching him, especially my brother James. "How strange", I wondered, sitting there too, "So proud of Michael Jackson… with his obvious feminine characteristics…someone for whom he didn't know". Yet, with family, I guessed that was different. I just sat there quietly with my siblings and their children as the brightly lit Christmas tree lights blinked on.

Liquor bottles had all been emptied and more than likely an argument or near fight had come to pass, just the same Christmas lights blinked on the tree. Everyone gone now. Emotions stifled, Michael Jackson and all. I felt the need to go out and hit up a crack house. My seasons' greetings set forth puffing and sucking air on what we crack fiends called a 'glass dick.' The only way I knew to relive all those loose ends to what I either refused or could not cope with.

Red, Delicious (1987)

3 am. If I'd made it that far usually, I was good to the end of my shift. John, the night desk person, came into the switchboard room to light another cigarette, chain smoking. "Round trip to NY, LaGuardia-$117," the airline ad in the newspaper read. "Hell! I can afford that." I thought reading it. On that chance, though, for the next few months, I lived and breathed my excursion to New York City. It proved further evidence I really was beyond the bounds of the Midwest, beyond Fort Wayne.

Working 3rd trick put more time on my hands than I could handle. Though it was a drag, many a night, I had cut short partying with friends. I needed to be at work by 11:30 pm, as a switchboard operator downtown at the newly built Hilton Hotel.

For certain, I'd aced the interview for the position. I had possession of gay, cosmopolitan manners; I could speak 'White' enough to sound 'professional' over the phone. I snagged the job that seemed to fit me and was all that mattered. I had been working temp jobs in various factories.

On any given night, I could be found hanging out at Dave's crib, which happened to be located right on the town's gay cruise strip. Dave, older, White, who looked like a tall, holdover from the hippie era, with his long slightly, grey hair. He smoked weed constantly. A scene of young boys, hustlers, mostly white high school dropouts, gathered most nights at Dave's 2nd floor Victorian flat. All of us toking hit after hit with the sound of his extensive music collection blasting in the background. Dave was the Beatles greatest fan, in Fort Wayne at least. His original ticket stubs to their 1966 concert at the Memorial Coliseum, hung framed on the living room wall.

This little White hood rat named Johnny would soon become my constant sidekick and partner in crime. First saw wind of him one night hanging around outside the Old Forge, lesbian bar. I looked up to spot this diminutive, White spitfire jump out of a car, walk up to the gathered group of us on the front steps. "What's up bitches?" He yelled out like here I am, something to be recognized.

"Who the hell he thinks he is!" I thought, seeing him. Anyway, more exciting than the folks I was hanging with, I wanted in. I craved whatever he was on, the excitement in the least.

Johnny had been my entre into hanging out up at Dave's. Most of the gay folks I knew from before LA, now, bored me. Many had moved on, grown up really. Others had since graduated into bar hags, budding alcoholics. Drinking never really turned me on. I sought something else, something more to the edge. What I carried; an addiction hungry to be satisfied. The wrong side of the tracks hoodlums up at Dave's was the gravitational pull of the thrills I sought.

A few dudes were hanging out there hustled themselves for sex from time to time, with older men who picked them up. Jeff, a kid only 17, had snagged himself a regular older benefactor. The benefactor relocated to Fort Wayne, working at the General Motors assembly plant that had recently moved from Wisconsin. He supplied Jeff with enough funds to keep the beer and weed flowing at Dave's.

Part of that exciting, thrill-seeking crowd gave Johnny and me the reputation of tearing the roof off any place we encountered. Soon enough, we were wherever the party was Hell! We 'were' the party. After a time, you can get to believe your own press.

At Dave's one Friday, ready to get the party started with a friend of mine. Dave greets us, saying, "You got a car?"

"Yeah, my friend does," I answer, wondering what Dave's up to. Next thing we know, we're in the car with him giving directions.

"Turn here, make a right at the next stoplight." He told us. Soon enough, we pull up outside of a house in the Lakeside Area. Dave informs us that we are at Jeff's sugar daddy's apartment. Jeff and the guy were in Chicago for the weekend. He informs us that some of our affiliated hoodlums have already broken in and stolen the TV and stereo system. I had known Jeff's guy had a vast album collection. So, in I go, the little criminal I was, grabbing up arms full of albums. On my way out, I spotted a 35mm camera and took that too.

Meantime back at the ranch, alongside partying, I sought out everything I could get my hands on about New York. I cashed in some of the stolen record collection at the Wooden Nickel record store. I myself was building my own substantial music collection. They knew me well at the "Nickel."

I planned out every bar and nightclub I wanted to go to, where to cruise for sex. I found cheap lodgings at a YMCA in Midtown for $15 a night, unbelievable for the prices in New York now. I had no clue, at that time, of the history of the "Y" and vintage gay society.

New York boosted my reputation. Neither the gay folks I knew nor the hustler crowd at Dave's had been much of anywhere beyond the Midwest, if anywhere.

Work proved another scene of high drama.

The Hilton Hotel was built as part of a publicly-funded downtown revitalization plan. Out-of-state developers had sold city leaders on building a convention center, including the hotel, with tax breaks. Less than a year after the grand opening, the money stream had gone bust, leaving the city basically owning the hotel.

I got hired in the period while the city looked to sell the hotel. Corporate chaos ensued. Months passed as we were unsure if we would still have jobs.

Being city property required hiring from all strata of the city's population; White, Black, educated, poor, dropouts. In that time, on paydays, employees made a mad rush to Lincoln National Bank, which held the hotel's account. Those unlucky enough to be last in line to cash their paychecks might end up having to wait to get paid. The account has run out of money.

The assistant general manager, a woman most employees called the 'bitch', in fact, held operations together despite all the chaos. I happened to get along fine with her having no problems with a strong woman in charge.

Eventually, the hotel was purchased by a management company headquartered out of Florida. All previous management was let go, including the 'bitch'. To me, it seemed unfair; she had kept the property afloat.

To my benefit, our new front desk manager was a Black, gay man, Ray Calderon. Almost immediately, I became like the teacher's pet of our staff. I experienced being a professional 'inside' member. I got away with murder. Ray viewed me as his protégé. My being Black advantaged me, in his opinion. *"Who could have ever imagined for once being Black and gay advanced my career prospects?"* Just the thought of that idea could spin my head. Still, the monkey of the addiction left me clueless about the opportunities.

The transition members of the new management staff arrived in the city. "This list is the big corporate wigs, arriving soon. Be on your best behavior." My boss instructed, handing me a two-page list of corporate names.

"Who me?" I replied, full of sarcasm. Looking over names on the list, I took notice of a pattern. Each and every single last name ended in a vowel. The switchboard room opened directly across from the executive offices. People I'd never seen previously moved in and out of those offices. I observed what seemed to be that each person had dark hair and features, dark for White folks at least.

My mind and intuition are always open to the unexpected of what others may fail to see. I knew it was a stereotype, but I knew what I was seeing too, Italians, East Coast, money from Florida.

"Ray! Come here for a minute." I summoned my boss to air my suspicions. "The names on this list all ending in vowels and the way everyone looks. Is this the Mafia?" I questioned in hushed tones.

"I'm not saying nothing." Was his response, neither confirming nor dispelling my queries. Like something I'd read about in some juicy thriller or in the movies, I couldn't believe I was working for the Mob, in Fort Wayne, Indiana. Nothing much seemed different, even If I did work for a tentacle of the La Cosa Nostra.

Clearly remembering the first hotel Christmas party, the one which our new general manager got blasted out drunk. Now, anybody could have been a drunk, not just the Italians or the Mob. *Very unprofessional though*, it left me thinking.

Saturday, April 26, 1987. I boarded a plane bound for New York City, the Big Apple. My first time on an airplane, by myself, with a ticket I paid for.

Anxious, excited, I could nearly be contained. Not too excited to not have missed my original flight, arriving late. "Ah, shit!" I mumbled to the pain of a toothache as the plane left the runway. This would be the first of many teeth to have to be removed later. Not a clue did I have of that being evidence of my habits, the drugs, catching up with me.

Now, I was really something. My heretofore insignificant, Black, queer, self-gifting myself this present, for my 21st birthday. A weekend trip to one of the most vibrant, exciting cities in the world. *What a way to greet legal adulthood!*

Departing LaGuardia Terminal, my first test; making the bus connection through Jackson Heights, to the #7 subway line into Manhattan. I made it. Looking to the west on the platform above the city streets, my eyes spotted that renowned profile of towering edifices poking up high into the sky. I appeared as if I was headed, just mere miles away, to the Magic Kingdom, and not the Disney one.

Walking up the steps to the street from Grand Central Station, my senses felt whiplashed. Everything seemed so huge, the buildings, the traffic, the people rushing about. Manhattan Island a giant man-made terrain and here I was about as insignificant as ant.

Gaining my bearings eventually, I made it to the YMCA on 34th Street and to my cubicle of a room. Night fell. Staring out my room window, on the 15th floor, my eyes took a view of the city's millions of lights all beaming, blinking.

Test number two; exploring gay nightlife in New York. The first place to mark off my list, just off 8th Avenue, west of Times Square. Once inside I got a drink. Upon showing the bartender my ID, he said to me. "It's on the house." He then informed me of a dance club he thought might more suit my tastes.

Later, I found the place he had directed. I immediately got the just of why the bartender had recommended it to me, as I entered the club. Not a single White face did I see. I held a stereotypic image of Black establishments. Thinking back on it, now, I had never been in an all-Black 'gay' club. Back in LA, I had been to an all Latino, gay place. Yet, here was a first in New York another whiplash to my cultural senses.

A steep cover charge I took as not a good sign. Feeling so out of place among that crowd, the hip hop-flavored sounds, to have stayed longer would have had me putting on a front. Truly, it was not my scene.

Leaving that club, next, I walked down to the piers facing the Hudson River, west of Greenwich Village. With the hours passed and failing to find the right club, pursuing getting laid seemed a good consolation. Certainly, I knew how to pick up a guy, no matter what city I was in. A guy with dark-haired looks, Italian maybe, spotted me. He parked there in a Lincoln Mark V with a half vinyl top. Scoping him out over our small talk, he handed me a flyer to the Tunnel Bar for the following night. Heated up as I was, he stopped me before we would have entered into unsafe sexual activity.

In real-time, I witnessed New York City's gay community deep in the throes of coping with the HIV/AIDS epidemic. Contrasted with how I came to know it in LA. This disease was real, not something happening to other people, somewhere else. I accepted the guy's careful admonishment.

Catching the subway back up to the Y, I disembarked into Pennsylvania Station, right below Madison Square Garden. Carefully scanning the scene, I noticed quite a few funky and hip dressed, young folks scattered throughout the station platforms. A handsome dude of some ethnic distraction that would never be found in Fort Wayne looked my way, cruising me. Within not too much time, we ended up locking lips hot and heavy in one of the shadowed corners.

Once again, a coupling carried nothing further than getting hot and having a hard-on. Neither of us had a place to go for a more private encounter. That guy, whatever his name was, informed me that all the hipsters and club-goers happened to be waiting for trains on the Long Island Railroad, riding back home to the suburbs after partaking in the nightlife in Manhattan.

The next day, Sunday morning, had me heading downtown to the World Trade Center towers. My eardrums felt shattered on the elevator ride to the 103floor observation deck.

That stolen 35mm camera came to good use up there, capturing astonishing views high above America's largest city.

Afterward, I gorged myself clothes shopping down in the garment district on and around 6th Avenue. I'd come prepared with a money belt to safely store my cash. Still, somewhere between all the shopping, snapping pictures in Times Square, and rummaging Greenwich Village records stores, I lost a wad of traveler's checks. Immediately, headed to a payphone to in the lost checks to American Express.

The flyer I'd been given to the Tunnel Bar had to be used before 8 pm. That left me no time to go to the Y and change into a 'clubbing' outfit. Waiting in line, one behind a velvet rope, yes, those infamous lines outside a New York club complete with a bulky-shouldered bouncer. I presented my flyer and got chosen over two other guys standing next to me. Those guys looked as if they had spent the entire day getting dressed to get inside. I proceeded inside the doorway, my head spinning from having gained entrance.

The Tunnel had a reputation as a hangout of the post, disco elite: Keith Haring, Madonna, and such. I must have arrived past the era of that fabulousness. That night the crowd proved minuscule. The DJ's music sucked, too, some high NRG gay disco shit. I could get that anywhere, Fort Wayne, in fact! The Tunnel failed to impress.

Through the weekend, something seemed off as I roamed the canyon ways of Manhattan. By Sunday, I got a clue to what I was sensing. *"Where were all the White people?"* I wondered out loud. Yes, I had seen White people, mostly gay folks. But I wondered about the regular, family-raising type, White people. Where were the kind of folks I grew up around that populated places like Fort Wayne? Little evidence of those people did I see that weekend.

My last day in New York, Monday, I wanted to do some last-minute shopping. First thing, go get my lost traveler's checks replaced. Ever after I swore by them for traveling.

Entering the subway train that morning, the hordes of people overwhelmed me. Nary an empty space in the train cars. It was then that White people appeared rushing about on their way to work. *"That's it!"* I thought. *"White people were in Manhattan. They just didn't live here."*

I boarded the Broadway line for Central Park West on a mission to get to Strawberry Field: the memorial to John Lennon. Once there, using a 35mm film canister, I filled it with a slug of dirt from the memorial. My souvenir present for Dave; the tireless Beatles fan he was.

Coming back home, I was, now, bi-costal. I thought quite a lot of myself having that reputation. What there was of gay life in Fort Wayne, now, bored me, so I encouraged friends to go on excursions to Chicago's nightlife.

A ragtag group of us took off to the WindFy City, one Friday night, six of us all in a minivan. Johnny and his boyfriend, Doug with his green, county-hick partner, my friend Gino and myself crowded all with me as the big city tour guide.

Once arriving in the city of the tall flickering towers we first stopped in a cozy, leather-themed bar on Clark Street. The place nothing more than a pick up joint with video screens playing hard core porn all throughout the bar. I was in the mood yet, we were to stay together, meaning none of us was to depart the group for a meaningless fuck.

Afterward we headed to Club La Ray's. I had been there before. La Ray's; an all-Black club as finely appointed as any other 'gay' club, the White ones that is. 'House' music', blasting out, all the rage at the time, in fact had originated in such locales.

That night's largest contingent of White people had arrived with me. Sure enough we got a few stares. Most folks though were bump'n to the music, doing their own thing, could have cared less. My group was the ones more put off. "What! You're not afraid to be here? I'm surrounded by White people all the time." I queried my White compatriots, especially Doug and his guy. The shoe was on the other foot, so to speak. *So, pick it up and get down with that Mofo!* I implied.

Johnny, never one to back down to a challenge took it all in stride, getting out on the dance floor with me. Anxious or not he didn't let on.

A later excursion to Chi Town had me lodging at the Mies Van Der Rohe designed Hilton at O'Hare Airport, my room complements of being a franchise employee. Such fancy digs had me spinning to say the least.

Somewhere in the night, at a club, I got myself picked up by a guy who drove me around in a limousine. I had too much to drink. Back at the room, I know I had sex that night, yet, upon waking up the next morning, the limo driver and the guy I fucked were nowhere, along with half my money.

Anyone else, under similar circumstances, would have had enough of living the fast lane. Still, my distorted need for thrills meant, yes, I lived hard...partied hard.

No one ever told me it was going to be easy, living fabulous.

Place Like Home (1987)

Around noon or so, I turned over and dragged myself out of bed, my couch, really. Luckily, I got in at least a few hours of sleep. Increasingly I became a 'rock star'; vernacular for a crackhead. The love and excitement of crystal meth lingered within my being despite the resulting drama. Nobody I knew in my hometown of Fort Wayne had even heard of crystal, let alone knew how and where to get some. Crack cocaine just happened to be the next best substitute, at the time, like water flowing, it was plentiful.

I lived on my own in a small, high-ceilinged studio apartment. My little studio, one of about six or so converted from a building that at one time had been a Victorian Era convent. My sister, visiting me one afternoon, tried to convince me of the benefits of me moving into the house she was leasing to buy. Just that day, it somehow sounded good, something made the scheme seem like a reasonable idea. *"I could save money... on rent".*

Stacy, my nephew, just two years younger than me, my sister's only child would be residing at Sandra's house as well. We grew up more like brothers cause of our closeness in age, in spite of my being his uncle.

The house, a Cape Cod Cod-style three bedroom on Werling Drive built during the post-World War II era, in suburban areas of the town. Increasingly such areas were all Black, the former White residents having fled to even further out suburbs.

Miscommunication began between my sister and me from the start of my moving in. The basement I claimed as my 'apartment.' I had assumed that we agreed on that as my living space, the reason why I paid rent. With that intention, I felt free to decorate it as I pleased. Sandra seemingly had other plans.

Less than a month after my move-in, the gas got disconnected. *"I know she wasn't... expecting me to be responsible...that bill was past due before I got here."* Standing on principle, so I believed, I refused to pay more than the share I had agreed. On principle, the house, our house, was without gas.

Gas heated the house and the hot water. It being summer, we were only out of hot water. Getting dressed and cleaning up required the task of putting a soup pot on the stove to boil water. True, a pain in the ass but something I learned to live with, standing on principle.

Having an active social life- single, gay, and over 21. I meant to exercise my adult vices. Even so, that might include dropping acid here and there and maybe partaking in smoking some crack. Not fully in my own house, such vices had to take on clandestine applications. Often, it seemed that I only slept on Werling Drive. Causing tension further, "What was I doing coming home so late? Sandra would query me.

My response was, "whatever, out with friends," implicating I was grown and answering to no one, paying my own bills.

Car troubles: I was now on my third vehicle. The first was a Volkswagen Rabbit that blew a clutch even before my first payment was due. I returned the car to the lot from which I purchased it, on South Harrison Street. That proved quite a challenging ordeal trying to drive the car only able to get up to a first gear, with the gear case roaring loudly. The proprietor refused to offer me any resolution, so I left the car, the keys, and walked away.

Next, I brought an orange 1974 Volvo. Man, I loved driving my orange, 'Swedish' tank' as I called it, until one day, the real axle slipped out while I was driving it. It lasted for a year. Knowing the car was finished, and beyond repair, I got out and removed my license plate, gathered my things, and literally kissed it goodbye, leaving it in the middle of the street, axle half off and all.

My last vehicle was a faded yellow Pontiac Sunbird. I purchased it used from the Recycler Newspaper. I don't believe the car ran for more than a month or two.

On one weekend night, my nephew allowed me to drive his car this before my Sunbird soon expired. His ride, a Monte Carlo, with low, bass woofer stereo system, the kind you could hear and feel the vibration from, about a quarter-mile away. I didn't have any interest in the obnoxiously loud bass woofers. I planned on enjoying the nice clear sound of his system. Driving that night with music loud, my flavor of sounds bump'n like the B52's, if I recall it right. One of my cassette tapes got stuck in the stereo. My every intention meant to inform my nephew that I would help to pay for whatever repair was needed, even if I was slow getting around to it.

Monday afternoon, boiling water to wash up for work, Stacy comes demanding, right then, I pay him for a new car stereo. Taken back at his insistence and more so his threatening me for money. "I'm gon pay you for it!" I know, I told him, indicating no need for him to be as upset as he was. Ego wounded, whatever slight sense of my manhood as well, I told him if he didn't back off me, "you'll get it when I give it to you!"

Always previously throughout our youthful years, I'd physically commanded the upper hand in any altercation between Stacy and me. All of a sudden, he blasted a punch that nearly took me out—triggering me to use all I had to fight back. His blows overtook me, no relief, really pounding on me. Realizing I was not going to win this one, I yelled out.

"Alright, hell!" Stacy continued to pummel me. It was then I felt unsure if I might survive. He beat me like I was some stranger. Nearly, I feared my life.

Bruised, bleeding, breathing hard, I laid there on the living room floor after Stacy left the room. I needed to call work to inform them I would be late. Walking or more likely crawling across the carpet to the phone, not sure of that part, I reached out to grab hold of the receiver yet, could not lift my arm. My mind, muscles, made the impulse again, same response, nothing. I panicked, in shock, my arm, shoulder, something was broken. It seemed just minutes later, an ambulance came blaring down Werling Drive, up to the corner in front of the house.

Once at Lutheran Hospital, they prepped me for surgery. Sandra had arrived along with Stacy by then. She cussed both of us out for "stupid ass fighting!" Stacy stood leaning against the wall crying, tears streaming down his face, saying nothing. Witnessing his grief left me at a loss to square his brutality, his anger, less than an hour before. Intuition reasoned that the anger got directed toward my 'faggyness,' even after I had given up the effort to fight him.

The surgery relocated my right shoulder socket. Afterward, I lay in a hospital bed in traction, feeling nothing, a result of the anesthesia and pain medication.

Family members came up to see me. My brother James memorably shook his head in disgust, looking at the results of machismo in action. His witness seeing me laid up in traction, he genuinely seemed unable to connect the dots of all the aggressive, bullying the male family members afflicted on each other growing up.

Friends Johnny and Doug as well visited me. It lifted my spirits that folks cared for me outside of my blood ties. I requested Doug bring me some trail mix.

Worse than the weaning off of pain medications was being immobile. A nurse looked upon me kindly, I recall, as I cried cause of having to use a bedpan. The trail mix containing raisins helped lead to such embarrassment. I pleaded with the doctors to allow me to at least get up to the toilet.

My boss accommodated my convalescence at work. For the next six weeks, I carried an upper-torso brace for my arm. Along with an outrageous hospital bill, memories of the beating lingered on familiar wounded emotional ground. Life on Werling Drive now lived in complete tension. I knew I had to get out of there.

Soothing some pains while heightening others, Johnny treated me to numerous bouts of smoking crack.

Finding release through sex always provided me an escape to coping with reality, temporally ceased. Even pleasuring myself met an impasse. My right limbs were out of order. Should I should have gotten a clue, even back then, I had more than one addiction. By the end of those six weeks, my need for sexual release, had me learning to how to make use limbs on my left side, to take care of 'my' business.

During the last weeks living there on Werling, one evening, a childhood friend of Stacy's, Louis, happened by one night. His mother, now, had a much-rumored reputation of being strung out on crack, having been a close friend of my sister Sandra.

As Stacy fell asleep in front of the TV, Louis and I started talking. "Yeah, you know my mom's and Sandra one time smoked some rocks... a time back." Louis let out, dropping a bombshell on my sister's habits of possible drug use. I had no proof of whether what he was saying was true. More to the point was how he wanted to steer the conversation to talking about smoking crack. One junky can almost literally smell another dope fiend. His tactics worked. I had some money, and I knew Louis probably had good dope connections.

Soon enough, we were in a cab that dropped us off in the basement of a crack house on Winter Street. All my previous crack-smoking activities had been with at least one other gay rock head—this setting by appearances Black and straight. Paranoid on being spotted as gay, I put on my best dope fiend persona. Luckily, for me wearing my shoulder brace drew me some sympathy, past any detection of my faggotness, among the assembled crackheads.

After smoking up what money we had to buy dope, I returned back to the four walls of my basement. On the return, I carried new family suspicions, more tension.

Probably the worst 'indoor' living arrangements of my adult life finally ended after just five months. I found myself an old quaint flat on South Clinton Street, only two blocks from my job at the Hilton downtown. The separate entrance and high ceilings sold me on the apartment plus, now, Pearl Street and the bars were within walking distance.

Back in comfort of my own place, I'd escaped the tensions of familial wounds. On the surface, at least, I escaped. Inside torments remained, festering.

Not Good, Bad and Ugly (1988)

White dress shirt, bow tie, and black pleated dress pants, my uniform on, now, I was ready for work. Late again. I called ahead to inform the other staff that I would not be on time. My tardy arrival had due to a fabulous overnight excursion, taking in the highlights of the gay club scene in Chicago. *"A person had to make life worth living...didn't they?"* I'm sure I rationalized.

Coming in the employee's entrance, I put my nose up the eye screen to clock in—numerous warnings I'd been given regarding my tardiness. Ray, my boss, my gay boss, happened to be out on vacation at the time.

"This is your dismissal for not following the procedure of being on time for your assigned shift." The assistant manager firmly stated, placing my termination paper in front of me. She had always had it out for me. Yet, I provided the rope for my own hanging. The switchboard position happened to be the longest I had ever held a job. I squandered the advantage of having a boss who was both Black and gay. Mired in the muck of drug-seeking thrills, I knew not how to get unstuck.

I had just found a new apartment only two blocks away from the job I, now, no longer worked. Devastated, I knew I had fucked up. Dope-hazed denial mixed up with pride pushed me to glaze over the circumstance my life was now headed. So, I applied to Wendy's Hamburgers located in the next block; it seemed a good answer to stay employed. *"Wendy's had whole wheat buns... a salad bar. More than that... it was not Mc Donald's."* I rationalized some hopeless remaining pride with a little side of snobbery.

A chick I knew from back at Wayne High School, Katrina; worked at that Wendy's. We'd not seen one another for years yet; she still remembered me. I almost couldn't fathom wrapping my head around the fact that she was, now, married and had three kids. Soon, I don't know how Katrina and I both found out the knowledge of each other's crack use. Maybe, it was just how one addict could sense another. We each shared where the locations of the latest crack house were and which had the best available dope.

My best buddy and partner in crime; Johnny, had moved out of town with his boyfriend, most likely with the added benefit of getting away from our forays smoking up crack. That left me partnering with other lesser associates to smoke up crack, not losing a beat... Doug turned into my next crack 'road dog.'

It was Friday night, payday, Doug along with his boyfriend at the time; Tim picked me up with some dude Doug knew from his old neighborhood. We all pooled funds together, intending to score a sufficient supply of crack rock to smoke well into the night.

The best crack houses were in the hood, Black hood, that is. With the rest of the car's occupants White, as was so often, I served as procurer, having at least the correct skin color to purchase the product.

Tim, the 'boyfriend,' along with his two brothers, sometimes hustled on the gay strip. Nobody in that family seemed to work. I met the brothers hanging out smoking and drinking up at Dave's, the scene there always frequented by such White hoodlum types.

The younger brother, Mark; an underage and real scammer to boot. I never trusted him as far as I could spit.

That night, Doug was still at work at a fabricating shop on Harrison Street, just south of the railroad viaduct. Tim was to drive Doug's car; I had the money, and the new dude was to ride along while I copped. "Don't go home and get Mark!" Doug ordered Tim before we took out on our mission for crack.

Minutes later, Tim pulled up in front of his mom's house. Mark ended up in the car. *He didn't have a dime.* Immediately, he started talking shit, fiend'n for a rock hit. Against my better judgment, my true and practiced crackhead judgment, I should have called the crack run off, right then. I knew Mark coming along was nothing but trouble.

Yet, onward we went. Mere minutes later, our car pulled into the parking lot of Eden Green apartment complex, stopped and turned off the lights. Built in the early 70's as part of Fort Wayne's urban renewal, the complex, now, lay waste in the depths of holding forth as an open open-air crack market. Sandra, Aunt Deborah, and Uncle Don's family had all once lived in the complex in those early years. Here now this night, in the dark, I creeped crept through the worn, grassless lawns where I had once roamed as a kid in the playgrounds.

Tonight, Eden Green was the playground of dope dealers and junkies. I was playing the part of junkie.

"Ya'll all stay here!" I insisted, knowing their White faces would make us targets.

"He just try'n to... get more for himself!" Mark shot out, influencing Tim. Again, I slipped in my street smarts. I should have demanded they stay in the car. In too deep now, jones'n for a crack hit, I relented and let Mark and the new dude follow me into one of the dank apartment hallways.

"Hey...I need a 20," I asked one of the runners hanging there in the shadows.

I passed him a ragged $20, he hands me a really small rock of crack.

"Ha ha...we got more money!" Mark's dumb, White ass snickered at the B-boy that sold me the little rock, as others in the hallway heard what he'd said.

"Get yo ass back in the car!" I demanded, under my breath, furious that he was going to get us robbed. Reluctantly, they did as I told them.

Undeterred in my mission, I slipped across the parking lot to another building in the complex., knowing there were more dealers with a better product. True enough, I copped about $200 worth of crack inside another apartment. Coming out of that building, looking across the parking lot I see that Tim and the car are gone.

They had left me there, my gay ass with a pocket full of dope, among all those fiends having had seen me arrive with the White boys.

Playing it cool. *"I gotta get out this muther fucker."* Looking straight ahead, I walked to be back of the complex, up and over the fence; once out of sight of the apartments, I took off, running, running as if my life depended on it. So sure, some scandalous broke-ass crackhead saw me copping all that dope.

Blocks away after crossing over the railroad tracks, finally, I slowed down, no reason to give a cop cruising by reason to stop me with all that dope I had on me. Eventually, I made it over to my 'crack mentor,' Robert's, house on Lewis Street.

Back when I finally had made the decision to try smoking crack, I knew of Robert's reputation as a 'rock star' for smoking dope. The intention in trying something new meant to go to an expert. He ended up teaching me well enough. Many a night, creeping, Robert ended up smoking up more than enough of the dope that I brought.

Inside his house that night, I noticed him serving up some White truck driver dude on his payday. By the night's close, the sun coming up, surely the trucker would be broke, doped out, and missing whatever valuables he had not already sold to continue smoking.

Glass pipe, straight shooters came out quickly. Proudly, I put a fat-ass crack rock on the brillo for Robert to smoke up. Fiend 'in, I myself got some relief from all that happened, smoking fat rocks too.

Geeked out, I go ahead and leave for my house. Thinking to myself, *"I deserve to smoke up more of the dope... I took the risk, and they left me... there alone."* Once I reached my apartment, that I'd just moved into about two weeks before, I discover the kitchen window busted and my oh so valued record albums missing.

Enraged. Furious, almost hyperventilating, I swear, it seemed I never ran so fast in my life. Doug's place on West Washington, about ten blocks away. I got there in less than 7 minutes flat, pure cocaine-fueled adrenaline madness.

"Open this fucking door...now, or I'll kick the motherfucker down!" Doug knew I meant exactly what I said; let me in. Like a madman, once inside seeing Tim, I yelled. "Where's my motherfucking records!" I learned Tim directed Mark and the new guy to my apartment, where they broke in to steal my music in place of the dope.

All three of us pile into Doug's car and speed off to the Gillham family house, now, at about 2 in the morning. After much cussing, going back and forth, I paid those hoodlums money for the return of my albums. Insane, pumped up on crack, I still refused to turn over the rest of the dope in my possession.

Fired from my 'good' job, in my new place less than a few weeks, now, having been broken into with a busted-out window, I had paid most of the rent money to get back one of my most valued possessions.

Late that night-morning, back in my apartment, I smoked the rest of the crack—more than I ever smoked before. Well into that next day, locked in my busted out, kitchen windowed apartment, I continued on puffing, smoking crack.

My heart, my chest, heaved. Smoking blurred and seemed to ease the pain of my reality.

Deep down in the crack hole I had smoked myself into. Living, what was left of my life, revolved around frequent smoking binges.

Turning tricks on Pearl Street, I meet Norman. Freckled, light-skinned black, gay, he danced as a member of the local ballet company. Beyond all else, over time, Norman continued to show up at my house, knocking on the window, became an addicted binging crackhead. He intended to have sex with me. I let Norman carry on with his fantasy. Always, the scene throughout those nights ended up with us smoking crack instead. Typically, after the small talk, I would convince him to drive to the ATM machine right around the corner, then off we went to the latest clandestine crack house. 2or 3 more times each night, it was back to the bank ATM, buying more crack and so on. With the sun's rising, Norman would know that's the signal sign to leave, ever so promising himself never again to do what we had just done.

Like the trickle-down economics of the 80s, crack cocaine trickled across the gay scene too. The 'in crowd', thrill-seeking folks found their way to find themselves gathered around at 1127 South Clinton Street #4; my place. Smoking crack.

Some of those people, I knew, felt they were themselves not a 'crackhead.' They ended up smoking after a night at the bar. And since the scene of such crimes never took place at their living quarters. They did not find themselves waking up to the physical aftermath. I did.

Others looked down on my infamous activities. A few even seemed to witness concern. Ricky, who I knew from high school, and had fucked my boyfriend at the time, just so showed up at my door one evening. Due to the fact we had fallen out of touch, over the boyfriend fucking, we caught up with one another, over smoking a joint. Ricky voiced a concern that I maybe was falling victim to a drug habit. Denial mixed up with good helping of lingering resentments led me to see his warnings as just further vindictiveness to my condition. He'd be the 'last' person I'd able to hear some truth about my addiction.

Miss Bobbie, a very attractive transgender queen who I took note, because of her very handsome Latino boyfriend. She asked me to take her for a ride one night as we hung out on the Pearl Strip. We rode around in my car as she fired up a joint. Then she said to me, "I don't know you that well...But... you know you need ta leave smoking them rocks alone." I didn't know how to take what she was saying to me. Denial kicked in. I just believed Bobbie had heard all the gossip folks were saying about me. *"People talk shit!"* I reassured myself. In turn, I brushed off another instance when someone showed genuine concern for my wayward junky ways.

Delusional maybe, still, I felt that I was not completely off the deep end with my habits. Working at Wendy's one night closing up, my eyes looked down from my register to spot a wad of cash. Looking around to see if anyone else had seen it, too, I slipped the bills in my pocket and continued my duties. I cleaned the restroom and the salad bar. While out cleaning the salad bar, the place was empty; I started counting the $20 bills. *"1,2,3,4…10,11, 12.,"* thinking of each twenty as a crack rock. My mind I considered, even if I got away with the money, I'd probably end up killing myself trying to smoke up that much crack.

Shortly afterward, that night's manager came out yelling, "Lock the doors!" He had money missing. I turned the money over to him. I was doing my best to make a joke out of it, telling him how I had found the cash under my register. A week later, I was fired.

A snitch coworker went and told the general manager about what had happened that night.

Even at that point, all was not lost. I still could count on a friend or two to be in my corner. Craig, a friend I'd known and hung out with since I was in high school, agreed to help me out in my situation. He fronted me some money in which to sell weed in order to catch up on my back rent.

On the night he picked me up to drive over to his dealer's house to buy the weed, all seemed cool. Craig just so happened to drop $100 on the dealers' living room floor as he was busy making the transaction. He'd got so caught up rolling up a joint and talking shit, high.

Sitting on the couch, I look to spot Benjamin Franklin lying there on the floor. What can only be justified as part of being a dope fiend, my first notion was to get up and somehow smoothly move over to where I could put my shoe on top of the bill, which I did. Eventually, I shoved it into my pocket when they weren't looking.

Driving me back home, Craig all of a sudden pulled to the side of the street. "I lost some money!" he said in shock.

"What!... Where!" In one of the most low down moves I ever made, I calmly got out of his truck and walked around with him pretending to help look for his lost funds.

I smoked so much crack that night I nearly felt my heart pound out of my chest. So desperate I was to escape my guilt.

Truth, my own actions had smoked me into a deep dark hole. Having fallen in, I lacked any ability to climb out, not even able to at least stop digging.

The Breath Taken in Between (1989)

Jerry scooted himself up to the black, mirrored, fiberglass coffee table. The one I constructed myself in a whirlwind of creativity and sweat, with materials from Home Depot, furnishing my first apartment. That same table now served more as the venue at which any number of crackheads, veterans, and novices alike, waiting their turn to inch their puckered lips, containing the narrow-tempered glass stem ever closer to the blue flame. Carefully, that flame ever so efficiently heated the baking soda- rocked base cocaine. Then, it released the chemical mind-altering ecstasy, pass the copper-brillo through the glass chamber up into the anticipating mouth, and into the lungs, bloodstream; the brain

Not uncommon to one and all, at such moments, personalities transformed, inhibitions could and would be let loose. Anything might be expected. Oftentimes, I just laid back to take in and watch the nearly nightly, possibly sexual, turn out. This the prize of holding the smoking venue.

This particular cloistered evening did not disappoint. Jerry exhaled a huge cloud of coke smoke, saying next, "You know...I wanted to come smoke just so...um... I could ask to suck yo dick." I heard him say as I put the 151 proof Bacardi- flamed torch to the pipe, taking a nice and long, languid hit of his dope. Surprised but not shocked, I coolly played off Jerry's sexual advances. "What about... Joe?" I responded, referring to his Black, rough trade, old man.

"He don't have to know everything. Besides... you know he in jail." With my encouragement, Jerry carried on smoking up. Time passed; the crack got smoked. He forgot all about his efforts at trying to suck my dick, he being, now, more interested down on the floor scanning the carpet for possible crack pebbles that, of course, were not there.

Quietly inside, I savored my revenge, my vindication. Jerry had been the guy with whom I lost my virginity, my first sexual partner. Then, I, a 16-year-old, naive horny teenager.

After what I felt and thought had been lovemaking sex, Jerry later denied to everyone we knew that the tryst had ever happened. As if he had been ashamed to have been intimate with me. I assumed, wounded as I was, that Jerry's ashamed was of having been with a Black boy.

Time had his true nature, his true lust, won out in the end. "*How dare he come at me, now, in such a sneaky way…*So what if he still looked just as good-looking… with his bleach blond hair. And no, he never apologized or even acknowledged his past actions. *"Shit! Crack transformed me too,"* sometimes for evil. I loved watching him practically beg to have me that night. *"Who had the last laugh now? Bitch!"* I wanted to yell at him.

With my bestest road dog having moved away, I gravitated back to one of my old haunts, hanging out at Dave's place. Long-haired Dave's eccentric burnt-out ways allowed me some comfort in contrast to his condition. Dave seemed to just live to enjoy his cats, his music collection, smoking much weed, and the boys; always the young almost jailbait, no account, wayward White boys. His place seemed to be a more interesting scene than anything going on at the two gay bars.

In the current starring role up at Dave's was Rich. Different than the other boys, Rich did claim to be gay, nothing flamboyant but gay. In so Dave took on more of a role of mentor to him than the other hoodlums hanging around. Rich had snagged himself a wealthy, older closeted benefactor in exchange for the use of his young flesh, of course. Soon, in exchange Rich earned his own car and seemed to always have enough funds to keep weed and other party favors flowing.

Sitting in Dave's living room more than likely high one night, Rich did something strange. Later, I put the clues together to his behavior. After having come out of the shower, I look over across the living room to see Rich getting dressed and rubbing his hand back and forth over the crotch of his boxer shorts, staring in my direction.

"What the…" I say out of my stupor. Coyly, he just smirked at me. Not ever really even liking him cause, our personalities clashed, I thought nothing of it.

A month or so later, I spot Rich and Dave cruising by me as I'm walking down the Pearl Street strip. They pulled over to ask if I wanted to toke on some weed with them. Why not, I figured. Next, after a joint or two, Rich drives to drop Dave off at his house while signaling me to ride along with him.

Rich while riding around some more suggests and then convinces me to take him over to my place to smoke some more. *"Why is he being so nice to me?"* I silently wondered.

Leaning back on my leather couch that I had scored out sitting next to the dumpster in the back, Rich passed me a fat joint. "I'll let you fuck me...if you... put on a rubber." Said so nonchalant and matter of fact, I choked, inhaling the weed hit. I knew I heard what he said, but I didn't really like him. Yes, there he was with his long smooth body now, topped with a head of bleached locks. Always, one of my weak points; is a handsome dude, a white one, offering sex.

Clothes soon were shed, lights turned out and we fucked on that same leather couch with a condom as per Rich's request.

Strangely somewhat, I made love to him. He ejaculated first and still laid there and gently held on to me as I did.

Conventional notions of sex and intimacy be dammed, I felt that night, for in those tender moments, we made love to one another without having to being in love.

His instance on having safe sex meant he cared enough about himself and, in turn, his partner.

I made the mistake of telling Gene that I'd slept with Rich. If Johnny had still been around, such shared confidences would have been among buddies. Gene jealous probably blabbed to Dave, and it all got back to Rich. He seemed more upset that Dave had found out. Nothing else intimate ever again happened between us.

Regular sessions of smoking crack meant there's a price to be paid. My rent was many months behind then. I came up with a scheme to solve the problem. For two years previous, I claimed two of the young hoodlums at Dave's, Tim and James Gillham, as dependents on my tax returns. I got them to agree to getting $50 each in exchange for giving me their social security numbers.

When my federal refund check arrived, it was large enough to buy an 8-ball of coke. I meant to sell it in order that I'd get caught up on the rent. On a Tuesday, when the check arrived in the mail, I called Gene to make the arrangements for buying the 8-ball, the most dope I had ever bought at one time. Gene came over to my apartment with some big, Black dude that I didn't even know. The dude appeared to be straight, already, I started to sense something not right. I knew that trick though.

First, he offers up a small amount of dope, then, he ends up smoking an even greater amount of my dope, once I was already too high to really know what had happened.

The sky had turned dark when Gene returned with the 8ball. Powder cocaine got cooked into the crack then, I acted as the proverbial kid in the candy store, forgetting all about who smoked as well as how much got smoked. Through the crack smoke, everything got blurred.

Then, by surprise, there's a knock on my door. It turned out to be Johnny back in town for a visit. Good finally, I had a good excuse to end 'that' smoking session putting Gene, his boyfriend, and the big, Black dude, that didn't know, the fuck out my house and off my dope.

Johnny and I leave my apartment and the coke haze to go to the Forge bar. He was now of legal age to drink. Genuinely I felt glad to see him. "Chile! ...Put someth'in on that pipe." He requested as we were inside the bar restroom.

"Johnny... I'm out!" I tell him, not even believing that fact for myself. In the space of just a few hours, I'd consumed a whole 8th of an ounce of coke.

"No, for real... I'll spot you something," He asked again with the implication that I was holding back some of the crack. But It was all over for the night. The 8-ball hurricane ended. Sadly, that also was to be the last time I ever saw Johnny, never even knowing what happened to him.

Waking up the next morning still, I could not believe what had happened, what I had done. I now had less than $100 left of my refund check. Any day, I could still be evicted, and there was nothing to show for the money spent. *"Like duh!"* What had I expected with my brilliant scheme; pay my bills and still be able to get high? *"I knew better"*, whether I wanted to accept that fact or not.

Depressed, desperate, what was I left to do? Go for broke; I go ahead and smoke up the rest of my refund. The rest of that day, I smoked alone, running back and forth across the railroad tracks to the crack house.

With the sun peeking out the next morning, emotionally, I wanted to die; I just needed to end it all. I hadn't felt suicidal in over 3years, one of the longest stretches since I first attempted at the age of 15.

The apartment looked a mess; dirty clothes, crack pipes, and paraphernalia were strewn about. I took a razor and began cutting my arms just below my wrists. Never one for afflicting self pain, now, a kind of masochistic thrill, came over me cutting, seeing skin cut and the blood dripping down. Surely, I must have done it incorrectly because I did not feel faint. *"Shit! Now I had scars...How would I explain that?"* I thought afterward.

Feeling even worse and believing I still had to finish myself off, I got up from the floor in the living room, walked into the kitchen, and opened the cabinet under the sink. Pulling out a plastic bottle of ammonia, *"This will surely do it."* Steeling myself for what may have been my last moment alive, first, I pulled my face and nose back from the noxious odor and lifted the bottle up to my lips to swallow. The liquid ammonia never did not get down my throat. The split second upon touching my tongue, I coughed and violently spit out the swallow, and fell to the floor dazed. Eventually, I washed out my mouth, wiped my eyes, still, utterly hopeless but alive.

Attempting to slit my veins, trying to shallow ammonia, thrust my addiction to crack cocaine into stark reality even I could no longer deny. The bubble of delusion and denial seemed ever so slowly about to bust.

Near this time, I'd been over to visit my Aunt Deborah, who lived close downtown, as did I. In random conversation, the subject of my crack-smoking slipped out. More so, I divulge that I was near about being evicted. She suggested that I seek the help of my sister Sandra. Sandra had many a time dealt with such financial matters herself. Knowing sure well I needed a lifeline, any lifeline, even from my sister, I agreed the idea of asking her for help it seemed more reasonable than any plan I had. It had just been more than a year since I had moved in with my sister and ended up with a dislocated shoulder from the fight with my nephew.

Sandra came over to my apartment a few nights after I discussed my situation with my Aunt. My nephew Stacy showed up along with my sister. I had not seen him or had any contact since the fight that broke my shoulder. Sandra sitting in one my Eames wrought iron, wingback chairs, that I had stolen, in an understanding tone, laid out for me how she would get in contact with my landlord to set up a payment arrangement for the back rent. And I was going to need to turn over my paychecks to her. Sandra's words gave me some feeling of relief, some comfort. It was a feeling that I had someone to lean on. "It's going to be alright...everybody has problems sometimes." Although, when she gathered herself to leave, she said to me, "You'll be fine... just stop do'in that c-o-c-a-i-n-e, " spelling out the word in admonishment.

The front door closed behind them. Speechless I was. *Did my sister just spell out words?* After, I had just basically admitted the shameful fact that I was a junky. Her son, only two years younger, was he not an adult too. Plodding the path from my own crack-induced hell, I wobbled on, any and almost everything feeling so uncertain.

Have Pipe, Will Travel (1989)

Friday, I know it was, there I was, back at my old 'hoestop,' a LA Metro bus bench at the corner of Santa Monica and Holloway. Time, late morning, I believe it was. I was still young, dumb, and at that point, possibly out of cum. Sitting there again, feeling I'd escaped, I thought the Midwest. Fort Wayne, Indiana. Escaped the shame, guilt, and failure of what had resulted from being a dope fiend.

In Indiana, a week earlier, I was awakened one morning with an eviction notice. Upset and in disbelief, I'd been left with the understanding that my sister had done as she promised and helped take care of the issues with my back rent. After, I had turned over all my paychecks to my sister. Though, yes, I'd not stopped smoking crack. How I'd gotten to this state in the first place. The lesson I learned; take care of my own problems myself.

Hope had been that by trusting and telling the truth, especially to family, things would work out. More so, I did not have to only rely upon myself in a crisis.

My state tax refund came just within a few days after the eviction notice. I came up with a plan of action. The solution was really the same action I had done earlier when I was 16 and 18. I decided on what I'd later learn in recovery as doing a 'geographic'; moving to a new place and taking with me the same problems. So, with my last earnings working as a busboy at the 'good' Mexican restaurant in town and my refund, off I go. Greyhound may have had some travel offer at that time because my cross-country, one-way ticket allowed me to choose my own route itinerary. I chose to go to Indianapolis, Chicago, then St. Louis, then continue on the usual route to LA, along Interstates 40 and 10 through Oklahoma City and Phoenix.

Bags all packed and ready to go. My recollection tells me that the bus was not to leave until five or six that afternoon. What to do? Go buy a crack rock. Afterward, smoking and getting stuck, I barely was able to catch my bus all geeked out. I even had to spend extra money to take a cab, to be on time, just three and a half blocks away.

Safe on the bus, I settled in, still a little geeked, 'straight shooter' in tow. We arrived in Chicago around nine o'clock that night. Where I, jones'n for dope, got the notion to cop some more crack. *"A little for...the road. You know."* Trying to run away and get high, smoking up, at the same time.

With my layover, I left my bag in a locker at the bus station, walked out on the streets and caught the 'el' going northbound. I'd slightly recalled knowing that Bughouse Square (park), on the near north side, had a reputation as a hustler hangout. I got off near there in search of finding a crack rock. Looking around, I spot this skinny, light-skinned sister who looked as if she knew what 'time it was'. Jackpot! She hooked me up with a quickness, the exchange made. Treasure safe in my pocket, I got on my way back downtown to the bus station.

"Fuck!...It's powder," I mumbled to myself. Sure, I did recently learn the 'skills' of how to cook up powder cocaine into crack but hell, I didn't have any utensils to cook it up. Still, wanting to smoke so bad, I poured that powder into the straight shooter. Made it back to the bus station and there inside the men's restroom, I discovered it easy to disguise the flicking of a lighter with all the other noise going on. I didn't really feel the usual blast from the cocaine, *"But something was better than nothing... wasn't it? "At least it was real cocaine."* That same certain chemical taste I did recognize. *At least it was real shit.* Felt really proud of myself, that I could, even here in the big city, cop dope and not get ripped off. The straight shooter got so hot, while smoking, I dropped the pipe right out of my singed fingers. It cracked as it shattered on the floor of my toilet stall. I stood up and made it out of the restroom, looking as if I hadn't a clue what had just happened in that stall.

Cannot recall or remember much about anything else on the rest of that long bus ride, doing my best to forget or having dope withdrawal, probably a little of both. Finally, three and half days later, I arrive and step off the bus in downtown LA. I slung my bags on my shoulders, put on my 'city' game face, though by now, this was routine for me. I headed west from the Greyhound terminal, remembering the five blocks walk to catch the #4, Santa Monica Boulevard bus to Hollywood.

Out and back on the Boulevard had me feeling within my element. Like as if I truly belonged there. Now, all I needed was to locate some speed, the real dope. "Shhhiit," I said out loud. Looking about to see if anyone heard me, really if anyone who might have noticed me might be exactly who I was looking for.

It was the week of my 23rd birthday. Whad'ya know, I ran into Matthew, aka; Yukmouth. He being the one I knew to trust to first shoot a needle of speed into my arm, back during my last go round in LA. Now, I knew for certain I'd get the real connect. Matthew looked worse for the wear. "Juan! Aw naw...for real, what's up?" he excitedly greeted me with his crooked rotten-toothed smile, that once had gold caps, worse than I'd remembered, still, 'Phine' looking in a rough, now older sorta way. More importantly, we got dope and got tweeked.

Paul, I saw a day or so later at Oki Dogs (the hotdog shop known for drugs). Everything started feeling like it all blurred together by way of the street, crystal meth, and turning tricks. Paul still looked as fuckable as ever, small, not too thin with his dark-haired, Italian- like looks. What had changed was how the way he seemed distant, colder. He copped for me, but he seemed distracted, like he really didn't remember who I was, but he played along anyway.

The goal was to escape my situation, escape my reality, to kill myself by way of shooting too much methamphetamine.

So, there I sat that late morning, as mentioned, on my bench, not dead. Homeless. Penniless and, needless to say, pitiful.

Sitting there, I prayed, *"God, whatever I've done, I have no one to blame. Give me strength to face what comes next."*

A thought came to me. Months before back in Indiana, on a subzero freezing winter night while walking home, I remember gazing up at a lit-up liquor store sign. It read, "What one desires most, one soon becomes." I continued on walking, braving the wind chill, and thought about what I desired most was to have a sugar daddy. A backup plan to support me while I did whatever I guess I needed or desired to do.

An hour or so later, sitting on that bench, along came this gold Mitsubishi that pulled around the corner and stopped a few car spaces away. Slowly I walked over and got in and started up a conversation. As memory goes, I told the truth regarding my homelessness, leaving out the drugs part. This man reached out to give me a hug, and not exactly in a sexual way. He was a 60 plus-year-old white man with a tight-curled perm and deep tan. Not exactly sure how I knew, yet at least for the near future, all was going to work out. As I leaned over and hugged him back, I cast my eyes upward to thank God. I had me a sugar daddy.

Fountainology (1989)

July fourth, our nation's celebration of its independence, saw witness to me getting my own independence from Dale and of my starring role as a 'bought' boy. Finally, I achieved the dream of my own apartment, located near the corner of Fountain and Edgemont Avenues in east Hollywood. Turned out to be my one and only apartment in LA.

My landlord, an older White couple, welcomed me with the warning; that they didn't tolerate drug dealing in their building. *"Fine...not a problem."* I thought. He never mentioned anything about using dope so I'm good.

Looking out the big window in the living room you could see the royal blue glow emanating from the tower on the campus of the Scientology religious cult of the stars, a 20-storey building that appeared to loom over the whole neighborhood. My dream was now set. Here I was on my own, in my own place, in the city that opened my eyes to all things that glittered. Soon, would I come to see that freedom is not free. Living life on Fountain Avenue burned like a candle lit at both ends.

I reunited with John, my surfer blond running buddy back from my earliest days on the streets in LA. Back when I returned to the city as a high school dropout. Back then in those days everyone we'd meet on the Boulevard wanted to fuck John. Just the previous year, I came to Los Angeles on vacation and stayed a few days with John and his entourage. The entourage followed because, now, John was living large dealing dope

I believed us to still be close, this even better, because I now had a reliable connection. No longer did I have to face the chances of getting burned (ripped off) buying speed.

John no longer called the Boulevard home turf. Now, North Hollywood, over in the "Valley" was his stomping grounds. Hollyweird, I'd soon experience had become a less hospitable place for tweekers.

Out on the Boulevard looking to cop a hit of dope, I took the path of least resistance and walked down to Oki Dogs, now, almost four miles west of my new apartment. I was having no luck, not with anyone I felt I could trust, when along comes this diminutive, wavy-blond, tweeker-looking kid. Couldn't have been no more than about 19. "What's... go' in on?" He questioned, sparking up my attention. "You... looking?"

"Yeah.... why, you know something?" I responded to him knowing surely this tweeker-looking kid was not a cop.

"Naw... I'm trying to find some crystal too," He assured me his tweeker status. "I got a car... ya know… maybe we could find something together."

Despite everything all moving so fast, I clicked that since he had wheels I could go out to the Valley and cop from John. I told the kid that I knew where to cop good speed out in the Valley. Like on a determined mission, off we went to his car; a Pontiac Le Mans, the little hatchback model. He handed me the keys to drive. Now, things were really moving fast, too fast maybe. No mind, when you're involved in getting high, perceptions always get blurry plus I was fiend'n for a hit.

We get to North Hollywood and both score dope of our own little supply. John smirked at me while hooking us up. He definitely was curious about the "kid". I told him I'd met him at Oki Dogs just that night. Not wanting to fix up a hit at John's house because of all his tweeked out entourage and hangers on. Not that they expected for me to share my dope, still, I sensed their jaded stares messing up my high. Not gonna happen, if I had anything to say about it. Besides, I still carried an attitude somewhat snobbish about being the Valley anyway. *"Real tweekers… are in Hollyweird!" "Okaay!"* I'm thinking.

Again, with me driving, we both came back to Hollywood and to my apartment. Out came the needles, door locked, it was, now, way past time to get high. I was nearly in a state of salivating, desperately anticipating. Superstitious, I was about having anyone watching me shoot myself up, so I went into the bathroom. Feeling like I was a veteran junky, now. I'd only been able to shoot up my own veins for just a month or two by then. I finished up as the rush of methamphetamine blasted my brain. Slowly walking back into the living room, high as hell, startled, as I looked down to see there was the "kid' bent over on the living room carpet, on all fours with his pants and underwear slid down past his calves. Meth became my favorite drug because it always made me super-sexual and horny as hell. This whole setting seeming like a pornographic fantasy. I got down on the floor and slid my fingers across his smooth buttcheeks simultaneously as I removed my pants and grabbed hold of my dick. I slid my fingers across his butt cheeks simultaneously as I removed my pants and grabbed my dick. After that scene opened up, all that I can remember for sure was that we probably fucked in every room of the apartment, until I needed to get ready for work about maybe 9 hours later. Then as LA's noted sunshine beamed, we both gathered in the bathroom to do another shot of speed, me, right before I needed to compose myself and show up for work. I was gonna trust leaving him alone in my apartment, if at least because I intended to drive his car to work. I left that morning, closing the door behind me, the "kid" still tweeked up, naked.

Arriving back home that evening the house smelling like sex. At least on that night, I proceeded to get around to painting over one wall of outdated paneling among the bouts of more sex with the "kid". Progressively, we started getting on each other's nerves. On Friday, payday, John promised he'd deliver dope to me. That night after I got off work, he arrived to my apartment with a 16th ounce of crystal meth. Smirking this time as well, John warned me to be careful. "This is powerful shit... gurll!" He campily admonished me. I paid him no mind. *"Whatever."* Dealers always be talking shit trying to over advertise the dope they're selling.

I guess, just looking around the apartment, it was somewhat obvious the "kid" and I had been fucking, and he was obviously still there. John soon departed and out came the needles. For some reason I didn't even bother with fixing up the hit in the bathroom. Sitting right across the dining table from one another I fixed up shots for both of us. Each syringe with the exact same amount of dope. I encouraged the 'kid' to go first, sitting there eager with just his pants on. He barley pulled out the rig from his vein. Instantly, I saw him fall back out the chair and to the carpet on the floor. I thought, *"he's faking... It's time for him to go... tonight."* I sensed he was just fucking with my head, my emotions, overdoing it. Like he's saying, *"I'm so fuk'n high you can do anything... you want to me...as long as there's some dope."*

Turning my head away from looking at him I do the hit of dope I'd fixed up for myself. Slowly, as I pulled out the needle, barely able to hold it between my fingers, all the sudden I'm down on the floor too. My chest, my heart beating so hard and fast I felt as if I might be having a heart attack. I could not move or control any of my body. Cause my head and brain exploded so that I felt no access to my limbs. I could hardly see. Barely, I could hardly I see. I swear to this day, it sounded and felt like I could hear the trees breathing outside my living room windows "Swoooooo, whoosh, swoooo" I heard it.

"Oh shit!" I'm thinking, *"I done did too much!"* What was I to do? Still, I couldn't fucking move laying there splayed out naked on the floor, needles out with bags of speed on the table. *"God, help me! Help me!... I'll never do this again,"* I prayed. Weekends usually meant the LAPD had the helicopters out, in Hollywood, circling overhead. Every now and then, splayed out in my physically comatose state, I'd see a bright flash of the spotlights as they beamed by. Noise of the helicopters mingling in with the breathing sound of the trees, just as loud if not louder. My mind wondered, *"If the cops come knocking on my door, ...I'm gonna jump right out that fucking window."* My paranoid fears seemed reasonable due to the fact of my state of not being able mouth words or speak. I knew I couldn't talk my way out of getting busted. So, the idea of making a run for it was reasonable, tweeker reasonable.

God did answer one of my prayers. I did, finally, start to come back down to a more normal high. We of course did more dope and continued using each other's bodies as inanimate sex toys, as opposed to real live human beings, all emotion gone, just sex. I can recall us arguing over which sex positions.

I needed to get some time away from the 'kid', plus, I had to go out and sell some of that 16'th of crystal, having purchased it with money intended for my rent. Nervous, anxious and extremely high I cruised in his Le Mans out to the Boulevard.

A rumor had surfaced, months earlier back in Fort Wayne, about a guy I knew; Paul. The rumor, among folks I knew, was that he contracted HIV and now had AIDS. Paul, a super-sexy dude with dark hair and sparkling green eyes that most everyone wanted to fuck. He knew all the guys wanted to jump his bones and carried himself as such. Somehow, he rubbed me the wrong way, probably just jealous of his looks. Paul disappeared. No one had seen or heard of him, giving more credence to the rumor.

That night, I pass by and see Paul sitting on a bus bench at the corner of La Brea and Santa Monica. I turned the car around pulling into the parking lot there at the Carl's Jr. Hollering out his name he turns to notice me. I knew from the fact that he was in LA, about as far as he could have fled from Indiana, the rumor was true, he was HIV positive. "Chile! ...What chu doing here?" Paul questioned me stunned.

"I live here!" I confirmed like a smartass. Catching up with each other I inform him that I had some crystal meth for sale. Always one to go head first into anything, Paul just couldn't resist turning it down with my prodding him on. I knew he had no clue what the effects of speed were and therefore clueless to what he was getting into. Buying a $20bag he opened up the car's glove box to snort a line. "Aww hell naw! I shouted, ... "Not in here!" I hipped him to the acute dangers of getting busted by the LAPD, then, suggested that he take the dope and snort it in the restroom, inside the Carl's Jr. I drove off and left him there.

Days later at Oki Dogs, I ran into Paul. "Damm,..... you fucked me up!" He blurted incredulously, "That shit had me up for 18 hours.!"

I just smirked, no one had held a gun to his head.

Back at the dope, sex pad, my apartment, the 'kid' sketching out, had begun to scratch and pick on his body to point of, now, having open almost blistering scars. I made claim that he needed to somehow go out to make some money. I was done supporting his dope use.

Next day, I took off in the car, only after I called myself hiding the last hit of speed inside a metal, Band Aids container. Immediately, on my return to the apartment I found him in the bathroom and, yes, the dope gone. I made sure I had parked the car far enough away so the "kid" could not locate it. Finally, mad and pissed off, I gave him an ultimatum; either he brings back some dope to replace that last hit or I was not telling him where was his car. Oh, and yes, he had to leave my apartment. "Doing my last hit," I fumed, "ungrateful ass... motherfucker!"

When Monday came around, there was no sign of the "kid," with me definitely in freefall, crashing from all the meth I'd polluted my body with. I drove the Le Mons to work on account of being lazy and coming down. Coming home from work that day, I neglected to strategically park the vehicle. As it got dark, I got awakened by banging on my door. It was two cops with the 'kid'. I argued to them that he may have some disease, he looked the part with the blotches all over on his skin. One of the cops chewed him out. Still, I had to turn over the keys, finally, ending that dope, sex and drama blitzkrieg. And that was only just the first week of life in my new apartment.

Out at John's place, in the valley, I happened to run into Jerry. Jerry; a skinny redheaded tweeker, who I had also ran around with us back in my early days out on the Boulevard. One time, both Jerry and I, high as fuck, standing out on Santa Monica Boulevard for some reason needed to know the time. I suggested to him to go over and ask a sheriff deputy, who was already interrogating some other hustler, to inquire about the time. Minutes afterward, I look over and I see Jerry getting handcuffed and put in the back of a patrol car. It wasn't funny at the time but we laughed a hoot about it later.

Jerry had somehow caught a ride, met me and came over to my place in Hollywood. We were talking, about the 'old' times, then, he starts to tell me how John changed, since he began dealing dope. Telling how devious and manipulative John had treated Jerry as part his entourage. Such actions offended the sense of camaraderie, I remembered there was or used to be, among us hustlers out on those streets. I felt it unfair, with all the shit we put up with selling our bodies, that we treated one another so shady. My respite back in Indiana, away from the 'Boulevard', had shielded me from those rough edges of street living and drug life. My big mouth got a hold of me. I said, "If I see John doing that to you... I'd turn him in." It didn't occur to me in those moments how Jerry's own junky habits set him up to getting abused in such ways.

A couple days later, John shows up at my apartment with detailing to me some plan that sounded way like he wanted me to allow him use of my apartment, setting up a satellite 'Hollywood' location for his dealing dope. Sure, I'd probably benefit getting some speed for my own habit. More though, it offended me that John just assumed that I'd go along with having my house used for his purposes. Even as a speed freak junky, in no way did I want anyone to have that kind of power over me. I had just left Dale, where I didn't even have to work if I had wanted, I'd left him for 'same reason, because I did not want someone controlling me. Besides, I had promised my landlord that there'd be no dope dealing in my apartment. As twisted as it may seem I did take some pride in being able to keep my word. John left after I had in a sense told him no that day. Hours later, he returned saying he had some "bomb" dope, that he had already fixed up for me, already in a syringe. "You just need to do it down your throat!" He told me. I protested about how strange it was to do it that way. Still, hanging on to the belief we were as close as we once used to be, I trusted him and let him shoot dope down my gullet.

The shot of speed burned my tongue and throat a little while it tasted horrible, and I felt no rush, what a tweeker lives for. Then John took off, saying he had business to take care of. Something I couldn't quite grasp definitely felt like it changed between us. A day or two later upon waking up I discovered that my throat burned whenever I tried to swallow. Naïve and trusting as I was, I just figured somehow, I was sick and coming down with something that had messed up my tonsils. Scared, like I had broken something in my body, for two days the only things I could eat were popsicles and ice cream. Finally, it came to me that the hit I allowed John to shoot in my throat was what fucked me up. Slow and painfully, in this case, I came around to the idea John being just as vicious and devious as Jerry had mentioned. Also, realized that Jerry must have gone back and told him what I'd said about treating friends that way. *"Had LA... the Boulevard...changed from how I knew it and remembered?"* I wondered.

Believing in that notion somewhere somehow, I got introduced to another tweeker in John's entourage; Todd. A thin, really tall White boy, kinda clean cut looking, suburban bred. Todd drove around the streets in this big jacked up Ford station wagon. Though I didn't have a clue then, it's possible Todd sought to hook up with me sexually. Yet, after the throat hit, I kept a standoffish posture with anyone in John's entourage of tweekers. I had no history to trust them.

One weekend out looking for dope as usual, I allowed myself to be talked into riding out to the desert near Palm Springs to cop some speed, in Todd's beat up station wagon. The plan involved Todd, me and another tweeker, who I didn't know, pooling money to buy a substantial quantity. Surely enough, off we go out to Palm Desert which to my discovery looked nothing like its wealthier neighbor community. This locale full of trailer homes and forlorn apartment buildings appeared like 'Deserted Palms' and had been taken over by legions of White gay speed freaks and the like. Palm Desert, I'd come to find out later, served as location where many gay pornos were filmed.

Once there, Todd pulls the station wagon up near this wild thicket of palm trees and desert vegetation. He then tells me the dealer won't sell to them with me around, so I needed to wait for them. Wait outside under the palm trees and dust until they complete the deal. Weary and reluctantly, but I agree. "*Shit...we had come this far.*" Only when I'm standing there seeing that jacked up station wagon pulling off do I, then, realize that I just might have been fucked. How well did I really know Todd? Top it off I now was stuck out there in the literal fucking desert, temperature nearly 100 degrees, 90 miles from LA. *"How the fuck could I have been so stupid!"* I cussed at myself, *"I knew better... than this shit!"* Pissed, I still did my best to stay calm and not think about my dire circumstance.

45minutes later, Todd and the other dude pulled back up to get me. I was fucking pissed as hell. Todd tried to play the scene off as if it was funny. Barely, I spoke a word as we drove the freeway back to LA. And, just like the dope addict I was, the afternoon's fucked up happenings faded away once I got high. Dope must have been good.

Coming up with rent for the next month, I was fucked. I'd spent it all on dope. Todd happened to be living out of that jacked up station wagon. We agreed to a deal, both out of addict desperation, of having him share my place to help on the rent. Somewhat I'd since forgiven him for leaving me, not high but dry, out there in the desert. We got along as much as two tweekers can without getting on each other's last nerve. Then one evening, both of us high, I told Todd exactly what time to come pick me up out on the Boulevard. "After two, the cops know... nobody's out there… cept tweekers and broke hustlers." I clearly informed. Instructions were exact because I would have dope on me, for sale. In no way could I take any chances on getting stopped by the cops.

2AM, last call, rolls around and no sign of Todd. Paranoid, I panic. And if that was not enough to be paranoid about, I add to the drama, slamming another hit of dope making things all the worse. Then, I recall myself hiding the dope packets under a dumpster in back behind the dry cleaners on the corner of Fairfax. Later, as the sun came up, I remember being on my back, under the deck of that same dry cleaners, (not too proud of this) jacking off. By the time I finally did get back to my apartment, I had lost the dope and Todd was gone. He had to go, I determined, locking up the apartment door knowing he didn't have a key. He returned, days later, for his things. Todd and I ended all partnerships, dope, financial, sex or otherwise. Come to think of it, John and I never crossed paths again either, all those times.

All the tweeker madness, my own and dealing with others, left me off balance, not quite sure of the world I had known in LA. Delusional, I carried forth with the sense that out there along that Boulevard there still existed a bonding, a commonality, in which we street folks treated one another with a kind of dignity, that only we understood. I can laugh at such thinking, now. Night after night it seemed I'd run into some tweeker, hustler, we'd shoot the shit and cop some dope, making our way back to my place to get high or crash for the night. And, not always did such mean I wanted to or even expected to fuck them.

One time this tweeker, remembered nameless. A White, Southern accented hustler with wiry blond hair, sporting cheap Naugahyde, Cuban heeled boots. Dude carried a feminine but street wise manner. Back at my place, surely both of us tweeked out because I clearly recall us jabbering for what seemed like all that night. Sharing tales of street life and other opinions. He told me his belief that gay people were purposefully meant as God's design of natural population and birth control. Ass backward as that sounded at first, sitting there taking in what he said, it really did make some sense. To this day, I still feel some truth to that uncommon wisdom coming from that air-headed tweeker.

Other varied instances of bringing home assorted street folk led to me having my underwear stolen. Having to nearly threaten to call the police to get another freak case out of my house and picking up this worn out straight porn actor, who stiffed the cab driver on the way to the apartment while insisting on doing a three-way with a female. That request didn't happen. I even paid this one hustler after sex, with what he termed 'walking money', if he promised to come back to apartment in time to wake me up for work that day.

In the last days before I left sugar daddy Dale, not even caring about him, I spent a night on a crystal meth- fueled sex romp at the Hollywood Spa bath house. I kept a little shaving bag containing my dope, syringes and tourniquet. When my room was up for the evening, packing up, I left to return to Dale's, taking the #212 bus all the way back down La Brea Boulevard from Hollywood to Westchester. Coming down from the high, on the long bus ride back home, I fell asleep and damn near missed my stop. Awaking in confusion, disoriented from speed aftereffects I departed the bus, forgetting my little 'bag' That 'bag' contained my ID as well as needles and my dope. A day or two later, I called the bus transit lost and found. The clerk answering the phone informed me, I needed to come down to a different location than the usual lost and found to claim my belongings. I blew it off, but carried concern about possible repercussions.

With the multitudes of dope and speed freaks coming in and out my place, I started worrying if the police were just watching, waiting for the opportune moment to bust in on all the dope madness. Sure, as well, the massive quantities of methamphetamines I pumped in my body tended to make one a little paranoid, to say the least. More than a month had passed since the loss of my 'bag'. I concluded, wisely I thought, it was better to go to them and see if anything was amiss as opposed to having them come to me. Lord only knew what condition they'd find me in. Besides, I actually needed my ID.

So, one morning I made my way downtown to the office the transit agency had directed. For courage, I did a hit of dope before leaving my apartment. On my arrival I was directed into a paneled inner office conference room containing a long table. Then, in came more cops, dressed like FBI agents, all stiff and I guessed supposed to be threatening. "Are you Juan Salter?" One of them said in an official tone.

"Yes, I am," coolly I responded.

"Is this yours?" Another one asked while spreading the contents of my little 'bag' out in the middle of that long table.

I lifted up slightly in my chair, looked across the table viewing my things, especially my identification. With apprehension and astonishment, I noticed the dope and the needles were not there. Thinking I was in the clear. "Yes, it is." I answered smirking on the inside.

Come to find out, after time had passed, evidence had been confiscated. They at first, so sure of themselves started to quietly question one another. I sat back mildly beaming from ear to ear. They had not expected some no account tweeker to actually come venture into 'enemy' territory. I remember one of the dicks (detectives) getting deep in my face with one of those instruments, with the tiny bright light, to check my pupils. So close to me I could smell his breath. He stated to the others, "He's clean."

"What dumbasses!" I mumbled.

Finally, I was informed that when my bag was discovered by the transit cop, he had pricked himself with one of the needles. Still in their official tone, meant to scare me, they basically ordered me to submit to an HIV test. Two police detectives would come to pick me up the next day, at my apartment.

The next day, a Friday I remember, a rude knock comes on my door. Me, high as usual and some other tweeker in the apartment taking a shower after our activities from the night before. Off I was taken in an unmarked vehicle to some police clinic in downtown LA. My wrists cuffed behind my back, during the ride. My blood was drawn, luckily brown skin helps hide needle track marks. Soon, I was told that I was HIV negative. Later, I wondered how the police were able to get the results so quickly, this being the early days before rapid testing.

With that done the two detectives decided to be assholes and keep the back windows rolled up and not turn on the air conditioning. Still tweeking, I sat in the backseat of the unmarked police car handcuffed sweating buckets. In August LA it gets more than hot enough with the windows closed. Dropping me back off at my place I strutted away from the car proudly, thinking I'd outsmarted the tough LAPD.

That was not to be the last of my encounters with the LAPD. On a typical evening I took off walking down the Boulevard, after having come home from work, probably as far as Oki Dogs. Still craving that 'Hollyweird' thrill I had once known. Nothing much was happening that night, so off I took to walk the more than 3miles back down the Boulevard toward home. Just before I got to Highland, I spot a police car slowing down just on the other side of the street with the cops giving me the once over. Knowing I hadn't done nothing, I wasn't high and didn't have dope on me, so, I stared back at them. Like, "what the fuck you looking at!" I continued walking but within like seconds, "Get on the fucking ground!" I heard one of the cops scream at me. Both of the cops, now, stood with guns aimed and pointed directly at me.

"What did I do!" I pleaded scared as shit, as I hit my body on the sidewalk.

"Face down...shut up!" One of them yelled, his black boot directly on the back of my neck, pressing my face in the sidewalk concrete, as handcuffs were put on my wrists so tight, they cut into my skin when I moved.

Defiant, "I didn't do… anything!" I pleaded and yelled. Spit coming out my mouth while tears started to run down my cheeks. Frisking me while I laid down flat on the ground, they screamed for my ID. It was there in my wallet but it was my Indiana driver's license. Finding that out seemed only to serve to make them madder. My breath was so hard and loud, now, I had never been so mad, disgusted, so violated in all my life. My body was picked up off the ground and thrown into the back seat of the squad car. In a minute or two, we hear over the police radio something about a black male suspect, in North Hollywood, more than 10miles from where we were. Minutes later, I was pulled out of the car, uncuffed and let go. I screamed at them, "Aren't you going to apologize!" Even still there with the probability of them further roughing me up, I didn't care being so fucking mad. Just like that, they drove off as if nothing had happened. Just unreal, I'd had two loaded guns pulled on me without a doubt they would have shot me dead, if I'd made one false move.

All I had done was just walk down the street. *"How can they do such a thing?"* I walked, still huffing, the rest of the way home. (The theme of the LAPD continues in another later story)

Guns drawn at my head were my proverbial last straw. LA did not love me anymore. It had changed. I understood how come John and his tweeker entourage had left for the Valley. My beloved Hollywood no longer put out the welcome of at least tolerance to us freaks. West Hollywood had gone gay upscale, always had been to a degree. What was left felt more brutal, maybe it always was, now, I realized the truth. In the next week or so I lost my job at Metro Traffic and, then, I studied up on moving me and mine to San Francisco. The 'fire' had left LA or LA was on fire, either way I burned.

Rock-N-Roll (1989)

On a kick, I decided to quit doing speed after about a month into my life in San Francisco. Figured I had opportunities to start a new life in a new city. I had set out on my own to the City and there I was. Came to my decision by what I had witnessed living in and around the City's Tenderloin District. The TL(Tenderloin), as we locals referred to it, seemed in reality to be a heaven for junkies' and drunks'. There in those 20 or so city blocks, it was not uncommon to see someone openly shooting up dope, turning a trick and most definitely buying and selling drugs. In 89' crack cocaine was the drug of choice. At night the streets really became a free for all, the place to sell, buy and use dope, including the buying and selling of the people who used the dope.

In almost the exact opposite of LA, the cops in San Francisco took the approach that at least the crime and illegality was localized in one area of the City. As a dopehead, if you stayed in the TL, you were allowed to basically free roam. In the daylight the gloss came off. Drag queens still be out and about showing worse for wear. Druggies strung out and out of pocket loomed desperate for the next fix. Heroin addicts in need of a 'wake up' staked their corners to panhandle or doing whatever needed to be done to get money.

Another fixture different from LA was the abundance of soup kitchens that served free meals. Glide Memorial served three meals a day, 7days a week, bag lunches on weekends. Saint Anthony's on Golden Gate Avenue served lunch at 10am every day. One could eat as many times as you wanted so long as you got back in the line again which snaked down and around the sidewalk for nearly two blocks. My first time succumbing to this necessity reminded me of seeing old photos of 'skid rows', in The Depression. A twinge of guilt and shame crept in. *"This is what my life has become?... Was I not raised better than this?"* Dope and living the kind of life to obtain them helped to keep the shame in the rear view.

For nearly three weeks I set out to be a young, black and gay upstanding citizen of the City. True, it occurred to me that I had a problem with dope but with determination I felt that issue could be licked. I searched for work, the legit kind, as I continued hanging on Polk Street where hustlers sold their wares. I grew frustrated due to so many of my associations still being connected around dope.

Some days when not searching for a job, I would go and spend time in the main library. Reading, particularly non-fiction, remained a safe refuge for my sanity and keeping a sense of myself. Books would serve immensely in my continuing education. Up in the stacks I perused "The Great Divide", by author Studs Terkel. The book; oral personal histories and opinions of individual Americans living in the Reagan Era. I know I could have added my own opinion of the Reagan Age. Easy to read and not requiring me to read it from beginning to end, another aspect of my affinity to non-fiction. I could read as my interest carried me along.

'Home' was a hotel room with a bed and a sink located at 6th and Tehama Streets, in the South of Market District. The building looked like something out of the Gold Rush Era, wooden, bay windows about 3 or 4 storeys tall. Such architecture in the City fascinated me, having lived in LA where almost no area contained buildings as old as were whole sections of San Francisco. The two cities in the same state seemed of such opposite characters.

Soon after arriving I met John, a cute, small white guy about thirty with thick, long hair. I fall for men with long hair. We met up on Polk and he, later, invited me up to his apartment. Feeling so excited about meeting and fucking with this super handsome dude, after that night we made no further plans to get together. Finding, in the end, he just wanted sex, took away the thrill of his beauty and attractiveness.

Later on, I met Gerry, an olive-colored guy who lived down on the Peninsula, Silicon Valley Area. The sexual encounters at least felt more fulfilling, he enjoyed kissing and caressing as did I. Gerry compensated me for my services, the pleasure all mine. Gerry compensated me for my services, the physical pleasure all mine. His cat named Juju, was declawed, allayed my phobia of cat claws. He worked in some business related to the San Francisco Giants. Driving the freeway to his house I had impressed telling the origins of my first name; in honor of the baseball pitcher, Juan Marichal, who had actually played for the San Francisco Giants team.

In securing employment, I also proceeded on another notion of why I had come to San Francisco. I had felt the need to make myself available of service to my fellow gay brethren whom had succumbed to the devastation of HIV/AIDS epidemic. Through research I found the Shanti Project. I walked to their office on Market Street and applied to volunteer.

I got myself around town mostly walking not having the funds for bus fare. On the day that I signed up to volunteer, I remember it being rather hot, not really common for San Francisco. I started making my way to eat at a soup kitchen run by Catholic nuns, on Fourth Street, by the dock area. Just so I happened to stop for a rest from the unusual heat, at the Caltrain Commuter Station on 4th Street.

Parking myself on a bench outside the station, I sat taking notice of the commuters busily moving in and out of the terminal. At what I'd learn later was exactly 5:17PM, there arose a very loud rumbling. Electric cable wires of the Muni trolley buses started to swing heavily, up and down and side to side, just over our heads. Within the terminal station, constructed of precast concrete, erupted the indescribable noise of multi-ton heavy concrete blocks being slapped against one another. During that unbelievable happening, I remember seeing this middle-aged woman sitting across from me, at the other end of the same bench, not much more than an arm's length between us. She turned to look toward me at the same exact moment my head turned to look at her. As I live, I was certain she must have had the same thought as did I. "That's…the trains... isn't it?"

Both of us would have said, if we had spoken. Immediately after that thought, I began assuming that, "Yes"! We were experiencing an earthquake, right here and now. It was California and earthquakes did happen here. Only near the end of the 25 second or so main tremor, I realized that this particular quake was a '*motherfucker*'. When it first finally stopped, I remained there still and completely frozen on that bench.

I began panting. "Haaah, Haaa!...Haaa!" Like I'd just ran a 100-yard sprint, in seconds flat.

In the immediate aftermath most people seemed caught off guard, me included. Finally, I got up off the bench to continue walking the rest of my way to free food. I ate my soup prepared and served by the nuns almost the same as I'd done before. Only when I started to make my way back to my hotel room did I begin to really notice that the traffic signals were out and traffic had backed up everywhere on the streets. The Goodyear Blimp floated by up in the sky, above the Bay, out towards Oakland. It happened to have been circling overhead for the scheduled third game of that year's World's Series, between the Giants and the A's.

Walking back, I turned the corner on 6tt Street, and just could not believe what I was seeing. There in the middle of the street pavement lay an open crevice, about 5 feet wide, that stretched for several blocks. *"This is just fucking unreal...like a movie set... but, this shit is really fucking happening!"*

One or two fire trucks were parked in my block. Fire and emergency crews stood accessing dangers and blocking access to buildings. My hotel just so happened to be one of the ones they were refusing to allow anyone to enter. Walking over I approached one of the firemen, "Hey...I've just recently got here to the City. Everything I own is in there…. I have nowhere to go!" I insisted to him, pleading.

Other residents pleaded and yelled at the firemen. All the sudden in frustration one fireman piped up, loudly, to all who demanded, "You'll ...look at that…. see that smoke! "We have more urgent problems to deal with. The city's… on fire!", he turned and pointed northward, toward the billowing smoke up in the sky. "Your building is unsafe. If you go in its.... at your own risk!"

I grasped the perilous situation. What was I to do? Further, I recall a small Latina woman screaming, nearly in hysterics. From what I could grasp and understand, her father, a senior citizen, still, lay trapped up in the hotel and she knew nothing about his condition. The emergency crews had made clear that they needed to leave and go address the fires burning out of control. That woman continued screaming about finding her father.

In that moment, like never before in my life, I somehow coolly braced the situation, in spite of dangers, and found the will to be calm and collected. I knew exactly where I was. I needed to go up into the partially collapsed hotel.

Small aftershocks quakes continued on and off. The Latina woman calmed somewhat at my urging. She informed me of her father's room number. I went in. Plaster and fallen debris lay in the way with the stairways leaning precariously to one side. Carefully, I climbed up. That man's room just so happened to be on the top floor. When I finally reached his door, I yelled out. I heard him respond saying that he could not move. His door was locked. Now, fantastic as it sounds, like on TV, I stepped back, turned to my side and slammed forward as hard as I could. My full body, adrenaline flowing, hit the door and it busted open. There inside, I saw an old man with a walker, prostrate over the toilet. Plaster and wooden slats from the walls had fallen around and on his back. I determined that he wasn't seriously injured more just in shock. As well I guess I was in shock, because I fail to remember any details of how I helped that old man out of the hotel and down to the street, with all that was going on. Then, I made way to my own room. I grabbed a jacket and the book "The Great Divide", that I'd been reading from the library.

Now, where was I to go? I knew no one. So, I made what I felt was the best decision, to go and be around people of my element; Polk Street.

Night fell. It started to get dark, really dark with electricity and lights out all over the city. Walking my way up to Polk I noticed some bars being open. People were inside drinking by candlelight. Residents that lived in buildings above the storefronts, stood about, out on the streets and sidewalks. Nervously, I walked up the street. It, then, occurred to me that as the hours wore on and with people outdoors drinking, getting intoxicated, the scene potentially could get dangerous. Amongst that atmosphere, this White gay guy with a receding hairline, walked up toward me. I could see with him, on a leash, held a rather large vicious looking dog, a German Shepherd maybe. He approached and spoke, "Man that quake was a mutherfucker! ...You wanna go somewhere... and fuck?" I just stood there and stared back at him with what must've been the nastiest look of disgust. The dog barked toward me.

"Like really... What kinda fucking freak are you!" I thought. Disgusted was the least of my reactions. I reasoned he'd come out, in the middle of that disaster, just to take advantage of some victim, certain, I had the demeanor of his perfect mark: young Black, desperate, out there on Polk. Probably, had the dog with him in case his 'victim' retaliated. In later years I would see that same guy up and along Polk Street. Always, I'd sneer disgustedly at him. (We would meet later when we both were in rehab from drugs).

There I wandered around in the pitch black darkness. To my surprise and my good fortune, of all persons I recognize Geoff cruising in his Jeep down Polk Street.

I yelled out at him. He turned to see who yelled and stopped, and let me in. Finding him that night proved evidence that there must have been a God taking care of me.

He drove out to the Marina District, one of the most affected areas of the earthquake. Houses stood half collapsed, sidewalks and streets with gorges in them. Some houses and buildings were still on fire and burning as we drove nearby. I happened to notice that the Marina area, unlike the rest of the city, appeared laid out totally flat.

In those immediate hours after the quake the world outside of the Bay Area knew the extent of what had happened and the status of the recovery. The City was completely without phone service and electric power.

I carried a sense that, like probably the rest of the city, having no clue if 'civilization' as we'd known it would return to normal tomorrow, next week or next month.

Down the freeway Geoff drove to get to his house in Atherton. Sex that evening provided me a feeling of something calm and safe.

The next morning power had returned to the suburbs on the Peninsula. Geoff made me breakfast and provided a handful of change, about $6. Saying, it was all he had. He dropped me off at the Caltrain Station in Atherton. I didn't even bother with the little money he'd given me, grateful of the fact I had had somewhere to sleep and had been with someone I knew the night before.

What irony. *I happened to have been at the CalTrain station when the whole disaster started in the first place.* There I was about to ride a train for the first time in my life (excluding subways and zoo trains).

I boarded. The ticket conductor stated half-jokingly but clearly, "Train maybe late... but ya can't beat the price." He was signaling that the service was free that day. Good for me since all I had would just have amounted to the fare.

I rode the rails back to the City. Like a scene in one of those disaster movies, looking through the windows outside, it appeared like some version of hell when I stepped out the train station in Frisco. Still, without electricity, street lights not working. People were out milling about in the streets somewhat aimlessly. Somehow in the chaos, I found out about an earthquake relief station set up by FEMA.

I could tell a rush was on to the Moscone Convention Center on Howard Street. I simply needed to follow the direction, folks who looked like I did, where they were heading. Denizens from the TL were well represented in the cavernous center. Cots had been set up to sleep and rest and it seemed as if every hour or so they were setting up feeding stations.

As if those of us who were without shelter or any information on where or how to obtain some type of living arrangement needed to be kept well fed. I witnessed what I call the Tenderloin mindset; to horde as much as you can, especially if it was free, no matter if you needed it or not.

On the evening of the second day after the quake local politicians arrived at the convention center, of course with news reporters in tow. I waited in a short line to speak with the mayor at that time; Art Agnos. He happened to be there with U.S. Congressperson, Nancy Pelosi. That being my first time having a face-to-face conversation with a politician. I fail now to remember anything I said to them. What I remember making an impression was their behavior. Agnos had the personality of a slicked up, used car salesman, in which he spoke a mile a minute yet, looked right through me. He was campaigning in the middle of the crisis, even as most citizens represented in that convention center didn't even vote. Pelosi, on the other hand, came across completely the opposite and did not pander. She seemed calm and listened respectfully to me, even if I was in reality a downtrodden druggie. Later, her political career would rise but, then she was relatively unknown outside the Bay Area.

In the next two weeks or so I found myself shifted into the population who were truly without shelter because of the earthquake. This as opposed to the many folks doing their best to scam in on the possibility of receiving free FEMA aid; as previously mentioned; the Tenderloin Mindset.

After leaving the Moscone Center some of us were to be settled temporarily on a Navy carrier, docked in San Francisco shipyard. Standing waiting in a long line to board the ship, some of the sailors began disembarking. I stood there surprised with my mind somewhat blown. So many of the sailors I was seeing that evening looked in appearance as if they were headed off to the nearest gay bar. I had heard rumors somewhere that the

Navy, of all the military services, held a reputation as hideout for closeted gays. There was the rumor, proved true, right before my very eyes.

Through the Red Cross, I ended sheltered at a middle school in the Marina District. That same district being one of the hardest hit areas of the earthquake also was known as one of the more expensive residential areas. Even so, some people there also had had their homes or apartments completely destroyed. Eating breakfast one morning, in the school cafeteria, I looked over to spot an older likely, wealthy white couple being served the same food as I was, by the Red Cross.

FEMA paid to relocate me in my own studio apartment at 351 Turk Street, in the heart of the TL. The building having once been a YMCA residential hotel, probably with a history of housing gay men, back in the day.

You could say it was not too bad for having arrived a month before to San Francisco, with the clothes on my back, a 35mm camera and bag of speed in my pocket. Ah yes, my respite from the dope life soon ended too.

Billy Wayne (1991)

Love at first sight, probably not, more likely lust at first sight. Writing, here, his first and middle name still brings to mind sweet and melancholy memories of the one who came to love me and left me with an indelible lasting impression.

Memories. In the deepest throes of my addiction, my love affair with meth alongside meeting the guy who would have been the love of my life led me to ultimately choose dope. The loss of being in control with the vulnerability of intimacy, I ran away from. Then, once again, I was alone wondering what could have been.

Out on Polk Street, one Saturday afternoon, that same block as were the Bagel Delicatessen and the QT gay bar, I saw him standing there alone on the corner of Austin Alley. Lean and tall, with long, ponytailed blond hair slung this stunning young thing sporting a fringed, black leather jacket, slick as could be. *"Was he new...I never seen him before?"* He caught my gaze. Somehow, I boldly sauntered my way to approach and chat him up.

He said his name was Billy. We got to talking, nothing much just bullshit, then, he asked "You know where I can get some rocks?" I stared back at him as if he asked the silliest question.

"Why, you looking to get someth'in?" I responded.

"Yeah...shit yeah! I ain't probably go 'in to pull another trick… anyhow! I heard him say.

"Damn! He is so cute." I thought, detecting a Southern accent as he flashed his overbite-toothed smile.

He followed me as we walked down to the Tenderloin to cop two crack rocks and we headed back to my apartment, which was nearby. As we walked, I was keen on his every move. He trusted me to cop for him. And, I didn't get a vibe that all hell was about to break out, once he had the dope, trying some kinda scam to leave me hanging. Since I had a buzz from doing speed, hitting on a crack pipe didn't mean that much to me anyhow. I was more interested in feeling out this fine-looking, new hustler. He was new and I'd gotten to him first.

Billy had his own straight- shooter crack pipe. I noted this sign of him being a real crackhead, despite his good looks and being will kempt. Neither of us said much of anything as we smoked. Too much talking while hitting on the pipe got on my last nerves anyway. *"Shut the fuck up… and smoke!* I'd usually think. When all the crack rocks had been puffed into clouds, we parted ways, still, in good standing though for dope fiends. My interest had been peaked for more.

About a week later, I bump into Billy again. "Wanna go get a rock?" He being more insistent this time. Off to smoke we go. On this particular occasion Billy literally did let his hair down, long blond and beautiful as it was. Once hitting the pipe, he took off his shirt and got up to go peek out the window, from 12floors up. *"Who the hell he thinks he is.... This is my house.... I don't care if you do got dope!"* And, his taking off his shirt didn't faze me either. I guess he figured if dope was out, and he'd bought it, then it went, naturally, I was supposed to get all sexual on his whim. *"Nigga please!"* (even if he was a White boy: I could have told him.) That smoke session got cut short. *"Smoke yo shit and get out. I don't even care if you tweeking... diggin in the carpet."* I wanted to tell him. *"Teach that fucker... disrespect me!"*

Seeing Billy once again out on the street, I decided to talk him into getting some speed. I might have offered to buy that time. It was my turn to treat. We had hung together three times now and throughout, often he'd flash that bashful, toothy smile and stare back at me with his gorgeous brown eyes. Like a good 'White woman', it was the third 'date' (dope encounter) and safe to screw. "Hey....you wanna... mess around?" I got through my lips and out my mouth as we both laid there on the carpet thoroughly tweeking out.

"Yeah... I wondered if you were gonna ask." He agreed, looking hot as ever.

I fell deeper in lust as my hand, fingers reached to touch his slender smooth loins. In those moments my sexual ideal realized. Aroused all just the same to be right there touching, holding, rubbing and kissing the lips of that lovely man. Billy shied from too much kissing. Neither one of us rushing to fuck the other. To me Billy was real, there in the flesh, why upset those glorious, sensuous moments just so someone could be penetrated. I desired love making natural, as natural as it could be with both of us all hyped out on speed.

We cuddled, post orgasm, laying still, there on the bare carpet floor of my bed less studio apartment. Billy shared his middle name with me and told that he was from the town of Dixon, Tennessee, near Nashville. I shared with him that I had never been in a relationship. Billy said he considered himself to be more of a bisexual, especially since having been in a relationship with both a man and a woman, at the same time.

"That night I first spotted you...I thought... that fucker is so fine wit his long hair and pretty eyes," I told him, "from Tennessee no doubt...with a twang!"

Further in our conversation Billy stated that he was presently staying somewhere only temporarily. So, I offered to keep some of his things stored at my place. Thinking the offer being not too pushy.

At the end of that week Billy had moved in. Though unstated he and I were, now, an item details yet to be filled in.

In quiet down moments, both of us shared with one another our background history of abuse, his more so physical, than my sexual abuse. Our bonding grew despite some tensions.

As a couple we were a 'mixed' marriage. No, not the I'm Black and he's White thing, but of me being speed freak and Billy basically a crackhead. Conflict and clashes of the mixture were sure to ensue.

Out on the hustler stroll, the favorite flavor was young and white. Now, I made do with what I had. Still, Billy was the real thing, in that sense. No jealousy on my part, except that Billy carried a cavalier attitude over the fact of him making money every night on Polk, sometimes two or even three times. Never mind that nearly every last dime earned got spent smoked up in crack, leaving us just as broke the next day. Adding to my sense of injury, since he earned the funds, so it was his choice of dope. To his credit Billy never was he greedy. He shared as much as he smoked, dope fiends notice that kind of thing.

Billy came back to the apartment after being out working the street, with this Latino crack dealer in tow. I recognized dude as same person I'd noticed cruising me before, out and around the Tenderloin. The setup, that night, was to smoke and fuck. I did my best to not be interested, giving Billy disgusted dirty looks as the crack pipe passed amongst us. And just for extra drama to round out the episode, "Mann! This shit... ain't no good. I could'a got a rock for ten!" Billy accused Jose or whatever his name was of scamming on the dope. Exactly the type of mess I feared might happen. Somehow, I managed to get the dealer dude out of 'my' house without having to give up dick or without a fight breaking out.

"Whaat!" Billy glared at me with his pretty, but now bleary, bloodshot brown eyes of his. I said nothing. What was the use of making an issue of what had just happened, feeling conflicted all the same? I knew what it was like to be fiendin for the next hit, desperate. I didn't want to come down on him and take on the role of being a fucking nag.

Was I in love? Billy was what he was, stunningly gorgeous at that. I knew full well he was a crackhead, just as I was a speed freak, so, I just figured I had to learn to live with him and love him. No, he's not perfect. I consoled myself all the while straining against my street instincts. I felt overwhelmed.

"I've never been willing to accept the ugly parts...with the good". Overwhelmed at being involved with a sweet beautiful man who said he wanted to be with me. *"Maybe... this is how all couples are."* Such went through my head often being with him. *"Maybe... that's why I've never really been in a relationship... I've not been willing to accept the ugly parts."*.

We happened to be up usually early one day within the bright daylight hours. One of us thought, probably me, that it might be a good idea not to start out the day with our typical crack binge. "Have you ever been out to the Haight?" I asked Billy.

"Naww." He responded in his 'in the hills' accent.

"Let's do that... instead." Was my 'let's be normal' suggestion. One of us came up with the notion we could cop some weed while out here. Weed more for Billy. I didn't really smoke weed on account of I considered myself a proud full-on speed freak. As best I remember we had about $13 total. With $10 going to buy the weed, meaning there would not be enough bus fare for both of us, to get there and back.

"Know what... why don't we walk ...since we ain't got enough for both of us to catch the bus." I told him.

"Walk!... How far is it?" Billy questioned my reasoning.

"Aw, I don't know.... maybe a mile or two." I shot back, "It's nice out, sun shine'n!"

"I'ont wanna walk that far!" he whined a bit.

"Then maybe...., let's walk there and take the bus back." A compromise I suggested.

"Let's just take the bus and we'll figure it out." Billy ended.

"Alright, you gon'e need a jacket." I further implored him, because he did not realize how temperatures would change once the fogs rolled in, especially like they did out in the Haight.

"Look out there.... it's nice! I don't need one!" He answered me, looking out the window to see a cloudless sky. Deciding to pick my battles, I just let him be.

Once we got off the bus in the Haight, Billy and I strolled down the street taking in the sights. I felt as if I was floating on air. There I was alongside this lovely man, figuratively, literally, on my arm. As I beamed, I realized at the same time, it was the first time we were out in public together, outside of being in the locales of the Tenderloin and Polk Street. Somehow those places didn't count as 'public'.

We stopped in a record store, only browsed though, cause we were still essentially broke. Finally, we finished the browsing street scene, then, made our way into Golden Gate Park. Minutes later we ended up striking up a conversation with a rather attractive female, who copped weed for us. I sensed Billy's attraction and felt jealous. I did the best to hide the fact. Jealousy never before reared its head, around Billy, yet, when some cute girl showed up it was different. Most of the time we were around other guys, so I never really took notice. No competition did I feel with another man, but a vagina and tits were out of my league.

Soon joints got rolled, smoked up and we got high, really baked as I recall. I tried to play it cool, masking my irritation, jealousy. Billy eventually looked toward me and took notice of my feigned laughter and fake smiles. He, then, graciously adiosed us from said female.

Then, somehow, we ended up at the park's kid's playground. Before we knew it, we lost ourselves on the swings, running around and jumping on the merry-go –round. Marijuana helped with the loosening of inhibitions, mine for sure.

The sunshine faded early, it being February. As I'd forewarned, the Frisco fogs rolled in steadily and thick. Appearing as if plumes from a fire, the fog noticeably chilled the air. "You ready to go... Damn! It's cold!" Billy announced, scrunching up his shoulders looking at me. Giving me a look with his poor, innocent eyes, I could have just about slapped him in the back of the head. Now, I sensed it was time for us to hurry up and rush to the bus stop, mind you we're still very stoned and all.

Half way walking down Haight Street, frustrated, I finally blurted, "Damn... Billy! Did you think I was just lying to you…. about how cold I said it was gonna get?"

"I don't know." Was his reply, revealing to me how Billy seemed to operate without the least bit of forethought. I let it go. And to make matters even worse, now, we needed to 'jump' the bus fare; sneaking in through the rear door of the bus without paying. Although chances being slim, we could get busted and arrested, not forgetting we were stoned besides.

Billy and I stood there in the chilly air to wait for a bus that was crowded, less chance of us being seen coming in through the back door. Once we got inside the bus, we sank ourselves low into a seat together. I took the opportunity, then, to lean in close to Billy. My earlier frustrations melted away as I felt his warmth next to me. I turned and stared into his soft brown eyes, not for too long, before being noticed by any other riders. I recall reaching out to grab ahold his hand, feeling our fingers glide against each other's. A sense of feeling loved and wanted came up and washed over me. I felt comfortable in the small body language of affection; although still, I feared saying, "I love you," out loud. In a sense we were really 'riding high', as the City passed by on that trip back to the TL. Remembering us there, being in San Francisco, on the #71 bus coming from Haight Ashbury, no one could have cared less what Me and Billy were doing.

One night in the aftermath of smoking up, I put on my 'jam' song. "She's the wildest one in the wild... kingdom.... She's the wildest thing that floats doowwn!" ("Junebug" by the B52's) I sang an animated performance of that tune, loud screams and all. Billy laughed at me staring up at my big, Black being, gyrating to the campy musings. In such moments I felt the closest to that langy man-boy, safe enough to open up the things I'd kept hidden.

I liked and loved Billy for being open minded to his intelligence, being open to learn new ideas I shared with him, in spite of his coming from down home origins. He revealed to me that going to school had provided him a place of safe refuge. Safer than he was in his abusive home.

In typical fashion of our dope incidents, I would cash my general assistance welfare check. Billy and I roamed up, down and around Polk Street desperately searching for a connect to purchase meth. When we did finally come across a dealer I knew and trusted, I got enough dope for the both of us. We made the deal. "Now... let's go home an fuuckk!" Billy stated bluntly, what was so true right out in front of Maurice; the dealer.

Door safely locked back at 251 Turk Street #1205, baggies of white crystals opened up and contents watered down, hypodermic rigs drawn up, arms tied off, needles pricked into pumped up veins.

"Ahhh!" One of us more than likely moaned just seconds after the chemical rush hit the bloodstream. The brain.

All super sex crazed and horny as I became on methamphetamine, alongside Billy with his long lithe and beautiful body, I never even tried to fuck till it hurt, as was the standard method of sex scene on speed. Instead we kissed, caressed and eventually ended up sucking and blowing off one another. Truth be told, all Billy really had to do was just kiss and hold me just long enough and tight enough, then boom, I'd blast off out my dick so strong and intense, I'd be moaning loudly and convulsing as if I was in a seizure. Then he'd come off too. Afterwards, we lay together spooned up against each other.

Spooning afterwards, Billy already half asleep, I lay there remembering back years before having sex with Art, who seemed to nearly yell while cumming, during our sex. Now, here was I, reliving the near same situation with Billy, roles reversed. I lay there silently praying to God in gratitude, feeling gratitude for having this lovely man held in my arms, part of my life.

As well I felt remorse. Thinking, maybe, Art had had similar feelings of love and lust, the way I felt for Billy. Back then I cared only for my feelings. It crossed my mind, did Billy really feel the same love for me as I did him, more reversed roles?

Holding him, feeling my breath as it bounced off Billy's neck, I recalled all the people I had fucked over. All the actions I had done, justifying the means to pursue my dopefiend ends.

In particular, I recalled a guy, Geoff; back in Fort Wayne. He had come from a small town, country background. I used to get him to buy us weed and beer, then ignore him when I got what I wanted. Now, laying there that afternoon, I could see he had just wanted to make friends, the only way he knew how. Callously, I could have cared less about his feelings at the time.

Outside the sunlight faded behind the window drapes as tears rolled down my face. I moved to hold Billy even tighter, feeling ashamed of what I had done to Geoff and he being not the only one I treated that way either. Billy laying still in my embrace moved something deep within my being.

Weeks drew on with us as a couple. Our 'mixed' marriage strained; tensions arose. Who knew two selfish dope fiends didn't make for the best relationship communication?

Billy finally agreed, at my urging him, to apply for and get food stamps. When the day came for him to go pick them up, he ended up cashing them in and coming back home with crack, without having come to consult with me. "Whaat..., he answered to my disdainful looks. ``Was I supposed to come home ...and see if we needed to save some for food?" Billy asked and reasoned aloud, sitting on the toilet, after we'd smoked up and the refrigerator still lay bare.

With the few dollars of food stamps that were left we walked up to Cala Foods to at least buy something to eat for that night. I regrettably recall Billy being upset that I wasn't enthusiastically excited about his wanting a meal of his comfort foods; boxed macaroni and cheese with hotdogs. I can, now, realize my inflexibility and my stubbornness.

Billy always seemed to gladly eat anything I cooked or suggested.

Nowadays, I just inform everyone that I'm a snob when it comes to my taste in food.

When I cashed my welfare check, having anticipated that exact day to get high.

I told Billy, specifically, to wait for me at the apartment.

An hour or so later, I'm as high as fuck, I hear him down on the street below.

"Juan... Juan!" yelling up for me to come down and let him in.

By then I was so completely tweeked out, greasy, sweaty, selfishly angry and most certainly naked. After a while he stopped, "I'll… get him later…when...I'm not so tweeked. Serves him right!" I thought. "Not being where I 'told' him to be." This my justification of my junky desertion of the man I was supposed maybe to be in love with.

Next night around midnight, when I'm starting to come down and all out of dope, I hear Billy call up to me from down on the street again. I take the elevator down to go get him. He comes back up with me looking like a mess, sucked up, cheeks protruding. His always beautiful brown eyes looked like dark sockets, his pants hung off his already thin frame.

Just as the elevator doors closed Billy began spilling the tale of his having been out on the street, since the day before.

How he had shouted up my name and got no reply.

Feeling guilty, I didn't let on how I had heard him yelling, yet still, I was too selfishly high to answer his calling up to me.

Inside the apartment as I looked over his condition, I guess somehow he felt he had to spill the beans that he had also gotten high. "Jose got me high. And fucked me." Billy said out as if in confession, sheepishly looking back at me.

Jose; a rather low life street denizen known for not being the cleanest person, who I assumed, specifically, aimed to get him high because it was known that Billy was my man.

Hell! I hadn't even fucked him. Billy, it seemed couldn't have sunk much lower, speaking in relationship terms.

Yet, not a single word of disapproval did I utter, even as much as I wanted to. *"Why bother the milk had already been spilled, seal already been broken,"* I thought. Looking at him in his dejected state said all there was to say. Maybe Billy fucking someone else, even if for dope, was justified payback to me for not stopping and going down to get him when, I was so high and tweeked out.

In the days following we talked over our situation being together. I told him that I felt his actions showed how he was not concerned about where we were going to end up, with my eviction due any day. Billy told me of his feelings of how he felt being controlled by me and saying I never really trusted him. There was definitely some truth to me having a lack of trust in him.

If Billy wanted to go, I wouldn't hold it against him. But, if he was going to stay with me, leaving me to always be the responsible one, then, he needed not go against what I had decided was best for both of us. If long ago memories are correct, the next day Billy came home, once again, with some crack ready to smoke just the same as we had been doing. Probably reading my feelings from the looks I gave him, "I'm sorry... but I really don't like living here!" Billy said in a half-angry tone.

As it came to be, I was the one to make the final decision to split.

In spite of all the feelings for Billy, somewhere inside, something beyond my fear of being all alone, I felt better, more stable, being alone than just left feeling alone. A decision to return to the life I was used to.

So, we separated, Billy and I, and a few days later he moved out.

Months out Billy and I continued to see one another out and around Polk. He'd offer to get me high, the same as when I first met him. Still having feelings for him and still being a true dope fiend, of course I go along. He would get so high he'd be 'noided' (paranoid). By that time, I was homeless myself with sometimes living off and on in temporary SRO hotels, when I'd actually use the welfare funds to get a room and not dope.

I sensed he felt safe when I was around. Even out on the street, in some dark alley, I assumed the role of the responsible one; the babysitter.

Our last get high, in an alley, happened to be the last I ever saw or heard of Billy. Ever after, I longed and wondered how it could have been different. I had no realization of what we had until it was no more. Whatever happened to my Billy Wayne?

C-Notes: Calling the Kettle Black (1991)

Earlier, as we walked up the hill on Geary Street between Polk and Van Ness I soaked in the rather handsome looks of the middle-aged man with dark Middle Eastern, Semitic features. I always considered men from that part of the world the most beautiful anyway. This guy intrigued me. I'd never knowingly met someone from Israel. The sex happened with rather much ease.

Afterwards, I could not resist asking him his opinion on the ongoing Palestinian- Israeli conflict. The first "Intifada" (Palestinian uprising) was still fresh in the headlines. "Yes," he said, "the whole situation... is horrible... They're not angels you know!" I remember his reply to my queries of the Palestinians.

"Actually... aren't both peoples in some ways...like cousins?" I furthered, proud of myself for having such worldly political knowledge, especially coming from a street hooker. He firmly pressed a $100 bill into my eager hand in exchange for my services.

Graciously, I thanked him. And no lie.

It was not every day that the leasing of my flesh commanded such compensation, not even close.

"In less than a half hour...who else... makes $100 an hour?" I thought conceitedly.

I'd spent the first part of that evening over at Drew's apartment.

Beyond our usual standing dinner date for sex, particularly this evening it was actually just dinner followed by us watching something, probably PBS, on television. The last few days after the Thanksgiving holiday and the end of the month found me busted and broke. I had called up Drew to just have somewhere to spend some time and get a free home-cooked meal.

Last year, I did the 'rounds' of taking in multiple free meals on Thanksgiving Day. Afterwards the effects of gorging on all the free food, way past the point of my stomach being full, left me bloated and disgusted with myself. I resolved this year to have more self-respect and not put myself in similar fates with less wear and tear on my body as well as my pride.

Throughout years' experience of street living, I could grasp the inescapable demoralization of actually being out on the street, homeless, with nowhere to go on the holidays. No amount of denial took away the literal reality of being a junky loser out there on the street on Thanksgiving or Christmas Day.

Maybe, just maybe, if you were blasted, tweeked out of your fucking mind high, then, you might be able to escape the fact that almost no one else happened to be around out there on those streets. Furthermore, usually it proved problematic to exactly time the peak of the get high to last all that day, long enough till the streets went back to the usual.

Back to where it's easier to blend in as just a plain ole every day junky that nobody notices.

No. My resolution meant that I would have to make a diligent effort to get myself invited somewhere even if it required me having to dry out a bit from my usual lifestyle of tweeking.

Walking back home from Drew's I took the route that passed by Layfette Park with the queers hiding in the bushes dick sucking, on the way toward Polk Street. Who do I run into but; Oreo, tantalizingly beautiful biracial youngster who more surprisingly seemed to be hot to fuck me too. At 26, I was older. Such attractions boosted my tarnished ego and my sense that I still had it 'go'in on' "Hey Juan... what chu do'in? I got a me a room." He spoke enticing me with his sparkling light brown eyes and mischievous smile. I couldn't say no. I could tell that he was high as well. "You wanna get... tweeked?" Oreo asked me, walking me up the street toward his room. *"Of course, I did."* But I felt somewhat leery on account of my own tolerance. Oreo being relatively fresh to the tweek game, he could get twistedly high on very little quantity. I, on the other hand, needed a quarter gram bag or more, by myself, just to get me started feeling anywhere close to being high.

Once inside Oreo's locked door room at the Shang Gri La Hotel, which was the farthest from what the title suggested, he passed and gave me a nice amount for a dope hit. Still, I was having trouble comprehending all what was happening; dope and a beautiful, sexy young boyish man to do with as I wished. Fates seemed all in my favor that night.

Perched on top the toilet seat, in the bathroom, I emptied out the quarter gram of crystal meth into the cap of a Clorox bleach bottle. The one which I'd used to sterilize the syringe.

"What the fuck!" I shouted, disbelieving my eyes. The tiny round piece of cardboard in the cap sucked up all the liquid in the dope. The dope just like disappeared. With me in full panic dope fiend mode, Oreo consoled me to simply add more water to what would be the solution of dope. Yet, I knew doing so would only further dilute what remained of the crystal to point that after shooting it in my veins, I was left feeling like I hadn't done any dope at all.

As beautiful as Oreo surely was, my frustration at not getting high left me jaded and fiend'in. I thanked him anyway, really, hoping he'd offer me another hit of dope. Finally, I just left him there tweeked out in his room. As much my mind, my fantasies, relished thoughts of perfect sex and drugs it never seemed to turn out as planned. One or the other always failed to sync up.

I envisioned myself, in my drug-fueled delusions, as living out fantasies of sowing my wild young oats, sexually that is. Crystal methamphetamine alongside gay San Francisco provided the ideal backdrop scenery and the flesh to make a reasonable facsimile out of reality. Nearly 24/7, in those days, one could find someone or multiples of persons tweeked up and on speed out and about looking to get a fuck on.

Sunday nights usually proved slimer odds getting picked up on Polk, whether a trick for money or whatever party favors I could get myself involved in.

This night the cosmos smiled upon me. Standing on a corner, I caught this tall looking, red-headed dude circling around my environs. A Thunderbird I noticed it was with an attractive younger guy, looking rather timid riding along in the passenger seat. The redhead; Rik, did most all the talking in his cockney accent that I barely understood every other word.

Rik had that English bad overbite. *"What? They must not believe in dentistry over there."* Rik had that telltale English bad overbite. *"Even the Royal family had grills like... White rednecks over here."* I wondered as we conversed. The deal was; they were a couple out that night looking to spice up their sex life with a three-way, spicing up with Black American buck too.

Rik asked if I partook in doing some lines of speed to heighten the sexual adventure. *"He had to ask?* The shy fella looked pretty enough to eat!" Yes, that Sunday it seemed all cylinders fired in sync.

In short order the Thunderbird headed to the 101 Freeway for the drive down the Peninsula to where they lived. I felt it had been implied that I was hooking. Though, actually, I would have been game either way, a paid hoe or slut whore.

All hopped up on crystal the festivities were set to begin. "I want you to fuck John." Rik requested, ordered really. "But, put on a rubber!"

In such times the monkey on my back; addiction, led me to believe that all the sex and the drugs meant I lived the 'high' life, in the fast lane (pun intended). Dope helped to deny the degradation. In reality, I was there playing the role of a living, heavily breathing, human sex toy in someone else's fantasy. I need not think or feel. My real purpose was to perform; a stereotyped image, deleting my having any feelings or emotions about what was happening there in real time and space.

Post all the poking, sucking, rubbing and sweating the scene proved unsuccessful in meeting the fantasized expectations, for all involved. *"What was wrong with me? Was I not fucking two very hot and attractive men, blitzed out of my mind? Whilst, getting paid on top of it all."* I thought, trying to make sense of how the experience actually felt.

Rik ended up having some courteous home training. He politely compensated me for my performance, dependent on if I rode the bus back to the City. "No problem," I responded in gratitude for the fact of having something tangible to show for my ultimately demoralizing experience.

He dropped me off at a bus stop bench just as the infamous Bay Area fogs began to lift giving the early morning sunlight a crisp haze. Soon, the San Mateo County, Samtrans bus pulled up, and I boarded, to continue winding its way down the serpentine path of El Camino Real, all the way till it became Mission Street, just inside The City. With the streets nearly empty that morning the driver slammed the wheels of that bus as if he was driving his own car. The long-articulated bus swung back and forth with velocity, passing each curve along Mission Street.

Pupils, now, fully dilated for sure. The long ride back to The City to the Tenderloin and Polk Street gave me plenty enough time to ponder the emptiness of the episode I had just played a significant part in. Moreover, to escape from my wretched feelings, escape from the actual reality not the fantasy, I could not get more crystal in my veins quick enough. *"How could what I imagined being so right turn out feeling this wrong?"*

No problem. Even in the bleak quiet early morning hours dope still could be had out and around the plucky environs of Polk. Surely somewhere, somebody, still, roamed for that ultimate sex romp not yet achieved. The dope that fueled those often seedy, sometimes degrading ends kept the dealers in business aplenty. One hustler dude, relatively new to the scene, happened along my way sensing my desperate dope fiend'in demeanor. Fiend'n not from a lack of dope cursing through my bloodstream, but, fiend'n from the need to wipe away and try to escape, the reality of what I had allowed myself to succumb. Dude told me he had "the bomb" dope! What would, he claimed, "knock my friggin socks off!"

"Yeah... whatever." I heard it all before. *They all say that when they're trying to make a sale,* I thought. For some reason, most likely paranoia, I was feeling too spooked to do the dope

deal out on the street. I insisted he follow me back to my place, 351 Turk Street, where we'd complete our nefarious exchange.

Up there, in my apartment, on the 12th floor, door thoroughly locked, hustler dude took out his quarter gram baggies of crystal meth. With one dangled between my greedy fingers, "Its fucking green!" I shouted in disbelief. "I ain't neva seen no green shit like this!" I barked back at him. As bugged out as he was himself, he looked at me earnestly, swearing up and down that that dope was the real thing. *Fuck naw!* I couldn't take no chances. I needed that chemical oblivion so desperately. Dude looked harder, rougher, than I figured I could take on physically, in other words, kick his ass, if the dope turned out to be bunk. Erring on not taking a chance on that mint green- looking crystalline substance. I declined buying dope from him and asked him to leave my place. I quite clearly remember him making a stink and being particularly pissed off at my accusation of him selling fake dope.

Frustrated and, now, really fiend'n for a hit I searched and roamed until I copped some speed from a more familiar connection. Days later, hanging out with one of my dope addict associates I hear one of them say, "that green speed go'in round.... is the shit!"

"No wonder ole dude got so upset at me believing his dope was bunk shit." I responded to hearing about missing out on some hella good dope.

Everything that goes around eventually comes around. The sexual fantasy tryst with those British guys, for example, had me in a role, the object of someone's fantasy. Yes, I know, I was out there selling my body for money and drugs.

"Duh!" What was I expecting to happen? Lo and behold time came to pass that I would offer to pay for someone else's flesh to be the object of my own fantasy. I had done such once before, back in LA, but that time was by default. This instance, in The City, was intentional.

Despite my ego deflation of having to 'pay' someone, I still believed that could get for 'free' any number of sex partners. Only this way I'd cut through the bullshit and get on straight to the 'meat' (can't stop doing those puns).

That fateful soon to be unordinary day, I roamed, searching the sidewalks and alleyways of Polk. On a mission for crystal meth and sex, either or, and or both. I spot this lanky, not too rough, dark-haired White hustler; Dallas, I discovered his name to be.

Giving him that once over, steely-eyed look of a speed freak I ask, "you know where I can find some... water?" 'Water'; one of a number of street vernaculars for crystal meth, meant to be incognito in case cops or narcs happened round.

Speaking under his breath, "You look' n? How much you want?" Dallas answered me, taking in my cues, giving me the once over, checking for cops. I, in no way fit the bill of a narc.

Making negotiations of amounts and specific prices, somewhat embarrassing, more due again to my ego, I made him an offer with the words "You wanna make $25 bucks?" Quickly coming past my lips, remaining nonchalant on the details of what I was seeking.

"Yeah... Ok." Dallas accepted. Correctly I'd accessed him as ready to get even more tweeked out than what he was already and open to whatever came about to make that happen. More likely, he happened just to be selling dope in order to supplement his own high.

Back at #1205 with the door firmly locked as always, my boombox radio blasting, I purchased about a gram or so of crystal and then handed him a well- worn 'Jackson' and a 'Lincoln' for the service he was about to render me. Dallas says, "At least I can...do another hit of dope", grinning in a way only another speed freak could appreciate. I came back out of the bathroom after a fat, heavy 30cc unit of the chemical fire, that I'd search the ends of the earth to obtain, delightedly had been pricked in my one trusty vein. Saving me from the embarrassment of being in the role of a john instead of hooker, Dallas quickly striped off his clothes, revealing his smooth pale lanky desired loins.

Naked now myself, I reached to rub, no less groped his long legs and smooth pink, pimpled ass cheeks. He followed my request to spread them as I near literally drooled jacking myself off. Betwixt his splayed body and my fantasized desires, we moved, slid, touched, licked and writhed around on my furniture- less carpet floor for what seemed like endless hours.

To this day, from that experience, I hold the belief that every hooker-sex worker, making a living selling something essentially not earned; their flesh, needed to have himself the experience, at least once, that I had had that tweeked out afternoon. I needed to be the 'trick'!

To experience what it felt like to be on the other side of that equation, and the mercy of my desires. Dallas played along his dilated pupils stared, distractedly enmeshed in the lurid pages of my porn collection while I pressed my lustfulness. I asked him questions on his sexual fantasies and of his first time getting fucked.

That afternoon, tweeked to the gills, my desires fulfilled. Id 'more than enough gotten my money's worth. I got pure hedonistic pleasure. Looking at the incident another way, addiction had driven me past the point of seeking mutually desired sexual endeavors.

Playing a role in a twisted dope-sex game, I became the game. Willingly playing and getting played.

In those times, days and nights, it seemed as if my whole existence entailed an endless series of dressings and undressing, pursuing opportunities to trade sex for money or drugs and simply sex and drugs. All the same, exposing my flesh and so on and so on.

Coming out my building on another random drug-fueled night in the Tenderloin, I encounter a lithe Black transgender queen, who spots me as an open mark for sexual tricks. "Psst! Hey you." Out of the shadows I hear her signal to me. "Come on ovah here!"

She had rolled herself downstairs, out of the public housing high-rise directly across Turk Street from my apartment building. Rolled cause as attractively as she presented herself, she was bound in a wheelchair. Probably, another one of the evident victims of the HIV/AIDS epidemic.

"Come on up with me baby." She requested my attentions giving me the 'look' and acknowledging that nothing else really needed to be explained as to why I happened to be out so late, alone, on those dark dangerous streets. Exchanging such street coded language, I grasped that she had some crack cocaine. In fact, crack was the trade opportunity she proposed.

True, I was a hoe. Many a time I traded a grope, a head job or jack-off for an offering of dope. Still, my dope fiend'n mind pondered the thought of sexually servicing a drag queen, one in a wheelchair no doubt. I'd definitely done worse, only this would be harder to fake. *"Maybe I could get away with a quick and fast one...smoking.... up the dope first."* Scandalously I thought.

"Come on now!" She insisted, "we go'in up to my place." Her insistence signaled that she was no novice at this game. No chance I'd get away without fucking her and getting her off. I'd never had sex with a woman with tits and a dick. The thought of doing such would really be 'working it' for me. Naw… I'ma gonna go." I blurted out riding up in the elevator just as she reached and started to grab at my dick, through my pants.

"Aww, don't stop now! I'ma smoke you up reeal good." Came her pleas of enticement. Using the word smoke as if I was an inanimate object to be sucked up in a glass pipe. I stepped back into the elevator when we had got to her floor, leaving her there even more hungry for a piece of dick. I decided even as much I wanted more dope, I was not that desperate, not yet anyway. A few years later, I did get involved in a drug-sex scene with another guy and transgender female. Again, I cut my participation short when that queen insisted I fondle her tits, it was too much for me.

Departing from the john's hotel that evening with a green paper bill, legal tender, the one with the two zeros after the one, tightly tucked away in my pocket. Usually a $30, $40 trick meant I'd be tweeked out for maybe two or so days.

With that piece of paper, I had enough to get twice as high for twice as long. Anticipation of getting high, craving the chemical ecstasy, manifested bodily in a loosening of my bowels. This happened so often to the point that, after time, when I finished my work with a john, I made sure to take a shit before leaving their place or hotel in order to circumvent the involuntary body reaction.

All too often what followed next became a vein-shooting, drug-induced, sex-hunting, craving, masturbatory blur lasting nearly 72 hours non-stop with no sleep, little if any eating. That's what usually became of the earnings for which I plied my 'tender loins', all easy come and easy gone just as quick.

Well into the third or so day shooting up crystal, tweeking, the limits of my physical-psycho endurance set in. My bones and joints ached, the skin on my genitals rubbed tender, paranoia, psychosis creeping into my brain with my senses hearing, sometimes seeing, things not actually there. I'd be walking about fully talking out loud to myself, and answering back. Any sudden unfamiliar moves out on the street, in public, by any person known or unknown had the potential to send me off spinning on some drug-crazed psycho tangent. Any sight of the cops, in such conditions, would prove an instant freakout.

With what my head was assuming alongside my fragile mental state, made me out as a good candidate to be, needed to be, arrested and taken somewhere.

The 72 hour or more tweek time, from experience, signaled to me time to throw in the towel and head toward the crash, the come down. Even if I could put up with more old men groping, clutching, at my dick. It required twice the number of johns to maintain that same, now fading, level of tweekness.

By that morning, I knew the high to be over. It just so happened I felt hungry. Hunger for food, a sign of normal humanity returning. Taking notice of the time, if I moved quick enough, I could go get in line in time for free breakfast at Glide Memorial Church soup kitchen, just a few blocks across the TL from my apartment.

Just a day or so before I carried a $100 bill in my pocket, yet, I spent it all on dope and such. The pint-sized studio refrigerator at 1205 Turk Street, captained not a crumb. I'd not eaten a meal since before getting that C-note. The ugly side of tweek'n, the crash, depression, had me deep in its grasp sitting at a cafeteria table shoving scrambled eggs and possibly some bland-tasting oatmeal pass my lips. Paranoid that someone, anyone, noticed me struggling to practicing chewing and swallowing my food, as if somehow my tongue, teeth and jaw organs had forgotten how. My fellow diners, society's dregs, that morning, down and out, many looking disheveled and or just downright filthy.

Maybe because many of them dining alongside me happened to be older Black men, my thoughts turned to, of all things, to thinking about my father. *"Fuck'in no good... drunk mothafucka!"* Grumbled a voice in my head. On it went, *"he don't deserve shit from me. Smelling like liquor... on his breath whenever I saw him,"* continued the voice. Truly, I held hate for the man who had made me, who brought me into being.

As I struggled to scarf down those free eats, the only method I had to feed myself, yet, another voice cleared across my chemically fried brain waves.

"You got a lotta room to talk... fucking junky!" It screamed in my head, *"Can't even feed yourself!"* This voice came through, *"pot calling the kettle black".* Truth one out loud and clear. Really, I had no right to look down on, despise even, my daddy.

His drinking, his on addiction. A monkey lived on 'my' back, no more, no less as bad. *"Hell, my daddy worked each and* every day *and at least and supported all his children."*

That voice continued, giving my dad credit for more than anything I could claim.

Sitting there dejected in the throes of my own reality, what was my existence, tears welled up ever so slightly to fill my tweeked out sunken eye sockets.

I recalled a memory from childhood of my mother telling me of my dad's mother having died when he was only 11years old. I knew and definitely understood the deep grief from losing my own mother. Right then and there, tears broke loose across my face and down my cheeks. Turning my head downward, I feared someone might take of notice my emotional meltdown.

Beyond that particular tweek, crash and burn I, from then on, held much more empathy for my daddy; William J. Bailey. On his next birthday I made sure to send a card. My brother Craig told me, years later in my recovery, how that small gesture had made my dad feel better. He died within that same year of cancer.

The slow process of healing began. Healing from self-loathing. Loathing my Black maleness, of being no better than 'that' Black man, my father.

Indeed, could I live up to what he had accomplished even in spite of the affliction of addiction.

Time would only tell.

Out of a common pain, a hopeful seed had been sown.

Streets of San Francisco (1991)

Not paying rent for more than a year and a half gets you served with an eviction notice. My attainment of a humble 12-floor studio abode was part of relocation assistance due to the Loma Prieta earthquake. Given this new start, I had intentions to take advantage of it and be responsible. Addiction crumbled intentions, well-meant or not. I may have paid the first month's rent.

Lucking out with San Francisco's strong tenant's rights made evection a prolonged process. Knowing it was coming, when the notice did arrive, I was in no shape to pay back rent; I of no job and nearly unemployable. Great idea; take my last general assistance check, buy some speed and sell it. My reasoning, if I made a profit, I could at least earn a grace period on the eviction.

With my brilliant plan in mind, on the court date, I trotted my disheveled, sweaty personage to city court in the grand Beaux-Arts, San Francisco City Hall. The first time I had ever actually entered the building, now I even had real business reason to be there. In spite of my paranoia that all the uniformed officers were watching me, looking at the image of a drugged-out tweeker, the ornate marble fixtures and grand stairways throughout the hallways, I found impressive.

I waited on a bench in the courtroom for my case to be called; I was barely able to sit there still without twitching, and drops of sweat poured down my face. Reality, like a ton of bricks, finally hit me when the judge informed me that I needed to come up with at least three months' rent to even stall the eviction, just till the next court date. Felt more than foolish that my tweeked-out brain had allowed me the think that just the act of me showing my face in court would stop the eviction. "Did they not understand I had my rights," went my screwed-up state of mind.

Logic is the furthest from your mind when one is doped out. I could have at least taken some money to lease a storage space. But I chose to get high on the money. I had and intended not to be present when the sheriff came knocking to officially and legally put me out on the street. All my keepsakes, pictures of my youth, young adulthood assorted mementos all were to be lost. Some other whacked-out tweeker, dumpster diver would soon have himself a field day with my treasures, the minutiae of my life. I left with a bag of clothes and my radio boom box. My new living quarters would now be Polk Street.

After a while on the streets, I would soon discover the art of squatting, taking residence in empty, abandoned buildings. You needed to be on good terms with whoever had first opened up the squat. Kinda like the White settlers of historical lore, whoever gets there first gets rights to make the rules.

My initial squat experience came about minus an actual invite. A fellow hustler junky, Scott, whom I knew from back in my LA days, brought me along one night to an empty office site up on the corner of Van Ness and Pine Streets. We entered from the alley by climbing through a window. The 'owners' of the squat showed some displeasure at my presence, due to them having dope and in the process of getting high. Both Scott and I were ass out; no dope, no money. Ignoring their selfish vibes, all I desired was a place to sleep and come down from days up run of speeding and tricking.

Welcomed or not, I went off to stake out an area to sleep. Scott came up behind me; I could only notice that he was within earshot. I slowly crept into a nearly black room dimly lit by the night's sky through a small window. "Hey! What is this dark space?"

I eerily remember myself falling, like weightless, as if in a dream. Next thing, "Whaa!... Get this shit!" I yelled while proceeding to jerk the oxygen tubes out of my nose, lying on a stretcher riding in the back of an ambulance.

Learning later, that 'space' I recalled asking Scott about turned out to actually have been an elevator shaft I'd fallen down from two storeys up. Scott relayed to me how the 'hosts' of the squat had refused to call 911. It would have ruined their getting high and all. Lucky for me Scott called anyway due to me laying there unconscious after the fall. That's my rough welcome to actually living on the streets of San Francisco.

I lay on a gurney in the emergency room later that night at San Francisco General Hospital. The doctors needed to apply a catheter to my dick in order to check for internal bleeding. What I can only describe as the feeling of rough-grade sandpaper being slid across the most sensitive tissue of my body, my penis, is the sensation of being catheterized. "Ahhhh!! I screamed, surely loud enough to be heard across the whole floor of that hospital.

"That didn't hurt that much." Retorted a White male nurse who I sensed was gay.

"Then... let me put one down your dick... bitch!" I howled at the indignity of his comment about my pain.

Frisco is its own little world in terms of public services. My little incident at 'General,' what we used to call the public county hospital, had been relayed to my welfare case worker. Probably sending in my name for payment. This made me eligible for temporary disability. All such happened beyond my knowledge. What mattered most to me was the checks kept coming every 1st and 15th of the month.

Around this time, I started lodging with John, another druggy hustler I met through Scott. The apartment was in a building called the Argyle on McAllister Street, in the Civic Center. John had been living there with his Asian transgender girlfriend, Pepper. They'd come about the digs from FEMA relocation funds after the 89' earthquake. Pepper happened to be in jail while I stayed there.

John, White maybe 30, hustler and heroin head got nicknamed the 'Bird' for his rumored reputation of being well hung. Always having steady clientele, I guess the rumors had some truth.

John and Pepper, as did many other residents; drug addicts, never paid their rent at the Argyle. During my time there, it seemed as if half the folks living in the building were in the process of being evicted. The utilities had long since been disconnected inside John's apartment.

A typical night living at the Argyle would include smoking or shooting up what dope we had. Sprinkled throughout the night well into the next morning, other junkies, usually crackheads (I hate that term), came knocking on the door. More than likely, the dope fiends had scored some crack cocaine rocks yet roamed, looking and needing a place to smoke them up. John never ever failed to allow them to come in. The rule was they could use the pad to smoke as long as they shared with the 'house,' no matter how small the crack stash. By the time the dope was split amongst John, me, the buyer, and whoever they had with them, the high result was not worth the drama and aggravation of having to put them out when the crack had been smoked and gone. It was not uncommon for said crackhead to be upset at being dope-less. John seemed never to learn. The next night some same similar scene started all over again.

The Argyle faced the back of the main library, heading across the street to hideout some time till the nights, I began my affinity for reading biographies. It began with "Dream Girls,"; the story of the Supremes by Mary Wilson. I simply devoured that book. Finishing that, I moved on to "Call Her Miss Ross," the unauthorized biography of Diana Ross. As an effeminate boy, in my early youth, I had idolized the glamour and stardom of Diana Ross, the movies, and music. She was the first super 'diva.'

Often, I'd be seen carrying these 300 or more paged hardcover books along with me up to Polk. One could find me sitting in my favorite spot, next to the QT Bar, reading, till I'd notice a new trick or one of my regular johns pass by. Those books may have been the first ones I had ever read cover to cover.

After a typical drug-fueled night at the Argyle pad, I half awoke an early morning as I heard John defending me to some dope fiend who had been dissing me and my gay ways.

"Yeah… so what if he's gay! He ain't never done me… no wrong. I'd stand up for him, against anybody!" I couldn't believe my ears what I heard John say. "Man, if yo go'n talk bout him, you gonna have to leave!" The dope head shut up talking shit. I felt vindicated and proud; still, I never said anything to John. Hearing what I'd heard was enough for me to leave it at that.

On one of my last days at the apartment, John surprised me. "You want… somma this?" He asked me, sitting on the floor with a spoon, a lighter, and a syringe, to cook up a shot of black tar heroin.

"Nah, man, I always get sick and throw up and shit," I responded back.

"Cause you do too much. You cain't start out do'in this… like that." He advocated with a kinda soothing dope fiend encouragement. I took him on. John shot my vein with 5cc units of heroin. True to his word, that time, I did not get sick or puke. Actually, I enjoyed it. All throughout my body flowed a mild, warm haze sensation I'd never felt before. Not all that bad, really.

Later, I brought back a john to the apartment. Being on that heroin, I had a raging hard-on. "Maybe heroin ain't too bad." The thought roamed my head.

Now Heroin. Maybe? Now even further proof of my having graduated full-on to a homeless hustler junky, a veteran. "Gotta do what you got to do. These streets ain't no thang!" I consoled myself.

Behind the Golden Gates (1991)

My General Assistance checks arrived on schedule on the 1st and 15th of the month. I lodged in an apartment with a fellow hustler, dope fiend, John. The pad, in reality, was really nothing more than a crashing spot with private amenities to get high. Nightly crackheads (a term I hate) knocked and dropped in, looking for a place to smoke up.

On Polk, I ran into this thirtyish, White guy for a paid sex date. Younger than most of the johns that picked me up, we took off to the apartment. I signaled to John that it would be worth his while to let us have the pad so I could 'work.' After services had been rendered, much to his satisfaction, he wrote down his phone number. He told me to give him a call if I ever needed relaxation or just a come for a swim at his place up in Marin County.

Waking up the next morning, I needed to be in court on a prostitution charge. The case had dragged on due to my homeless, junky circumstances. It was the first time I got popped for hooking in San Francisco. Over the years, I'd become wiser at spotting a vice cop up on the hustler stroll. Still, everybody has an unlucky night.

`I had told John not to forget to wake me up. Chances were that he'd be up anyway to get his morning fix of heroin or possibly still up smoking with any number of crack fiends. He never refused to open the door if it meant getting a free hit.

Getting up around noon, "Fuck!" I thought. I knew missing court meant a warrant was out for my arrest. I took off walking to the police substation on Bryant Street. I figured it better to spend a night in jail than get picked up by the cops on Polk, where the cops might find me tweeked out high. Having not yet issued the bench warrant, the court clerk gave me a new court date. I checked before leaving just to be assured I was not gonna get arrested.

With a new court date, I thought all was good, but not quite. That night up on Polk Street, the beat cops happened to be out and checking for outstanding warrants. I got stopped and checked off to Bryant Street; I went cuffed in the back of a police cruiser. Who was I to be mad at, John, for not waking me up on time or the incompetent court clerk?

I sat in jail that night till court in the morning pissed off for sure. I made a plea to the judge to represent myself in court. To me, my situation, being a homeless hustler, presented difficulties in keeping court dates, to say the least. I had not been arrested for drugs, robbery, or actually hooking but for missing a fucking court appearance. I just wanted to get it all over, even if it meant going to jail. My ignorance glared. The judge, deputies, and lawyers all appeared stunned at my request. Before my public defender had calmed me down and somewhat explained the law to me, I had allowed my case to be amended, which meant my prior arrest record from LA could be relevant in the case being tried in San Francisco County. Yes! I know now for sure what amending a case in court means. What happened in that courtroom would later come to affect the outcome of my life.

To my utter surprise, the judge, Tomar Mason, I never forgot that name, apologized for my having been arrested after I had tried to turn myself into the court. There I was, a broken-down junky prostitute getting an apology for the justice system fucking up. Judge Mason vindicated I was more than my accused crime and that I valued my time and freedom as any other citizen. The case continued on.

Back at the Argyle, John and I kept up our daily, nightly, tricking, doing dope, all while holding a venue for addicts to shoot up and smoke. Both of us knew for certain any day, and we'd be evicted.

It was a Saturday that Miles, another hustler who often crashed and consumed dope with us in the apartment, found me up on Van Ness Avenue panhandling. I must have been exceptionally hungry, having awoken too late to make myself available for free eats at any number of soup kitchens. Miles had been to the Argyle just to discover that the apartment had finally been padlocked.

My check was due on the 1st, the next Tuesday. In the meantime, I'd be ass out homeless over the weekend; adding to injury; I was not even high. A thought came to me. "I could call that trick in Marin. He did say I could come anytime I wanted to get rest away from the City." I reached into my wallet for the scrap of paper where I'd put his phone number. Anxiously I called. He agreed I could come out. Absolutely broke, I borrowed the $3 for the one-way bus ride to Corte Madera in Marin County.

LA has Beverly Hills, Brentwood, and Hollywood Hills. Frisco has the wealth, exclusive equivalent of Marin County. The suburbs north of the City are actually one of the wealthiest locales in the whole country. The world-renowned Golden Gate Bridge connected Marin to the City. I settled into one of the plush seats of the public busses that served commuters going to Marin; crossing that bridge, I took in the majestic scenery, the place where almost every tourist to the City comes to capture the view that contrasted against me escaping my broke down living circumstances heading out into the high coastal hills that seemed the barrier to where the real money lived.

Soon after, I arrived at the bus stop, and he picked me up. My eyes grew wide, passing by huge estates and mansions, like out of the lives of the rich and famous. The car approached one such estate and drove through a heavy iron gate up to what was his parent's expansive villa. I actually got dropped off at the guesthouse as my host walked over to the main mansion to scrounge the kitchen for something left over for me to eat.

Full, somewhat relaxed, I fulfilled the promise and enjoyed a leisurely romp in the marbled stone pool. Heated waters further relaxed me. I then got summoned to ply my trade. Cocks got sucked, and legs flew overhead. He being not much older, allowed me to go beyond my standard hooker performance. Sensing my surroundings assured me I'd be well taken care of for my 'work'. No blatant figures were discussed, all the more not to break up the lovely atmosphere with such vulgar details.

I slept well, must have needed a good rest; no wonder how many days I'd been up previously. In the morning, we went to breakfast at a restaurant, nothing too fancy, nothing too shabby either. After eating, he handed me $10 and told me to wait for him in the same shopping center. My street senses weakened out amongst all the highly manicured landscapes and matter-of-fact displays of wealth. Minutes after having been left there alone, I thought quite panicked, "Did that fucker just ditch me!" Insulted, "And he got a good fuck for $10!" I did my best to play it cool; no sense in making my broke, Black self more conspicuous than I already was. I ducked into a coffee shop, ordered a strong brew, sat down, and read the Sunday San Francisco Chronicle.

To my relief, he did return an hour or so later. I continued as if everything was cool. On our return to the 'estate,' I learned knowledge of his family owning a winery and vineyards; real money. In real terms, this guy was the definition of idle rich. Not having to work for a living, whenever he desired some fun, he'd come over to the City and pay a boy to play with him. Hence how I came into the picture.

As the sun got low in the sky and it was dark, I told him of my need to get back to the City. Soon we both got into his car to leave. He drove; next thing to my amazement, he pulled up to the bus stop. "I'll see you sometime." He spoke as he reached into his wallet to hand me $2 for the bus fare.

"This is it!" I asked incredulously, almost out of breath.

"Well, yes…you never said I had to pay. You told me you wanted to come for a swim." He responded. The words he said were true, to what we said to each other over the phone.

"Yeah, that's what I said, but…you know how you met me. You knew what I did." I said, making my point. "This just won't do!" I finished and then stared out the car window.

He put the car in gear and drove off. I figured we were headed to a bank ATM, or he at least was going to drive me back across the bridge to San Francisco. Even if I had taken the bus, by the time I would get back to the City; the bars would be closed. It being a Sunday, the pickings are slim anyway. He pulled the car up somewhere on the street and asked finally, "You're not going?"

"No!" I confirmed, "Not just with $2!"

He opened the car door, got out of the car, and walked into some building. I looked over to see where he'd gone. The street was quiet. To my shock, I could see that it was a police substation. "This fucker gon' get away with not paying me!" Thinking fast, I recalled the advice of my old street partner and mentor, Michael Chaffin, back from my early days being on the streets in LA. "Go off! If they don't pay you. They have more to lose than you do." He once told me. I knew the cops would be coming for me soon. I got out of the car, mad as fuck. I started kicking, slamming, and jumping up and down on the car. "Crack!" Finally, the passenger side window busted. Out of the side of my view, I saw two officers headed my way. Knowing for sure I was going to jail; I put my arms up over my head with my hands in the air. Marin guy started screaming about all the damage to his mother's vehicle. "Bitch…shouda thought bout that…when you gave me that $2!"

One of the cops came toward me, grabbed me, and put me in handcuffs, saying, "Have a seat," putting me on the curb, "You must be tired…after all that." Surprised at his attitude, almost playful he seemed.

Minutes later, the same officer came back to me to get my side of the story. The truth was to my advantage. I told the officer that I had met the guy on Polk Street in San Francisco. The officer's eyebrows raised upon hearing that fact, and he turned to look over towards the Marin guy. I told the cop that we had had sex, and he refused to pay me.

Of course, I would be charged. The cop put me in the back of a patrol car and took me off to be processed.

We both kept quiet riding in the patrol car, except for the noise coming over the police radio. The car pulled into the Marin Civic Center Building. "Aw, wow!" I can't believe I'm here." I said aloud, moving around awkwardly in the handcuffs to get a better view out the car window. Even in the dark of night, I felt in awe of where I never imagined I would be.

"You know this building?" That cop asked me, surprised.

"Oh, yeah, I've been looking at pictures of this building since I was in grade school," I answered him, still gawking.

"This place is pretty famous," he shot back.

The Marin Civic Center was designed by probably America's most famous architect, Frank Lloyd Wright. He intentionally built and designed it into a series of small hills having low sloping roof lines. The structure was meant to seem like a part of the natural landscape. What I had only before seen in books I now was actually there, in spite of the circumstance of how I came to my viewing.

The White officer, looking to be no more than his late thirties, took down all my information while again telling me what I was being charged with. In the midst of everything, the officer told me that he had once been on the police force in the City. He next blew me away by telling me, "As an officer for the County of Marin, I have to tell you to leave him alone out here in this County… But," and he kinda looked away toward the windshield as he said this, "if he comes back over to the City…he's all yours." That cop knew what time it was, practically giving me permission to get my due.

For over the next year, I kept getting arrested for bench warrants to appear in court for the case in Marin County. I kept blowing it off. I just so happened to be too busy as a meth-addled junkie hooker to be bothered with such matters. And besides, it would at least take about $10 just to take the bus up to Marin and back, just to appear in a courtroom. "$10… that's half a hit of dope!" Finally, my bail was up to $100,000. I was not getting out of lockup simply on a sworn promise to appear in court. They extradited me to the jail in the Marin Civic Center, a section, I found out later, that had not been designed by Frank Lloyd Wright. Next, I got shipped out to the county penal farm.

I requested a jury trial. I carried some confidence cause two of my regular johns had promised me they would testify for me as character witnesses. At least commit to testifying that I was not violent. When Marin guy realized his picking up and paying boys for sex in the City might come out in the open courtroom, spoiling his rich, respectable, wine heir reputation. All charges got dropped and without restitution. Rich boy was about to learn he could not play in the dirt without getting dirty himself.

Yes, I got justice. It only required that I'd be locked up for 30 days at the penal farm for it the come out that way. They put me in the general population even. Marin County Jail did not have a gay ward.

The morning I got released from the penal farm, Drew had left me with money on my account. Walking me out towards the chain-link fence gate covered with circular rows of barbed wire, the deputy pointed out the direction to the closest bus stop to catch the ride back to the City. I had nothing except the clothes on my back I'd been arrested in with a $50 dollar bill in my pocket. Hearing the gate clang behind me, I walked, stepping with a little swagger, feeling I'd come out on top, having beaten the case.

In short order, the bus arrived; I boarded, looking quite rough. Obviously, as I had figured, no one on board had changed for a fifty. I relayed to the bus driver how I had just been released from jail. He allowed me to ride without paying fare showing some sympathy for my hard luck story, but not without throwing a lookup disgust like, "Man…yo sorry ass…make us Black brothers look bad."

Arriving back on the stroll in Frisco is like coming 'home.' What's a homeless speedfreak hustler to do, having nothing but a Grant in his pocket? "Duh! Cop some speed and get high."

Out looking to cop dope, I came across Tracy, a White hustler who occasionally sold crystal too. Tall, thin with this Andy Griffith 'Opie' red hair and sexually was into Black guys. Tracy was not my type, though, at least not at that time. He sold me a half gram of dope. "Chile, it's good shit, betta watch out!" he forewarned.

"Yeah, Yeah…whateva." I blew off. Every small-time dealer talked shit about how good their dope was, nothing new.

Holding and homeless, I had nowhere to go to fix up. I started walking down Polk Street towards Civic Center and SOMA (South of Market) as I often did when having dope on me. A seedier locale meant one might blend in more, a just a part of the whole degraded street milieu. A crazy thought came to me. I remembered when I last got arrested on the Marin case. The first-floor restrooms were being remodeled down at the Southern Police Substation on Bryant Street. With luck, a city government contract like that takes forever. All the cops would be on the first floor. "Besides," I thought deviously, "they'd never believe a dope fiend would have the balls to go to the police station to shoot up."

My left arm tied off, I pushed in the needle till the tiny bubble of blood registered in the clear part of the syringe that I'd directly hit a vein. I pushed the plunger in. "Ah, chum!" I coughed, then, within an instant, I soon felt the powerful rush to my brain. That body numbing all-consuming rush. Sitting astride the toilet, my pants half down, needle by my side, many minutes passed before I regained coherence enough to get my wits back, realizing where I was. "That red-headed bitch was right… this is gooood shit!"

Tweeked to the extreme, I did my best to coolly pass unnoticed by the cops at the entrance metal detectors while walking out of the police station. So tweeked out as if like I walked on air, just above the sidewalk going up 6th Street. I stopped in the little convenience store on the corner at Howard, often, I frequented the store when I'd lodged in one of the cheap hotels nearby, and the proprietor recognized me as I entered. He was in the middle of some rant about all the crackheads roaming around and trashing the neighborhood. I went to the cooler and purchased a Sprite. The meth had me gagging with thirst. Barely listening to him going on, I did my damnest to keep from bursting out in laughter. He was utterly clueless about me being so high, right there in his face. So friggin high my ears heard non-existent ringing sounds. Politely, I plastered a smile as I left the store feeling quite smart-assed.

Chemically, full-on and ready. Justice served. Back in the City, my city, I rejoined the riff-raff hordes out in the full chaos by those Golden Gates.

"Bruno" (1991)

A friend of mine, David; often used to say the phrase, "Like it was the thang to do!" Having the full-on monkey on my back, my addiction to methamphetamines, the places, behaviors, degradations happened as normality. It was just the things that were done. "You mean to tell me everyone's not sucking dick for money to poke track marks upon their arms in order to scavenge in trash dumpsters, in hopes of pursuing more sex and fucking?" I would've said at the time, implicating folks whom thought such living at extreme, were damn fools.

I had my own private living quarters. I had gone big too, a huge warehouse-sized space with such amenities of electricity and lights. I'd taken over a condemned abandoned garage. Formerly the place had been a car audio installation facility. This is why I loved being out late in the alley's dumpster diving so much. I just happened to discover the place unlocked, late one night, roaming via alleyways off of Van Ness Avenue. Typically, if you were out looking hard enough, I could be spotted out there under dark night skies sweating, breathing hard, teeth clenched, way too high, tweeked on speed, paranoid and unable to look at another human being in the eye for more than a mere few seconds, before my dilated pupils would scan back toward the ground in search of more possible 'treasures'.

Squatting had the effect of lessening my homelessness, at the least it kept me inside from the elements. The squat gave me a place to get high and tweek as long as I wanted with no one around bugging me or begging to share my dope. Someplace to rest up, in spite of all the dirt and grime, when my chemical fuel ran empty and the withdrawals got ugly. Most of all there were no cops to give me grief. It was all mine, mine, mine, a dope fiend living the good life.

In the year I wound up being evicted, twice. Summertime climate in Frisco brings in chilly wet, fog cover. No place to be in shorts. Still, generally it doesn't rain either. The extra brisk summer months roll into the drier hotter fall, when the City actually gets summer like temperatures. The City was habitable to living outdoors if need be. The same climate that had gathered out the hordes of White, 'Summer of Love' children and hippies, back in the day. As a strung-out speed head hustler like me, I made efficient use of the more forgiving natural elements. More than not, often I was too high and unconcerned to care about the weather. "What weather?"

The dry season in California parched enough to make way for wildfires. It may not rain a single drop for a month or two. The natural phenomenon still, so strange to me one from a temperate climate and weather. That October, the scorched dry hills above

Oakland and the posh suburb of Piedmont sparked into a massive fire. One evening, before it got dark, I shuffled down to Civic Center Park right in front of grand City Hall. My purpose for the journey, I needed to obtain my one meal of sustenance for the day. The free eats provided by Bay Area-hippie, central casting; Food Not Bombs. Usually, their hot meals prepared from excess leftovers of local restaurants. It made for quite hardy, tasty vegetarian soups with bread, always bread. That early evening as I waited in line, I could turn my head and just look up to the east and see in the sky a thick black, grey plume of smoke. It billowed up toward clouds and an already risen full moon.

Jokingly, I overheard some other raggedy denizen in line say, "Earthquakes...wildfires and full moons...the world's coming to an end!" I laughed slightly. I had survived the 'big' earthquake, just two years previous. Still living in and with the aftermath of my own personal circumstances combined with the, then, and the present environmental surroundings seemed to ring truth to what that homeless freak had spoken aloud. What did I care? I had a solution, just get good and tweeked and go back to hide away in my boarded-up abandoned abode.

Having that place to steal away sheltered me from the reality to where my body, my mind, escaped when high. I holed up in there for a good 3weeks or so. Just me and what other vermin that surely lurked and scurried around the place as did I. Street survival instincts told me not to share my secret squat with anyone else, less some other careless dope fiend get caught coming and going by authorities. I slipped following my own advice and brought Miles up to the squat. Miles and I had just shared digs in last place we got kicked out of. Maybe I felt a little obligation, loyalty maybe. Sure enough within a few days, I came back to find the squat, my 'home,' padlocked and more securely boarded up. Lesson learned.

Really desperate, more tweeked and strung out, I moved all of me, myself and I a block away up on Franklin Street to what was the loading dock of a funeral home. The dock descended down and away from the sidewalk. Undetectable to passersby. Somewhere along I scavenged a refrigerator –sized cardboard box. I slept there a few days. I recall the comedown and withdrawals, I only came up and out of the box to eat, piss and take a shit. I had carried a short existence there like character in the novel "Invisible Man." Peeking my head out, I could even estimate the time of day due to the angle of sunlight. Just so I could tell the time of which free eats were available. When the time change rolled around, I recalled being pissed off. "Damn fucking daylight savings!" I mumbled or shouted out loud. I felt impressed with myself for eschewing the need of artificial time keepers such as watch or clock. Coming down from a meth high I indeed talked to myself, odd looks from bystanders be dammed.

I had screwed over my regular appointments with Drew; my college professor benefactor. We had a Sunday dinner and sex date. I could go over have healthy meal and get a needed good night's rest and we'd finish up our 'activities' the next morning. I stood him up, being too high and paranoid to leave the squat and make the call. He, now, days after refused to take my calls.

Life in that refrigerator box got old real quick. Taking refuge in the squat had gotten me spoiled, tweeking unencumbered by any distractions except my own.

I remembered, then, the warrant for my arrest from a prostitution charge. With winter coming on soon it was true jail was at least 'three hots and a cot'. Besides, I figured I could get out from dodging the warrant and be done with it. At first opportunity I found the two cops that I knew that regularly patrolled Polk Street and turned myself in for arrest.

Just like that I'm on the way to San Francisco County Jail in San Bruno, California to serve 45days incarceration. Early in my time in the City I noticed how people up on Polk Street, especially speed freak hustlers, who disappeared for months at a time. On their return to the street, I'd ask them, "Where you been at?"

"I was in Bruno." I'd hear them simply reply. Not knowing myself that 'Bruno' was the colloquial for county jail. For all I knew and suspected, San Bruno as being someplace where they had a top rate speed connection. The dope being so fuck'n good they had went ahead and stayed in 'Bruno' for a month or so. "Shit! I wanted a connect… in Bruno too." I guessed somehow; I just hadn't reached the correct level on the crystal meth hierarchy to get an invitation down there. I hoped someday I would. "Man, I was naïve".

Now, my wish come true. I had my invite to 'Bruno', chauffeured by the county jail bus, with a quickness, plying down Interstate 280 Freeway at 60 miles an hour.

4South tier; protective custody which included the unit for gay inmates held at county jail. Coming in upon my arrival as I scanned the surroundings and looked around it seemed like a Polk Street reunion. Inside was my friend David, Toby, Seattle Mike; a small- time dealer who was rough trade gorgeous, alongside many other hustlers and assorted tweekers I had seen around or copped dope from before. Just like home away from home. You had to be careful to not get too used to the familiar seeming atmosphere. lest you'd not get too bothered by the sound and finality of those heavy steel gates closing with you behind them.

Mack, probably not his real name, was my first cell mate. His moniker meant to indicate and signal his street cred. Light-skinned Black with an overbearing macho demeanor, yet here he was on the 'gay' tier. He viewed me as fresh meat. Being an out gay, in his world, that meant I had won the gay lottery and should feel lucky being locked up with the finest 'real man' on the whole tier. I was not having it, not my type. Mack was just beside himself that I held no interest in fucking him. After a while he got the clue that he had nothing coming.

There was this one hustler on the tier I would have cashed bad checks for. I always had cruised him out on the streets. Steven was his name, thin White guy with dark hair and sexy dark eyes. I made an effort to cat-call some comment every time he passed by.

Veronica, a transgender queen on the tier, I'd never seen or met before. We grew into somewhat of a friendship on the tier. She had immigrated from the island of the Dominican Republic. After meeting and talking with her I impressed her with having been named for Juan Marichal; a sports hero in her country. I found it interesting how I'd gotten used to the lilt of her accent when she spoke. I'd miss understanding a word or two in conversation yet I got what she meant, even when it might take a few seconds more to comprehend.

Jail life works backwards. I mean the structure is turned inside out in comparison to life on the outside. It was nothing to how many inmates loved to see a fight on the tier, even if such a fight caused everyone else to be on lockdown for hours on end, maybe even a whole day, in our cells. To them the thrill and excitement was worth the restrictions.

On such a lockdown I lay on my bunk and took to reading a National Geographic magazine. The pages of which I'd actually been engrossed since even before I really started to read. As a little boy I looked at the exotic pictures to escape to faraway places, and tried to figure out words in the captions. Who'd know that that skill learned so long ago would come to good use locked up in jail. Mack, I began to notice, became agitated when I took to my reading. I escaped, not wanting to be involved with all the verbal 'checking' of one another, that goes on up and down the tier. There's even more so all the telling tall tales, detailing vividly how good the times had been out on the streets. How high they were living before they had got busted. Especially, leaving out that, now, they had nothing to show for their ball 'in live styles.

In time I discovered the source of Mack's agitation. He was illiterate. His agitation sprung from jealousy that I could read. I could escape from the bullshit monotony of jail, though those National Geographics.

To the good, Drew accepted my collect calls from jail. Even better he agreed to put some money on my books. Desperately I needed double-bladed razors. The jail issue, free single blade razors caused my skin to rash and break out in a bad case of razor bumps.

All else you can really legally buy in jail is snacks and candy. So that's exactly how I spent my money.

"Salter!" the deputy called out my name from behind the gate at the front. I walked to the entrance gate and read him my inmate number. He handed me a clear plastic bag, half the size of a large trash bag, contents full of candy, chips and whatnot. Like dogs salivating to the smell of meat all eyes turned my way as I walked by and hoarded my bag of treasure to back to my cell. In jail terms I now had some 'juice'.

What's the point of having juice if you can't spread it around? I made the rounds to pass out goodies to friends; David, Toby and Veronica, letting them pick out what they wanted and I even made certain to drop something off to Mack, like as if I was some small-time king maker. My intention to show him I harbored no hard feelings after having turned him down. In a way I really meant to convey that I considered myself no better him, keeping his secret that he could not read.

Moments passed by sitting on my bunk back in my cell, out of the blue I turn over to see Matthew slowly linger just outside my cell. Big -eyed blond hair Matthew, I knew from around seeing him hustling out on Polk. For certain I'd found him attractive, still, out on the block he never even gave the time of day, let alone recognize me. Here now, he was his 'gay for pay' self giving me a coy look as if, now, I could have my chance to demand my sexual wish. "For a damn candy bar!" I thought, looking at him there, his still 'fine' self dressed in a jail orange jumpsuit slightly disgusted. "Now… I was good enough for him… cause I had some candy!" This a prime example of how jail life is backwards. No longer did I desire what I once thought was such a catch. Maybe because now, it was just so easy. To cut it short, I said to him, "Here boy… what chu want… a Butterfinger?" Matthew perked up with his sheepish eyes and accepted my offer the 'free' candy I passed through the cell bars. I understood how low some folks could go just being locked up. I figured Matthew would give the same, "Fuck you," attitude back out there on them streets. Pondering that incident with him that day, among others things I'd witnessed, I knew maybe I must have been made from a different mold.

My cellmate, then, was Duane; a small, somewhat scruffy White, tweek head. He had a missing top front tooth as did I. As I remember he had both top teeth missing from his grill. Duane would tell me how he got his money out on the streets by creeping late at night, popping open car trunks. "You see them blinking…little alarm lights…I don't fuck with them," he told me one day laying back stretched out on his bunk. He'd sell what ill-gotten gains he obtained to dealers in exchange for crystal meth. Duane mentioned in conversation that he was not beyond selling his body, just that if he had his choice, he preferred not to have to. I could appreciate wanting to have that option.

Being in such close quarters and sharing such similar street backgrounds I grew to like Duane. He not being exactly my 'type' either. He did fit the White, speed freak personage I'd been known to fuck with. One evening after the lights were out, I crawled down to Duane's bottom bunk and laid myself alongside his body. In the dark and shadows we made motions as if to have sex. Somehow, each movement and motion we made in effort felt awkward. Add to that, we were doing our best to make as little noise as possible. Only just to not bring any unwanted attention to our goings on. Still, like when I was jail years earlier, in spite of all the anonymous, drug-fueled sex I participated in out on the streets, I simply could not replicate sex, no matter how much I wanted to, in such seemingly forced conditions and with the lack of privacy.

My buddy David noting the such phased him. He carried fucking at any possible chance he could. I could literally stand two feet away and watch if I'd wanted to. One time I almost did as David just started to suck this dude's dick, just as sure as we'd been there talking right before. He'd always been just as loose on the outside so it should have been of no surprise.

Toby, who I'd known at little bit out on Polk. Over those days we ended up getting to know each other more. I just seen him as the White gay hustler, not all that good looking, average. He had these baby-fat cheeks with dark brown hair. Toby freely shared his being HIV positive and found himself down here hooking the streets from Canada. It intrigued me, him hailing from the Great White North. If I remember correctly, he actually had a felony; armed robbery. He fit right in comfortable with the jail atmosphere. I just never figured his little, White ass to have been so shady.

Taking his HIV status in stride he bided his time till he'd get out and continue right on using dope with his boyfriend on the outside. Toby, I could sense, accepted the inevitable death sentence of his status, even at the ripe young age of 24. There were days I recall that he just stayed laying in his bunk all day, feeling to weak be up and part of the action on the tier.

We passed the Thanksgiving holiday on 4South. Somehow, I seemed to pick fall as the perfect time be locked up. I remember had been in jail Thanksgiving 1984, back in LA, my last time of extended incarceration. Right before the Christmas holidays, it was my luck to get an early release date, something to do with having served 'good' time. Whatever the reason I felt happy to get hell outta there.

"558143…Salter!" A deputy barked down the tier of cells.

"Yes" I heard and answered.

"Roll it up!" Came the deputy's command for me to gather my bedding and meaning be ready for release at any moment.

Different than some of my other 'street life' associates, I had no qualms leaving the sometimes festive gay tier. Never did I get used to those iron gates closing, locking me behind them. I felt a spring in step as I sauntered toward the main tier gate. I sensed apprehension departing my fellow inmate friends. At that time, a crowd was grouped around the table nearest the TV. In my final pass through I heard, "Salter…you alright!" Affirmatively declared by my old cellie Mack. In his own way he wanted me to know he carried no hard feelings. I'd made something of an impression on him, maybe that even us 'out' fags were more than just objects of sex.

My early release stipulated that I be under the supervision of someone responsible for me showing up for my probation hearing. Drew had come through and agreed to vouch for me. Add to the fact I needed someplace to go. I being just at homeless as I'd been when I had entered 'Bruno'. I have no clue remembering how I made my way back to the City. I did have money on my books, sufficient funds to make use of public transportation.

Good ole, liberal-minded San Francisco implemented diversion for those of us arrested on misdemeanor crimes, such as prostitution. The diversion program offered me the option of completing and obtaining my high school G.E.D. The bonus being if I completed and got my diploma, the prostitution charge would be deleted off my criminal record. The City's district attorney's office believed and intended to go after the root causes of why people did these type minor street crimes.

A week or so after being released, I felt anxious like a kid on the first day of school riding the Muni bus out to the adult education center off of Hayes Street near Masonic. Close to a decade had passed since I'd been anywhere near being in class or school. I had failed to graduate my senior year in high school, lacking only two credits. At the time, 18 years old, I felt absolutely fucking through with high school. Desperately, all that mattered was to be done with Fort Wayne so I could get back to LA and West Hollywood 'fabulousness'.

Sitting across the same kitchen table I had been many at time, in Drew's Pacific Heights flat. He encouraged me. "Juan…your smart and intelligent as any…of the students I teach in my courses." I heard him say to me sometime before. When I left the school that day, I had signed up to test out the subjects I needed to get my G.E.D. My first exam was math. I carried the most anxiety about taking that test, I knew to be the most difficult subject for me. Yet, without practically any study at all, I passed it. In spite of lacking skills in that subject, I had mastery of test-taking skills, like answering the questions I did know and move pass those I didn't to come back to them if I had time. By the beginning of New Year's I officially was a high school graduate. Internally my self- esteem and confidence boosted. I guess those educated folks did know that having me doing this would be more productive than just locking me up in jail.

Had I broken the mold of graduating to a life of further criminality? It happened I had chosen a new path at a fork in my long and twisted journey.

Right-N- Wrong (1992)

It happened to be crisp spring noonday slinging around The Bagel Deli at the corner of Bush and Polk Streets I catch up with Scott, one of my tightest street buds. He'd been away from the scene having taken a little excursion to Reno. Probably, I hadn't even really noticed that he'd left town. First seeing him back on Polk, "damn, girlfriend! I startled him, "What chu do? You... look different."

"Been up in Reno" Scotty replied to my query, "Ain't had no Her'ron… That's it!"

About this epoch, the young White hustlers around the stroll, started finding it just as slick to inject heroin in their veins as well as the usual suspect drug; meth. Speed always had *been* the mainstay up and down Polk. It kept you horny anyway and ready. Then, you could kinda forget the sex your having with some old man crawling on your body. Now, it seemed almost chic to be doing something different that that 'ole' speed shit. Nonetheless, whatever the 'kids' were doing, I was having none of it. I hated the high on heroin. Every time I'd tried it, it made me sick to my stomach with me ending up puking somewhere. *"Aw hell naw! Who needs that shit?"* No thanks, I'll stick with the teeth grinding and horniness.

Still, Scotty looked so good, so different, better. With somewhere in that, I came up with I needed to get clean. Wow! I got clean not because I'm 26 years old and I have nothing to show for my life, besides pricking a needle in my arm to shoot dope, but got clean and sober cause my dope-addict friend looked better. So, I did. Kinda. Never much of a drinker, and weed I could take it or leave it. I had no problem giving those up. My downfall, my poison, has always been the euphoric whirlwind of methamphetamine. Each and every time meth brought me to my knees. So, I started attended 12 step meetings both, AA and NA. I had familiarity with recovery through an outreach worker at the Larkin Street Center. Larkin, provided HIV counseling us hustlers and sex workers. That same street counselor directed me where to get free therapy at 18th Street Services on Church Street out in the Castro. I began to talking to a therapist once a week, attending meetings and I stopped using dope.

I mentioned 'kinda' got clean because, still, I was hanging out and tricking. Out on Polk, I did become one the best dressed hustlers. Now, I had more money to spend on clothes. In hindsight I now know that prostituting my body continued adding damage to my emotional self. In due time, surely, I'd return to shooting away the pain and hurt, numbing it with speed.

In the rooms of 12 step meetings they referred to it as being on a 'Pink cloud'. All my new experiences and meeting new people, some that were good looking too. I felt as if I was on a high. Whatever this was, whatever was happening, I felt good. Paying no attention to when other addicts shared in the meetings. When one of them spoke and let go of some of the emotional bruising that had led them to be addicted in the first place.

In that short time, I was 'dry' and abstinent, I just so happened to cross paths out on Polk, with a john who also was in recovery. The guy was in town on a business trip with his boss. In similar fashion to me, this guy held on to the delusion that he'd still being able to hang out in gay bars and pick up young guys for sex. Gene was his name; a middle-aged black man, of light complexion. High strung and meticulous. Over the course of the few nights I ended up tricking him twice. The last time we were together Gene succumbed to all his demons and relapsed. "Juan...you know where I can cop some crack?" I remember him asking me that last night up in his hotel room. I lied, telling him, I hadn't a clue here to cop some crack. All the while still gladly taking the fee for my 'services'. Sure, I felt some empathy for Gene, just the same, selfishly I felt glad it wasn't me relapsing.

"All right...Imelda…bitch!" Miles stung greeting me on Polk, as I strolled by. Miles; of the previous summer residing at the Argyle Apartments, much dope and no utilities. His remark signaled notice of the number of new pairs of shoes I now, recently, owned. In jest, similar to wife of deposed Philippine dictator Marcos, found to have may hundreds of shoes, in full closets, all the while millions of the Filipino people lived lives in desperate poverty.

Under clear skies that early afternoon, I related in conversation to Miles how in more than four years living in the Bay Area, I'd never even stepped foot in Berkeley. "Biootch! I used to hang in Beserkley… all the time." Miles shot back of such experiences under his belt.

"Let's go! I got money… my treat." I proposed the excursion. I felt proud of myself for coming up with the idea of having some clean and sober fun. Next thing, Miles and I took off heading down toward Market Street to board the BART subway train for Berkeley. I fed cash into the automated ticket machine to purchase two fares. Miles got my attention. "Buy the cheapest fare!" I did as he instructed me to and we proceeded on our way. I recall looking around at everything I was seeing as if was all new. New to me, viewing experiences without the fog of dope. New, venturing somewhere I'd not been before.

In those first few years I'd traveled to the East Bay maybe twice. Seeing the same things and places over and over. Usually, I roamed and ventured within less than a 10 or so block area that made up the Tenderloin. And that being just a small part of the 'village' that was San Francisco.

I know we exited at the downtown Berkeley station. Cause, I visually marveled at the 60's Brutalist architecture of the station's rotunda. Miles led, navigating the way to down and around Telegraph Avenue. I probably appeared as if I was a tourist, looking around at everything all wide-eyed. That lazy afternoon we were tourists venturing outside our usual 'home' of hustling and drugging.

The few blocks right close to the flagship campus of the University of California. Up and down the sidewalks and corners on Telegraph, the aura, patina or just the plain dirtiness of 60's flower children appeared to linger in the air, on its last breath. The unmistakable smell of marijuana waffled by in the breezes under our noses, walking among the sidewalk vendors and hippie -clothed White folk present. If one happened to be searching for the idea of Berkeley in the 60's at least you could purchase it in the tourist trinkets and drugs sold along the avenue.

I reminded Miles of the need to stop somewhere to grab a bite to eat. Yes, I gained back an appetite practicing an amphetamine- free diet. He and I walked around some more before getting bored and deciding to make our way for the journey back to the City. When the BART train departed West Oakland Station and dipped into the tunnel beneath the Bay, I noticed my shortage of funds. Looking over at Miles, "no problem gurrl", he counseled. Knowing we lacked the exact fare amount to exit, I followed Miles' lead as we exited BART at the Embarcadero Station. Following him, we, then, proceeded to take the disabled access elevator up to the MUNI level train cars. We caught the next MUNI trolley to Civic Center and coolly walked to exit, smoothly saving about five dollars off our fare. Clearly, the day's tourist excursion had ended. I was, now, back to the familiar world of low-life scamming, hustling and numbing life's pains.

Indeed, I'd come about that 'disposable' income for the Beserkley excursion due to a trick the previous evening. Todd; late twenties, White with a healthy compact build and thick brunette curls. He'd first picked me up on Polk, for what felt a seemingly surreal encounter. Surreal, cause Todd himself sparked hotness in all sense of that word. And, he loved to kiss as well as sucking dick. *"Yes, hookers are not supposed to kiss clients."* Surreal, again, cause I got paid $100 for what my body and my desires would have gladly done gratis.

Most certainly I'd mentioned all the details to Miles while he did his best to tolerate my outsized ego and attitude that day. Dreams of sexy Todd screwing me at $100 a pop had me floating, my head way up into the clouds. *"This clean and sober thing felt almost as good as gett'n high...especially my wages were better,"* so I thought. After that night's hot and heaviness, Todd promised we'd met up again later this evening.

Just as balloon it either floats up and away or it pops. My oversized attitude and ego and eventually, my foundation less sobriety, fell to earth, crashed and burned. The trip to Beserkley simply served as respite. Back on Polk Street with all its hardened grit and grime, hours ticked away as my anxiety grew. The red, of the stoplights looked redder and the green look more neon. I wanted, desired, no, actually needed Todd to return. Seemingly, only upon his return to scoop me up from this grime, I'd be still able to pretend and keep the pain and fear at bay. For sure I was clean from drugs. Yet, what about my life had really changed. Everything in my life felt fine, exhilarating even, so long as things went my way. Life felt fine if the world outside of myself substituted gratification for the empty hole I still, felt and gnawed my insides. Amorous and thoroughly pleasurable encounters with Todd did not and could not, cover up for intimacy and companionship I desired sharing with another human being.

Around 9oclock that night, a Sunday, whatever within me could no longer mask the ever-present feeling of loneliness. A loneliness that felt as if having been brought so much closer to the surface, without the usual buffer of meth. With Todd a no show, I had my excuse to resort back to what I knew best. Back to what I'd known to be an instant pain relief; dope. Right then, that evening with those bright traffic lights blinking brighter, it seemed I just couldn't get high enough, fast enough. So desperate I was that got ripped off. Copping dope from someone I didn't know because I just couldn't wait getting that first hit. I hadn't been ripped off buying dope, in like eons, well-seasoned doper I was.

Those 30plus days of life, clean, without the chemical escape route; methamphetamine, evaporated as a warm soothing glow came over me just as the needle point punctured my arm, my veins, leaving a small bubble of concentrated blood and dope at the entry point of the syringe. As like an old friend, a familiar intimate lover had returned to keep me safe. Returning to protect me from danger, real and imagined.

My life returned to me feeling like whole, carrying alongside the emotional 'hole' in my being. A life I could handle.

There I stood, sun shining, traffic flowing, back on the 'block. Back on the auction block; Polk Street. Just a typical afternoon living the life of a no account tweeked out hustler, except something seemed weird, not as it used to be. Out of the corner of my eye I spot a group of maybe five or so young, Black brothers walking together up Polk, in a pack. This not the usual sites around those environs, I stared not too hard, just as they rounded the corner of Bush Street and coolly walked went up the incline to Van Ness. A strange sight cause, the world the way it was, and is, a bunch of youthful black male bodies together incited suspicion. Even I was not immune to reacting to the stereotype, not proud of it, but that's probably how come I noticed them in the first place.

Whether you'd call it intuition or street smarts, something told me these fellas some an intended mission in mind. Surely, I figured, they were not unawares to the racist implication of their presence, in these parts, would bring. Furthermore, I also could tell they seemed not be just your everyday hood rats and gang bangers. Just as quickly as I'd noticed them, they had disappeared somewhere up on Van Ness.

A rumor circulated up and around Polk, later in the day, about some chaos happening. "Some Black dudes... gone up to Good Guys and...just busted out the store front glass... stole some TVs on display." That's the story I'd heard. Putting two and two together, *"it musta been dem young brothas... I'd seen.'*

The rumor mill drummed up thick that day, all around the atmosphere seemed thick with an anxiousness. Somebody had mentioned they'd heard there was some kind of protest going down somewhere along Market Street, downtown. That was nothing new. Always there happened to be some kind of protest march or another going on in Frisco, especially, since President George Bush; George I, had taken the country on a military excursion, to kick some ass, in the Mideast.

That day's protests of rage responded to the atrocity of the 4 White LAPD officers having been acquitted of all charges for the violently brutal and near death beating of Black motorist; Rodney King. It seemed like every few minutes or so a cop cruiser raced up to Van Ness and that burglarized Good Guys store. Just the same craziness, every other minute a cop car raced, sirens blaring, in the direction toward downtown and all the commotion going on there, like the police couldn't keep up with it all.

Soon enough something in the atmosphere hit me, I too took off down to Market Street. I could hear the action and commotion before, I even came upon the scene. Pent up outrage and anger I'd withheld, filled my being. Noise of the protest shouts, like a vibration, in increasing decibels, took ahold and overwhelmed me, my senses. Loud sirens blared as if coming from all directions. The echoes of which filled the space all down in front of the buildings on Market Street. A genuine mob of people, folks young, black and white, Latino and others. All of the City's struggling to live, near-about starving hordes, appeared to having had taken over the whole street, the area really. All traffic, cars and surface transportation, buses, ceased to moving. This definitely a fete, since it was near evening rush hour. A phalanx of SFPD officers armed and dressed in full riot gear appeared by then and moved in formation, down the street, ever so slowly. As the crowds of protesters grew and grew more boisterous, the police definitely pushed and moved quicker.

The mob grew even angrier. Storefront, plate glass windows got busted out, both sides along Market Street. The loudly shattering glass gave a thrill to the crowd, feeding the chaos. Chaos that seemed to feel good. Right! The idea that an all-White jury from the suburbs did not or refused to see the violent terror of that 'beat down,' the violent beating whole world had seen; 10 or more officers of the law participating in a free-for-all whipping of a Black man. *"What the hell? Was this fucking... Mississippi 1964? Hell, fuck'n naw!"* LAPD once nearly had me too at their complete will and mercy, for something I didn't do. I enthusiastically joined in the mob as it pushed passed Civic Center, near 8th Street. Passing by the Radio Shack near around 9th Street, having closed early. I could see and hear someone kick out the storefront glass. I too ran in alongside others grabbing a handful of blank VHS video tapes. Within mere minutes the sore lay cleaned out, looted, amid the shards of broken glass. The loud noise, sound of sirens and the enraged mob played on.

Somewhere around the intersection of Van Ness and Market Streets, I spotted my counselor from 18th Street Services. He there himself walking in and among the crowds of protesters. My relapse having happened since my last session with him. See him it dawned on me how much had taken place, in and outside my life, in the 30 days since I'd been clean from dope.

Memories of being there within what happened, that moment, in solidarity with those Black brothers. In the streets protesting(looting) with Black sisters, there in those moments with my white gay counselor alongside my street-honed self, all of us moving, acting as one. That day has never left me.

Tear gas canisters floated in the air or rumors of such did. Soon, I got the hell outta there in short order. San Francisco got put under a martial law curfew that night, as South-Central LA exploded and burned in an aggravated upheaval. Sitting alone on the creaking bed in my flop house hotel room. I listened to reports of all the goings on, from NPR. Listening, reeling and taking in the day's thrills and feeling justified in the incitement. *"Burn...the muthafucka down!"*

Sleeping Dogs Lie (1992)

It just so happened we almost ran past one another at the old main library in Civic Center, the building suffered heavy damage in the 89' quake. He'd been one of my most regular customers. Though, he was different than most other older white men who leased the services of my youthful black male flesh. From that very first encounter Drew and I seemed to click on similar frequencies, beyond the exchange of sex for a fee. No mistaking though, still, each time it was about the dick. Yet, the chemistry between us before, during and after the dicking helped to make for a certainly more comfortable if not completely unpleasant experience.

Maybe it was Drew seeming to be wiser than the average fellow. He took me back to his place right after we'd just met passing each other on Polk Street. I say wiser, thinking about it later, cause the cab ride in itself could have been a sorta testing of the 'goods'. If I appeared to fidgety or shady, he could have had the cab driver drop him off somewhere other than his place. And, besides, he'd have the taxi driver as possible backup in case things got a little out of hand. Maybe because, that first night, I inquired about the sleek black African sculptures dotting the decor of his apartment. Or maybe his occupation as a college professor seemed to draw out my natural curiosity for how the world worked. Often, our later 'sessions' were filled with more time over dinner, wine and discussion than the actual slamming of our bodies between the bed sheets.

Many a time I spent my downtime when not speeded out, filling the space between my ears with something of substance, within those walls of the library. Something positive to try to counteract the damage and negativity I often pumped into my veins and my soul. Drew may have been surprised to see me that day, but not surprised to find me coming out of a library.

Walking with him that day, I fessed up and revealed to him my addiction to meth and my having been evicted from my apartment. Drew concluded that embarrassment regarding my unfortunate circumstances as to the reason why I had lost touch with him. I never told him it really had more to do with me having been so fuck'n high out of my mind that I didn't show up and even call with an excuse the last we had arranged to meet. In other words, just plain old junky rudeness and selfish inconsideration. Now, with hindsight, coming 'clean' to Drew eventually, though unawares then, the long emotionally painful journey leading to me getting clean from dope had begun.

As Drew and I reconnected our relationship, similarly I reconnected relations with my Aunt Deborah. I even mentioned Drew in my letters to her. In fact, they ended up sharing letters to one another. Never did I explicitly mention the 'raw' circumstances that which put Drew and myself within each other's company. I assumed she could figure it out between the lines of what was said and what was not said.

In the midst of my reconnecting I happened to mention to Drew of a desire to go visit back 'home' to Indiana to see my family. He told me he would buy me a Greyhound ticket to help me in that pursuit, on account that any and all money I had went to fund the addiction pumped into my bloodstream.

Right before I was set to make my journey, we went out bar hopping to celebrate Drew's 62'nd birthday. Drew's birthday just two days before my aunt's, two people dear to me both Virgos. What were the odds? Starting out at about 4pm, we found ourselves at some meant to be chic gay bar, down in Hayes Valley, an up and coming spot of gentrification. Always I enjoyed conversations and debates with Drew, alcohol only seemed to heightened the effect. Hours flew by paying no mind to how we must have appeared; young Black buck with this old (in gay years for sure) white man buying him drinks and being loud. Before we even realized night had descended. Our bar hopping turned out to be just a hop.

Many years of experience meant Drew could handle his liquor. Me, on the other hand, absolute lightweight, I felt as if I could hardly stand up. We finally left the bar and hailed a taxi up Franklin Street pass Cathedral Hill to Drew's apartment in Pacific Heights. "Hey....I'm just too...wasted to... do anything." I told Drew just as we exited the taxi and I tripped and nearly fell on the sidewalk. That signaled no sex was happening that evening. Probably, I could have performed just enough to get the job done, me being a professional hoe and all. It was only that I hated the effect of being drunk. Besides, I needed to sleep it off as I was to be on a Greyhound bus the next day.

Sun bright not too early in the morning, I boarded and stepped down a familiar seeming narrow aisle. It'd been awhile since my buttcheeks had taken a seat on Greyhound. Now, the total bus and all the seats were non-smoking. From what I could tell not all the riders had clearly' received the memo' as to the new law. So, at regular intervals along with the regular stops, our diver pulled the coach over to the shoulder on the interstate to let us smokers get our nicotine fix. Noticing this somewhat sweaty-haired, white dude who appeared to have a heavier habit that most. "Whosevers...that's smoking in the restroom...the vent blows out up here in the front. By law, you cannot smoke on the bus!" Our driver demanded over the PA, just after that same dude had just exited the john.

Later, as I was headed to the john, I spied the dude, lookin even sweatier than he had looked before, taking a swig off a half-gallon bottle of what looked like some cheap gin or vodka. My speed freak junky ass always on the lookout to catch some 'legal' junky doing bad. Passing by him and shook my head, registering my disgust, as if I had some right.

Out in the salt flat deserts west of Salt Lake City our bus pulled over and stopped for another smoke break. As I stepped off the bus, immediately I felt the intensity of the desert heat sucked at my exposed skin like it was roasting in an oven. Seconds later, that sweaty-looking dude attempted to disembark the bus, mis stepped and proceeded to tumble down the embankment leading up to the roadway. He awkwardly stood up as a cloud of dust settled back to the ground around him. I shook my head again, looking in his direction. The indignity. None too soon dude would experience just how hot dusty the desert could be.

He continued on in his inebriated condition fucking off the warnings given out from our driver. Lesson: Don't fuck with a Greyhound river. At least not in the vast desolate nowhereness of Wyoming.

"I will not warn you... bout drinking alcohol on this coach!" The diver sternly put out over the PA, as he drove somewhere high up in the mountain ranges east of Salt Lake City. No specifics as to who the driver had intended his warning. The rest of us passengers knew. By then, the dude barely even bothered trying to conceal his gin bottle. He had meant, in his staggered reaction time, to zip up his duffle bag, on the floor near his feet, containing the liquor bottle. Only when the wafting fumes from the alcoholic spirits drafted up among the noses of the rest of us.

"Man..yo bag leaking!" Did somebody yell to get his attention. He finally peered up though his bloodshot eyes to notice the trickling stream leading to just under his shoes.

"Huh" was his incredulous response. A burst of laughter could be heard among us fellow passengers.

Wide open skies began to emanate the sunset as our bus exited the interstate and pulled into a combination Burger King, gas station, bus station, a common part of the commercial landscape out in the empty interstate stretches. When the bus stopped, "we'll be stopped here twenty minutes exactly!" Our driver informed us riders. When a few of us returned to board the bus within the stated time frame, having relieved our insides or loaded up on artery-hardening junk food. Our driver, having had enough, stood up and looked directly at the aforementioned, now drunk, dude, "Sir... you have to leave this bus... Here!" He ordered him to exit. Intently eavesdropping, I heard the dude being informed that, when he was sober, another bus would be along at the exact same time, 24 hours later. That was that.

The coach, then, pulled away from the Greyhound station, Burger King, mini mart, that I also noticed was closing as the lights had turned out. Seemingly they had waited for our departure to close shop. So there with a classic red-orange sky over a mountain backdrop, a cloud of brown dust enveloped the drunk dude, all alone there in the semi gravel parking lot. He probably would soon pass out. Our bus moved on minus one problem, at least.

I sensed the life I had created, more like the mess I called a life, fade the further I travelled away from San Francisco, past the lands west of the Rockies. My travelling 'home' meant to settle some scores. Settling some scores with myself and settling scores with others. Taking a vacation from my home of which I had none. I possessed a particular geographic area, a patch of terrafirma that I regarded as home. In spite of real-world realities expecting a 26-year-old adult being able to have a domicile of one's own, roommates at the least. Still, on this journey I actually had a round trip ticket that allowed me to return 'home' if only in the metaphorical sense.

This time, returning to Fort Wayne did not have me with my tail between my legs. Returning on my own terms, certain of my having a welcome to stay at my Aunt Deborah's. She in some ways my soulmate, she the first family I ever told I was gay. We had since reconnected within the year via letters and birthday cards. I had dropped an emotional bombshell. In one of the letters, I mentioned the fact of remembering having been sexually molested as a young boy, by my next oldest brothers. A fact, I myself, more clearly had come to accept. Accept the murky reality of memories I had held for as long as I could remember. By writing this to her I needed and believed, I could rely on her confidence. I realize, now, how desperately I needed to reveal, to someone, the pain of that emotional numbness. To my utter surprise, my aunt told me she confronted my brothers; which she wrote to me that they denied it. Inside I felt relieved. Rejoiced really. Finally, the burden of that secret no longer only weighed down my shoulders. Now, somebody else had to carry the load of that pain.

Calling after arriving, not exactly sure if I'd informed her beforehand or if I just showed up without any pre-warning. My reputation typically had me springing such surprises upon family folks. Aunt Deborah had acquired a diagnosis of lupus; the autoimmune disease, since I'd been away. I noticed how the symptoms in many ways were similar to H.I.V that I had much familiarity. Both diseases attacked the person's own body. She could no longer work and now received social security disability. Further similarity, many of those I knew afflicted with HIV as well received social security disability.

Observing her during my stay my aunt appeared as I'd remembered except for gaining some considerable weight. "My medicine makes me big and bloated," she told me as an explanation of the weight gain. Never having heard of Lupus before, what did I know?

Settling in those few days I felt a sense of emotional warmth, being 'home', among loved ones; comfort. The life I had chosen of dope and living at the edge of adventure, periodically homeless, resembled traits similar to being in a combat zone. Safely indoors close to my aunt, whom I dearly loved, made the world feel right. In spite of the "Leave It to Beaver" relational warmth, my origins leaned more to the dysfunction of "All in the Family." We talked, shared and caught up with one another. I even took the risk of revealing my addiction to meth with her. To my surprise, she shared with me her own having used speed pills; black beauties, back when she attended University of Wisconsin in Madison. Madison having the reputation of being the "Berkeley" of the Midwest, for its liberal and open ways.

Still burning from the financial misdealing I had had with my sister, prior to my leaving town 3 years earlier. I made the decision not to even acknowledge or speak to her during my visit. Demonstrating, I felt, my displeasure at her basically using the money I paid her to help me not be evicted. This had been also after I disclosed to my sister the desperation of my drug addiction, the reason for my being in arrears on my lease in the first place.

No other family member doubted my tale of 'getting fucked' dealing financially with my sister. She carried a noted rep for having treated 'family' as such, especially in any concerns with money.

On one afternoon of my visit, My Uncle Don dropped by to visit my aunt and me, with cocktails in tow. Probably a bottle of Cutty Sark or some other scotch too strong for me to handle. "You might as well... get over that!" Uncle Don said with a chuckle, in regards to my being made whole in dealing with Sandra's ways. Uncle's acknowledgement of her 'wrongs' toward me, ironically, by his own witness, comforted me. *"Hell! At least I was not the only one who should have known better"*

The red brick, row house apartment of Aunt Deborah's became a venue of impromptu family reunions. The wife of my nephew Stacy; Katrina, came by to introduce me to my first grandniece; Moneca. The two-year-old, biracial toddler sat smiling and beaming as any cute toddler does. No one, nor had I, made any reference to the odd fact of my nephew Stacy just so happened to be absent. He didn't personally come to share with me the proud joy of his first born. For certain I knew he'd been the one to arrange the visit of his mate and child. The thought did pass my mind, Sandra might have just as well set up that 'family moment', fully aware that her own relations failed to fit that 'wholesome' setting. Stacy, probably having to pick a side; his momma or his uncle. Family.

I'll never forget that day though, cause it made both Aunt Deborah and me tickled. Little Moneca let out a sigh, "Huh... grandma," at her hearing of her grandmother being discussed. A truthful sign that the shit-nanaghans related to my family transcended even the barely verbal toddler.

An unexpected yet, feared reunion came about with the appearance one early evening of my brother James and my nephew Tarakus. As memories of my molestation as a young boy became unrepressed, James as one of the perpetrators with his subsequent teasing of my afterward expressions of femininity, my weirdness, all bubbled up to my emotional surface simply as rage. Once, I remembered dreaming that I had killed him. Coming after him, in the dream, with a butcher knife in a monstrous fit of anger. Recalled crying also, the morning after the dream fully comprehending the substance of what I had dreamt. What I felt. I feared such powerfully repressed emotions, ever since I finally actually acknowledged the memory of the rape as fact.

Within a minute or two of his crossing the threshold of my aunt's front door, James gestured to me to speak with him alone. Tarakus and Aunt Deborah got caught up in greetings. James acknowledged and told me that he had been confronted by our aunt, about that dark, horrible incident; my emphasis. "We...was kids Todd! I'm sorry..."

To this day I feel God intervened, in that moment with my flesh and blood brother. Parts of my world, my being, my existence started to complete into some form of wholeness. To hear my macho brother, in real time, admit that, "Yes," not only did that fearful violent act happen. In fact, the people meant to protect me, keep me from harm carried responsibility.

"Now What!" God seemed to speak to me. In essence saying as true as that was, it was, now, in the past. *"What was I going to do about it?"* Surprisingly, in my feeling of numbness, I did not hate James. Deep down all I really wanted was to have the truth admitted. And he had.

Though stunned, I felt okay. Still able to stand both physically and figuratively. Stand as I had done since the afternoon of that terrifying hurt. Yes, I had weathered close calls to my demise, most at my own hands. I still stood. Stood for integrity, for love and for vindication. My relations with my brothers James and Keith were in no ways healed, yet no longer breaking. I loved James for helping give me my truth. Now, God had left the final result up to me.

Momma had named Tarakus, born within the year of her death. His name a made-up set of letters and sounds she had heard the summer before at a friend's family picnic. Born with a birth defect similar to what I'd had when I was born. Both of us born fighting for life. I loved Tarakus dearly as a baby and a little one. He had admired his Uncle Todd reciprocally.

Most of his childhood I'd been off being a confused wondering gay, drug addict. I supposed his coming over with his dad that unusual afternoon, having due to his fond remembrances of me. For then, he was just of the age when my 'gay uncle' status equated to something like; Superman to kryptonite, for a pubescent Black male teenager. Being from a family, a people, not knowing the manner to accept and nurture a boy who grew to reject the confining expected gender roles for a Black man. In the reunion nephew Tarakus surveyed the image of his uncle, flesh and blood, of his own blood. What he actually concluded of who and what I was, surely, he lacked the words to articulate.

There having my childhood sexual abuse confirmed left me with a least one certainty; acceptance and acknowledgement of my being an addict, a dope fiend. My river of denial had burst a dam. Still true, deep emotional pain, a hurt burned at my inner being. I soothed that pain with dope, crystal meth as my balm. Aiming to numb the outer shell, the body, to match the long-ago numbness hidden down deep within. .

The next afternoon I sought to connect with an earlier site of refuge, the library. The place a many a gay, queer boy hid out amongst the books, in an atmosphere of the intellect. Having forgotten something, possibly misplaced, I called back to the apartment from a pay phone to check if I left whatever it was there.

The phone rang for an extended number of rings. I knew my aunt to be home so I stayed on the line. "He...he...hello... The voice dragged with a raspy tone.

"Debbie!... This Todd", I said, responding with emphasis.

"Huh"...after a pause, "Oh...yeah... ba baaby." She finally spoke with some coherence recognizing my voice on the other end of the line.

Whatever I'd called for remained insignificant to the 'live' exchange that I had just experienced, as I stood there still at the payphone after hanging up. As an addict, one can spot another addict a mile away even, insight gained from my lived experience, articulated that interaction with my aunt.

Back out on Polk, in Frisco, the era of 'Heroin chic' was in full bloom. A number of fellow street associates had begun to switch over to using heroin, opiates. (this the early 90's, not the latter Heroin 'epidemic' of 2000 teens) mostly the straight hustler types. I had been familiarized with the tell-tale signs of a heroin and downers high; the slow almost incoherent speech patterns, the nearly android body movements, the eyes rolled back in their sockets. Being used to my family drunk or stoned, maybe, this was 'out there'. My brain needed to graft new emotional coping methods. An elder, a loved one, a 'junkie'!

Was I to confront her? Who was I, 'the pot calling the kettle black?" I relied and fell back to familiar coping strategies of my family; I kept secrets. Having been emotionally released from one hidden secret to hold a pact to another, *"One step forward two steps back, you know?"*

Meanwhile, however all warm and fuzzy my reunion 'home' had been, the monkey I carried craving for a hit of dope, to cope with reality, clawed its slimy way to the surface to be

fed.

'People, places and things.' I have come to recognize such dangers since in recovery. Seemingly innocent intentions, I sought to reconnect with some old friends. Gay life in Fort Wayne meant nightlife in the bars, so off I went. Headed out on my last night in town to discover that the main bar was in a new and larger venue. That particular bar; "Up the Street", I knew to be owned and run by a short, racist prick. I was only there for the night so I rationalized my going in, keeping my resentments intact.

After some time trying to sip the lone bottle of beer I could afford, I recognized someone from years before. I recognized and spoke to James. Giving him an extra raised eyebrow look as he played a game of pool. *"What was he doing in the gay bar?"* My look was meant to say. I knew him from smok'n crack back in the day, when he was 'straight'. I had tried to make a move on him sexually during one night of our heavy 'puffing', only to be rebuffed. Now, I knew my 'gaydar' hadn't been malfunctioning that night in regards to him. We only spoke for a hot minute.

Eventually, I did run into Geno, after I had left the bar and was out walking on Pearl Street. We both went back a ways, especially speaking of using drugs. From the first time he came over to my house when I was still in high school, he with his rock hard stomach and bulging biceps, that afternoon, proceeded to smoke a fat joint of weed, with my brother Keith and me, sitting on our living room couch. Geno and I had been tight as 'rock heads.' When he offered to catch up with me on my last night, the way junkies do, how could I refuse? Defenseless, in my element, I got to smoking, "like nobody's business", with him and some older white dude, as his trick for the night.

Broke and geeked out I slithered my way back through my aunt's door at about 3am, not a word to day to my condition. "Yes indeed, the pot and the kettle were black!" Reunion over. I kept my shame to myself on my way out, via a Greyhound ticket.

Olive- Branches (1992)

'Having a moment of clarity,' didn't have much meaning to me till much later in my recovery. Even deep back in my using life glimpses of profound epiphanies, came piercing through my delusional bubble of dope and denial. Only now, I realize the sheath surrounding my hurts cracked every so small, allowing a tiny bit a healing to begin.

For about a month that summer, I'd abstained from all mind altering substances. Although; I held firmly to the addict lifestyle, eventually leading to a relapse and the continuance of my addiction, at full speed (pun intended). In spite of my relapse, a fellow recovering addict, whom I met at AA or NA, I don't remember which, a big White guy, with a red-haired beard and receding hairline. He offered me a place, one night, to sleep off my withdrawals. Whether his intention meant to keep in the recovery loop or offered out of physical attraction, nonetheless, his name not remembered yet, his kindness was, even 20 years later.

Even in spite of my drug- delusional thinking I thought, "What… a Black gay man isn't allowed to be seen as a regular human being!" That's what I was. I dawned on me that those like a Senator Helms, in a way, were perfectly fine with Black gay folks, like myself, to continue harboring self-loathing. Destroying their lives just as I happened to be doing.

I remembered my red-bearded recovery friend inviting others over, other gay men, to view the premiere showing of "Tongues Untied". The documentary being somewhat of big deal in gay circles. Another of the benefits and support, living in the gay 'mecca', being amongst the comfort of one's own that even trickled down to my lowly station.

With my eyes and ears fully transfixed on what emanated from the TV screen. Riggs began by narrating the tale of his having fallen in love with a White guy, during his years in high school. Telling about when he knew he was gay. "That's just like me!" I could have blurted out, in response. Seeing other Black, queer lives on television, speaking in their own words, not hiding who or what they were frightened my senses, at first. The years of negative social conditioning coming to the fore, in the moment. Slowly as the minutes passed my spirit within said, "Yes!" Owning and accepting the 'real' images my own eyes were witnessing.. I drank in the notion; there's nothing wrong with me. Full-sized, masculine, feminine, androgynous, lisping, sass-shaying, Black men are, and were just as human as anyone else. This in contrast to the "Men on Film" hyperbolic, stereotyped characters played on the "In Living Color" television show, whom some people saw as so funny, at the time. Being there that night, I may for the first time in my life, fully, acknowledged my own humanity other than having had unconditional acceptance from my mom.

Marvin Riggs' biographical vision helped me know and become more, Me. At the conclusion of the program, "What did you think of it?' My friend eagerly asked me.

"I...I...ah" my mouth literally seamed to hang open. It was exactly and everything all in the same. My own tongue untied left me with so much to say as well leaving without the words and not knowing where to start.

In spite of that film's metaphorical "look at the man in in the mirror', it proved not enough and at the same too much to scare down the demon of addiction I'd become so comfortably, emotionally numb to. My relapse drew me back into my meth odyssey, deeper than ever. At the same time, things were different. I knew, now, without a doubt that I was 'fucking up'. Something held within me kept certain knowledge, a knowing, that eventually there was an end to my 'travels' with dope, my old companion; meth. Clearer than before, the longer I continued travelling on path of speed the uglier the trip was gonna become.

For no specific reason around that same time, I gathered into my sphere of junkiedom some compatriots, of the female gender. One of whom ended up becoming one of my closest friends, even beyond the degradation of those drug times.

Tanya, a petite, blond spitfire full of street and sass hovered me in first. More than likely we'd probably crossed paths procuring dope. At one time she lived in the same apartment building as my connection, halfway up the hill on Bush Street, just after Larkin. Days and many a night my junky self, coped my narcotic poison and shot up in that apartment building, only to find myself way too high to be out on the streets. I'd end up tweek'n out in the stairways or the basement. And yes, "Why not?" I'd even go up and tweek out, high as a fucking kite, on the roof of that apartment building. Crawling around, peeping and hiding in the shadows at night by the light of the moon and stars. Crazy to think about it, anyone residing on an upper floor of nearby apartments had to have been witness to a crazed, zoomed out, Black tweeker, up there on a roof; me.

Tanya might find me in the lurking, tweaking in the hallways, spotting how high I was she'd invite me into her apartment. In a subtle way, my large, Black male body served as some protection. If she only knew, I couldn't really kick ass. I was too scared. Tanya's demure stature could imply to any shady dope fiend to take advantage. And besides, me being gay, she didn't have to worry about me making a move on her. More often she'd leave me alone at her place. While she was out doing whatever she did to get her hustle. Tweeked out I'd end up cleaning up the apartment. Part of that deal, any leftover bags of speed I might scavenge in some crevice was mine; a junky's bargain. Not till way after we had met one another did I find out Tanya was a stripper. Early on I didn't know or care how she made her money. Who the hell was I to judge?

My girlfriend Jill, just so happened to be a bank robber. No, that's not hyperbole. Jill used her pale, red-headed, suburban White woman, looking self as privilege to just walk right into a Bank of America or Wells Fargo branch with a stolen checkbook. Make a scene, typically, as a distressed house wife in the midst of a divorce or some other housewife drama. About 8 out 10 times it worked. She'd walk out of the bank branch with cash, tears still streaming down her pale freckled cheeks. Some other hustler prostitute would have stolen a checkbook somewhere and had brought it to Jill to make use of. Jill would pay them off or split the proceeds in dope, after she had gone to a chosen bank and did her thing and robbed it.

Jill enjoyed my company as well, cause I happened to be for real gay. Not just a dude who posed as one to make a living, then, to claim being straight and make a move on her, especially when the meth, freak juice appeared on the scene.

In a demonstration of the continued ugliness of being hooked, Jill called me up to her room at a cheap hotel on Polk. The only dope she had left to share that afternoon turned out to be a syringe full of a thick hit of speed, all ready to go. The only problem being, within that clear, icy to the touch hit of dope, lay a perfect bubble of blood. Jill's blood. Jill already too high herself, failed to hit a vein with the needle and she was afraid she would miss, which caused a severe burning sensation within the vein and basically wasting the effect of the speed high.

Certainly, the fiend'n doper I was, no matter knowing with confirmed or unconfirmed sureness that ninety percent of everyone I knew and associated with were HIV positive, along with hepatitis etc. I shot the big hit of speed with evidence of danger. Forgetting all concern, just as that toxic, possibly deadly, poison intoxicant zoomed via my bloodstream to my brain. Afterwhich, I too was 'zoom'n'.

The best of all my 'girlfriends', my road dog, street confidant stood as a rather tall scrawny, knock-kneed, blond chick who wanted to be called; Olive, like Popeye's girlfriend. She passed the average rating department while going down the line of God passing out looks. That drew me even closer to her. Olive didn't come off as conceited, better than anyone else. And as an advantage on those streets, in terms of personal safety, the plainer-looking a White girl was fended off unwanted sexual motivations.

In and out of homelessness I navigated and maintained somewhat decent physical hygiene with access to a phone and mail in times of the most destitution. The Hospitality House on Leavenworth Street, right around the corner from where I had an apartment, served mostly single men clients, most of them Black. It happened to be there one afternoon, to my amazement, I spotted that same bony, White girl; Olive. She checking for mail at Hospitality House too. Her young White femaleness stood out, like a cop in a crack den. Nonplussed, she took her odd presence in stride. Olive simply was handling her biz'ness, no more no less. That stood out to me, cause most of the White, hustler milieu cast aspersions at the types of Black men up at Hospitality House. As if their own drug addictions and the resulting destitution were in, absolutely, no ways similar.

Olive a Midwestern refugee too. From Kansas and the state of "Misour-y" as could hear her pronounce it. She ended up on the City's streets via a path through New Orleans and Texas. Small bands of various filthy, 'gutter punks' (the term they used themselves) began to populate the environs around Polk Street and such. They came on heels of the rise in use of black tar heroin; 'Heroin Chic'. Many of these White kids came as couples, as did Olive and her boyfriend, Clay. The dudes sold their bodies, dropping their pants turning tricks on Polk while their girlfriends plopped on the sidewalks begging for spare change. 'Spanging' they called it.

Soon enough it seemed like they were all over Polk. All dressed in dirty black clothing, bondage belts and Doc Marten boots. The look, attitude and drug life coincided with a gloomy music scene coming out of Seattle, grunge and punk. Certainly the White hoodlums (my term) were definitely grungy. Even us speeded out tweeker hustlers never practically laid down on the sidewalks. At least we tried to keep up appearances. It was just expected that you'd gravitate deeper down to the 'Tenderloin' when you simply didn't give a fuck how you appeared.

Olive and that punk crowd did hip me to squatting; taking up residence in empty abandoned properties. By 'squatting' it seemed like we weren't homeless junkies, at least not the homeless part. Having a place to 'crash' in the midst of drug withdrawals, away from the harassment of the cops, plus, it being safer to shoot up indoors with some privacy added to the benefits of squatting. Surely, some of us were fucking in the squats too.

The key to keeping long-term residency in a squat (a month), secrecy. You only entered or left the premises being as incognito as was possible. The less folks who knew of the location the longer it remained like our own private residence, within our own street family existence. Usually, in the end, enough fiend'n desperate junkies would disclose the location of the squat in exchange for a hit of another junkie's dope stash. Surely, within days half the hustlers and dope heads on Polk were coming in and out, at all hours, day and night, before the 'authorities' had to put an end to the madness.

Yet, contrary to that first rule, one particular careless, dope head hustler; Ron, tracked the cops to the squat that was on the corner of Van Ness and Golden Gate Streets. They'd tracked him after some nefarious or another action he'd gotten into up on the stroll. As it was just so happening to be raining that particular evening, coming down in a good pour.

The San Francisco Cops took assessment of how many of us there, that would be put back out on the streets in the rain with nowhere to go. They only arrested and carted off that one hustler himself. In so, the police allowed the rest of hustler junky types to remain in the squat, knowing full well we were trespassing and more than likely consuming illegal drugs. That was tenor of those times in the City.

I recalled squatting at the same location, or maybe it may have been the building right next door, for what felt like nearly a month. One of the two buildings still had the electricity running, luxury digs for sure while it lasted the gay pride festival held each year in Civic Center Plaza, in front of city hall, actually was just two blocks away from where I was squatting.

The arrival of the 'national gay holiday' that year seemed to fill me with dread. Unspoken, unarticulated, at the time, what did my broke ass possess to show pride? Normal-like, straight folks, fail to fathom the scope of gay pride weekend in San Francisco. This happened to be the epicenter, the 'gay mecca'. Festival attendees, arriving from all over the world, in some ways were almost on spiritual pilgrimage. An over-sexed, boozed out, drug-addled, hedonistic pilgrimage nonetheless.

By then, I knew and was aware of the history of the actual protest- rebellion, the last weekend in June 1969, in New York City's Greenwich Village. Which, now, was memorialized by the pride festivals in June. I knew the reality of the protesters being a bunch of faggots, drunks, drag queens and hustlers which had all gotten fed up being harassed and continually busted my crooked cops. A weekend long riot ensued from a police bust at the Stonewall Inn, a seedy, Mafia- infiltrated, gay dive bar.

By 1992 gay pride festivals had become fully commercialized. Backed and supported by liquor and beer companies that'd slicked things up, seemingly squeaky clean, almost middle-class White.

Closing the door, I shielded my dilated eyes from the bright sunlight. Sneakily I slipped into the Mickey D's just across the alley from the Van Ness squat. Most certainly sweat had started to bead and roll down my forehead, not due to heat and humidity. No, profuse sweat just the physical manifestation of dope fiend, junky anticipation. Anticipation that the body could not hide, despite social conditioning on the meaning of a sweaty personage.

Just as well, McDonalds had a working toilet. Needing to take an enormous shit, a further bodily anticipation sign of dope dependency. Barely could I stand there in line, let alone be able to look the young cashier in the eye while buying at least the required 99 cent,

Sprite soda. Like a child waiting for a treat simultaneously needing to go to the potty, I fidgeted nervously. Just wanting to get it over with and get inside the john.

Not wanting to be seen or noticed, either from the McDonald's staff barely wanting to touch me or my money, with good reason, to other customers almost at the point of beating down the restroom door. Often, it took more than a normal courteous 5 or 6 minutes to take a dump, wipe, draw up water and the dope, tie off and hit a vein. Finally, unlocking the door, I'd leave walking out amongst glass- eyed stares of disgust, will deserved. If I'd done it right, what did I care. "I'z tweek't" by then. "Man! That's shit was good." I raced, with my body seemingly screaming. No ways did I feel in shape and presentable to go out among the throngs at gay pride. Out among all the beautiful, gorgeous bodies of all shapes colors and flavors. The proudly gleaming gay crowds. What pride did I really have; there was I, just a low-life, homeless junky whore.

All alone, I climbed my way down to the first floor of the squat. Blistering bright, June sunlight broke through the windows. The only brightness among the filthy surroundings, the garage-like space literally splayed with refuge. The smell ignored. Easy to accomplish when I got so high to point my senses went to overdrive, almost in reverse. Either that or I, myself, smelled so bad I commanded my olfactory nerves to turn off. I did have some decency. At least I went next door to Mickey D's to take a shit. Fellow squatters be like, "Fuck it!" And go downstairs to do #2.

Here on a bright summer day, Pride Day, I scavenged and picked through useless trash. The smell of excrement concealed in the air. Surely, rats probably crawled underneath. All this due to my state of intoxication. My pride.

Sunday morning, right before the Pride parade was scheduled to proceed down Market Street among the many thousands of queers, faggots, queens and dykes, etc. By happenstance I met with an attractive dude visiting the festival activities from Detroit

We both, in homage to the 'national gay holiday' atmosphere were pumped up high on meth, in the throes of pursuing sex till we dropped. Having looked in one other's eyes with approval for fucking, not many words required.

We decamped to his hotel room at the Holiday Inn, on Van Ness. The site of where I often slyly made my way, past the front desk, to the first floor restroom to coolly shoot up dope. In the span of mere minutes, we were naked on the carpeted floor of the room. We advanced to becoming sweaty, sliming back and forth. Total sexual inebriation. A nasty scene ensued devoid of any intimacy, unless the sucking and poking of holes, bodily appendages substitute human intimacy. Pleasurable or not neither of us could stop, let go and pull oneself away. Detroiter had to pay extra fees as the phone, more than once, interrupted our animalistic sex ritual, informing him he was late checking out of the room.

What did I care? I had nowhere to go, I could continue the sex feast at least till the dope ran out. The times, my existence.

Meanwhile back at the ranch, one of my first times squatting, I remember looking around behind us to see if we had been followed, just like a tweeker would do, as if our junky asses carried some top- secret info. Olive and Tommy took the lead as I followed up the stairway in the darkness, guided by only the dim flickering light of a disposable lighter. This being my first time ever squatting in a vacant building. Mustering all my courage to trust Olive, not Tommy, to spend a night illegally trespassing. Both of them younger, White and less concerned about making an issue that could bring on an incident with cops. "Plus, what mice and rats!" My mortal fear. Weren't they to be expected lurking around in a dirty abandoned building? Again, trusting Olive and having a real bad desire to sleep indoors that night, it happened to be chilly out with me being on the backside of a comedown.

After some time in the dark, we settled a 'suitable' room upstairs. One of them lit a candle they had found; someone having left it there previously. Seeing my surroundings in the fuller, yet dim, light, I began to feel calmer and more at ease. "This' almost like somebody's… bedroom." I said, as they both giggled to my left field comment.

"Olive's bedroom" Tommy came back.

"Right, right" I heard Olive respond, over her giggling.

As we all laid down on the floor carpet, each having built some form of a makeshift sleeping cot, from clothes and jackets with backpacks serving as our pillows. There may have been one small blanket. Both of us 'men' being chivalrous, that evening, gave the blanket over to Olive. I remember laying there and the conversation turned to discussing either when each of us first ended up on the streets or, me, my first incident experiencing knowing I was gay.

As bad and mean as those streets were, I'll always say, "I grew up there." Meaning; that's the place where I learned and began to form my ethical nature. The ethics I carried till they were amended in recovery. In those few tender moments, even among dopers, life tended to became more real. We bared, sometimes with our clothes on, glimpses of our real selves, with one another. Not too often, we felt comfortable to let our well-built amour down.

"I'm half a fag!" Tommy interjected across the room lastly that night, seeking effort to bond with Olive and me. I knew also that he'd never admit to what he just said out on the street. Tommy felt comfortable too, there that night, safe with that plain, funky, tweek-skinny White homegirl; Olive.

The Gig Was Up (1994)

Once, talking to a street outreach counselor, I described my drug use and addiction as maintenance. Certainly, I was a junky using way too much to hold down anything close to resembling a steady legit job. Just the same, not so desperately strung out to the point of committing felonies for my habit with a direct way to a life in prison. I held myself in proud esteem to be in a low-bottom holding pattern, as addicts go.

The ingredients that glued together my junky status included a welfare check, possessing relatively still youthful 'loins, marketable out there on a dark street corner plus, and lastly, a volunteer commitment I did once a week. This my only true link to the 'real' world, the world beyond the drug-hazed fog in which I habituated. Possibly, my attempt at normal human living stemmed from having actual four walls with a locked door and regular access to a toilet and bathing facilities and, let's not forget, heat. This contrasted with other periods of my addiction era where I'd be. *"Fuck it! I don't need no a fuck'n room...I got this!"* Was I going soft, losing my 'game'? Beginning to get used to actually sleeping in a bed when I finally did sleep.

Addiction continued. No longer did I hold notions other than seeing myself as anything but a dope fiend. Twisted pride and denial led me to hold up my drug habit as a sorta badge of honor. The Good Lord made everyone from housewives to doctors to policemen. Eventually, in the scheme, some people had to be junkies. At least I knew my place in the world. I maintained and stuck with that reasoning or unreasoning as it was, as long as circumstances remained relatively the same. The four walls with the door that locked served to keep the world and the progression of addiction at bay, for a while at least. If the rent got paid and I didn't burn down the place, I stayed contented and alone in my own tweekdom.

One day addiction's progression totally humiliated me with good reason. Having been up for days, high, tweeked and locked deep inside my skid row room, cracks in the walls, radio loudly blasting out tunes, various porn images splayed across the room floor and the bed. This, the throes of a compulsive masturbation marathon, me butt naked, sweaty, greasy from nearly head to toe, teeth grinding, mouth and jaws locked. Bam! Bam! Bam! A fiercely loud knock seemingly attacked outside the door, followed a minute or so later, Bam! Bam! Bam! Expecting absolutely no one, there was no way I was answering that door. *"Stay absolutely...fuck'n quiet....don't breathe"* I tried to act so as if whoever, some fiending tweeker probably, would just finally decide to give up and go away. Next, to my utter horror and surprise, I heard the lock turn, and the door began to open as I was naked and panicked; split second, I rushed up to get behind the door and tried to shove it closed.

"Board of Health monthly inspections!" Some non-descript city bureaucrat shouted out. Surely surprised too.

"Poor thing!"

"Ha...huh, what.!" Abruptly returned to the world of the present, my words almost unintelligible. Feeling maybe the lowest I may have ever felt in my life. I darted my eyes away from the stares of the two other humans standing there. My filthy, animalistic, drug-fueled bubble having been popped. The whole matter was over in five minutes tops. Embarrassed and humiliated as that whole demeaning scene made me feel, another shot of chemical delusion pumped into my veins made it disappear. Good thing that I'd had some more meth on hand to soothe such debased 'rough' spots.

My high would stretch for as long and as much as the selling my ass could pay for. Somewhere slightly under a gram of meth sustained me for a length of complete 48 hours or so. My typical john paid around $30 per fuck act, in turn, purchased about two $20 bags. By day three, in order to be able to get high enough to feel a "rush," the real purpose a 'speed freak' does dope in the first place, my tolerance required doing 3 quarters to a gram in one single shot. Anything less, after that many hours up, just led to what we called 'sketch" or what was really psychosis; hearing and seeing delusions of things that actually weren't happening.

Selling my flesh carried a marketplace to dope tolerance limit. Day 3 usually means time to wind things down, no matter how much my body and my being still craved and fiend more meth. Yeah, just about 3 days signaled it was time to put my worn-out mind, worn-out body, and most certainly worn-out dick to rest and get some well-needed, humanly required sleep. When I was high, the constant companion of my radio switched either from loud music, up and down the FM dial as moods took me, or to National Public Radio. Certainly, I may have been the most intellectually informed tweeker in San Francisco, the Tenderloin for sure.

Another extended night's high, I recall; a Sunday, I believe. Just as I could feel my eyelids start to grow heavy and close for the first time in almost 50 or so hours, I heard the news over the radio, "Los Angeles police are investigating the death of the wife of former pro football star, O.J. Simpson."

"Why in the hell does that washed up fucker's wife make national news?" Hazily I wandered before I soon crashed off, comatose-like, into almost hibernation. I'd sleep for nearly the

whole next day or so. My pattern, when I could best keep to it, okayed me to sleep off the weekend of intense tweeking. Withdrawing from meth's downside, side effects throughout all of Monday, therefore, I'd be recovered just enough to be some ways nearly presentable as a human person; Tuesday. Recovered just enough to rejoin the 'real' world, like my volunteer commitment at Project Open Hand. The only effort in which I earnestly did my best to show up was not high on dope. My gig volunteering, I believed, allowed there to be some integrity associated with my name, in spite of me being a junky.

That particular Tuesday, I awoke from my near coma as NPR on the radio still announced headline news about O.J. Simpson at the top of each hour. Project Open Hand was located at the crossroads of Church and Duboce Streets, a major bus and trolley stop. My weekend of tweek left me too broke to even have the $1 bus fare. So, I walked quickly along Market Street the mile or so distance. Traversing the stoplights and blocks along the way, my thoughts couldn't stop pondering why *the* national media concerned itself with the domestic concerns of a kinda washed up, minor, Black celebrity. *"She must be WHITE!"* I maybe said aloud to no one except the airspace in front of me. *"Yeah! That's it. It's because she White, that its national news."* I arrived walking in at my appointed time commitment, 1-4 pm.

"Chile...you done heard bout O.J. kill'n his wife?" Was the blurted greeting I got from Lester, a fellow volunteer, on my arrival. Usually, it was normal for him to fill me in on the latest gossip. A 'queen' from the old school, back in the early days of urban gaydom. Lester appeared as if he could be of Black and or Latino heritage. Anyway, "back in the day," as I could hear him say, "all of us folks who wutn't White had to hang together." Meeting Lester gave me an actual link back to a Black gay past, a fringe benefit of living in the gay ghetto. In the 'ghetto,' one experiences and mingles amongst all elements of the 'life,' all colors, black, white, brown, yellow, and those in between, those of high and low class, rich and poor, alongside those of idealized beauty as well as those with looks that they'd be grateful if anyone noticed them at all.

Brett, another fellow volunteer, a white guy in his forties, befriended me also at Project Open Hand. Often, he delighted me with his 'tales of the City' of earlier days when gay baby boomers flocked to San Francisco in the '70s, turning it into the mecca it still was when I fled to its shores. Brett's tales came with less 'color,' both figuratively and literally, than the bawdy stories Lester shared.

That day though, the murder of Nicole Brown Simpson, the White blond former wife of O.J. Simpson, spewed forth from many tongues as if it was the most important thing in the world.

"She's white... ain't she?" I questioned Brett. He nodded in affirmation of that fact.

"Yeah, she was…" he answered, acknowledging the nagging, unflattering racism as the reason for all the over-blown media coverage. Someone somewhere even found a television to put into the lobby that day for the sole purpose of not missing any of the latest gory, salacious news coverage. It was now nearly a decade; I'd lived on my own, without a television. In the days and weeks to follow, all the wall-to-wall CNN cable-style news slash entertainment caught me off guard, absurd to say the least. Later that week, without a TV, even I heard of the 'freeway police chase' seen around the world covered by every station in real-time. All this happening in the city I formerly called home, just some 395 miles to the south.

Project Open Hand (a meals program for HIV/AIDS patients) integrated me into further 'community.' Yes, I participated in a community of dope-fiend'n, hustlers, and hoes. Living the reality of such, being almost totally self-centered and addicted, left me in a world of doping alongside the ins and outs of selling my body to obtain the drugs. That was the breadth of my life.

At Open Hand, I chose to be there. It required me to make some effort to remain there. Some of the same circles of my drug life intersected at POH too. By sheer luck and blessing, I happened to somehow remain HIV negative, but I volunteered just the same as others who were positive. Meaning, on some level, fully selfish me gave of myself for something outside of my own self-interest. The gesture was not totally altruistic, and often, I supplemented feeding myself via meals from my volunteering. There, I had this time as my own; I felt comfortable dressing to please no one other than myself. In contrast to the hoe stroll, when I attired to present the most masculine image possible, which wasn't much. I sauntered in on Tuesdays in pants as tight and feminine- reflective as I pleased, dangling bracelets and earrings to my delight. My tall, long, then skinny, Black self came reflecting the gender androgyny I packaged myself. My most inner self. That androgyny I'd been ever since a boy. More than a time or two, I showed up naturally 'fabulous' to feel right at home.

Being in Lester's loud, visibly hood if not Black manners and presence allowed me to envision someone like myself having lived in an earlier time and era. He'd come up and of age in Detroit. Back when the Motor City still promised dreams to working-class folks of color. "Chile... Daddy Franklin's (referring to Reverend C. L. Franklin, the father of the 'Queen of Soul,' Aretha Franklin) church the chill'ren..carried on! Yes, we did!" He told me how church services included numbers of gays and 'queens' populating the pews, sing'n, and shouting on Sundays there. I remember him telling me a scandalous tale of, "deal'n her'ron up in there too." There was no way to prove the truth of what he told me. I did know that that congregation held prominent regard in the life and lives of Black Detroit following World War Two. Listening to NPR, I knew of Martin Luther King gathering at Franklin's Church during times of the Civil Rights Era. My own aunt and cousins lived there during those same times. His stories pricked my ears and a budding interest in things historical. Lester connected me as a Black gay man to the times, those places and spaces I was growing in desire to learn more about. Through him, I could see myself as having been one of the 'chill'ren' carrying on back in the day.

Lester's boisterousness no less diminished due in essence to his own ravages of HIV/AIDS illness. On what seemed like any typical Tuesday, volunteering, the sun shone brightly at 1 pm, when I was always due to start my shift. During a moment when we both took a break when we had few if any clients being served. I sat down at a round table across from Lester. He looked over to me, squarely in my eyes, in a manner more serious than was his usual. "Juan...you know my doctor says... I only got a few weeks or less... to live." Lester spoke to me plainly.

Incredulous and somewhat shocked at what I'd just heard him say, I returned, "Child'e what you talk'n bout...them doctors don't know everything." Scared at what he was saying, "quit talking like that!" I ended. Undeterred by my meager attempt to be upbeat, Lester felt that he was simply stating the fact of his impending mortality. "Naw...now really gurl!" I tried to change the subject, as I recall. More so out of disbelief at the fact that Lester seemed to be trying to tell me goodbye. Minutes later, after having had our morbid conversation, I remember overhearing him in the restroom behind a closed door, coughing so guttural and loud as if to sound like his lung were about to come out of his body. *"Man... maybe he really is sick,"* for a few seconds, I allowed that thought to pass for a moment.

Arriving the next Tuesday, at 1 pm. "Hey, Brett," I said, greeting him while putting on my apron to work my volunteer shift.

"Juan...Lester died," Brett gently informed me, looking forlorn, "His memorial is this Saturday." I'd heard him, heard what he said. But all that afternoon, I felt stunned, just absolutely stunned. The whole atmosphere there now seemed different, different as if a powerful wind swept through the place, leaving all objects and things intact, only carrying away ghosts and spirits. None of us could touch it, yet, the spirit of Project Open Hand had gone. Some part of my spirit was gone too. I had not believed him. *"He was right. He knew he was going to die!"* Such thoughts rang loudly around my head, remembering our conversation just the week before.

That same day that I'd heard of Lester's death, I awoke from a deep nightmare late that night. My body felt chills; I recall haunted visions all cause I did not tell my friend goodbye when I had had the chance. Wednesday, the next day, I distinctly remember it being the 10th of the month. That date I knew, anticipated, because that date, each month,

I got disbursed my food stamps. $150 worth that I took to the Tenderloin and semi-clandestinely (it was seemingly out in the open) traded them in for cash to the Asian 'mamasans' hanging around just outside the check cashing outlets. Cash so I could buy dope, usually meaning I'd be good and tweeked out for a good day or two maybe three. Plus, it meant I could get high on my own terms. Not having to perform or suck dick at the whims of some older man.

Yet, that particular Wednesday, the 10th, I made my way to a payphone to call Drew. I called to ask him if I could come by, not to pick up a trick, only just to have somewhere to be. I did not want to go back to my room, where I'd woken from that nightmare. Drew had since retired, and I figured for certain he'd be at home. Upon my arrival, walking me to the kitchen table, he offers me a drink. He wondered why I'd requested to come over in the middle of the day on a Wednesday. "Lester... at Project Open Hand died yesterday," I informed Drew as he poured me a glass of the white wine he was drinking. "I just...didn't want to be alone." At a loss for words to convey how monumentally spooked I was. Spooked to the point of my super junky ass passing up the chance to get high. *"Stop the presses!"*

Drew encouraged me to stay and have dinner with him, giving me space to talk it out, whatever the hell I was feeling. Looking back, even then, as a strung-out dope fiend, I couldn't mask feeling empathy toward my fellow human travelers.

What had bolted me out of my usual drug-hazed, jaded numbness lay in the fact that I had witnessed a man, Lester, clearly look me straight in my eye and tell me he knew that he would be dead soon. Remembering that day, the way in which he showed no sorrow, felt no remorse, no bitterness to that fact. Thinking of my last encounter with Lester. I had seen and had been a witness to the bravest encounter I'd ever seen or would see since. Lester understood and accepted, like all 'acts' in this world, that they eventually end. That experience, at the least, beheld a man accepting his fate, if not so boldly, yet, ready and willing to meet his maker.

On the day of Lester's memorial that weekend, I'd since returned to my reliably junky habits and ways. The actual afternoon, my state of sweaty, sleep-deprived, teeth-grinding tweekness left me nowhere able to show up and make a respectable appearance at a venue such as a memorial. Deep down, as much as I truly wanted to honor him, I took solace. *"Chile...Lester could understand a sista...got ta do what they gotta do!"* Anyway, memorials are meant for the living; surely, as I knew, Lester no longer lived in this worldly flesh.

In the aftermath of his death, Brett and I ended up forming a closer bond in his absence. As I think back on the times Brett and I shared, I believe he may have been in recovery from alcohol and drugs. Brett regaled me with stories of the 'hippie' days in and around the tail end of the 60s. "If you were cute...and had long hair...you'd get anything," I remembered him saying to me with a twinge of lingering bitterness. He left out the fact that one also needed to be white to be thoroughly included in those festive days. I guess being blond implied it. Somewhere in our conversations while volunteering, I must have mentioned my unfamiliarity with the other 'left' coast, Berkeley. So, we decided to make a mission to go there together, at Brett's urging.

Brett arrived on the agreed date and picked me up from my skid row welfare hotel room at 6th and Mission Streets. A bright afternoon as I remember. Maybe to assuage my evident embarrassment, he shared that he'd once lived in similar environments at times in his past. We took off cruising up and out beyond the dirt and desolation of 6th Street. At 65 mph, like some California fantasy, we crossed over the Bay Bridge in his blue convertible MG, top-down, no hair blowing in the wind, though, neither my kinky tresses nor Brett's baldness, sun shining on our backs.

We parked the convertible and walked to a restaurant of Russian cuisine located on Telegraph Avenue, deep in central Berkeley. Brett intended to introduce me to something I'd never experienced; borscht. I had recalled reading, in the "Good War" by Studs Terkel, of this having been the staple food of Russian World War Two survivors. 'It's...not really too bad." I stated in approval, now having eaten for myself. *"If I'd been one of those desperate starving Russians... I could've eaten this every day."*

Brett's friendship and tutelage proved short-lived. He, too, died within a few months after Lester. To me, he'd always appeared upbeat and healthy. So, his sudden demise and death caught me off guard as well.

Thinking back today, maybe Lester's seeming braveness in the face of death provided Brett an example to have the courage to face his own.

Nonetheless, such was the hard reality of HIV/AIDs in those times, precluding the antiviral drug cocktails that would soon enter the realm to extend people's lives and change the nature of the disease's grasp on the community and the 'life.'

Disillusionment from an over-mediated era forsaking holding up the truth, yet giving back un-reality. What felt like reality. Having been within the touch of witnessing a brave soul meeting death just as boldly as he'd lived, without fear...to say I'd been changed is an understatement.

Hollyweird (1994)

Homelessness honed and helped refine hardcore skills as a junky hustler. Getting evicted the previous year left me with absolute 'freedom' and abandon to pursue the depths of crystal methdom. Now, I'd only be available for 'outcalls' to turn tricks. Throwing any pretense aside, I accepted the fact that every dollar earned leasing the use of my body got spent toward filling my body, those same loins, with meth. Some of my so-called clientele had use of me on a regular basis such as a college professor and a plumbing hardware salesman. Turning a trick with the salesman might entail an excursion across the aesthetically beautiful world renowned, Golden Gate Bridge to his home out in Marin County.

One of oddest 'regulars' was a compact nondescript, Asian guy; Mike, who worked at some well-paying position in the City government. Very meticulous about hygiene he always insisted on me using double condoms. Mike picked me up out on the street and we'd walk to one of the hot tub spas. The spas, thinking on it, were a special quark of San Francisco. They just had to be a legitimate front intended in the service of prostitution. You could rent a room with a hot tub for use by the hour.

Definitely I earned the fee for my services. Oftentimes it was hit and miss, then finally, after hours plying my wares to no avail I'd hook up with a john. Sometimes, right before the point I'd almost given up.

That all that changed one particular weekend, the hooker gods seemed to smile down upon humble me. I began and took off on a 48- hour long continuous tricking binge, one seemingly right after another. Such never had happened before or thereafter since.

Friday evening just as the sun was about to set, casting a hazy orange glow across the sky overhead, I ran into Mike. We walked and agreed to our usual exchange yet, when he learned of my homelessness, he offered to get me a room, a cheap flop house room, a room nonetheless, down along 6th Street just south of Market. "I want to...get with you again... tomorrow," Mike tells me and, then, I realize that getting me the hotel room was insurance to guarantee use my body the next day. Anyway, facilitating two guaranteed for sure tricks lined up, worked quite alright for me too.

Mike's thing', what he desired; was to see himself being fucked by a Black man while dressed in black fishnet stockings, a garter, and bra and lastly, yet oh so important, 4-inch, black patent leather pumps. One wall of the spa room was covered in mirrors, enabling him to watch himself in action, all a part of his trip. I got the sense of Mike being deeply closeted about his homosexual proclivities. After he'd go on his wild 'trip', he could slip back into obscure normality. Just another inconspicuous Asian guy in the City, San Francisco, especially, being the most Asian of American cities.

This evening, as always, Mike took me to the hot tubs. He seemed to be more flush spending cash than was his usual. My usual, immediately afterwards, to go cop some speed. On this evening to tweek through the night in my cheap dirty hotel room with no radio or TV; no noise. Tweeking without some noise distraction, indoors at least, is like as if hearing the paint peeling. This left me in a room up on the fourth floor to hear all the sounds emanating up from the street below. All the sounds and noises of down and out drunks, junkies and crackheads roaming in the night. Tweeked out on meth heightened my hearing, to the point where it felt as if I just might as well had out on those filthy sidewalks and alleys myself. It seemed like I could hear every conversation, every drug hook up, every eventual argument and a fallout amongst junkies, over who got the larger share of the dope stash, over who and who hadn't paid for the dope, giving them rights to do more of the dope. The voices and the yelling peaked around half past 2 AM; the last chance to buy booze for the night. As liquids and chemicals passed through the mouths, veins and bloodstreams, noises became fewer and farther between till, there seemed to be just one or two lone voices mingled betwixt loud lurches of Muni buses and garbage trucks making early morning rounds. Then, once again, the sun rose. Having risen as I'm there more that wide awake, buzzing, needing, craving to do my last remaining bit of dope.

That last dope needed to last till Mike was due for me, again, at noon for my next bag of tricks, round two. If nothing else came through before then, Mike would be just in the nick of time as my high would be wearing off. In spite of meth withdrawal making my nerves on the edge of fraying, considering myself the 'professional' I felt I was, most certainly I'd be able to maintain sexual performance enough to get paid. 'Concentrating' entailed me thinking of how, no fantasizing, how good that next shot of dope was gonna feel. I psyched myself up to ejaculate as was needed.

Morning blurred by spending the hours lurking, feeling dirt in the air, fiend'n, in and out of the porn peeps up on Polk. Thinking, walking the booths, I'd just might get lucky and snag a quick suck or jerk, easy money with porn for extra stimulation.

Mike showed up at noon, exactly punctual, exactly at the predetermined location, like a stereotype for Asians. All I could care about was getting the sex done and over with, anticipating, craving, that next hit of dope. Just like a speed freak, once the 'run', the high, begins and you never want it to end.

Right away, I see Mike toting along a rather large duffle bag with us this time. Always he'd have a bag full of his needed 'accessories'. "What did he have up his sleeve ...up his fishnets... more like it?" Once we got inside the room at the hot tubs, I see him reach in the duffle bag and pull out a tripod and video camera. Mike started setting it up, aimed toward the mirrored wall. "You taping this… so you don't have to come back," I voiced out my assessment of what I was seeing.

"No, no…. That's not...it," Mike lied answering my response, in his soft-spoken Asian manner. It was obvious. I knew what was up. He'd record the scene to use for his pleasure, at his leisure, whenever. Thinking now, I could have refused being recorded, giving him the need to return again for the pleasure of my 'services'. Probably, Mike even with all that preparation, still would have gone ahead and paid me for our transaction in spite of my refusing to be videotaped. At the least, I could have charged more for being filmed.

Nevertheless, as a broke down junky hustler my primary goal dealt with just getting him off. The quicker that happened, the sooner and the quicker there'd be meth refilling my veins. What did I care there'd be a porn tape with my face, my body, and all I'd got in payment was $30 alongside the ending of a regular customer? "Fuck'n junky!" What did I expect?

Finished the scene with Mike. Off I went in pursuit of my next hit. Now, on day two of this run. Desperately in need of a fix I go and cop dope from Joel; just some hustler I knew, and the fact that there happened to be no one else out and around at that moment. I trusted him and he sold me a fake hit of dope. Off wherever I went to shoot up, minutes after pulling out the point(syringe), I didn't feel a thing. "Imma… fuck you up!" I shout as I see him. He darts away with a quickness at my approach coming up Polk Street.

All in the process of that fuckhead Joel acknowledging his scheming, and that, "Yes!" I could kick his ass. Just before blood pours, it happened to end because I was spotted and picked up by another of my regular johns. Lucky for Joel.

David lived somewhere down the peninsula, south of the City. I'd been to his home to trick before. Lucky for me, that day, he had a hotel room up in the City. Always, he'd have me lying on my stomach, then, he'd climb on my back, dick between my legs, to simulate fucking me till he shot off his load. Again, what did I care? The quicker he got off, the faster I'd get to continue my stream of crystal meth.

Now, this time back on Polk, I show a little more patience and got hooked up to the real shit. "Awhh…! The blast that refreshes." Just like that tagline in the soda commercial, junkies' humor. Walking pass where see Joel standing, delivering a smirk, signaling that he owed me and yet, his scandalous ways had not fucked up my getting high, not this day anyway. "Yeah," just knowing he'd not got the best of me. I'd get my revenge when he least expected it. Tweeking, right then, I couldn't be bothered with his low life ass.

As the sun crawled lower across the sky, later on day two, there I was my junky tweeked out self, again, selling my ass right at the corner of Polk and Myrtle Alley, just between O'Farrell and Geary. The apartment tower that faced O'Farrell Street had a windowless alcove, the fire exit at street level on Polk. The spot chosen for displaying my wares. Driving past in a car one would barely even notice a Black, dope fiend'n hustler holding up a wall. Just as I liked it, almost incognito.

Standing there right before it really got dark, a grey Chevy Malibu drove by. I'd seen the guy circle the block more than once. Yet, what I noticed more was that the type of the car, looked like the ones the vice cops used. Standard vehicle, plain, no frills, those used as unmarked. "Naw Naw…. Hell naw!" I blurted out to no one but myself. "This hoe know better... than that damn obvious cop car." Just then, the Malibu had circled back and turned onto Myrtle Alley, pulled ahead a little and stopped. Curious at least, I slowly sauntered toward the car and took notice, what my eyes were seeing. Oddly, the driver looked too old to be a vice cop or any cop really. Still, I felt spooked by his car looking like unmarked police. Add to that, I also, just couldn't believe my luck, one trick right after another. That's how I'd always gotten busted before, just when it seemed to be too good to be true. It was!

As the car stood there stopped, he wanted me. "Get in!" He said through the downed passenger window.

I'm thinking, "Whatever you do... don't mention nothing… bout no money." While opening the passenger door and I got in.

"What you out doing?" The driver asked me, looking way too old to be a cop. Yet still something made me feel leery.

"Look'n to get in ta some party'n" I responded in my slickest street-honed hustler tone, "You know."

As the Malibu rounded the block and headed west up Geary, "How much are... you talking about?" the old dude prompts me for a price or maybe a setup.

"You know...just get into it really…we'll see how go" I obfuscate answering him. Believing I'd be safe from being arrested as long as no 'price' was actually mentioned. Within a few nervous minutes old dude pulls the car into the parking lot of a senior apartment complex, just south of the prominent St. Mary's Cathedral, derisively referred to as the washing machine, due to its modern Brutalist architecture.

For certain, now, I knew this old guy was no cop. He looked as if to be 70, if not maybe older. Following him entering his small apartment I can detect the old dude's tweeking. I've yet to mention a price. Of course, it's just implied were going to have sex or some facsimile of.

This was just the weirdest. Even for my jaded hella, been-around-the block ass. The senior gentleman led me to his freezer, where there laid two cold-chilled syringes filled with speed. Amazed at what is happening and, actually, just a little anxious 'pops' being too damn old to be slamming dope. And going against my streetwise judgement of 'never letting someone else fix up my hit of dope. But who was I trying to fool? Just like a broke ass junky, I knew that within minutes, more dope, more speed, would be searing through my veins into my bloodstream, my brain cells. "Thirty dollars." I mumbled out the hard currency price for my 'services'. Not too sure if he'd actually heard me say it, before I shot up his cocktail of dope.

As much as I considered myself a professional 'hoe', performing my best, if only just to keep a satisfied, paying, return customer. Still, I loved meth even better and if given enough, at some point I just became fucking 'twacked'! There I lay all bare-assed, heart racing and sweaty, as the hardcore gay porn played on the TV screen across from where we were on the couch. The remote control was so greasy to be useless, as was I useless to perform. The best I could do was to grab my dick and stare, eyes dilated, at the naked moving images. Too high and out of my mind. My senior citizen customer and addict constantly, as was his due, reprimanded me to get busy servicing him. Which I'd half-assed proceed to do till a minute or two later I'd wonder off. As a hooker, I know I cheated him. What could I have done? I simply was too frigging high.

The scene hours later, after all the groping, sweating and frustration of not getting his 'nut', the old fella gave up and, still, paid me. We got dressed, got back in the Malibu and he dropped me off in front of Frenchy's porno store. With my junky tolerance level, I knew a $30 hit could only make fiend even more desperately for more dope. No matter, I stood there that brisk late evening, early morning, pupils dilated like saucers, funky, teeth grinding, homeless and beginning day three of a dope high. The best solution to my dilemma; porn, more sex and maybe I'd score another trick to get an even bigger hit of dope.

Dilemma: a situation requiring a choice between equally undesirable alternatives. That was my life. Each day my eyes opened. My lungs breathed air. Of the choices I'd made up to that point, all seemed equally detrimental, and they were. The pull and pain of being a junkie draws you in too far to be able to get back out. "Here I am. How do I survive with what I got?" In hindsight, that question was my method of operating.

Functioning with no hindsight, ergo, how I always ended up in a dilemma. Besides, dope helps to put a positive spin on some fucked up shit, at least it does in the present moment.

Ass out, homeless in Frisco. My road buddy for the trip was Miles, a young and pretty boy. In spite of his youth and beauty, Miles was nobody's fool when it came to dope and those streets. The slickest streetwise hustler, under 20, I knew of. Way more skilled than I had been at that age. Currently he was staring as the main boy, fuck toy of Hollywood Dave; a small time speed dealer. Hollywood; trailer trash background with always an ever-present baseball cap to disguise his balding crown of long stringy blonde locks.

I circled among, mostly White speed freaks working off and coping with the streets in San Francisco. I'd heard mention this Hollywood Dave's notoriety. That, "he'd just as much rip you off as sell you some bang'n good dope." The deciding factor on being ripped off depended oftentimes on whether Dave was interested in fucking you.

What added to the nefarious reputation as a shady dope connection included him being known for fuck'n um young. Not little boy child young but definitely teenage, under 18, jailbait. Many of us hustlers ourselves, having started our careers sucking dick for money and becoming dope fiends, more than likely were somewhere south of being legal adults too. None of us really had any cause to judge. Still, society's mores lingered even among us, as to someone being a 'chicken hawk' exclusively. Nonetheless, holding a juicy bag of meth as ransom for taking advantage of some young teenager's loins carried with it a certain stench, even out on those mean streets.

Miles, as Dave's main 'boy' had a direct line to obtaining good dope. Yet, even still a pattern seems to have formed. When we both purchased dope together, it always turned out to be the 'bomb', getting me quite high and satisfied. Other times Miles procured meth for me only. What I got back turned out to be highly cut or just plain ripped off altogether. Miles, when I saw him afterwards just shrugged. "Gurrl you know how he is!" I'm thinking, "Why the hell am I going through Miles' ass for!"

A later incident proved a change in my opinion of Hollywood, leading me to a much better dope connection whereby my career in junkiedom furthered too. Hanging around David; one of my few Black, 'road dogs', as he just happened to roll up to Polk one night in a hot stolen car. David didn't hustle. He mostly showed up on the scene already high looking to get a fuck on or as many fucks as he could get. We first met one another from back when he and his twin brother lived in the same building as I, on Turk Street. We all had long since lost our apartments due to irresponsibility of our drug use. David's twin, by then, had also died of HIV/AIDs. Such the life of the times.

David, that dark shady night, nonchalantly explained away his thievery "I....was out at General (SF General Hospital)." Probably, at one of the clinics to get treatment for his own HIV. "I'm there...there's this car empty... running...keys in the ignition...so, I hoped in and drove off." David said it, as if that's what anybody would have done, given the same circumstances.

Night settled in, hustlers and the johns doing the cat and mouse dance of circling and being circled with all usual sleaze and slime. David, then, surprised me by giving me the keys and leaving me to deal with the 'hot' car. The vehicle happened to be one of the last models of Chevy Novas. Ones that looked like a Toyota Celica. Just as he had stolen someone's car as if that was no big deal, I got it into my head I could easily exchange it for dope. I convinced him the car needed to be gotten rid of, asap, might as well be for dope? Las Vegas bet, he left me the car, just to chase after some hot and inebriated hustler so, he couldn't be bothered.

Under the influence of my drug-addled brain I believed that I'd be stopped by the po' lease, they couldn't prove I had stolen it, only that I happened to be driving it. Paying no attention, seriously, to the fact I lacked a driver's license as well. Craving for that next fix will have you in all kinds of dilemmas.

"Why not get dope for a stolen ride?" The felonious illegality of it all was just a side issue. David trusted me to come back with the 'goods', I too, believed I would do exactly as promised.

Headed off to the apartment building on Bush Street, the same one I'd many of times turned my money over to Miles, only to be burned by that Hollywood Dave dude. Tracking down Kevin, who actually lived there. Kevin, who happened to be 'tight' with my bank robber, homegirl, Jill. "I wanna gram ina half" I insisted with a crazed look emanating from dilated eyeballs.

I'll...go tell Hollywood" Kevin shot back at me. Indicating a sign that the 'car swap deal' did have possibilities.

"And....a....a...I'm only deal'n whit um direct or noth'n" I demanded as the sweat of anticipation ran down along my forehead to coincide with the urge to loose my bowels. Kevin sensing, I meant business told me follow him up to his apartment. A few minutes later Hollywood comes in to sit on the edge of a mattress. He then proceeded to take off his right foot Nike Hi-top and fingered a slit in the tongue of the shoe. I took notice for a somewhat skanky guy he had sexy toes. His beaten battered fingers slid out a fat mini-Ziplock baggie of meth. "All.. I's got on me now... is this...bout a half and a quarter" Dave tells me, looking up at me with his dark dilated pupils. "I can get you the rest...

tomorrow." Like a dog to a sirloin, seeing the dope colored my already flawed decision making for sure.

"What if he didn't come through on the rest of the deal? David would be in my ass!" I had no intention to cross him. For certain David could fuck me up if he wanted to. Still, he had to know the car needed to be gotten rid of, "I'm doing that!" Such questions buzzed in my junky brain as that Ziplock of methamphetamine, right there, settled the decision. Either way I'd handle things after getting high, knowing that that baggie, kept safe deep inside his Nike was the 'real' thing.

"Yeaaah!...That's right" I murmured out as my brain cells felt that 5- second jolt, just as I pulled the point out of the crook of my arm, licking the dark purplish red, methamphetamine-soaked droplets of blood that always leaked from my poked vein. "Good fucking dope handles… everything," thought afterwards.

The next 12 or so hours, half a day, were a meth-addled blur. Filled as was usual probably hunting for sex or with just as many hours passed, eyes glued to viewing porn at the sex shop. If I happened to have gotten too high to be in such confined spaces among people, I'd likely be found traipsing rodent, vermin-like in dark recesses of alleyways searching, bent over, diving in refuge bins.

Next afternoon running, still, on meth fumes as my body, my bones, began to ache, painfully showing manifestations of the wear and tear I put upon mortal carcass. Just the same, then, I possessed not one drop of dope to show in exchange for having sold that hot vehicle. I decided it better and less shady to come clean and show my face. David, at least had to take into account I wasn't hiding from him. "I'd actually only done the amount of dope that woulda been my share anyway." I told myself, using dope fiend'n rationalization.

More than likely I walked all the way out to David's aunt's garage, nearly two miles or so away. All that way from Polk, on my aching blistered feet. For sure, I know I wouldn't have hopped on a bus, cause whenever I was tweeked, the closed ventilation on a bus always had me sweating bullets. Really. Like running a marathon, sweating, paranoid that everybody's looking at me. I scrambled up to the white clapboard garage door, of the address David had given me, on a street between Fillmore and Divisadero. David was being allowed to reside in his aunt's garage. "I'm...spossed to get the other half when… I call um today" I tell David in my best pleading earnestness. Some 'straight, rough trade' brotha, there also in that garage, held more of David's rapt attention than whatever my speed freak ass had been concerned about.Yet, I felt it right that I'd come over and shown my face.

Waiting by a payphone, I dialed his pager, via my dumpster-dived scored, and stolen, Pacific Bell corporate phone card. About 5 minutes later, Hollywood called me back to set up where to meet him for the residual dope quantity. They pulled into the strip mall parking lot, David and I opened the doors and got in that, still, 'hot' vehicle. David wanted to make sure he got at least some of the dope this time. "A half an a quarter...right," I say out to Dave and Kevin. Kevin serving the role as chauffeur for the day. As I was passed, across the front seat, the little baggie, sure enough, it was 3 quarters of a gram. Exactly almost as if it had been weighed on a scale. As a seasoned dope fiend, speed freak I sat there in the back seat amazed. Not only had he answered the page, which he didn't have to, he also kept his word on the dope deal. No scam whatsoever. That just didn't happen on them mean streets. Keeping his word allowed me good standing with David as well, saving my ass that day.

After all the scandalous talk I heard of him we developed into an extended 'dopeship'; the cross between dope fiend and connect. What serves as a friendship in such dependent associations. That treasured association as it was, helped provide steady access along to road to be even further strung out.

Silly freak Tweek'n for Kids (1994)

I simply grew out smoking marijuana, my first drug of choice. Put another way, I 'graduated' up to bigger and better things, substances. About the time of high school, one real good joint, nowadays called a blunt, really have me flying high. But anything beyond smoking two joints was a wasted. If I toked more I didn't feel any higher. Ah, the good ole days. Nothing heightened the atmosphere or scene going on by smoking more than that.

Early days in my love affair to speed and career on the way to being strung out, the high fit me just right. Doing more dope made me higher and I could feel it. Again, for the time, a relatively modest amount crystal meth lasted a good long while in my system. That 'good long high' threshold lasted most of my twenties. Eventually, that came to its end. 'What goes up must come down'.

Simple physical body tolerance grew over time. I needed more and more speed to maintain the high I'd come to know and love. I craved more too. Then, the twisted handle of addiction took hold. Then, even as my body craved and could handle more meth, my mind and my psyche flew off the other way. The more dope taken into my body the screwier I seemed to become. 'Sketch', the term we called it on the streets. Actual psychosis is what it was. The ugly hateful, delusional, multi-headed creature via methamphetamine abuse began making a recurring role in my life. The existence I called my life.

Typically, my habit was to cop a half or just under 2/3rds gram of dope. Did a good fat shot up into my veins, the one vein on the backside of my elbow. I would do about half of the half. The shot would have me flyin, tweeking a full 12 to 16 hrs. Going into day two, I'd do the other half of the dope which would carry me flying through to day three, well past the 48-hr mark. Right about then danger began to set in. The point past the red mark on the metaphorical dial. The point that, in order to get 'high' I'd need to shoot up nearly a whole gram of dope in one single needle hit. That would really only maintain that current level of 'tweek'. A shot of that much dope cost anywhere from $80 to $100 to purchase. Even on my best nights selling my ass on Polk I didn't pull in such rates, not all in one session with a john, two to three maybe. Fiending for hit, what speed freak junky is going to wait that long to get a full $100? Danger sets in, cause, if I got any dope, less than a gram, I'd go ahead and shoot it anyway. Even knowing I was not going to get any higher. What's more likely to happen, at that juncture, more speed on left me frustrated, jones'n for more, irritable and paranoid.

Salvation could be on the horizon if I would choose to simply take my ass to sleep. Even the sun eventually goes down. After a good 15 or so hours of sleep my body would feel rested. An appetite reappeared, craving something sweet. After I'd stuffed my pie hole sufficiently, that in turn put me in for another round of near comatose sleep. Sleeping for two days and not getting high. Afterward I considered myself a normal sober humanoid. Another physical telltale sign of normalcy had me over a toilet seat moaning with a painful bowel movement. Three to four days of not eating or taking a shit, what did remain in my colon came out hard as a rock. Fun stuff.

Yet, by this year, this period, sometimes even after nearly two days of resting my body, I could still discover my brain and psyche spinning, screaming. "Motherfucker… I'm not through wit yo ass yet!" Just the normal act of walking down a street, out my eyes, I'd spot or see something, someone, that could and would set me off. For sure I knew 'they' had been following me, spying on me. Intricately involved and paying attention to my every broke down, junky ass moves. Sure, today I know all of that sounds crazy as fuck. But in those meth- fueled remnants everything felt live and real. Often, my brain cells led me to be screaming out loud, full on conversations. Ranting out in public view to persons I felt with certainty were driving me crazy. Insanity I displayed in the least.

My time up and around Polk Street and the Tenderloin I witnessed numbers of delusional freak characters, walking around all alone. Likely you'd hear then coming, due to their screaming into the airspace, at no one, around themselves. "Girlfriend...you shoulda seen him...back in the day… he was so fine and sexy...Look at him now!" I know I heard some veteran queen, hustler, mention sentiments about someone as such, remarking, "it's what happens when you do too much." Meaning too much meth. Such speeded out zombies seemed to just roam the streets, almost like a warning sign. And there was me, on the tail end of every other tweek session or so about ready to join their ranks.

"Is that what my ancestors, who suffered to survive through slavery… through back of the bus racial discrimination and the like," I be wondering, "after all of that, their reward of perseverance would turn out to be my loser ass… roaming the streets of Frisco, talking to myself." Damn! Some posterity.

As desperately as I wanted to deny, it proved harder and harder to keep telling myself the giant lie, that tweeking no matter the circumstances, in the end, was all the party, I believed it to be.

Prime example: Out Wednesday night displaying my carnal wares, as per usual, on Polk. Recalling the night as a bust, my feet started heading back towards my room empty handed and not high. All the sudden I come across this White dude, not too bad looking, just a little pock marked, in his thirties with head of short blond curls. "Hey ...you wanna go party with me?" He propositioned me directly. I wizened knew 'party' to mean; fuck for dope, no money. "I'm up in Two Rock...I'll bring you back," he followed up selling the proposition.

I got the gist that Two Rock was somewheres out past Marin County. Hell, I wasn't doing nothing. "I'd just be skipping the middle part of having to cop dope...going straight to gett'n tweeked and fucking someone I, maybe, didn't want to." Rationalizing. Besides, Friday coming up, the first of the month, and I'd have a (welfare) check waiting on me by the time I got back.

Not paying too much attention on the trip travelling up. Riding in the dark, his ride, as I recall, a remodeled Buick Skylark from maybe like 1964. All I probably looked out as we drove over the Golden Gate Bridge, always a magnificent sight to behold whether or not I was high.

Less than 10 minutes of arriving at his somewhat shabby looking locale, dope got brought out and shot into my veins. Next, I lay there naked as the night is long. A VHS porn video played, on o small TV/ VCR all in one, on the floor across the bedroom. The guy with the blond curls- (referred to as 'curly hair") kept on his Speedo -type underwear, as if he doubted, he intended for us to be doing anything other fucking, that required us both to be buck naked. Noticing that fact, I caught a sense of his coy act of lingering in his underwear as a sign of him looking upon me as his captive creature. Whereas, I felt like, "Mothafucker... you know the drill; dicks, mouths, asses, fingers, gropes!" Business for me disguised the pleasure for him. "Don't play dumb!"

Such circumstances beyond 'formal' transaction of sex-for- hire, if the payor chose to fill me up with my favorite 'poison', then, he should not be too taken aback if I, the paid party, bit him by failing to fulfill my end of providing satisfaction. "Too bad. I'm...too fucking high!"

Curly Hair wanted, intended, me to be 'too high'. Willingly, to a point, I played along. We got busy sexing, then, soon I find myself sweating profusely, panting, almost like out of breath. Sure, amped up on speed one could end up breathless, sweating. But then I looked over across the room, through the dimly lit haze and glow coming emanating from the TV porno, to see glowing red lines of the heat coming from a portable space heater. I slithered over to turn it off. We got back to the action and in less than 15 minutes or so I felt the heat again, enough to have me nearly about to pass out, as hyped up as the dope had me. "It's too hot with that on!" I demanded, glistening in sweat but feeling the fact should've been clearly evident from sweat that had been dripping from my body.

The third time I discovered the heater back on, I'd had enough. "I'mma take a break!" I told him flatly, signaling it wasn't up for negotiation. My intentions getting him either come to my demands or leave me alone to tweek out. For sure, he did not want me to leave. Just the same, my dope fiend ass had not come way the hell out to nowheresville and not get pumped up much dope as possible, especially since I wasn't getting paid. The 'dance' implied waiting one another out. See who'd cave in first.

Our tryst pairing lasted into the next evening, Thursday night. Curly hair decided that adding another body to our mix would keep us riled up for more. This being the early 90's, the burgeoning days of the personal home computer and internet. Then as now, the popularity and explosion of the medium relied on its vehicle for furthering sex and pornography in all forms imaginable. Chat rooms for gay men to hookup and have sex, and in our case do drugs, parlayed us into meeting Victor; a good looking, Latino fellow tweeker possibly his thirties. Curly hair and I drove down to pick him up in San Rafael, the last stop on the Golden Gate Transit bus line, just as it was getting dark. We played dueling back and forth radio station on ride down, not a promising sign.

Round two, night two, dope injected and snorted into blood streams, clothing shed, sex organs, orifices displayed, probed, fingered, licked and mouthed. Arms, legs, torsos writhed back and forth across one another as sweat dripped and commingled bodily fluids. Purely mechanical as the act of sex could be we humans were and are connected via emotional sensitivities. But yet, the lives of gay men, we do this to ourselves.

By then Curly Hair completely had got on my last nerve. Dope or no dope I'd grown tired of his controlling and orchestrating. In general I was tired. "Duh, like 26 plus hours now!" Tired of moving, bending, contorting, being directed. Methamphetamine does not lead to sympathetic bedfellows. Literally. At least he had Victor to play with, I figured.

When daylight broke through on Friday morning, I decided, time go back to the City. That day. The 'master of ceremonies' was having none of that. How dare I come out and shoot up all his dope and he not be satisfied. Never mind the fact, my nearly weekend length performance and effort. Victor, I sensed too, saw through his madness so somewhere in the machinations slipped me $5 for bus fare, for a ride back.

Time and worn out brain cells account for the lack recollection, of exact details. Yet, I seem to remember us having driven Victor back to the bus stop we first picked him up. Why I didn't also get out and just ride the bus ride home, I haven't a clue, only, I surmise the reason to have been greediness and dope related.

Somewhere riding in the car, along those country back roads I got so fed up with Curly Hair's methed-out bullshit I, all the sudden, reached over to grab ahold the steering wheel. For sure, as the vehicle skidded to a stop and he regained control, I yanked out and snatched the car keys. The car a 65 Buick Skylark you could take out the keys, even in gear. There was only two keys on the ring. Across on the other side of the road, behind a wooden fence, grazed some cows in a field, smell and all. "Take that...you fuck!" I screamed at the top of my lungs as I wildly threw the keys across the fence and into what I hoped to be cow dung.

Even with the faded recollection, I remember soon after, the car stalled in the middle of the road, we were encountered by a sheriff patrol car. I didn't sweat it. In such situations I actually a little advantage; the White guy I was with, had no inclination to tell the authorities the real reason why he just so happened to be here, at this exact spot, 7:30 in the morning, with some young wayward, freaked out Black dude. On the other hand, I could tell the cops exactly why my drugged-out personage happened to find himself on the seemingly quiet country road, in broad daylight, high as a kite, alongside this 'upstanding' citizen of Two Rock.

At the end of the tweek explanations, the cops put me in the back of the squad car in order to drive me to my bus stop. All the more to get my shiftless, druggy, Black ass out of their jurisdiction. And, not be their problem. A long bus ride later I arrived back home to my rundown hotel room ready to end the memories of the two previous nights. End the memory with shooting more dope.

About this same epoch, I found myself meeting and getting picked up by an attractive, blond guy, no more than about 5 years older than me. He drove a convertible BMW and lived in a newly built, gentrifying, high rise apartments on Cathedral Hill. We happened upon me a night on Polk. I'd tricked before with other men I'd found to be attractive-translation; "I'd have fucked them without gett'n paid!" Somehow, this dude, this time, proved different than those others before. Maybe cause I was getting older or just a moment of clarity, I could envision myself, in another life, meeting this guy as a potential boyfriend.

This particular 'white prince charming' came with a twist. Here was this male gay man, sexually attracted to me; a male, black gay, even on just those base terms he was off. His sexual desire, fetish, demanded me punching my fist, as hard as I could, onto his testicles. Fucked up, weird. Who knows, maybe if I had not been so attracted to him or the idyll of him, the whole sex scene would not have fazed me.

This period of my sojourn some shit thrown against the metaphorical wall did not just slide right off or at least when it did much residue remained left behind. In times before, I'd just be a good little hooker, hustler, providing my services to a hopefully satisfied customer, making my money for whatever the guy's sexual trip. If he happened to be good looking and hot all the more benefit to me. I got to fill my bloodstream with meth, forget the downside of my actions and on to the next.

Things changed. With each pound of my fist, even in spite of copious amounts of meth, I just couldn't shake off the evil twist of my drugged- out sex nightmare. Longed desired sex-fueled fantasies amplified to the max when I'd be under the tweeking spell.

One lost well remembered weekend, reality, fantasy and sex-drug delusions all whirled together in an explosive epiphany that signaled emotionally the emptiness I could hardly longer deny.

Friday into Saturday began the tweek going. A typical occurrence with exact details either forgotten or unremarkable. Surely shooting methamphetamine, sex with some nondescript older gentleman for money in order to have more sex with another denizen, likely to be similarly tweeked out too many long hours spent holed up alone involved with porn and my hand.

Late Saturday early Sunday morn, I hook up with the BMW, blond high-rise guy. Looking out the window of his splendid view overlooking Cathedral Hill, the City, upon the rising sun, we did a return performance of me playing Muhammad Ali on his nut sack. Interspersing the scene, I ask him to pose in various positions to increase my libido. Needing to distract my mind from the picture of a young gorgeous, male specimen who only achieves sexual pleasure via this bizarre ritual. "Man...I'm really gett'n into this but...I kinda need to take care a something" I lie to the guy as I feel my high wearing off. I might have even indicated directly that I needed more meth, figuring how could he cast an opinion with his fucked-up fetish. "I'll be back in an hour or so." He agreed to the proposal even giving me his phone number. The idea and actually of ball sack boxing wore me out both physically and mentally. More dope I needed!

Departing from his swanky digs, sun bright now. I headed east, downhill through one of the alleyway side streets cross Van Ness, right alongside one of the recently converted boutique tourist hotels. Right there on the sidewalk, my dilated eyes cast downward, I spot out the corner a piece of luggage or maybe like a shopping bag. Assuming my most scandalous street mode, discreetly I moved toward the items, picked them up and quietly continued down the alley, not running and not looking back.

Finding some cubby hole or possibly a space between two parked cars, I scavenged among my 'finders' keepers', ill-begotten treasures. To my good fortune lying within a mass of tourist's clothing, not my size or taste, I find a book of traveler's checks. Treasure for sure but iffy for me. I didn't do checks, on account of getting a felony, if caught. Non-felony, county jail time was the extent of my willingness to do crimes and suffer the consequences of the jail time. Still though, I had no reluctance to pass the checks on to some other braver criminal in exchange for a fee, payable in meth.

"Uhm uhm..That muthafucka is so phine!" I pronounced out to my fellow hustler associates within hearing distance. Such opinionated comments stated my lustful desire of John Paul; 6 feet plus, long strawberry blond locks with kind of dirty Brad Pittesque looks. He having been a recent arrival on the Polk scene, not being yet a dedicated hustler, translation; not gay. That fact may have made him all the more desirable, live embodiment of my fantasies.

In the throes, of recently, I felt less and less in control of my fantasy world. Lustfulness overwhelmed my being, seemed hardly I could distinguish among reality and fabrication, deeply high on speed. Did it matter? Did I care?

There he was. Here I was with enough money to get plenty of dope and unfulfilled desires.

Cut to the chase; I returned back to Cathedral Hill to finish up action with BMW ball sack dude, got paid again and returned to Polk. After effects of scrotum boxing leaving me even more in pursuit of my own pent up sex lusts. I find and then buy dope with my regular connection making sure to drop the fact I had plenty money for more dope. I recall myself portraying a 'king of the world' like attitude. "Wanna git high?" I question John Paul almost like a command, "Come wit me!" That's where things get implicit. In my questioning it's implied, in this environment, we are going to be doing speed. I'd previously intoned from my vocal flirtations that I wanted to use him, use his body sexually in exchange for that 'gett'n high'. This, despite the fact I've already been up high now going on nearly three days and nights.

Putting out feelers, I hook up with John, a hustler druggie whom we both shared history on those mean streets, going back to days and many nights on Santa Monica Boulevard, nearly a decade earlier in LA. John being the link for me to barter the 'found', aka stolen travelers checks for meth. The link probably being his association to rough, drag queens who 'kept' John as a sexual trinket whilst they trafficked in felonious criminal activities, between turning tricks decked out in high, spiked heels on the hoe stroll.

Under an enclosure of thick plate, glass at a Muni bus shelter, on the corner of Larkin and Turk Streets, Me and John Paul, waiting in quiet anticipation, and the other John sat non-discrete to make our nefarious narcotics-stolen goods transaction. John, a skilled street veteran knowing what's what, realized I already had enough dope to get two persons sufficiently high. He could sense that the purchasing of more meth, as just an extra insurance policy that no-holds barred sex and freakiness was going down. As I may have even licked my lips closing the deal, signaling such implications in my body language. "Hell!...shit. I wanna go!" John whined, like a kid does when they think another's getting the bigger piece of candy or prize, meaning; "I'd even let you fuck me for that much dope." Never in all those years had I sensed him ever feeling me an any way sexual. Anyway, I wasn't certain if I felt flattered or just viewed his comment as evidence of him as a greedy, dope-fiend'n, hustler whore barking with his asshole for a hit of dope. Lines of intent, desire, lust and fiending often ended up blurred in our world.

Just minutes of arriving at my room, at the Delta Hotel on 6th Street, both of us pumped enough crystal meth in our bloodstreams that neither of our junkie psyches laid unsatiated. I lay across my mattress having changed into I what usually wore as my pajamas. John Paul across from the mattress sat himself on the floor, back against the wall, pulled of his Doc Marten boots and socks.

With him there barefooted, the epitome of my physical sexual desire, in the flesh in front of me, from the feet up where I enjoy beginning, fantasy made real. But that was just it; flesh only. In those moments, high or not, I failed to bridge the chasm. I lusted for John Paul, the human being, even though I knew nearly nothing of that human other than my carnal cravings. This conundrum despite the fact that I'd previously paid for fucking someone's body, in cash and for dope. Yet, my humanity, integrity maybe, longed for flesh, emotions and all. Methamphetamines, even massive amounts couldn't fill that gap to make the fantasy real.

Insufficiently, I lacked enough lust to demand that John Paul service me. Allow me to have my way sexually with his gorgeous virile loins. Looking back, it was within the bounds of what was expected by junkie, speed freaks. We who traded our loins for a 'hit', especially, that hit that'd "knocked his socks off"; literally.

That extra-long morning before the sun shone on day four of tweek'n, I discovered after all the effort, all the exchanging flesh, for money, for dope, for lust, deep within myself, in reality, I could not desire to be with someone who did not desire also to be with me. Discovered flesh forced, no matter how much dope, remained that; flesh. I never made a move on him in spite his inquiring of my assorted porn. We did it 'old skool' style meth, blabbing for hours. Did another hit that which neither of us got high on. We talked till we'd got on one another's nerves, till I felt no longer in lust of the flesh of that human.

Almost 18 hours later I nearly demanded John Paul leave my room. "I love you man..." I heard him say as we hugged, out on Market Street. Parting our ways grateful to be, still, friendly acquaintances at least, no hard feelings, no pun intended.

When Stars Fall (1994)

The airlines offer passengers discounts for frequent flyers. Greyhound, or what was left of the bus carrier, offered no frequent rider discounts. Hell! I had been cross- country on the bus nearly ten times in my life

I concluded my time as an American needed to come to an end. My above average intelligence, large-sized Black gay male body lacking the necessary capital for a successful crack at the American Dream seemed a failure. Europeans, to my thinking and research, were more willing to accept someone like myself as a full participant in their society. Being practical, I lacked the money or passport to go as far as Europe, so the next best alternative; French Quebec, Montreal: My destination and the answer to my dilemma.

I read of Black jazz musicians and writers leaving the States, particularly to France. James Baldwin had left for France. I became keenly aware of Baldwin through reading his non-fiction work. I saw him somewhat as gay, Black icon.

How would I handle the language difference? A failed attempt to enroll in a French course at City College crashed and burned. I brought some language cassettes to listen to on my Walkman.

I became obsessed with longing to flee to Montreal. A repeated topic for small talk conversation with johns picking me up on Polk. Something interesting to bring up in between the negotiation of price for which sex act I was to perform.

A one-way ticket to Montreal equaled about exactly the amount of one general assistance(welfare) check, with a little something left over. When I purchased a ticket it left me without enough to get a room. So, therefore I stayed overnight in Scott's room, a fellow hustler and dope associate. Both of us with a history of being out on the streets in LA too. Next day, to my amazement, that ticket came up missing. Eventually, later, I found out Scott went and cashed in the ticket for dope. I just so happened by such info by way of the other dope fiend which he had shared the dope with. *Shit, ain't no honor among thieves... and or dope fiends.* After that. Scott became persona non grata on Polk Street, when I was around. Eventually Scott paid me back the equivalent in dope later that summer. This after a couple of ass whupins beatdowns. To me, if you were going to live by the law of the jungle or 'street' *bitch you'd better be the lion and not the zebra!* I concluded through Scott's actions that heroin addicts tended to be a wee bit shadier than speed freaks. Either way my international escape plan ended up being put on hold for the time being.

A harm reduction program provided me a means to have a place, finally, to live off the streets. Still, the housing was to be in a fleabag hotel room in the TL(Tenderloin) or South of Market areas. They paid my rent out of my welfare checks. That would leave me about $40-50 left over for the rest of the month which I then added to my food stamp allotment.

On the 10th of each month like clockwork, I would go pick up my food stamps. Waiting somewhere in the next block or two from the check cashing place there'd be an older, Asian woman pacing along on the sidewalk, unassumingly. The 'Mama Saans' as we called them would be there to exchange $80 cash for my $120 worth of food stamps. *Don't cha just love capitalism...one hand greasing the other...all races and colors.* Off to the dope man I'd be bound.

My regular speed connection at that time was a dude Hollywood Dave happened to be actually in jail at this time. His boyfriend, sidekick, Michael substituted duty in his place. Michael Lennox a few years my junior, dope fiend thin, pallor-skinned and frequently disheveled hailed from a background of money. Rumor had it he had a trust fund to finance his dope habit. Michael had grown up as a youth in Luxemburg. Out on the street as a heroin addict, he needed a regular supply and protection. Ergo, why he hooked up with Hollywood. A bond mutually beneficial to both of them. Dave had the dope connections plus a street rep and delicately raised Michael offered a continuous money resource. Their partnership occasionally included sex yet, with no love lost if either strayed.

Michael began to hang around me out of a certain intrigue and wonder I believed. Yea, I knew he had money. Still, I found no fascination in that fact. He was still just another dope fiend to me. In other words, I did not beg and felt that other dope fiends who did had no self-respect. Like I really had something like respect with me shooting dope in my veins. Michael did serve for me as someone my age, with real actual experience and knowledge of life outside America. Often I filled our interactions and conversations talking up my intentions to leave the country.

"Juan... you don't know anyone in Montreal! How are you go'in to get by? He'd question me.

"I know I don't. I'll figure it out", I smugly answered. "I came to San Francisco... not knowing anyone."

Yes, I didn't beg for dope but, I sure as hell never turned any down either. Michael took well not to insult me by offering an amount of dope that would only make me fiend. I would have indignantly cussed his ass out if he did.

That late spring 94', record breaking floods devastated vast parts of the Midwest along the Mississippi River. As if that was not devastating enough news, along came reports from the African nation of Rwanda. A place I had never heard of or could not even point to on a map. Deadly violence among its different ethnic peoples spread to the point of up to 800,000 dead. I listened to reports of the massacres on NPR. President Clinton's Administration did nothing more than debate on what was the real definition of genocide. For me, Rwanda proved another of the reasons why I never voted for him. Yes, I always fulfilled my constitutional right of citizenship and vote despite living as an active speedfreak junky.

Bloody photographs of the slaughter in Rwanda came out plastered on the covers of Time and other news magazines and newspapers. Michael and I happened to be walking past some newsstand and he later referred to such pictures as 'porn'. His meaning went clear over my head in understanding his point at the time. (I would remember, later, his comments during the exploitive news coverage of such devastations as Hurricane Katrina and 9/11).

Browsing through the classified section of the local gay newspaper I took notice and answered an ad for survey respondents. Why not, it was a way to make some extra money. As it turned out a local law firm needed people to participate in a mock jury. Much later, I come to realize that participating in that survey may have been part of the process to build the legal standing for the landmark cases against the tobacco companies in the following years.

Serving on that mock jury paid out $75 for about two hours of my time. It worked for me. Other participants were a typical cross section of the City, young, old, White, Black, Latino, a business owner and was also equally divided between women and men. Our jury, as I recall, presented with the evidence sided 8 to 4 against the tobacco defendants. My vote being one of the four pro-tobacco. To me, it seemed as if most of the others felt like the tobacco insurers had plenty of money and were kinda pleased to see them get sued. In my opinion they did not take into account that the cost of suing would be passed down to the average consumer, in higher insurance rates.

The day of the actual survey also happened to fall on the 10th of the month, the same day as my food stamps allotment. Trading them in for cash meant it was payday for real and all without having some older man's dick in my face or mouth.

I meant to get tweeked enough to be cross-eyed. Promising my bestest, street partner, Olive that I'd have enough to get her 'twacked' as well. I told her to wait on Polk until I finished the survey. Sure as shit, a little past 9 that night, Olive and I were back in my drab room at the Delta Hotel on 6th and Mission Streets. Having secured sufficient quantities of crystal meth, I took great pride in being the one to get Olive high enough to be tongue tied. With that completed, my standard rule was I did not fuck my friends, especially females, *eww!* Still though, lower reach sections of my body were flaming and desperately needed release. What was there for me to do? It was off the porn peeps for me.

Hours later, more like maybe 9 or 10 hours later, my sweaty, greasy personage, finally, returned back to my fleabag room to check on Olive. It was, now, the close of festivities meaning only enough dope left for me and me alone. Olive had to go. Just in time, Michael had gotten into my hotel and knocked on my room door. Looking thoroughly deshelved as ever yet, he arrived with a stash of heroin that he nonchalantly shared some with Olive. By that point she desired to come down from the tweek clouds. My aim required getting both of them gone out of my room and be left alone with my fantasies, penis and my right hand.

Finally, at peace so I thought, then, 30minutes later a knock on the door. I knew it had to be Michael. Being so tweeked, worn out, my dilated pupil looked out the peephole, then, I slightly cracked open the door to exasperate, "Come the fuck in!"

I neglected any pretense of putting back on any shred of clothing. Michael with a slightly mischievous grin on his face, entered the room. The door got locked tightly behind him. More dope, more speed he generously offered. At that point, I really could not have gotten any higher, yet, still the greedy dope fiend that I was, I shot up some more in my veins anyway.

We talked about nothing I remember, after shooting up, laying across my bedraggled mattress, various porn spread out and me, still, butt naked. "Juan uh, uhh, think I'm.... falling in love with you" Michael worded, leaving me speechless. Unreal.

Thinking to myself, *"Did he just tell me he was in love with me? Me!"* "Michael, I don't know what...what...I had no idea, uh," is how I recall responding. (Knowing much much later that is not how to respond to that particular phrase) My response mechanism, action, was the action I knew well; have sex. Up until that moment Michel never had figured within my ideal of sexual attraction. Looking back now, the moment likely was just a drug-fuel haze, still, no one had ever said they were in love with me, so I'm not exactly sure either.

I got up to light some candles I had. *Yes...you know to set some kinda mood more than just dope and fucking.* We nastily, sweatily (not actually a word) got busy with dicks, mouths, asses, feet, hands, torsos moving and sliding back and forth. Michael's habitual heroin use had left his body with the residue of abscess bruises, all up and down the skin of his legs that were usually hidden by clothing. Telling me he was in love with me got inside my head and had emotions spinning, while the state of his physical body actually turned me off. Being told someone loves you had a feeling experience similar to losing my virginity; nothing to write home about.

In the days that followed our sexual tryst and his vow of falling in love, Michael made a promise to financially support me in my yearnings for escaping to Canada. One day, while typically high, we just so happened to stop into a travel agency located conveniently on Polk Street, to inquire about me, possibly even taking Amtrak up to Montreal. I shot down the idea, as exotic and adventurous as that would have been, due to the cost of a train ride.

Hollywood Dave, Michael's erstwhile boyfriend and protection, had just been released from one of his periodic stints in the slammer. His release due in no small part, now, from access to lawyers obtained with Michael's trust fund cash. Hollywood, when I dealt with him, let it be known that he knew of me having had sex with Michael. He seemed matter of factly nonplussed about it too.

Michael did his best to convince me to take along enough money so I'd appear more of a tourist in Canada. I humbly accepted just the cost of a ticket. My own foolish pride and respect felt the money from my welfare check would be sufficient to take care of what I needed in Montreal. Lacking my own hindsight, Michael did wisely convince me enough to go ahead and purchase a round trip ticket. Even though, with my mindset, at the time, I had no plans of returning to anywhere in the states.

In my process of preparing to leave for my 'adventure', I came up with the notion to trim down and take along with me only black and grey colored clothing. My practical genius, I reasoned, if by chance that I might have to spend a night out on the streets in Montreal, having the dark clothing would allow me to appear fresh. Just as well, monochromatic black happened to be all the fashionable rage then. With a change of a shirt I'd give the impression of a new outfit. I ended up continuing to dress in the same fashion way more or less for years. My wardrobe remains monochromatic black.

David, another of my street and drug associates, one of my few Black associates, got me hooked me up with his cousin in order to have my hair braided, with extensions. My hair as well would be set and have a hassle-free appearance should things get rough in my stay in Montreal. Drew to my surprise allowed me to turn his kitchen into a makeshift African hair braiding salon just for an afternoon. I think Drew just expected this 'fancy flight' of mine to burn out and I'd fall flat on my face, so allowing me to have a stranger in his home was just more like, *You silly fool.*

Having all I was taking with me pack, essentially everything I owned, I felt more than anxious and ready to go. Finally, *I was gonna make this happen...All the smack I'd been talk'n bout was gon be real!* It seemed unbelievable to me too. Yet, my history of taking off for who knows what. I'd done similar 'crazines's before. I got a hold of Hollywood to get a highly discounted bag of speed." One for the road", I told him, the night before I was set to leave. He made some comments on my hairstyle. I did look good though!

Bright and early, around 10, that's early for me, the next morning I arrive to catch my bus scheduled to depart at the Transbay Terminal downtown. The Greyhound terminal, since had been moved from seedier 7th Street, just south of Market. Where it was located back when my lowly ass arrived in the City, five years before. I think there's even a porn video with the 7th street station as the backdrop for a none to innocent young man/boy coming to Frisco...about to be shown the way and means to survive in the big City by a not-unhandsome experienced stud.

Meanwhile, my bus leaves out the terminal and winds up the last remnants of the Embarcadero Freeway, the freeway having mostly been torn down due to damage from the '89 quake, and begins the journey crossing the Bay Bridge, with a beautiful vista of San Francisco and the bay waters to stare at out the window, as go to make a stop in Oakland. Oakland just right across the bridge, still, mostly unknown to me having almost never leaving the City to venture there. Memory recalls passengers boarding in Oakland provided the ride with an authentic Greyhound atmosphere; all the sudden it got Blacker, louder and more ghetto. As the bus cruised, 70 mile per hour, past the outer reaches of the Bay Area I curled up and settled in to get some much-needed rest after being up for days, tweeking.

Our bus after passing through the high Sierras arrived in Reno early in the evening, with the sun still up, for a short layover. Having gotten some sleep and feeling a little refreshed I decided, here, to be a good opportunity to go to the restroom and shoot up that last bag of dope I had. I entered the restroom trying best to be nonchalant even though, I felt nervous. A bus station restroom you find passengers in various stages of using the public space like a home bathroom; brushing teeth, shaving or taking the extra-long shit. The kind with excessive farting and the smell. Even as I settled in the toilet stall with meth and syringe, anxiety around getting caught probably gave me problems. I just couldn't find a vein. Through the longer I took, the more nervous I became and the more I had trouble hitting a vein. Through the public address system I heard announced the pending departure of my bus. Fiend'in I really wanted that hit now. Finally, *fuck it!* I missed hitting a direct vein. "Just fuk'n wasted it," I huffed under my breath quietly to myself, as pain, burning, minus the euphoric rush, entered my arm. Damn near missed getting back on the bus. In fact, I ended up re-boarding on the second of the two busses on that same route. Yet, my one piece of luggage was still in the bottom of my original bus (an important aspect of this story and trip). Anxious, tweeking, I walked to the back and found an open seat. Sweating profusely. My body always did high on speed. Making matters even more intense, now, I was beginning a ride with a different set of passengers seeing me for the first time, all dressed in black, long braids and with eyes as wide as saucers. My presentation a little more freakish in appearance than usual.

Laying back in the seat on the 'new' bus I turned to look out the window to see bleak, monotonous desert landscape roll by as the bus traveled through the rest of Nevada. Despite having shot up speed, I must have ended up sleeping the rest of that night.

The next morning the bus pulled over and stopped on the shoulder of the Interstate for a smoke break. We were stopped out on the vast salt flats of Utah. I walked down steps at the front, to get off the bus. Stepping outside, out of the air conditioning, I felt the sun blaring, beaming, making my exposed skin feel as if I'd been set on fire. Quickly, I ran to the nearest spot of shade behind some roadside shrubbery.

We arrived in Salt Lake City mid evening for another layover. My mind still raced with the excitement of what lay ahead on my journey and also probably some effects of the methamphetamine in my bloodstream. When you miss going directly into a vein, the dope lingers in your system more slowly but longer. Walking around the area outside the bus station confirmed to me how bizarre Salt Lake City appeared. Recalling memories of having been there before on a previous bus trek back to Indiana. Everything in the city seemed to appear to be spotless, especially compared to San Francisco or any other city for that matter. I guessed it to be the result of overwhelming Mormonism that the citizens made it look like a city without blemishes. It happened to cross my mind as well how horrible it'd be to have grown up a freak, like me, in such a place.

10pm. that next evening, the busses heading east set off again. All passengers had to stand in line to board with pre-boarding passes. Greyhound and their poor and or lack of service they offered began to get me riled up. With my ticket costing over $300, even if I didn't pay for it, should have meant the company showed some appreciation to their customers. The bus driver's union just so happened to be on strike at that time. That fact figured into my pissed off mindset. Politically, I detested union busting, which I figured for sure was the greedy corporation's ultimate goal.

With the busses reading Chicago bound, the coaches headed out on I-80 up into the high Rocky Mountains and soon on into desolate state of Wyoming. I remember in being sometime near midnight that the bus in which I was riding broke down out there in the middle of nowhere Wyoming. Shortly, after the other bus following behind, pulled ahead and over to the side of the highway. We passengers were informed that we could all board the other bus but, that some of us would need to stand, without a seat. That situation would be all the way until we reached Denver, where there'd be another bus to take us the rest of our trip. That would be more than maybe 6 hours away.

That was the last straw, for me. No way was I gonna frig'n stand up on a bus for the next couple of hours especially when I'd paid full price for my ticket. "You... you can't do that!" I incredulously shouted toward the front of the bus. "It's illegal... to ride standing up!" My pleas went out mostly to the air as I looked around at the other passengers. Just then, a family of passengers who had two small kids got up to rush off the bus, along with the other passengers, to quickly see if possibly they might obtain a seat on the other bus.

Foolishly not knowing exactly what I was doing at that particular moment, I did it anyway despite the outcome. What even more surprised me about what was taking place, this young, White kid, no older than about seventeen stood at his seat and said, "I'm not going either." In spite of his youth, he presented himself with calm assurance.

"Good," I thought. *"I'm not the only one."* The situation became more real, then, with at least two passengers refusing to give up their seats. Intuitively, I knew the bus driver was going to have to remain with us. Then another passenger, a dark-haired, kinda short, dude with a pair of headphones on his neck leaned on the seat in front of him saying, "Man... hell! I'm staying too. I'm not... rid 'in standing in no aisle."

"It's against the law!" I pleaded my case to encourage others. Plea that fell on deaf ears.

30minutes afterward, there the four of us remained me, Troy; the dark-haired guy, John; the young kid and the bus driver all alone on a broken down, Greyhound bus stuck in the pitch-black darkness in Wyoming, on the side of Interstate 80. Lucky for me my travel plans included an exact destination but no fixed arrival date. I was in no rush. Ego feeling justified in not having allowed the greedy corporate, union-busting, Greyhound to charge me more than $300 to be riding, against federal transportation laws standing up without my own seat.

Meanwhile, in real terms, we would have to wait, right there, until the driver of the other bus reached a bus terminal that was open in order to send us help. That next open terminal could have either been Cheyenne or Denver more than three to five hours away from where we remained stranded.

"How long do you think.... it's going to be til they make it back to get us?" I queried the bus driver.

"Can't exactly say for sure." The driver responded back with what sounded like a southern accent. "It could take til morenin for sure."

I let out a sigh, "There's no way…. for what I paid (again, mind you I didn't pay for the ticket), that I was figh'in to get a seat. I don't care...Fuck no!" I looked back to Troy and exasperatedly questioned, "Did you see that couple? They had kids! There's no way that can be legal."

"Yea, the kids was already loud enough... jumpin all over the seats as it was," He shot back making the point that the kids had already been getting on his nerves.

"I just can't believe all those folks running like a stampede to get on that bus, to stand up for the next two, three maybe four or more hours," my words restating my shock at what had taken place. "Greyhound's gon…. to have to compensate me for this," I claimed affirmatively to the captive audience of three.

Settling into this new reality, all told each other our stories of how we ended up riding on that bus. John, the young dude, was on his way home to Denver. Troy, a dark-haired guy, originally hailing from New York State but, headed on his way back to Chicago, after some kinda misfortune in California. The bus driver, well, he just happened to be doing his job and probably was not too pleased to find himself stuck out in the middle of nowhere Wyoming with our smart asses.

Hours into the ordeal we pushed open the windows, in the emergency manner, to smoke. "They cain't do noth'n about the rules now." The driver signaled his ok to us.

It being August, sunrise came early. Outside the windows of the bus the view opened up and expanded for what seemed nearly an endless horizon across rolling hills of sun-burnt grass bordered in the far-off distance by high mountain ranges that appeared like black shadows.

"What's that?" John asked, looking out seeing some wild creature moving outside there among the grasses.

"That's a coyote," the driver answered back.

"Man... when they finally do come out to get the bus... all they're go'in to find is an empty bus with bones and carcasses picked over by the coyotes," Troy joked with morbid humor.

"It'll be posted in the newspapers and on TV... Four Greyhound passengers eaten to death by wild animals in Wyoming," I added, as we laughed like our sides would burst, the bus driver too. We needed to make light of our circumstances. In truth we still had no idea when we'd be rescued.

John was travelling back home from his summer vacation. Troy had been living out in San Bernardino. I viewed John as wise beyond his years for having calmly decided not to rush, like everyone else, to get a seat on the over-packed bus. Now, he just as well could have been young and foolish all the same. Tall with thick blond hair, his look went easy on the eyes too.

An hour or more after sunrise, we spot a black, Plymouth sedan with large CB antennas slowing down passing us on the other side of the interstate. The Plymouth, then, u-turned across the median and drove up and parked in front of the bus. We were to discover, to our grateful surprise, it turned out to be our rescue no matter how strange it appeared. In actuality, we were in fact stranded about 30 miles outside of Laramie. The driver of the Plymouth, a grizzly looking White guy about fifty, had the fortune of owning the only taxi in the whole town. Once inside the vehicle, our luggage in the trunk, he informed us that he'd rigged massive CB antennas to the vehicle, in order so that any phone call could be radio signaled directly to the car. This being more than a decade before the widespread use of cell phones. At the time, I sat in the backseat thinking, *What a trip. Dude had the 'hook up' for real.* He ended up driving and dropping us off at the Greyhound pick up location in Laramie. Lastly, before he left us, with a wide crooked-toothed grin he said how he was being paid by the mile plus his base fee.

Troy and I cracked jokes back and forth to kill the time. Our wait sitting in the elements on a ramshackle bench, outside a locally-owned gas stop, looked in the condition as if it had been built at the beginning of paved highways.

"You know.... that commercial with the two old geezers in overalls sitting out next to the Pepsi machine, surrounded by all the dust... and nothing else?" I piped up.

"Hell yeah!" Troy shot back.

We each looked back and forth at each other and our surroundings, made the connection and busted up laughing. Laughing until we nearly cried. Both of us seemed to recognize the absurdity in us urban freaks; I Black and gay, though not stated at that time, and Troy, White somewhat looking like a hood rat, out there stuck in nearly 100 percent, White hick, probably redneck Wyoming. "It's like we're fucking aliens from another world transported here to this strange planet," I observed to Troy and the others.

"Take me to your leader!" Troy mocked.

The bus driver, as I looked toward him between guffaws, wasn't laughing as the rest of us cracked up. He may have not so clearly realized our humor was making fun of the type of folks possibly similar to his own origins.

We passed the time till a bus arrived that afternoon. Anxiously those hours passed with me fully aware that not only was I the only Black person/body in the group, I was probably the only Black for hundreds of miles around, out there, still, in the high mountain nowhereness. We boarded the bus which took us through to Cheyenne then, to Denver. Again, I not only slept but really passed out along that leg of the trip. I awoke from a nearly comatose sleep as the coach played down Interstate 25, from the suburbs into downtown Denver. Glued to the windows, like a wide-eyed kid, I noticed the construction taking place of the city's new light rail line going in the median of the Interstate. The view of the enormous Coor's ballpark loomed above everything when we pulled in near the bus terminal.

Troy and I saw young John off as he saw his family waiting for him inside the terminal. "You take care man... and graduate." I said in parting, in the best older person, sage manner I could muster

"I will," John replied, his face registering a look of disappointment that his out of the way adventure with us was finally over. His family seemed polite to me in a kind of passive aggressive way, the way some White, middle class people are.

Then, I made sure to go and register a complaint with Greyhound. The station manager happened to be a clean cut, tall, Black man in his thirties. His coolness and resignation gave me the impression that he had the education beyond that required to be a manager at Greyhound.

"I expect Greyhound to compensate me... for my inconvenience and... the misplacement of my luggage." I demanded firm and calmly, in my best facsimile White America, diction and entitlement. In reality though, I'm somewhat sure my mind and body, still, coursed with the effects from the hit of meth I missed shooting up directly into my bloodstream, back in that restroom in Reno. As per what a manager is expected to do. "Sir...I'm very sorry that happened to you. We will do the best to get you to your destination without any inconvenience" I was told, minus any material compensation.

When the Chicago bound bus headed out of the terminal in Denver, once again staring out the bus window we cruised out of the city on the interstate and passed through flat, treeless farmland, dotted by patterns of circular irrigation systems. This was the Plains where nothing obstructed the view and the horizon spread out flat as far as my eyes could see.

Bored with the nothing sameness outside the window, Troy and I seem to hit it off pretty well. Both of us were prone to sarcastic humor that looked outside life's absurdities. As more time passed and mouths tend to run, I felt safe to share with him my use of speed. Likewise, Troy confirmed with me his own use of illicit drugs, mostly crack for him. Feeling more bonded to one another we settled into making wise cracks at the riders of Greyhound. A unique set of folks, we both agreed, mostly people too poor to afford any other means of travel and or those too unprepared at handling life's circumstances and deciding to make a change of location on a moment's notice. Years later, I learned the term for this; geographic. I myself fit into both of those categories. Like other passengers, on my third day of travel without a shower, my physical person began to get a little rank. With my braided extensions, my hair still looked fierce though. The speed buzz negatively affected keeping my body fresh and continued to swing my emotions up and down.

By now it seemed we kept up our own little party going in the rear of the bus. "Can you believe that... they have a disclaimer before an episode of "Bevis and Butthead (a TV show)?" I asked incredulously.

"Yeah really," Troy came back. "What kind of loser really woulda take that shit seriously? I am Chief Cornholeo. I need TP for my bunghole!" Troy mocked, imitating his best imitation voice of the cartoon character on the show. Cracking up and laughing loud enough for other passengers to turn their heads toward the back and give us dirty looks, as if we even cared what they thought.

Troy hipped me to listening to his cassette of the rap group "House of Pain." And to my surprise some of the tunes I actually liked, although it was hip hop. Our next major layover was Omaha. On a previous bus journey, I'd been in the city and was fond of its character, that I discovered within the space of a couple of hours. The city about the size of Fort Wayne, my hometown, yet it carried a more cosmopolitan, urban feel to me.

The bus arrived in Omaha on the weekend, Friday or Saturday night, if I remember correctly. The bus terminal located right on the edge of downtown. Stepping outside the terminal, Troy and I witnessed a small crowd of slickly dressed, mostly White folks lined up outside a club about two blocks ahead down the street. I knew about the old restored section of the downtown area all gentrified with fashionable shops and restaurants. I told Troy, "Let's go walk down the river area."

"Hell, why not", he said. We got some time to kill."

"It's just a few blocks down that way," I informed. Off walking we went.

Leaving the bus station, just outside there was some guy causing a loud ruckus, the dude slim with olive skin, dark eyes and jet-black straight hair. Being out in the middle of the country, the Plains even, it did occur to me that dude maybe was an Indian, Native American.

"You…you know who I…I am!" He yelled loud enough to be heard for blocks around. Right there, at that moment, he played out the stereotype of Indians; alcoholic and shiftless. Troy and I along with other passengers just stared at him, he couldn't be ignored. We just kinda shook our heads in mild disgust of the whole obnoxious scene.

As we passed by the crowd gathered outside that club. It was clear, to me, it was a gay club. Highly fashionable men standing in line alongside more than a few females looking rather masculine if not androgynous appearance, lined up men with men and women with women.

"You know man...I'm not into it... but I'd have no problem with gettin down with two of them women." Troy made claim, smiling rather deviously while pointing back toward some of the women in the line. The topic of my sexuality identity never came up or entered into our conversations, until that point. I took his statement of desire toward two lesbians as his small yet, covert way of signaling that he was cool with whatever I was.

When we finally did get to the 'olde' town area. Most of everything was already closed for the evening. Just as well neither of us really had any money to spend anyway.

Standing on a bluff overlooking the Missouri River I stood there staring out at the majestic, moving force that had in essence shaped the land features of the continent. That River sure seemed to beat out the power and mightiness of rivers where I came from.

Meanwhile, as we got back and approached the bus station, 'Chief Indian guy' was still there outside, loudly holding court.

"Wha…what you look 'in at? This was all... my pe, pe…people!" He shouted out, actually to no one in particular, gesturing by pounding his chest. "All of this!"

"He is telling the truth. At one time this 'was' all Native land," I said, affirming 'the dude's historical accuracy, looking to Troy for a response.

"I could take it all back...my people!" Indian guy claimed loudly.

We both quietly laughed, at his absurdity, listening. "Man all you can do sometimes is laugh... to keep from crying," Troy said back to me, in response to what we were witnessing.

"Sometimes man... you have to do both," I ended the comment, giving somewhat a final assessment, as Troy remained silent.

I could feel the speed in my veins wearing off by then. Since missing a vein, shooting up, I didn't get that 'rush' I carved. To the good though, the comedown (withdrawals) were expected to be less severe.

The bus rolled out of Iowa to cross the Mississippi River. I peeped out the window, even here where it is narrow, that River is something to see and behold. We made it on to Chicago, a city I always loved. My last visit in the town found my crack headed self copping dope inside of 30minutes on touching feet to asphalt, not knowing a single soul. To my surprise the Greyhound station had been rebuilt and moved. The station used to be right in the heart of the Loop downtown. The new terminal sited just outside of downtown on the edges of the commercial district. I assumed the powers that be had tired of having the elemental riff raff that frequents Greyhound being deposited smack dab in the middle of the, now trendy and spiffed up Loop District. I departed the bus to look around the shiny, Postmodern designed station to discover there were no lockers. If I'd wanted to go off exploring, I'd have to take my bags with me, giving me the look of a tourist out in that big city.

Chicago was Troy's destination. "Hey man take care of yourself." I told him as we said our goodbyes, thinking to myself how much I had enjoyed his company. Meeting Troy actually helped to make my journey more memorable

"Yeah, you know... maybe it'll be better this time around." Troy said back.

"Shit! You could always come to Canada... like me." I said sarcastically but meant it.

"I wish," he shot back at me, "You take care man. Be safe!"

The major terminal in Chicago gave me another opportunity to register a complaint about the bus being stranded. I asked the counterperson to speak with the general manager. The same as in Denver, the station manager turns out to be Black; a woman in her early thirties, very professional looking. After I explained to her all that had happened out in Wyoming. I also got the same, run around, corporate speak response as in Denver. All that this efficient professional Black woman could do for me would be to document my dissatisfaction.

An hour or two later, after I'd decided to remain in the bus station after all, the next bus destination read; Cleveland. I walked up on the bus, it contained the smell of some disinfectant they had sprayed yet it barely masked the odors of passengers, myself certainly included, days into a ride without a full shower. The bus was going to be crowded, as usual. *Not gonna have my own seat.* Scanning as I walked toward the rear, I spotted a seat next to a husky, White guy in his thirties with reddish blond hair. That guy was Jerry. We introduced ourselves to one another, making small talk. Found out he was headed all the way to Syracuse, New York.

Sunny afternoon, as I remember it not hot, it being August, much seemed normal, then, just as the bus happened to drive out of the view of the terminal, right before making a turn to enter the Dan Ryan Expressway, the bus pulled over and stopped. The driver, a Black woman, kinda energetic, from her voice, spoke over the bus microphone. "Hello everybody. I'll be driving this route today for another driver. I was hoping… to see if anyone had any spare double A batteries? I need some for my Walkman player" As some passengers actually scrambled and checked to see if they had batteries. Taken aback, myself at how odd and unprofessional our bus driver came across. Turning to my seatmate; Jerry, "That's all fine... and good that home girl wants some batteries. But I sure hope she knows what the hell she's doing." Jerry smiled a grin giving a look that questioned why I felt so uneasy. The driver, she got the batteries. I still had my doubts though. Already this leg of the voyage had gotten interesting.

Just happened that three buses left the Chicago terminal that hot sunny August afternoon, all headed and bound with passengers toward Cleveland. I supposed this must have been busy season for Greyhound. Frequent rider that I had been, I had familiarity with and knew the standard routes. So, I pricked up to notice when the other two buses took the exit to the Chicago Skyway Tollroad. Standard east routed, out of Chicago, buses used that highway. Just so, as well happened to be right around afternoon rush hour traffic. I leaned over and pointed out that fact to my seatmate; Jerry, how I believed our driver missed the correct interchange. "Remember... she mentioned she hadn't driven this route before." I commented feeling more than a little vindicated in my earlier suspicions.

The bus continued travelling along I-94 until we hit almost standstill in absolute bumper to bumper traffic. Our seemingly novice driver, I recall, announced over the PA system her frustration driving us into traffic. Such incompetence slowed us down one this leg of the trip by about 30-45 minutes. More confirmation of the blood-sucking, union busting, corporate greed of Greyhound, I thought.

Slowly, ever so slowly, finally somewhere around Gary, Indiana, traffic eased up ,then we continued along the interstate to the Indiana Toll Road. Quizzingly looking across my seat at Jerry, not sure whether I spoke anything, yet, we both noticed the bus travelling at a fast pace; speeding actually. My look probably said it all. Due to not knowing the route, our driver must have needed to make up for losing time by illegally going over the speed limit. Probably, I made some snide remark to that fact as a few other passengers, particularly the Black passengers, shrugged to pass off the driver speeding as just getting to our destination even faster, oblivious to or ignoring the risk to life and limb. There seemed to be a pattern on that journey. Folks were unconcerned about service and or safety as long as they had gotten cheap tickets.

I dozed off with the bus crossing through the northern tip of Indiana. I guess I figured nothing really to see, *Hell! I grew up here.* Woke up and looked out the window just east of the Ohio state line, where the Indiana Tollroad becomes the Ohio Turnpike. Finally, our bus made its first rest stop after nearly three hours. As we pulled into the rest area the other two buses on our same route were already there.

Minutes into our rest, some of us learned that the rest stop was required and was meant to be for 15 minutes. Just as I noticed the other busses turning on their engines to depart, our driver informed us that we actually had only five minutes to stretch and relieve ourselves in the restroom. "There are people still in the restrooms!" I insisted to no one in particular but, meant for the driver to hear. "What about that one lady?" I questioned, looking at Jerry. The woman in question was older and moved as such. I remembered her having her head wrapped in a scarf. Then, the bus driver repeated, "Five minutes... we have to go!"

"I know she's not go'in to leave that woman!" I stated loudly enough again, so the driver could hear but more intended, this time, to stir the other passengers. Surely, as I and the other passengers were afraid to depart and go get that woman for fear of being also left there. There was no doubt in my mind the driver would've had no problem leaving me and my pain in the ass, self at that rest stop.

The two other two busses pulled off leaving the rest area after their full appointed rest breaks, our driver closed the door shut, backed up and also left the rest area headed back onto the turnpike. "Ha… ah! I don't believe it. She's leaving that old lady! She paid for her ticket and she's leaving her stranded!" I nearly shouted, now, so the driver could hear this time.

"I can't believe it either." Jerry said, astonished.

Now, I was incensed. Incensed that the fucking greedy company had such unprofessional employees, incensed that that incompetent, bitch driver, who was Black, had just left an older Black woman stranded at a rest stop all by herself because, this driver didn't know or even care what the hell she was doing.

All the rest of the way on the turnpike to Cleveland I didn't care anymore if the driver could hear me complaining and bitching.

Still fuming, I filled Jerry in on my tale about the lack of service Greyhound provided me back in Wyoming.

And, it got better. Or worse, depending on whether it's humor or reality. Our intrepid driver happened to lose track of the other busses also traveling the same route. When our bus approached the outskirts of Cleveland, I recognized the bus having taken the wrong interchange ramp and was headed away from the city. Despite having never actually been in Cleveland, I knew which direction to go from my being a street map nerd, since childhood.

Some of the other Black passengers began looking at me disapprovingly for my comments. "She's doing... the best she can!" One rather large, Black man responded to me.

Flabbergasted, I said loudly, "This is Greyhound...We're supposed to leave the driving to her!" A few other passengers started to roll with laughter at my comment which actually happened to be the bus company's advertising slogan. Clearly, I could tell some of the older, Black passengers felt as if I was going over the top for rudeness.

"Fuck that old school, Black deference shit!" I thought. In short, because she was a woman, a Black woman at that, I should know better not to expose her in public.

Finally, that same large Black man got up from his seat and moved up to the front of the bus so that he could help direct the driver to the correct interchange ramps and lead in the direction to the Cleveland Greyhound terminal. Once we, finally, got there, no doubt, I proceeded directly to the station manager to register a formal complaint over the actions and incompetence of that driver. For sure, looking back, nothing ever became of that complaint. I felt even more upset about that driver than about my missing luggage and delayed travel.

Knowing the layover in Cleveland sure to be a few hours, I asked Jerry to look after my bag and I made my way to see something of what I could of the city.

I found my tastes partial to an old industrial city like Cleveland. Coming out of a small corner store, after buying cigarettes, I walked up to a small group of young, Black folks, nearby, and asked what there was to see in their city. They gave me no answer, appearing dumbfounded at my question. *Oh well...I tried.*

Downtown I found and walked in the direction of the Terminal Tower, one of the tallest buildings in the city and a fine example of Depression Era skyscraper architecture. Next somehow, I found myself out about the Flats, a revitalized warehouse district where chic restaurants and bars, for hip White folks, were located.

Walking around there I looked up to view lights trailing all along the underside of a viaduct and piers overhead. People mingled in and around the clubs and food spots. Noticing people out drinking and carrying on, I began to think of and be aware and conscious of my surroundings. Anyway, my funds were low so I thought it best and decided to get back toward the station.

I got a little lost walking back towards the station. Downtown Cleveland's street grid is on a diagonal. The Terminal Tower, lit up and rising up in the night sky, I knew to be at the zero point between east and west.

When I did get back, I took what time I still had to layover to clean and freshen my appearance. While shaving in the bus terminal restroom, in the mirror, I noticed my skin where I'd shaved starting to break out, not in the more usual razor bumps way I sometimes got. I was like, "Huh." Otherwise I really paid it no attention.

The next morning as the sun brightly peered into the station, our bus departed out of Cleveland taking I-90, New York City bound. My face glued to the window I took a superb view of the city's skyline as the bus snaked the expressway alongside the shoreline of Lake Erie. Peeking toward the other windows on the other side, across the seats, lay the aqua blue waters of the lake, shining beautifully in the sunlight. I considered how much I'd enjoyed exploring central Cleveland, despite having had no one to share that with.

Jerry and I decided again on being seatmates. I spoke of my exploits in downtown Cleveland. As our conversation deepened, along the ride, Jerry shared that he happened to be separated from his wife and children. In fact, the reason he was now headed home to Syracuse was due to his teenage son having gotten into trouble. In an odd phenomenon, on this particular trip, as had happened earlier on the journey with Troy, both Jerry and I revealed to one another our own familiarity with using drugs. Seemingly, just casually coming up in conversation. Jerry's habit happened to be cocaine.

Taking me by complete surprise, I'll never forget it. Jerry shared with me that the troubled son in question, also, just so happened to have been conceived during a drug-fueled swinger's party back in the day. "It could be... that I'm not actually his real father," he stated somewhat in jest. He further confirmed that no matter the paternity, his son was his son.

Thinking and taking in all what Jerry had told me, I mentioned to him. "You know it might be a good idea to have your son... come live with you. If you think about it, he's exactly at the age when drug habits begging to start to take hold."

Jerry listened to my seemingly sage advice while kinda staring off. "Could be...could be." Was all said in response.

"It might be a good idea, as well, in order to keep both dad and son straight." I ended my psychological assessment of his situation. I slept afterwards.

Next thing I knew, I looked out the window and we were in Buffalo. By now, I'm no ways at all tweek'n from that speed hit. In fact, the fatigue meant my body was in withdrawal. Discovering we had a short layover; I left the bus station to walk around downtown near the station. It surprised me that Buffalo had a light rail transit line. I got on, got a seat, turned towards the large window and took a short ride not too far out, crossed to the other side to ride the same line back towards downtown.

Later on, that morning the bus travelled on through to Rochester, then on to Syracuse, all across Upstate New York, Interstate 90 Thruway. I recalled memory of Michael telling me, "Upstate New York... one of the most underrated places in the country." Viewing the scenery outside those windows, with my own eyes, that morning, I could agree. Rocky low hills, containing the full variety of greenness impressed me, maybe it was just me missing the full change of seasons. Not something you see much in California.

Jerry departed the bus in Syracuse. Parting, I reminded him about my two cents worth of advice, of how to deal with his troubling son. As if I really knew something about raising teenagers simply due to the fact that I'd been one.

Leaving Syracuse, next it was off to Albany then turning north up towards the Border. My excitement and anxiety increased by the hour. This shit was finally getting real. Me, young, Black, and queer guy setting forth the experience of another country, another culture, even another language.

At the layover in Albany I got off the bus and headed straight to the station manager for complaint in regards to Greyhound's poor service. What would you know, the station manager, again, was Black. A light-skinned brother, clean-cut about in his fifties, sat at his desk while I detailed my travails. Soft-spoken, he inquired of my citizenship documents, and nothing that I needed to have ready plans for lodging in Montreal. A little taken aback, I felt as if he was questioning my intentions or at least changing the subject. At that moment in his office, the thought passed me that Michael had mentioned to me the same issues about having someplace to stay while in Montreal. Being headstrong and tunnel vision assured of my goal, I had put such concerns out of my mind. Coming back to the situation at hand I told the station manager I'd make lodging arrangements when I arrived at my destination. To his credit he did issue me a partial refund ticket that also could be cashed in. *Finally...some results for my troubles!*

Passengers, myself included, boarded another bus with the front marquee; Montreal. Nearly exhausted after more than three days riding in an aluminum can on wheels; Greyhound, I beamed inside lookin up at that destination marker. A few hours later, Interstate 87 our bus arrived in Plattsburg, New York, the last town before the international border. Before departure, a Greyhound official boarded the coach in order to inspect and check each passenger's citizenship documents. He made a definite stop at my seat because I was not in possession of a passport. I presented to him my California ID and voter registration card which was, at that time, acceptable verification for U.S. citizenship. He appeared somewhat incredulous at my documentation but allowed me to travel on, noting that I was likely to be checked further at the Canadian border station. Fully anxious now, I was more than glad to have passed that first inspection.

Finally, at the border crossing, all passengers had to disembark and pass through customs. When the line came up to me, I was asked to go wait inside the booth area. I was certain that my citizenship documents were correct, so I waited. Only when I noticed the bus leave the customs station, did I register distress. *What the hell was go'in on!*

In a small inner room, a Canadian customs agent began questioning me in regards to my travel plans. "I'm just coming for a visit. I've read all about Montreal... listened to the CBC (Canada Public Radio)." I answered him. Then he started asking me questions about my arrest record. Sensing this was the real deal, I answered truthfully telling him, "Yes!" I had a conviction for solicitation (prostitution) in California.

"Do you have any aliases?" the agent insisted.

"No!" I replied despairingly. I waited some more. Some other customs officers were processing these two large, Black women dressed in brightly colored clothing, speaking French. I figured them to be Haitians, maybe. Fumes of strong perfume mingled with body odor wafted through the air in that rather small space. "Maybe the stereotype is true, about the French and taking less baths."

My same customs agent returned and continued his line of questioning me about aliases and whether I'd been arrested under another name. My distress began turning to tears. I told of my just coming to visit and how this trip had been a dream of mine for over a year. "Have you ever used another name!" He again firmly persisted.

"No sir!" My answer.

"I will not be able to allow you to enter Canada. You will have to return to the U.S border," was his final word. And just like that, I was not going to Montreal. A vehicle drove up to take me with my backpack the short quarter mile back to the U.S. customs station.

I remained in shock, disbelieving what had just happened and what I was going to do next.

Entering back inside the U.S. customs station, a generic portrait of President Clinton hung blankly on the wall, a proud symbol of the nation. There was I feeling, anything but proud, desiring to escape. "Sir... you're free to go." The U.S. customs agent told me as I stood there all dejected in stupor.

I gathered myself up with my backpack and began walking a little despondently along the emergency shoulder of the northbound Interstate. Solitary, still in disbelief of the situation, I walked along as traffic sped by me. The sun overhead began to set there in far Upstate New York on that hot August evening.

Within a few minutes of having left the border, "Aww fuck! I don't... fucking believe this!" I yelled out loud, to no one but the open sky, the grass and the highway. "I did use another name!" I remembered having used an alias back when I had been arrested, over a decade before in LA. I simply had completely forgotten all about the, one-time incident, forgotten it until being out there alone on that hot forsaken stretch of highway, when it was too late.

What was I going to do? My return Greyhound ticket happened to be dated a week ahead of that day. I did have the refund ticket issued back when I was in Albany. I figured I could only use it at a Greyhound ticket office, the nearest one being in Plattsburg. Still continuing my walking, I recalled passing a road sign on the Interstate reading: 'Plattsburg 24 mi'.

Eventually, I walked up and off the interstate at the first exit. I could see a small convenience store on the road at where U.S. highway 9 ends. Walking in I purchased something to drink and a little snack. Leaving the store, I began the long walk and trek back to Plattsburg. *"Had I ever walked 24 miles?"* That evening for certain I was about to find out.

Most cars, now, drove one the Interstate. Cars traveling on the old US highway were few and far between. My mind got to wondering, paranoid a little, that not many if any Black folks lived up in that sparse rural landscape. Especially none that would have probably looked such as me; urban-dressed, braided hair. No, there'd probably be no hitchhiking for me. Walk I did.

Night slowly wore on out there along that bare undulating, countryscape. Darkness filled the vast sky like I'd never ever recalled seeing before. I started to wonder, worry, that my Black body, a rarity out there anyway, would assume an easy target on that empty and desolate roadway.

To my utter amazement, light did arrive in the form of stars, up all across the sky overhead. Urban creature that I was, I grew fascinated by the thousands, maybe even millions of tiny lights in that night sky. Walking on still, I pondered and grasped how ancient peoples could have looked up and seen those same stars in the night sky, as something heavenly.

A flash appeared out overhead above me almost like fireworks. *"Am I trippin... having a dope flashback?"* What I'd actually seen, after later reasoning, turned out to be a falling star. Never before had I seen such vivid brightness. I continued walking miles passing up farmhouses and the occasional crossroads with a few gathered houses and maybe a business or two.

The old highway followed along the same general direction of the Interstate and a rail line. Off in the distance, to the west of me, I could hear traffic sounds and once, that night also, a freight train echoed up across the otherwise quiet expanse of farm fields.

Dark nothingness, then all the sudden, there'd be another bright visual burst, trailing across the sky overhead. Luckily, for my sanity, the falling stars allowed my mind a distraction from my situation. I began to count them. I recall tracking over 15 falling stars during the course of that otherwise exhausting lonely night.

Well into my trek, more than two or maybe three hours in, one car passed me and pulled over to the side of the road well ahead of me. Uncertain what was up, I started to pick up my pace, just as the car sped off again, gravel rocks spinning out under the tires. Dumb ass youngsters pulling a vicious prank at my expense.

By that point, my calf and leg muscles had grown sore and stiff. Yet, I noticed the pain seemed to lessen if I continued on walking, not focusing my mind on it.

20, 10, then, 5 miles to Plattsburg the highway signs I passed directed. At some time, I figured it was past midnight, cause not a single business was still open. I trudged my weakening exhausted body and limbs across a suburban shopping center parking lot. I found a front edge with a building overhang, just in case it might rain later that night. Threw down my backpack, spread out a newspaper and gently braced my painful limbs to curl up for sleep.

Waking up cold, shivering, the morning after, my legs and feet still aching and painful. I thought it best to walk along the main streets toward central Plattsburg. Groggy and sore due to my walk, no hike really, from the Canadian Border and sleeping outside in the elements, any of my recollections of that morning are still somewhat hazy. Conscious of my large, Black male, conspicuousness I made my way with purpose. I somewhat remember a local police patrol car passing me while also giving a quick look over. I stopped in at Mickey D's for a little breakfast and to ask directions. For sure I was quite a sight to see by then. I'd gone a week since having a full shower.

The Mc Donald's happened to be located close to Lake Champlain. Standing outside, I could look out over to the other side of the long narrow lake and see Vermont.

When I reached the Greyhound ticket office, after pleading my case, the agent redeemed my refund ticket allowing me to travel back down to Albany. All I remember after the bus arrived was sleep. Ever so glorious sleep.

Back in Albany the same station manager at Greyhound must've had pity on my sorry ass. He had forewarned me. He changed my remaining ticket to allow me to get back to San Francisco. on the next departing bus. His secretary, a young, thin, very blond woman, processed my new ticket speaking incredulously, "That's awall ful... just awall ful!" Upon hearing me tell my travel details. Now, as in then, I will never forget hearing her thick, Northeastern accent.

I made a wish to myself to write that station manager a note of thanks. That older brother showed concern and took care of me almost as if I'd been a relative. But as usual, my dope fiend reality made the wish just that; a wish. The routing back to San Francisco had me transferring busses from the Port Authority Terminal in New York City. Yet, I was tired, dejected and slightly depressed, still, probably coming down off the speed too, did not even bother with doing a little exploration in the most thrilling city in the world, on the layover.

Later when I got back 'home' to Frisco, I settled, not too comfortably I recall, into actually being homeless for the better of the next month. Because I had cashed in my public assistance check fleeing to Canada, new regulations had been put into effect for general assistance welfare payments. That required that I have to wait more than thirty days to reapply for any aid. *Shit!...*Welfare was cracking down even out in liberal San Francisco.

Much of what I had been through on that trip changed me. I would not be able to exactly define what the changes were or what it meant, until much later, but life, living was somehow different.

Further adding insult to my injured being, that shaving problem I noticed back in the Cleveland Greyhound restroom turned out to be genital warts. A result of the surprising amorous sex tryst with Michael (from Michael). *Just fine.* So, there I was not only homeless but with nasty little warts covering my chin. More than the stars had fallen out of the clouds in the sky.

Up...Must Come Down (1995)

In the flick of a mere second, it happened; just as his finger grazed my finger, skin touching skin, my sense of touch synchronized with my sight. A vision of a long, tall, live, breathing, handsome male specimen of God's creation stood there before me. And as well, all within that mere second, the second after the feel of his skin, like a shock of static electricity, my body and whole being shuddered and twitched. Seemingly, within the blink of an eye, I recomposed myself. I put back on my street-hardened, drug-addled game face. "The nerve ofa...muthafucka! Oh, just a light." I mumbled under my breath, my body still reeling from the shock to my senses. My humanness.

That overly handsome fella, fellow street denizen, simply had prompted me for a light to his cigarette. I had been almost ready to bite his head off, thinking he'd asked to bum a cig. "Buy your own…fucking cigarettes!" Bothering me. "Muthafucka!"

As a watch ticked less than a minute or two, I steeled my tweeked out eyeballs back to peering into the windows of each passing vehicle. For each car, I hoped for a potential john desiring to lease my carnal wares. Hoping to continue my methamphetamine fantasy. My tweeked out dream that, in reality, was a 72-hour nightmare.

More and more signs foretold of my existence; my life as I lived it, had come to its near end or at the least reached a breaking point. I realized or accepted how dope had numbed me to the psychic and emotional connection of my body and senses. Sure, in my line of work, I used the body each and every day. It functioned on que, body fluids pumped, cursed, and erupted forth. Veins, nervous systems performed roles as needed, to have meth flowing to and through my brain as a utility to repeat the same process over and over again. Mechanics. Functionality. All of it devoid of emotion and feelings.

Over the course of years, more than a decade by then, the average hooker-hustler gets himself arrested. Prostitution or crimes committed in the commission of selling my body were the only crimes in which I have ever been convicted and which I have served time in jail. The vice squads were always rumored to having to fill quotas of arrests, in efforts to 'clean' up the City of its carnal sins. This phenomenon was more prone to happen in a mayoral election year. More than once, I ended up snagged in one of those not rumored but, for real, vice arrest sweeps, once in LA and then again in San Francisco.

Vice cops go out and cruise the streets in unmarked police cars to entrap a broken-down hustler- hooker plying his or her flesh for sale; illegally. During said sweeps, no sooner than one prostitute is arrested, typically just after quoting the john-vice cop a price for services. He is driven, handcuffed, to a central location, possibly some alley or secluded parking lot. Just as I'd remembered years earlier in LA, they took me out of the car and handcuffed me to another just arrested hustler until there were six of us all handcuffed together, chain gang style. Finally, as the last arrestee got booked, a police van arrived to transport us all down to 850 Bryant Street, the central jail locks up.

A few minutes after being locked inside the police van, all a sudden, I couldn't catch my breath. "Huh, huh...Huh!" I could feel my heart race out of control. I felt it bumping up against my chest. I panicked. All I wanted to do was get the hell out of the dark, cold steel-enclosed, locked van, to get some fresh air so I could breathe. My eyeballs bugged out there in that darkness. Cold sweat poured down my face. I sat there, chained up, hyperventilating thinking, "I'm gonna... die!" If not from losing my breath, from the irrational claustrophobic fear.

Chained and handcuffed, right next to me on the van's bench wall sat an Asian dude I'd seen in and around Polk Street but whom I had never met or even knew what his name was. Intuitively, he then allowed me to lean my head on his shoulder. As I recall the memory correctly, somehow, he maneuvered his hand to gently rub my arm and soothe me. There we were, two grown men, me nearly as big an athlete, cuddled, essentially strangers to one another in a locked police van alongside various other men.

By the time the van had driven us the mile or so down to the jail, I'd miraculously recovered my breath and my sanity. To this day, I have never ever met that Asian dude, never even found out his name. I'm left with the belief that had it not been for his natural concern for a fellow human being; I may well have died there that night in SFPD's van.

Today, I realize I probably had had a panic attack. Never having had one prior to then and only a very mild episode since. Looking back on it, I prefer to see that incident as evidence of a God showing up just when I needed intervention the most. Again, it just seemed another sign, a coincidence of a certain something having been changed.

Bout this time, I'd become experienced procuring 'chicken' for my main speed connection, Hollywood Dave. He at about 40 liked, no craved, to fuck what looked to be young adolescent boys. Justifying my part, they all definitely were past puberty no matter how young they looked. "I hadn't put um out there... on the streets!" I could have said, then, to myself, "they had a choice to say no." I rationalized, trading their asses for my next fix of crystal meth. More times than not, those 'boys' happened to be well on the path to being full-on dope fiend hookers. "I provided both parties a service; good dope for the hooker kid, a fresh new piece of ass to my dealer," more rationalization.

Along came one night, this pimpled-faced little guy with blond dreadlocks. I'd never seen him around before. As young as he looked, I knew him to be a perfect specimen for Hollywood's taste. The kid also just so happened to know a younger sidekick of mine, Lynn, a sweet-natured, androgynous youth having arrived in the City from the Navajo 'Rez' in Arizona. I took Lynn under my wing, as an effort to be responsible for another person of color out there on those mean, White, gay streets. She needed to know, in my opinion, that just cause the lights glittered didn't mean you'd find gold. Since the young kid knew Lynn, my proposal of him turning himself out for dope came across as a little less slimy than it really was.

Sure as shit, I had gambled right. I made the call and set up the scene that resulted in me getting my well-portioned hit of meth for the evening.

It so happened he; Jackson, had finished up doing his deed with Hollywood before I had even left Polk that night to head back to my room to shoot up my hit. "What chu gon' do?" the little punk Jackson queries me. Streets had taught me to answer him with another question.

"What... you wanna go with me? You know...you gotta have 10 bucks to go to my hotel."

The next thing I realized; Jackson seemed like he was coming on to me. Strange. Almost seemed as if he felt grateful to me for setting him up with a good dope connection. He had finished his 'work' and was now off to enjoy himself. A junkie hooker out for my heart. I could so relate to having had done your 'work' and now you were on 'free time' in hustler speak; any sexual activity intended for personal pleasure. In other words, you could exhale, relax. Relax as much as possible, a hyped up, tweeked out junkie who sold his body and emotional time for other men's pleasure possibly could.

For sure, I felt I could switch from one mode to another with ease. My mind could recognize and function differently between the situations. Getting aroused for the pleasure of someone who naturally didn't excite me, felt completely opposite from arousal for my own desire. Or could I?

Under dark night skies, Jackson and I proceeded on walking the route to my 'home', down Polk to Turk Street, then crossing over Market to 6th and Mission; The Delta Hotel.

Even prior to injecting even more dope, in my head, I struggled coping to the real fact of this kid, in street terms, seducing me. Was I not the streetwise veteran? The whole setup was the other way around from how it was supposed to be. Jackson young, white, about 125 pounds wet to my 6'2'', 180 and Black. Maybe, seeing too many unreal stereotyped gay, pornos screwed up my thinking.

Having already started some dumpster diving, from the night's earlier tweek, I also wheeled a shopping cart of garbage found 'treasures' alongside with this young street urchin into my hotel's elevator and pulled the old-fashioned metal cage closed behind us.

Sad and unfortunate, we'd parted company with Lynn. Neither Jackson nor I possessed enough dope for the three of us to get high. Besides, we all knew the score; Jackson's and my intentions were all about the fuck. Otherwise, there was no need for us to be together. For sure, I consoled myself; Lynn understood the ways of junkie, sex freak hookers. What are 'real' priorities?

Post the rumbling through my treasured garbage finds, veins got exposed and readied. Needle point in, blood bubble spotted, plunger pushed, makeshift tourniquet loosened, "Uh...Hum!" The cough. For certain, I modeled an example of bleaching the 'works'(the syringe). No need for that deadly roulette added amongst other deadly risks to be taken.

Next, Jackson exposed, bared, his smooth still very youthful body. I took notice of the hard-yellowed edges on the bottom of his feet. Signs, evidence of how the 'street' ages.

Surely, even almost romantic like, both of us needed application of soap and hot water. Single occupancy rooms, such as mine, lacked private shower facilities. The shower located two doors down. Gathered in our underwear along with my one dingy, long since being white towel. We locked ourselves inside the grimy communal shower room.

I pummeled his nimble loins. Simultaneously, I turned the dials for the correct water temperature and rubbed the remnant soap pieces into a generous lather. I could nearly lift Jackson up in one arm while gripping, stroking him with my other. My mouth and lips alongside actions of my tongue searched, licked, over every fold and crevice to be found.

Cleaned up somewhat, bodies still wet and moist with only a semblance of a towel for drying ourselves. Jackson followed me closely behind, back to my room, loin cloth style. Quickly, I unlocked my door, standing in the hallway, wet, butt naked. I may have had just a little smug intension, displaying evidence of what was to come with that nimble youngster.

Finally, all preliminaries out of the way, down to the fucking. Me into Jackson, right? "Everybody.... all the time... I get fucked." Jackson mentioned, probably a true statement.

Moreover, his idea just did not fit the scene. I heard him say next. "How bout me fuck'n you?"

"I don't... really get fucked," I told him, somewhat incredulously of his question. "And I'm Black and top and he's the tender White, much desired, fuckee. Why couldn't he just go with the 'program? How these things… are supposed to work," I'm thinking. Sex stopped right there, brakes slammed, as we both tweeked off on something else in the room entirely.

When the morning sunlight greeted our bleary, dilated eyeballs, we dressed and left my hotel for no reason I can't really remember, just the fact we're no longer going to be fucking.

Jackson ditched me without warning. Walking up the hill on Mason Street, my eyes cast down toward the sidewalk. I turned around and looked up, he'd vanished. No way could I be upset. I knew the game; just hooker junkies doing what we do...on to the next hit, more teeth grinding, dumpster scavenging, sex here and there.

The whole scene that evening, still, stunned. Having been so long since I had any intimacy with a person I actually desired. From somewhere inside me I knew there had to be some kinda catch.

For years I'd settled for illusionary fantasies of drugs, meaningless sex in substitution for any real intimacy with another man, for well, love. There I said it, Love. My familiarity with the whole drug sex thing never, never, worked out as has been desired. Somebody always got the short end of a deal.

Jackson leaving me, there, in a drug-hazed lurch, had jolted me back to reality.

Note; to later self, Jackson was 17, jailbait, no matter even if it felt like he seduced me.

Fall Down Seven times, Stand up Eight (1995)

Somehow, someplace, someone had informed me that I needed to be at the shelter on Market Street. The one near Van Ness, before 3pm, on Friday. Then and there, I would be able to get my name put on the list for detox to start the process of getting into a drug treatment program.

I got there on time, right at 3 o'clock. As I walked across the expanse of white-painted walls and fluorescent lights of the main room, I passed by hordes of men seated in folding chairs. Older rough-looking men, the type who spent their daytime hours in such facilities in San Francisco. I thought to myself," I'm headed beyond such pitiful fate."

When I reached the desk, I told the staff person the purpose I had come there for. Just then as I was speaking, I was told that I needed to wait due to a critical situation taking place. I turned to look over my right shoulder to witness this disheveled old White man in filthy clothing with matted-up mangy hair and beard. He seemed to be passed out there on the floor. The paramedics had been called and were on the way. I looked back again to see the old man involuntarily vomiting up fluids and as well a green-colored mucus had begun to stream out of his nose. I detected the shelter staff being leery about touching the man in all his bodily filth and uncleanliness. I thought I heard someone say the man, obviously, a wino, was in the throes of a convulsive alcoholic withdrawal, very near death, if not already dead. I'd seen much out on the streets, still, this scene hit me.

Finally, someone back at the desk told me to come back for the next appointment day. I walked out of there, amongst all the commotion, wondering if that old dude had actually died, right there before my very own eyes. I had never actually seen someone die. Although, I knew a lot of folks who had died. That scene, that day, symbolized the formal start of my journey getting clean and off dope.

For about a month or so, I had been clean and attending both AA and NA meetings. I still lived in my single occupancy room, on 6th and Mission Streets in the SOMA district. The same room and place I had been living getting high on speed. The drug life milieu still carried on all around me. Now clean, I had had just about enough of living in that environment.

I found myself at one particular meeting in which a group from Walden House Treatment Facility showed up to attend as well. One of the guys from that group, I recognized from seeing him back when we both were strung out in our depts of addiction. Dude, I always felt as being quite attractive. Some of the other guys in the group looked like guys I saw up around where I frequented using dope; Polk Street, the adult bookstore, and the like.

It occurred to me, "those guys... been where I'd been…doing the same things I'd done". Now, they too, were trying to get clean and turn themselves around. Different from other gay folks I had met in 12step meetings, these fellas were from the same street element I was familiar. "Maybe this Walden House...be a way outta of the fucked-up environment I lived." That night, I made up my mind I wanted to go to that same rehab.

My tightest using pal at the time; Olive, had left Polk and moved to Texas a year earlier. She had moved back to the Bay Area, and one night back in the City, she just so happened to have arrived back clean and sober. For one night Olive came back out to Polk Street to see us old dope fiends. Me, I was just so thrilled and genuinely happy to see her.

Clearly, I can remember a group of dope heads sitting out on the sidewalk, that night, talking loud and excited to be hanging with our old bud. Some other street associate came walking up to speak to Olive. In the manner that junkies do, excited to see her, he offered her some of his dope stash. Olive turned him down saying, "Aw naw! I... don't do that anymore." Stated as a matter of fact with really no explanation and without judgement. It just was like unbelievable. She'd blown me away.

Over my years up on Polk, Olive grew to be one of if not the only person I loved and truly cared about. In spite of all the shady ways junkies treat one another, even me, having sold her coveted punk-styled belt, one with all the studs on it, for a hit speed. Yes me, after all the times I had sworn up and down, I would never be 'that' kind of dope fiend to do such a thing to a friend.

Being there witnessing Olive clean and sober that night made me love her even more. I loved her even knowing she no longer was a part of that drugged-out scene. The exact whole scene I held onto as a part of my identity, who I was. Where Olive and I met and had come to bond with each another so tightly. Even with my jaded heart, I wanted what was best for her. Knowing that what was best would be for Olive to leave the 'lifestyle' and to get away from being around people like us, people like myself.

Somewhere across the Bay, over in Oakland, Olive found and now worked at a legit job. It was quite some time when I'd see Olive again, after that night.

Meanwhile, back at the ranch, back on Polk, a 'friend' happened to come by and gave me a bag of meth one Monday night. It turned out to be fake, bunk. Not knowing that fact at first, I hightailed back to my fleabag hotel room upon receiving the bag of dope. Once locked inside, I filled up a rig as was usual, shot it up in my vein, waited, and didn't feel a thing. "Maybe… this shit just a little weak…" I fixed up another hit. Still, I felt nothing.

Splayed out there on the bare wooden floor, a needle laying by my side. For whatever reason, finally, I had had enough. Enough of all the lying, enough of the scheming, selfishness, and just enough of out-and-out degradation. "There has to be... something else." I thought. Something like what I'd witnessed that night I last saw Olive. "She seemed to be ok... happy without dope."

Long story short, I resolved to be done with dope and started attending 12step meetings, later that same week. In a meeting, came across those former street folks, just like me, in a Walden House treatment program. And to the fact, I had witnessed that old wino dying, while I waited at the shelter. All of it added up to something else. "Maybe there was another way."

My perseverance and determination got me into the Walden House program. I showed up and got accepted into the outpatient day facility. Like clockwork I showed up early in the morning, Monday through Friday, to the location on 14th Street in the Mission District.

I felt my whole demeanor and outlook change. Inside me lay a happiness I had not recalled feeling since I was a boy. Later on in my recovery process, I'd come to know such feelings of elation, as being on a 'pink cloud'. "Who needed to be high?" Shit, I was floating higher than I had been in years and all without dope. "What could be better than this?" During this period, I was getting by only sleeping maybe 3 or 4 hours a night. Again, all without a drop of dope.

Drew my benefactor, during my using days, happened to be delighted with the fact of my no longer using drugs. Despite, his misgivings with us no longer having sex, he did nothing to thwart my turnaround. Truly, I took this to mean he really cared for me and my well-being. Lord knows he had weathered many of my flights of fancy while I was under the influence. Drew's support would later really be put to the test.

In a TX treatment, the modality is designed with the intention of having the addict be stripped bare psychologically, of all the survival defenses one picks up living the life of a dope fiend. Stripping away all that emotional scar tissue you build up surviving only to get that next hit, that next fix. The TX community is meant to be a safe place, amongst other recovering addicts, facilitated by trained addiction professionals. Putting it bluntly, I had signed up and was expected to get 'butt naked' emotionally within the group.

Determined, headstrong, and desperate I latched onto the expectations. I latched on as if I had been in the sea drowning and finally had reached a lifeboat. I can see now that getting clean essentially was my lifeboat. In similar fashion, just like when I was using speed, I figured, if a little made me feel good then more was gonna be the 'bomb'. I went into overdrive following the rules.

"Tell everything," they said. "Learn to snitch on each other." Honesty, as the key ingredient was going to save us. For me that meant, for once in my life, follow the rules! Each day as I continued to show up, clean, it felt as if another layer of my addiction had been uncovered and released. Each passing day, I'd show up and could sense the other fellow addicts in my groups started to be leerier of my presence. Some would flinch or stop conversations as I entered a room. Probably afraid to be mentioning something they were not supposed to be doing, that I probably would bring up in a group session. "Why wouldn't they want to be as free... as I was feeling?" Would be my thinking with no understanding as I unwittingly alienated myself from my peers.

July 8, 96: Forward

Soon some recognizably familiar junkie characters I'd known came into my view, still doing the same shit as before. That night, it seemed to me, the junkies were doing the same shit in the exact same place as before as I's last remembered them.

That day was July 8, 1996; a full 24 hours after my last hit of dope. My first day living not dependent on meth or any mind -altering chemical, now some twenty- something years later. I share nowadays that it felt, that relapse, like I was a 30year old man, by myself, playing with kid's toys; Matchbox cars. It felt like I'd, finally, outgrown tweeking.

Now doing drag. She as proof evidenced of the progressive nature of addiction, had sunk from a newly out of the closet young kid, whose mother was lesbian, to trying the best to be 'fabulous' in the gay 'mecca'. The reality had her as a drug-addicted queen at the homeless shelter. Yet, who was I to pass judgement, there I was too.

One of the ten being Michelle, formerly Michael. A short round Puerto Rican with a 'Latin' attitude to match the stereotype. We ended up bonding. Probably cause she being trans and me Black, neither of us were set to be involved in the fucking and bed hopping the mostly White guys where up to there. Jealous, resentful, maybe. More so, for me I knew, and my gut told me my life had to change. I was there for the long term and not at all interested in the typical bedpost notching so many gay men do to and upon one another, no matter how tempting it seemed. Clearly, I had had more than enough of my body and loins slung up against another man's, for nothing much more than just the ability to be slung. Been there done that.

Working at my job, I learned to prepare lattes and espressos, probably, wasn't that good actually. The gourmet- Starbucks coffee phenomenon just started to take hold and spread. Frisco being the dot com epicenter, folks required some kinda 'up' fuel to keep mostly non-existent dot- whatever business going.

This being my first job in recovery. I just so happened to work alongside a crew of mostly Asian -Americans. Although the City was the most Asian of places in America, except for Hawaii. All of my 8 years living here, I'd never ended up being in such close contact with many Asian folks. All the years I turned tricks, in the City, the number of Asian men that picked me up was less than 4 or 5 maybe.

The only history I ever had in the neighborhood was tricking with one of my regular johns who lived there. Though his name long forgotten, I remembered him for his often told often-told memories of travelling to black Brazil and cause he was so easy to get him off. Get him started, jack him off a little and then blow in his ear a couple of times, soon it would all be over. On more than one occasion, I'd found myself out there, late at night, negotiating which Muni bus would take me back to Polk, the quickest, after 'earning' my fees.

An unusual occurrence happened one afternoon while out working with Bernard. I happened to be waiting on him at some client's home or it may have been a work setting. In the room where I waited, a Major League Baseball game played on a television. I have no clue which teams were playing. As I sat there looking over towards the television, I found myself getting interested in watching that baseball game. Relaxing and enjoying it really. Watching the players, men in MLB have the most perfect male physiques of all professional sports, in my opinion. The whole idea of enjoying watching the game blew me away. Wow! I was actually enjoying sports. Enjoying watching it on TV at least, that seemingly unspectacular afternoon.

Since that day, I've gone on to be a fan in the stands at live baseball games, both in San Francisco with the Giants and also later to cheer on the A's in Oakland. Never have I become a fanatic, you know, knowing all the stats and stuff. From that day on I have been watching pro MLB games of a team I have some allegiance and affinity to. Mostly, it's been the Oakland A's.

A friend, Tom, and I, both residents in the transitional treatment house, still remained friends even after I'd blown up and stormed out of treatment to go relapse. We stayed close through his own relapse as well. Cause, every Black gay man needs to have that one straight, White dude that he is not attracted to be a friend. True or not, that's how our friendship appeared to shape out. Tom seemed comfortable around gay people. I felt at ease around him sharing my gay shit as well as recovery stuff and just life in general.

Recalling these memories having both of my parents deceased, I may have been overcome with my emotions, chugging along the 101 Bayshore Freeway on that game bus. Going to the exact stadium that my daddy probably had watched the Dominican-born, darker-skinned namesake, athlete practice his stunning craft. I imagined my parents' common bond for the love of the sport. Giving meaning, that they shared something in common beyond the physical coupling that obviously produced me.

Despite myself, the arduous journey, pushing beyond my comfort zone, proved well worth the effort. As the night darkened the skies, endless stars fell upon our light pollution-less spot. Our view high above with the sound of wave calming waters. Looking out into that night, my eyes took in the metropolis I called home. It surrounded us, lit up by a million lights spread out as far as my eyes could see.

Some other campers passing by our site, I asked to capture a picture of Tom and I with the vast San Francisco Bay environs behind us in the background. I still have that treasured photo. The effort up that mountain of Angel Island and its priceless reward, seemed to symbolize my uphill journey with rewards of living clean and free in recovery.

They Like Me! Really Like Me! (1997)

My life's little journey happenstance, twice, begat me a lucrative livelihood right at the tail end of the year in December. Both positions bookended desperate path trajectories. In 86′ the opportunity at a top hotel chain opened doors that could have led upward, if not for my additive nature, that started closing like a vice grip. Then in December 97′, the fates led me to a promising occupational arena. In that instance, having been clean for 1 year from meth, proved I had learned something from the previous decade living life as a loser. I walked into the interview from an ad, with my reasonable King's English vocabulary; using enough of the expected verbiage and adjectives that White people tongued. Aced the interview with little work experience in the field.

Hired as a monitor in a group shelter serving homeless families, I opened and locked the facilities outside of the regular office hours of our social service non-profit.

Having worked with and around the director of youth activities for over 4 months, when she quit without notice I was, to my surprise, offered that position. I then had a full-time job with benefits and a $24,000 salary. I officially held a professional title, with business cards printed with my name and all.

Emotionally at heart, I am an overgrown kid myself. I fit the job with a natural affinity. From deep within me I felt empathy for the young kids living there, with families in turmoil, wanting, needing, a safe place to be innocent in spite of the world's harsh realities. My new career reflected the forward growth for me both emotionally and spiritually.

Somewhere I hooked onto the notion that being clean in recovery meant healing and growth in three perspectives; mind, body and spirit. I kept a consistent regular attendance in both NA and AA meetings. I worked with the same sponsor I had before and after my relapse, who guided me, most importantly, through the 12 spiritual steps of recovery to a place of beginning emotional healing.

Just right prior to having my relapse I'd begun to jog regularly. In my using days, a clear giveaway that I was high would be the sound of loud music blasting on my boombox. My love for the music of favorite artists has carried a life-sustaining role for me. That connecting link of blasting favorite tunes loudly on headphones boosted my inner spirit, all the while as jogging positively uplifted me physically. Literally, endorphins generated through physical exertion got me feeling a mild high, a mild little tweek. Actual physical maintenance through some form of exercise I have managed to keep up all throughout my recovery.

Initially, my foray seeking a religious grounding left me spinning out on some metaphysical mission going one week from a Catholic cathedral to another Sunday at a Christian Science reading room to then, a Black Muslim mosque of The Nation of Islam. When inspired, I can really dedicate myself to something.

Fredrick, who I had met by way of my stint at Walden House Treatment facility, heavily endorsed his religious faith and was deeply connected with his church. He was one of 'those' people, you know the type, always quoting something biblical to any situation that came up. "That ain't nothing... but the Devil!" I could hear him say when something turned out not in his favor. As much as we got along as friends, I never really brought into his heavy-handed, 'God's this, God that' spiel.

Yet, I witnessed Fredrick was in flesh as evidence. Black, out gay staying and living clean from dope. I had to acknowledge there must be something 'real' in religion that worked for him and maybe could be helpful in my own growth. I did have a yearning for spirituality. All the same it pleased me to have a Black gay friend to relate to. Black friends as fellow travelers were sparse casualties of my using days.

The City of Refuge, the church where Freddy belonged, held services on Sunday afternoons beginning at one in the afternoon. That's, just so in case the 'child'ren' (translation to Whites and heteros: Black and brown gay folk), who'd gone clubbing the night before, would have enough time for rest and recuperation and still make it in time to get their church on anyway.

The Refuge's worship services just so happened to be held in the same building as a popular NA meeting I regularly attended. A meeting that attracted many Black and folks of color along with other low-bottom addicts who used dope similar to how I had used. I took the geographic coincidence as something like a sign from God that I followed the right path. My habit and drug of choice; methamphetamines, alienated me from such communities during my active use. Now clean, I felt and yearned for some restoration to places and communities I lacked. I wanted to be more whole, connecting to all the pieces that made up who I was coming to be.

The 'refugees', as City of Refuge members often referred to one another, worshipped in a manner and intensity way beyond what my forebears led me to learn practicing faith out in the open. These folks were 'holy rollers'; fallin down screaming in the aisles, God-praying people. I'd never known or could have imagined there be gay folks like that.

Once, way back when I was a boy about 9 or 10 years old, I attended a Black Baptist church service. I never ever forgot that afternoon. It happened on a weekend I spent with my nephew's mother's family. I remember feeling scared as I saw folks, big older women, jumping up, hollering, dancing wildly, screaming and being loud. And, as if that was not enough, it seemed as if church was gonna last forever. The White majority, Lutheran church my family belonged to in my childhood, no one screamed or danced out in the aisles. Church Sunday service was over and done, two hours tops, including Sunday school.

Being there at the Refuge, I, as an adult, in my mind and body felt some sense of alienation witnessing the full screams of worship and praise. I felt uneasy seeing them jumping up and dancing in joyful release. Feeling clueless, at that time, to the freeing religious experience going on in my midst. No one at the Refuge made me feel any less welcome as I appeared outwardly numb in my worship. So, I stayed nonetheless. Feeling enough 'at home' just to be in a place of God, present, just simply as my true Black queer self.

True, sometimes, I resented how when-God in the Spirit- showed up in the shout praises, it always seemed to be the same exact individual, 'saints', as we referred to one another. "Why was God...the Holy Ghost... always speaking…touching the hearts of the same damn folks!" I would think to myself, while standing aside making way as a 'saint' jumped up and hollered, feeling the Holy Spirit.

Now, I had a friend; Freddy and 'family'. A different Black family than the one which I came from in some ways I, still, had the experience of not being fully a part of, like in my own family.

My sponsor Christopher, a big gregarious, White guy I picked out from seeing him at my meetings. Cause, I remembered hearing him share once how he had stayed clean and sober even while seeking sexual fulfillment at the one gay bathhouse in the Bay Area, over in Berkeley. "I had to tell myself... once I got off...to call it a night…and leave," he said honestly, "not to stay all night, seeing how many I could pick up." His bravely sharing such possibly embarrassing, yet, practical aspects of being a gay man in recovery drew me to him.

When I got to working my fourth step in recovery: 'A searching and fearless moral inventory', my prayers were to be as truthful as I was able. In meetings I witnessed many addicts relapse and return to using for failing to be honest working that particular step. Since I had already relapsed, I vowed to myself not to be one of those who did. That last experience I had from being 'out there' again, if only for two days, led me to know and finally realize that I had a 'choice'. Afterward, I could no longer lie and tell myself that using dope was just my fate and I was destined to die alone as an addict, a junkie.

Baker Places; a transitional recovery housing program, the same recovery program that had asked to leave due to my lack of anger management, gave me another chance. They allowed me to return to live in a flat with four other gay men in recovery. I'd have my own room, chore assignments, plus we needed to attend weekly house meetings with a counselor. I was required to meet one on one with the same counselor. The flat was located on South Van Ness in the Mission District. All seemed to be looking up. I had landed in a safe comfortable place to further grow along my recovery.

That summer my buddy, Michelle, did an all-out effort to help me celebrate my first year clean. She ordered me a cake decorated spelling out my 1st year. Michelle, playing the role of the party planner extraordinaire, had our flat's back porch decked out with balloons and streamers. I, still, can remember the love I felt on that beautiful July afternoon, each time I look at the photographs taken that day. The memories bittersweet though. Many of the attendees that day are no longer in recovery, a few even actually no longer alive, due to devastations of addiction. There I was, in my dreadlocks, smiling widely with my missing front tooth. Yet, I felt filled with real, albeit budding, freedom and joy like I've never had before.

Addicts are suggested to refrain from sexual relationships for the first year clean and sober. Yes, nowhere in the AA "Big Book" or NA "Basic Text" is that statement actually written, yet still, some version of that maxim is often heard in the meeting rooms. My first year I kept true to that suggestion, preferring to practice the '3M' method of recovery: meetings, movies and masturbation. As the moon had passed by 365 times, more than eager was I to experience relationships, intimacy and sex drug-free. Not necessarily in that order. I felt like as if I'd arrived. In truth, I had all along desired some kind of meaningful connection in spite of my many fleshful experiences. Even back in the days when I pumped myself full of chemicals as a substitute, affection is what I really wanted. Having reserved my body and being for the requisite year, my Higher Goddess surely meant to reward my discipline and faithfulness with a boyfriend. Dream on Juan.

Jeff Potil (real name used in memorial) just so happened to be a Walden House client at the same facility as my own first residential treatment. Back then, during treatment, I hardly noticed or even remembered him. More likely I had been preoccupied and infatuated with unavailable Derek. Later on, Jeff and I would see one another around in 12 step meetings and may have possibly even gone out for coffee and conversation afterward with a group of other addicts. After one meeting in particular he leaned toward me, to tell me, "Man…I wanted to... just sneak up to your floor and come into your room one night."

"Really!" I replied to him. I really was surprised I never even knew. Yet, it thrilled and flattered me, the prospect of being desired, being wanted. So, I got up the nerve among all the flirting that we were doing. Bravely I asked and invited Jeff to come over to my house, one night, for dinner. He accepted.

Absolutely! To my mind things appeared to be flowing just as they should. Getting clean, working on myself and my recovery while staying celibate for a year. Now, here there was this handsome someone, tall and long just like I favored them. Jeff and I getting together appeared as culmination, the fruits of recovery.

The Friday evening of my 'date' I prepared a simple pleasing meal of baked fish, rice and vegetables. The kitchen rafted with cooking aromas when I heard the doorbell ring. Excited. I sauntered off to open the door and greet Jeff. As I remember it, we kissed, then he followed me up the long flight of stairs to our third floor flat. Feeling awkward excitement mixed with anxiousness, I invited him to take a seat in the living room and watch tv. I darted in and out to the kitchen, engaging in small talk, none of which I recall, till our food was finally done. "No guy has ever... cooked a meal for me." Surprisingly Jeff told me, between taking bites of his food. I had no clue how to respond to his amazement. Maybe, I could have shared that it was my first real date; ever. A date where within the first 15 minutes my clothes were still on, and were intended to remain that way. He and I both evidenced ravages of addiction and its dysfunction. Each of us is in our late twenties and neither having had much if any healthy experiences dating, sex and intimacy.

As an episode of the Simpsons ended, I vividly recall intensely lip-locking Jeff, there on the couch. He then departed, soon afterward, toward his own transitional living quarters elsewhere in the Mission. The night left me feeling clumsily unsatisfied. A sense, I guessed, the way one probably usually feels after a first date. I had no other experience to compare it with.

My newly dating 30-year-old self stumbled clumsily into the next step. "Was I in love? Was he with me? It was too early…to even be considering such" I wondered, if the ill at ease was what everyone experienced. Still, there in my newly budding drug free life, the fear that I feared ultimately; rejection. I felt I should be old enough to know how to navigate being 'with' someone. I didn't. I fell back to relying on my well- honed knowledge set. Sex. Sex always gave answers to bewildering cluelessness. "I know…what I'm doing…with sex!"

Conversing over the phone with Jeff we set up a Saturday night when I would go over his 'house', signaling but, not actually stating our intentions of fucking one another. More awkwardness yet, no confusion though.

Saturday night came, we did. After a cursory meeting of his roommates, whom I had seen around in meetings. We waited till an episode of whatever show on TV ended, it didn't really matter anyway. We eagerly departed off to Jeff's bedroom. Naked within minutes of closing the door, all besides Jeff's holey socks which I asked him to remove. Very intensely we meshed our loins together. Intercourse with Jeff being HIV positive, that fact I knew of beforehand. He never really allowed time or space to discuss or decide on safe sex condom use. Willingly, I participated in that non-discussion and decision making. Soon, too soon, it all was over. That was it. I sensed, felt, as if I had been a human dildo. That same gorgeous guy had just had sex with my body. Lying beside Jeff lightly holding him, feeling his body breathing, I wanted something more. I knew, in those moments of fleeting tenderness, surely, we were not in love. Sex hadn't answered my desires. Had my Higher Power let me down? I left that night wondering. For Jeff, I may have been a fuck, a conquest.

That first year clean in recovery rounded out on an up note. I had not visited nor seen my blood family in over six years. My last appearance 'home', deep within the throes of *addictiondom,* I had capped off with a late-night binge of crack cocaine use. That had me lying about my whereabouts and state of being to my Aunt Deborah who always had been my kindred spirit and ally. On this stay, I resided with my sister Sandra. Ironically, we were not even speaking to one another during that previous visit. Now, with hatchets buried, whatever, had been forgiven and forgotten. Sandra took great effort on her part to have a celebration for my 31st birthday. She had planned a barbeque cookout with a cake decorated with candles and all. I had not had so many birthday cakes since my childhood.

Family in the full sense of the meaning all seemed to make appearances. All my brothers and their wives and mates. Nieces and nephews and even some cousins. What meant the most to me, seeing my elders; my Uncle Don and my Aunts Mimi and Deborah. A real 'holiday'-sized event. My nephew Stacey's growing family all there as well. He and I had fought one another almost nearly to death, only less than a decade before. Right there beneath the sweaty heat of a hot July sun I had the feeling of being appreciated. I witnessed love within the full breadth of my family. Everyone there to celebrate no other 'holiday' event than my birthday, even if it was belated in July. "I'll take it!"

The epoch I lived as a junky always left me viewing my folks only in terms of what they had "did" to me. Standing around me, that afternoon, I blew out those candles gathered among loved ones aware of my queerness and my wayward life as an addict. Even if as much remained unspoken, family showed up to celebrate my humanness and give me love. The lines from actress Sally Fields' Academy Award acceptance speech floated through my thoughts. "They like me....they...really like me!" Before the elders and the generations; the prodigal son had arrived back home.

2K (1999)

"Sit!... Sit!" I yelled, snapping my fingers and pointing. The compact, pretty brown and white pit bull did as I commanded her tail wagging just a little. Whether it was the feeling of total control or just that brown and white cuteness staring up at me, I was hooked.

"We call her Lady", Danny, one of the neighborhood kids who frequented the after-school center where I worked told me, referring to the puppy's name.

"How much you want for her?" I asked against my better judgement. Knowing of how my boss counseled against exchanging money with the kids, non-professional and all that.

"You gotta to ask... my brother," came his reply. I thought, "You mean that older brother…the one who graduated…and hot as hell. The one I hated when he came around the center because I had trouble keeping myself from staring at him.

I actually said nothing but, "okay." Within short order, that afternoon, a price and purchase we negotiated. I now had my first, very own pet, finally at the age of 34.

I chose to name my very sweet and innocent puppy; Scoot, after my mother's childhood nickname. Taking care of a pet reflected expanding growth to my life and recovery. In reality though, I was almost clueless about raising a dog. Looking back, I understood nothing about how to house train a puppy. I ended up going ape shit when Scoot chewed the door frame to my apartment into literal crumbs, a result of being left alone inside, all day long, on a chain.

One of the funniest stories I tell, giving example to my learning curve as a pet owner. One week when I came home, I happened to notice small little drops of blood on the kitchen floor, day after day. I panicked. "Please please... baby!" I cried to the dog, as if she could respond to my pleas, but mostly to reassure myself. I was broke that week till I got paid, having just enough to feed myself and get back and forth to work and school. I felt just horrible that I couldn't be a better pet owner and take Scoot to the vet, because she was obviously sick, hence the bleeding.

On one of those nights that week, after an AA meeting, I went out to a coffee shop with Josh; a friend I knew through Olive, and some others. Josh was to meet us there after retrieving his dog from his apartment nearby. We all were hanging outside on the patio, probably to smoke, then, all of a sudden Josh came up with his rather massive male dog that shoots over to me and starts humping my leg, right in front of everybody. I had just told them of the travails of my ailing puppy. I was freaking out about the dog's actions trying to fuck my leg.

"You dumbass!... Your dog's... in heat". Mary, another friend in recovery I knew through Olive, blasted it at me. Duh! My own menstruating female dog had caused his male dog to hump me. Never having had a dog, clueless. I had feared the worst when I saw the drops of blood on my kitchen floor. It definitely was good for a laugh at my expense. I laughed at my own absurdity too.

Way back in 'gay' years, I'd known of an affiliation called Black and White Men Together (BWMT). Basically, a way for gay guys who dated and fucked outside their race to find each other. Also, way back in the gay time machine an exclusive partner of a gay man or lesbian used to be referred to as one's 'lover'. Both such references sound so outrageous to the ear, now. Black and White men have no trouble finding each other, now, on the internet. 'Lover, the term became more mainstream. The phrase today being; spouse or life partner.

Once, I had attended a convention of (BWMT) years previous. I'd come to the gathering as the young meat of an older White man, I'd met in my early hooking years. This year, I happened to find out about a similar gathering of such men following San Francisco's multifaceted gay parade and festivities. My own propensity to desire White men as sexual, romantic partners, I acknowledge in myself as not something I felt eager to shout from the rooftops. "Damn... snow queen!" I could hear my friend Joe, from the People of Color AA meeting, accuse me.

The gathering picnic was scheduled to be held at some large Victorian flat over in the Castro. Folks came gathered, grouped and mingled. Like in one of those time lapse scenes, I witnessed, close up, in a sped-up fashion, actions that I myself participated in that in a sense shamed me. Witnessing it in real time, I saw guys in the flat talking to each other, one Black, one White, inside and outdoors on the patio. It was just assumed that all of us were probably single and interested in a sex fling, at the least. After a time, I saw, when a possible hook up coupling hadn't panned out. Soon, other possible matchings I witnessed, another set of one Black, one White guy could be seen. Eventually, as the time passed by, the couple switching and match ups seemed to come about quicker and faster.

Really, I don't know exactly why what I saw going on surprised me, nothing I'd probably hadn't seen before at any gay bar or club with regularity. Maybe, I must have never paid much attention to such or more likely I was too high to notice. Maybe, seeing those guys each one Black and White, just continuing to go after another one, as long as it was of the opposite race, almost like everyone was interchangeable. Personality, character, all that kind of stuff simply was of no mind.

At this point I decided that I needed to leave the 'gathering'. Whether I was leaving out of disgust or lack of hooking up my own self, I'd seen enough. On my way out, departing the Victorian, I just so happened to see someone I recognized sitting in one of the rooms. Rodney, a White fellow my age I had met and knew from seeing him at 12-step meetings. Also, I knew him to be some kind of religious person. Having seen him once attending a service at City of Refuge. My church. Particularly, I'd remembered Rodney looking a bit out of place, that day, amongst the traditionally excited Black praise and worship goings on. I walked into the room where I saw him and we greeted one another. "Hey Rodney", I smiled.

"How've you been.... Juan?" He asked me in return.

"Who else... you know here?" I queried him with the unspoken implication that he had to know of the whole Black and White thing. "Maybe he was of the same preclusion?" I had had no idea that he was possibly 'available'. "I'm taking off now... But, here take my number." I passed him a slip of paper with my phone number written on it, wishing confidently he'd call while simultaneously vowing to myself never to be involved with an organized grouping of that type again.

True enough, as I'd hoped, Rodney did call me. Soon after we make arrangements, hooked up and fucked one another. Afterward, I guess we kinda stumbled somewhat into becoming a couple. I can look back, now, on that time as having been given a blessing. Blessed for having had the experience of sex and the added, longed for romance topping off my early recovery.

A phrase not uncommonly spoken of in the recovery rooms, "it's either romance...or finance", that lies at the root of an addict's troubles having to live life straight, no chaser.

Rodney lived at home with his mother down the Peninsula in San Jose, almost an hour away from Oakland. He'd usually spend his time in the City as an extended weekend excursion, where he'd have the need to crash on someone's couch during his stay. To my discovery, as we each learned about one another's lives, Rodney was enrolled and taking courses at a community college as well. To the good, we were sexually compatible with one another. That's needless to say an important aspect for gay men. He had a positive diagnosis and that made no difference to me. "Everybody needed practice...fucking...and staying alive." And I was to assume also, having met him before in the rooms of recovery. He practiced his own 12 step recovery program. All seemed well. Pistons firing on all cylinders. What more could I ask for?

Want to see your glaring defects of character? Get into a relationship. One hears that adage in recovery rooms too. I viewed my expectations of a relationship as realistic. In hindsight, I was so desirous of having romance I wanted perfection, almost a kind of fantasy really. "Who was supposed to call who? How often? When we were together…were we supposed to just be staring lovingly into one another's eyes?"

Spending time together with Rodney, over a weekend at my apartment, I came to discover I possessed a competitive steak. We played board games to pass some time. He won every frigging time. That same weekend nearly had us getting into a fight over which movies we were going to pick to rent and watch. I wanted to see "Deconstructing Harry", a Woody Allen comedy flick (I still enjoy watching although; it bothers me). Rodney, he grew excited with the prospect of having me see the "Matrix". I didn't know it, at the time, the "Matrix" had some kind of a futuristic sub plot of a world beyond race. Then, I just carried the opinion of it as some fantasy action flick. Not really my cup of tea.

In spite of tensions we carried on, if not happily. Lingering in the back of my mind I'm thinking. "Damn…a relationship ain't spost'ta be this hard!" Upon waking up, one morning with sun bright in the sky we both leapt up out of the bed to rinse out our mouths before making love. Loved morning sex, though not the morning breath. During our sex making, a call came that, obviously, I let go straight on to voicemail. One of my home group members from AA, had gotten the word of my having been fired from my job at the East Oakland rec center. Her voice came on, "Juan I'm so sorry that... that happened. I'm here for you... if you need to talk." "Beep!" Distinctly, I remember the voice and the call ending simultaneously at the exact same time as I climaxed. Still, my thoughts took in her loving offer of support as my spent body fell heavily into the arms of Rodney's gentle embrace.

My job that I had had was at the Discovery Center, an after-school program of the city's parks department in Fruitvale, East Oakland. It aimed at teaching hands-on applied science principles to racially diverse, working class, neighborhood youths. The head guy, my boss, a White fellow in his fifties with a Berkeley, leftist sensibility, specifically wrote the grant that funded the program and our jobs. Kids dropped in at the center each day and learned proper use of heavy drills and machine saws, under our supervision. For example, they would make rudimentary wooden- wheeled, 1 volt -powered electric cars. Our focus meant to teach them how to use the equipment while applying safety measures. While just maybe, they might become interested in some of the mechanical and science principles along the way of just building things and working with their hands.

This just so happened to be the time of the Pokemon phenomenon, particularly among the school-aged boys we served. It seemed to be everywhere. My neighbor and a past employer of mine, Lisa, told me one day in passing, how she had even allowed her own son to skip school one day in order that he could go to the premiere of the Pokemon movie. Cause those first chosen few, waiting in line, had the possibility to able to get a rare collectable card, only given out at the premiere. That day which as I remember happened to be like a Wednesday, a school day.

Each day I'd arrive to work, often by way of riding my bike and catching the MacArthur Blvd bus. Once I arrived, I'd change into my black t-shirt and faded black almost grayish jeans, kept on site as uniform to get dirty in. I did my professional best while working one day when one of the regular boys came in and asked me. "Can you loan…4 dollars for a Pokemon?" I just stood quietly and listened as he desperately described one of the characters that he had no clue that the cards only had some meaning to boys his age. The kid had come in that day after having just lost some card. I had seen and witnessed a group of the boys, outside the center, gambling amongst themselves to get the most sought-after cards. Looking at this breathless desperate 11-year-old, trying my best not to embarrass him. I remember thinking, seeing his reactions, how similar this kid appeared to be having a craving like a dope fiend hunting for the next fix. "These damn cards… got the kids act'n like junkies!"

My firing a result of an accusation of sexual impropriety with a child; not true. Still, just the accusation alone was enough to be believed. Due to me being suspected of being gay; true. That was all it took. The father of the kid I'd been accused of, stormed right in the center and punched me dead in my face. No police were called and of course, I left with my life. Upon hearing of my horrific travails, my sponsor supported me while generally being baffled and shaking his head as to why I even wanted to pursue a profession with such unjustified hazards. In hindsight, the theme of accusation, by way of being gay, did happen to follow my career pursuits, especially working with poor and minority populations.

My position at the park ended as the budding relationship with Rodney crashed. We ended up parting one another's lives not hatefully but, yet on unfavorably. Rodney may have been resentful that I broke it off with him. In essence, he got dumped. Always, I am the one to end things. The one to end any real intimate possibilities out of the fear of being rejected, so I'd do it first. Fear and my insecurities rose up to the surface when we were together alongside my expectation that being 'in love' meant perfection. Me even in recovery, still, a night owl and Rodney an early riser, for example, left the weekends we spent together with even less actual face time. I wanted the 'us' time so badly, yet still, so clueless as to what or how to get there. So, I bailed.

When I was still new to the City, a decade earlier, I had worked with the US Census. In fact, that ended up being my last legitimate job I held, before I got clean. Due to my dope fiendness I never actually even completed that job. Recovery allowed me to come around and complete that circle by working in the 2000 Census. That time around the area I enumerated was located in the East Bay and North Berkeley mostly. My work skills having been so improved, without the side effects of shooting meth in my veins, I got promoted to the position of follow-up supervisor.

Most memorable of my time with the census was working with one of my co-workers; an older Black woman, about the same age as my mother would have been. "You know you need to be careful…round these 'White' liberals." She somewhat whispered to me confidently one day working doing our follow up duties. I felt as if I needed to take her warning to heart, mostly due to respect seeing her as my elder. She graduated college back when few Black women obtained a degree. She had even written a children's book that had a Black girl protagonist. "I wrote it for my grandbaby." She told me the day she presented me with a copy of my own to keep.

The short time we were together fates had us sharing a two- way street of wisdom and knowledge. I came to discover her weariness of 'White' liberals as ringing true as I worked day by day, out surveying the environs of the most liberal bastion in the nation; Berkeley. The places I counted were White, wealthy, having all these barriers blocking the residential streets to through traffic. Endlessly, this frustrated my driving and locating places to park while doing my work. Not uncommon I'd encounter knocking on the door of addresses on my route, doors that were answered by persons of Latin descent with limited English skills. I concluded, maybe correctly, those persons to be the hired servant help. "So much for equality of the masses…here in Berkeley." I thought of the hypocrisy.

Maybe cause I felt like she was my elder, I shared with my co-worker some of what I'd call practical wisdom and coping skills when having to deal with drug addicts. In our time working together we had discussions in which she made the admission that both her grown daughter and son were each addicted to crack cocaine. Telling me how she had, recently, paid her daughter's rent at some low- end hotel. "I did it…she don't have to sell herself!" She insisted on her efforts to help her only daughter, just to discover later that same junkie daughter had gone ahead and spent the money intended for rent on dope anyway.

"What of your son?" I asked her, yet, I expected hearing some sexist reasoning, common among black families, of why she hadn't done similar actions for her addict son.

"He…can take care of his'self." She retorted insistently. Although I wanted to, I did not have the heart to inform her and shatter her delusion that men addicted to dope, especially in and around Frisco, were known to sell their bodies too to get a dope fix.

"In the future...you maybe should…actually pay the rent yourself instead of giving her cash." I advised her in relation to her feeling compelled to help her drug addicted daughter. Such practical knowledge seemed to give her comfort even in the midst of desperation about her children.

Added to my endeavors in the year, like the census, I got the notion of believing myself up to the task of working on a political campaign. All in effort to serve my community. For the better part of the previous decade I'd existed, mostly, as a parasite on the communities where I lived. Something inside me longed to give back, in a way put back, some of what I had taken.

2000 being a Presidential election year. Al Gore, the current Vice President, ran as the Democratic candidate. In my opinion he was a sorry excuse to represent the 'Left'. I wasn't buying it. Politically I detested the administration of President Clinton throughout the eight years he held the office. I'd voted during the period whilst still addicted to dope, yet, not for that Democratic candidate. With his promoting the 'War on Drugs' and all the resulting devastation on the communities and populations affected. I attributed that pain with a direct line to Clinton, given my own front row seat as witness. No politician of the era proposed rehab and treatment. "Lock they…Black ass up!" Was the unspoken, true sentiment of the times. The notion of those cruel policies perpetrated on Black and poor folks, fostered and pushed into action by Democrats made me sick to my political core.

Ralph Nader, the decades-long consumer and public advocate, was seeking a long-shot candidacy for the office of President. Let me state the fact here: I, nor anyone I worked with on the campaign that year ever expected Nader to actually win the nomination for the presidency. Many, as did I, believed that if he won enough votes and support, the ideas and policies he promoted might, might, be taken on by the eventual Democratic nominee.

On a number of Saturday mornings and afternoons during that summer I'd be found with my fold-up ironing board for a table, outside the Ashby BART station registering voters while passing out 'Nader 2000' campaign information to those interested. Man, did I witness an eye opening and an earful. "How dare you!" One White liberal lady, I assumed, shouted toward me for my not automatically supporting the Democrat candidate. Implying, cause I was Black that I really had no other choice. "You might as well… vote for the Republican!" I also heard in rebuttal on those long, yet, exhilarating afternoons that summer. Most of my fellow campaign comrades happened to be White, yet, I did recall there being a Black woman, supporting the campaign, helping me register voters on at least one Saturday.

The campaign held a significant rally meeting one night in San Francisco on Valencia Street in the Mission. Memorably, I recall a fellow Black man, close to my age, speaking up. "Right now, the campaign is not talking about issues...important to people of color." That statement of truth, I could tell, seemed to fall on deaf ears in that hall that evening. In retrospect I could sense, then, due to such facts, that much of our campaigning efforts were ultimately doomed.

Sitting there that night in the somewhat stuffy meeting hall, out of the corner of my eye, I remember looking across the room to see this one couple. A middle-aged, White, Baby Boomer man and woman appearing as stereotypical aging Hippies, as if straight from central casting. The real deal, there they were with long graying hair nearly barefoot except for their Birkenstock sandals, no tie dyes for them though. Being there in that hall with them, that night, I got a sense, a feeling really. There they were, and had been, standing up and fighting the 'good fight'. Ideas I believed in, they'd most likely had been struggling for almost as long as I'd been alive, win or lose. Appearances aside, I felt proud to be there amongst them in solidarity that evening.

The gifts of recovery just kept on giving, I rounded out the year traveling a weekend to Toronto Canada. I'd longed for years to be able to call myself an 'internationalist'. In a little less than a two-year span I'd visited as many countries, including Guadalajara, Mexico. Crossing the international border into Canada carried significant meaning for me. Six years prior, during the height of being in the grip of methamphetamines, I had sought escape across the border to Canada as the solution to my seemingly cursed life. The blunt fact of my not being allowed to seek that escape, to do a 'geographic', as we term it in recovery, began the process and journey of my getting clean and finally seeking recovery. For as far back as the age of 16 I had been fleeing from my problems, fleeing reality, by changing my geography.

Having then been denied, yet, my curiosity led me to venture and find out what the peaceful, if mostly frozen land to the North was all about. Getting past customs without a passport (pre-2001), I took this as a sign my Creator answering my dreams. Picking up the rental car inside the vast complex of Canada's largest airport; Person International, I drove off into Friday rush hour traffic. Driving the freeway had me a little off kilter by the fact of bilingual freeway directional signs in both French and English. Nonetheless, I navigated my way to the small bed and breakfast on the east side of the city. Intentionally, I had chosen that location to benefit my budget and the location being within one block's walking distance from the Bloor Street subway line.

Friday, that first night in the city, I set myself off to find the gay ghetto. Different than Frisco I discovered Toronto to be an indoor city. I could have guessed so due to the basic necessity of having to be indoors for nearly eight months of the year. That evening I found it to be not as cold as I'd expected it to be. As if by instinct, I found and made my way to the hustler's stroll. Confident of my pursuits, I even went as far as to walk up to this blond, slightly disheveled young specimen of male flesh. "Hey...you want a coffee…somethin'?" He looked me up and down and guardedly accepted my offer while directing me where to go. Once inside a small diner, sitting across a booth from this young guy, at 34, I didn't exactly picture myself quite old enough to be a trick. A 'troll' as we'd referred to older men back in my, not to recent, hustling days. I think I slipped the young man the Canadian equivalent of 5 bucks; walking money, paid the bill and then I gracefully made my exit from the diner.

Toronto's gay district, still, contained a plethora of bathhouses. Again, maybe, due to the weather. For the toll of less than $20, and it being a weekend, with reasonably good looks one could feel certain to get laid. That night, I did.

Addiction's 'dis ease', I came to discover in my time on this getaway can appear in many forms. Near the end of my active use of dope, I'd be thoroughly high on meth while at the same time actually spending as much or more money watching porn at the adult peep store as I'd spent on actual dope. The sex addiction, the particular hunger, sprung its deceptively pleasurable, hydra-headed nature to the fore on that weekend.

As well all my appetites took in extra helpings in Toronto. I ate thoroughly three times a day and shopped for clothes like there's no tomorrow. I purchased a 3/4th length heavy leather coat. In the ten years I had it, I think I actually wore it once. Yet, I just had to buy something leather, because I discovered leather goods particularly inexpensive there in Canada.

Toronto the 'good' opened up before me as I traveled the streets and ways and passed by many people of all races and colors, in particular numbers of black peoples (without the capitalization) more so than I'd likely would encounter in the Bay Area back home.

That sexual hunger swelled up within my loins, having been set forth on the first night in the city, desired me to have more. Be careful of your wishes.

Inside another cavernous darkly lit bathhouse, I slipped into his room. A man, long and slender, handsome. I somewhat remember him being half clothed in black leather if having anything on at all. Definitely this the most attractive man I'd been with sexually since having gotten clean. In that dark bathhouse cubicle, on the second night, we poked, prodded, rubbed, licked and sucked one another's bodies till we're almost made tender, almost sore. Sliding back and forth, dicks, tongues and asses. Periodically, he sniffed from a small brown bottle of amyl nitrate- 'poppers', a long-believed gay male sex enhancer. "That's ok…I'm good." I declined his courtesy of overing a sniff to me. The idea of, feel and 'smell' of sex, real sex, was all the enhancement I needed. That alone was enough to get me 'high'. Really. The potent racing of my blood throughout my body added with the erotic escape from the world held me gripped. Gripped feeling almost the same as I felt back when I was chemically induced.

"Toronto's… the shit!" Such sentiments whirled around in my head late into that same night after having left the baths. Making my way to the subway, passing by my path, this light-skinned, high fore- headed, Black man came into my notice. We both cruised one another and then stopped to strike up a conversation. Not being sure of myself or maybe just feeling guilty that I'd already had more sex in two days than I'd had in as many years, we just exchanged phone numbers. I did seem to remember the guy mentioning that he'd come from Djibouti, a country located in the horn of Africa.

Encountering that 'African' man that late night, actually that early Toronto morning, thrilled my ego. In the city I'd become hidden from my recovery support. The bathhouse milieu triggered me as well, having been such sites of my past using haunts. The deep underbelly of weakness; addiction, took hold. The next night, Sunday, in the 'grip', had me lurking through the halls of yet another bathhouse completely naked, on my third evening at such a venue.

Searching, as I was, for that same hot man I'd so enjoyingly fucked the better part of the previous evening or more likely just seeking another sex 'fix' to satiate the, now, almost burning hunger that could not be satisfied once I'd started. I knew not for sure. The sexual boosting of my primal ego led me to be traipsing through the maze-like, bathhouse corridors fully nude as if I was the hottest male specimen to ever grace that locale. Shoulders stiffened. "Hell! You should have seen…the guy I fucked last night." I would have told anyone giving me the odd once over. Unbeknownst to the fact that most of the other dudes, that night, just hoped to get a least one fuck on, paying my cocky, nude self no nevermind.

Canada's largest metropolis presented me with a gift. A gift I actually already possessed. Something I had never before acknowledged as anything to be treasured. That weekend all around me, I passed by and amongst other Black people, black men in particular. Yet, I seemed to perceive and felt a certain coldness. Ever since I've walked on this planet in the 'man-sized' male body nature gave me, I carried the White society's fear of that same Black male body. Along with that, an imperceptible, but definite, lift to my inner soul followed along by my side. I'd never ever realized this fact until I discovered myself roaming the streets, there, in Toronto, Canada.

The majority of people of African descent, encountered there, were immigrants. Diaspora black immigrants unburdened by the weight of America's slavery and aftermath. The centuries-long battering to the spirit, barred across generation to generation in the Black man's body. This discovery came about cause ever since 'walking' as a man, whenever

I'd pass by any other Black man (capitalized B), whether one homeless or suited, absolute strangers, we'd each acknowledge the other's presence. A certain, "What's up," signaled by unspoken language, often just a slight tilt of one's head or a second's look in the other's eye. Yet, an acknowledgement that signaled each of us, no matter our individual circumstances, carried weight. The burden brutally beat upon flesh, upon the bodies and souls of our ancestors, predecessors, our brethren. That two second 'sign' said, "We're still here…Brother… no matter what!" I'd not experienced nor felt that uplifting acknowledgement in three and half days.

Such left me off kilter, lost somewhat. That internationalism gave me the gift of 'home'. I had a place to be and a 'lift' to carry.

Erotic Neurotic (2001)

Jeff, a buddy of mine, true to his word one Sunday, drove over Oakland, rounded me up and took me off to the firing range. Since meeting Jeff in the rooms of recovery, we somehow bonded over thrill seeking. Many a times Jeff related his trill at desiring and seeking out transgendered hookers, amongst other things. Even with his adventures I considered him a friend and good guy at heart.

Once we got to the range, looking around, I took notice that the place seemed to be filled with the sorta fellas I'd most surely not want to be associated with otherwise, probably all George the II(Bush) supporters, I assumed. In those off-putting surroundings, the for real 'White' spaces, I let Jeff take the lead as well as being my tutor. "BOOM! BOOM!" I held the crafted steel firmly within both of my hands, feeling the immense power and projectile energy released out the hole at the end of it. Corresponding ripples of that same released energy shot back through along my arms and down my body. Puffs of smoke giving off a smell unfamiliar to me, filled the air. Jeff informed me that I was smelling gunpowder. "It's kinda like... having an explosion...in my hands" I related to Jeff, the sensation of firing the gun.

"Ha ha" With a wide grin is all he responded to observation, barely containing his thrill at showing me how he got some of his jollies.

"BOOM!" "BOOM...BOOM!" I could hear even louder shots fired coming from the booths inside the building.

"That's a…45!" Jeff informed me, meaning a 45-caliber pistol. Damn! I really do remember it being so fucking loud. I got back to practicing more shots with each one of Jeff's pistols; a 22 revolver and another one that you popped in an automatic clip, as I recall. Jeff helped me practice my aim shooting directly toward a paper target with the bullseye, about 50 feet straight in front of me.

In the car on the ride home back to Oakland, "So, you…wanna get you one?" Jeff asked me, seriously.

No..." I almost laughed. "I really wanted to try it out...shooting one, but...nah I'm good... I don't need one." My reasoning, although not outright saying so, I'd been getting along thus far in my life without having to pack a mini, hand-held 'bomb' at my side. "Hey, why change now?" I gratefully thanked Jeff for being my guide and taking me out to explore a new experience. That was all it was for. I've kept that day's bullseye target packed away somewhere, as a souvenir.

Drew was, still, financially supporting my schooling and as well-being the main 'cheerleader' in my corner taking on this new life in recovery. Taking up a suggestion from my boss at my last position, career wise, I started taking college courses in early childhood education. And, for my own desires I took courses in photography. I had a somewhat dream, fantasy more likely, of becoming one of the greatest high art erotic photographers. No matter how delusional, I thought to meld the worlds of porn, I knew, with my higher education, possibly turning it into some artistic vision.

Boldly I went forth. And to my surprise I had no trouble finding models. I asked some guys from my church and also, from my recovery meetings. Even some classmates offered to model for me, mostly au naturelle. I asked a dating partner I'd met online. My photography captured both men and women in my nudes. Even now I can recall how I deliciously I enjoyed feeling some slight power in having people take off their clothes, allowing me to pose them in my own photographic image. Hopefully coming up with some erotic artistic vision. Looking back now, I probably could have learned more about the actual mechanics of photography and the art, yet I reveled the experience. Now, I see that it was all part of exploration and the healing process I had to go through.

The final project, in my first course required us to finish the semester using the skills we learned taking a self- portrait. I decided mine was to be me completely nude staring straight at the viewer from behind a five-foot tall, rectangle of plate glass. It seemed only fitting that I myself should be photographed in the suit God gave me. Walter, another friend in recovery, played the role of photographer's assistant that afternoon when that revealing portrait was captured. He less likely to be awkward in that situation, because Walter and I previously had had sex and had seen one another sans clothing.

My self-portrait final actually consisted of two portraits. The second of which I was not actually physically in. That self-portrait featured a photo showing a chalk outline on a pavement, the kind police use in a murder crime scene. The chalk outline juxtaposed with a deep shadow of a figure, me, holding the camera and capturing the scene. The photo I shot in the alley up off Polk Street, a site where I had used dope many times before. Back when I was homeless tweeking meth freak. My aim and intention meant to display both compositions revealing a sorta then and now aspect. Oddly enough, it never occurred to me how exposed I would be, literally, presenting my nude personage in a photo right in front of my classmates.

Word of my nudity circulated around the photography department at City College. In the end though, the experience left me feeling somewhat free, like something I'd never experienced before, like, "Now what!" After having had that experience, I could kinda almost understand the mindset of a nudist. It's only a body. We all have the same parts.

When the summer rolled around, school was out, I needed to find another full-time job. My JCC gig only lasted while school was in session. That left me needing to find something temporary that I could quit by September. "Who was gonna hire me under such circumstances?" I wondered. The bright idea came to me; "work at Frenchy's, the porn store." Surely, they'd likely hire me under such circumstances and I got to thinking it could be a place to enter the business; erotica, even if it was just the cheap sleazy end of it. A starting point for my erotic photography. Conscious or unconsciously in the back of my mind, some part of me wanted to be back amongst the neighborhood of my old stomping grounds. Getting paid to be a voyeur of that environment so to speak. This really took something else to convince my AA sponsor of my necessary and purposeful need to be working in such environments. I chose to have the mindset of looking at it all as an adventure. Decidedly, I kept a journal detailing the ins and outs of where and what I would see in my daily travails at the porn store job site.

During the course of working at Frenchy's, off Polk Street, I'd run into Aaron. Back in the day, I'd once taken him under my wing as my little brother. My little White skinny heroin junkie, brother that is. Yet, there he was all grown up. I knew him back when he was still underage jailbait, selling his loins on the stroll to get a fix. Now, much over 18, and still, most definitely strung out. Appearing worse for the wear, at about 25 years old, he looked as if he could be almost 35. Aaron sheepishly smiled when we first ran into one another, after so many years. His smile displaying his missing front tooth, probably more than likely the fruits and result of living the dope life. Every time from then on, I'd run into him crossing paths, Aaron would try to hit me up for money. Feeling almost like I was being taxed. I considered it in some ways that it was just his devious way of getting back at me for being clean and his shame of still being out there stuck and strung out. I could see it in his face. And it still bugged the fuck outta me. Strangely enough I didn't run into too many other faces I'd recognized from my own using days. Maybe the scene hadn't changed but, least the faces surely changed.

Many days I'd bring my camera along with me to work and possibly take pictures of some guys I'd hoped to encourage letting me photograph them. The running cast of characters, customers and coworkers in and out of the store made up a motley bunch. From my trainer supervisor, who was from Iran to the Black security guard who hailed from Nigeria, Sammy. Who in the course of our time working together, informed me of his belief that AIDS was a White, Western conspiracy? Then there was my main supervisor, Mike, who had enrolled at San Francisco State taking courses on erotic film editing.

Then finally, there was Danny, a tall skinny White guy with a laughing grin. In the course of talking one evening, we discovered that both of us just so happen to be from the same small city of Fort Wayne. Each of us also having attended the city's Lutheran parochial schools.

This is where the recovery adage of, 'people places and things', came about to teach me a difficult lesson. Let's just say I became infatuated with Danny. Something about us coming from the same hometown just got into me. I couldn't shake it, like it was some kind of coincidence, fate. Being around the everyday perversion of the sex brought it out in me as well. One night I even asked and paid Danny five bucks to take off your shoes and socks and let me photograph his feet. Strange is as strange does.

After a month or two of this, what always felt like flirting, I got it within my head that I'd take Danny home with me one night after work. That night came about or I thought it had as I closed the shop and set the alarm to go home back to Oakland. Danny followed along beside me as I walked up to the bus stop on Van Ness. In my mind Danny was coming with me. Yes, I knew he actively was using dope. Probably right then, that very night, I got the sense cause I really, really desired him, I'd maybe even entice Danny to come with me with the lure of some dope. There hidden in basic carnal desire, "how bad… did I want to fuck him.?" Was the desire enough for me to relapse? Willing to relapse for the fantasy of having the guy from my hometown?

I made it home that night, traveling the long ride across the Bay Bridge to Oakland, on an AC Transit bus deep in the dregs of my emotions. Upon finally getting home inside my dark apartment, I neglected to turn on the lights, it didn't seem important. First, I dialed the number and called my sponsor all teary-eyed and blubbering. Yet, I blurted out to him how I'd just nearly relapsed after nearly 4 years clean. Told him the truth of possibly giving it all up, for a fuck. He comforted me by just listening to me moan at nearly two in the morning. On that phone call I released whatever it was I needed to get out and let go. I knew that I had had a close call with my recovery.

As another gift of recovery, I began cherishing an uplifting closeness with my Aunt Mimi. Her daughters, my cousins, lived out on the West Coast too. So, I would get to visit and spend time with Mimi out west and also see her when I'd get to vacation back home in Indiana. I had encouraged my siblings to the idea that we should give a surprise birthday dinner celebration that year, our aunt's 70th birthday. No one in my family has or had really lived much beyond that age. So, I assumed the time to be appropriate. After having the experience of losing my mom, one lesson I had learned from it all, was that you needed to honor elders and loved ones while they are still here with you. The birthday was in August. Which meant I would be back home amongst the family, in the sweltering humid summer temperatures.

Who would have known that in these interactions and visitations with family it always seemed to bring to the surface deep emotional reverberations? Somehow, during the summer months when I would visit, residing with my sister, each time I'd end up getting laryngitis. I figured because she always had the air conditioning in her home pumped up high. On this particular trip I learned, to my revelation, that the laryngitis, sore throat, actually resulted from the screaming matches I got into with particularly sore family members. Once again, recovery came around to show me that just because I am recovering, not everyone else was. Even more importantly, they were not going to do so according to my timeline. Stacey, my nephew, just so happened to be the antagonist in this incidence.

Over the visit I witnessed him drinking, tall-can malt liquor, seemingly almost continuously. Doing my best, I kept my opinions to myself, only when one morning he himself stated and questioned "probably… shouldn't be drinking this?"

"Maybe...not so much." I responded to him with a look that said, "didn't you just answer…your own damn question?" Remembering it back, now, I have not a clue what the argument started over, but we ended up shouting and getting into one another's faces loud enough to have awakened the whole apartment complex.

Recalling the near-death match that had taken place between us, a decade or so earlier, that morning at my sister's, we only shouted at one another. No physical blows took place. Shortly following after that particular shout match, blow up, I noticed how my throat started getting sore.

Aunt Mimi arrived in town from Flint, as we were all expected to keep the secret about the surprise birthday dinner. Each of my siblings were to pay their own way at the dinner with the exception of my older brother Steve, who I had agreed to cover. He, in the throes of his own active addiction, could not have been included in the dinner without someone helping. Overhearing such conversations about this fact, between me and my brother Craig, Sandra took this as an offense cause no one offered to cover for her son; Stacey. He for reasons similar to his Uncle Steve couldn't afford to go out to dinner with the rest of us.

I'd viewed the idea of the dinner as a gift of gratitude from among my aunt's nephews and nieces, not the grand nieces and nephews, anyway. In the end, Sandra got upset and said she would not be attending our aunt's birthday dinner. Plans went ahead without her despite the ensuing tension in the household where I was laying my head during this visit.

All of us dressed up and gathered at Hall's Gas House, Fort Wayne's reasonable version of fine dining. Aunt Mimi soon arrived at the restaurant and to the surprise of seeing all of us there, she immediately burst into tears. Tears of joy. I'd only seen my aunt cry twice in my life, the other occasion of note at my mother's funeral. Looking at her, I actually felt as if I was looking through her to see the little girl that, obviously she once was. This tender emotional display tapped into the child in me. Overcome in the moment, I knew and deeply felt the genuine love she had for me. She'd loved me exactly as I was. All of me. I too began crying with her and I didn't care and it didn't matter who else saw me crying or what they thought of it. Writing here the record of that memory, years later, I still remember the time as one the most joyful moments of my recovery.

As the universe would have it, my brother Craig paid for half of the whole tab at the dinner anyway and, in the end, it didn't matter who was covering for who. It was all about the simple joy of gathering with family and being in the company of those we love. Sitting across from me, Aunt Deborah asked me, "what happened…to Sandra?"

"She…decided not to come…when I said I was paying for Stevie and not Stacy."

She looked back at me, kind of shook her head and gave a roll of the eyes, seeing how my brother Craig had covered most of the tab so no one had to worry about money, "We'd need her bad attitude...here tonight…anyway." I laughed in agreement and thought, "Family."

Next morning on my way into the kitchen, Sandra informed me of how she had spoken to Aunt Mimi on the phone since the last night's dinner. Telling our aunt how her absence having been of pride. She said that Aunt Mimi told her she understood, she understood cause of her own such pride in the past. Again, 'families.'

I thought of myself being lucky, for maybe the first time in my life, I realized I had some meaning; some meaning coming from the family I'd been born into.

Before all of us out of towners were set to return back to our homes elsewhere, we all ended up coming over for drinks (alcoholic for them) and confab at my brother James' home. Upon my walking in the door that afternoon, Aunt Mimi purposefully greeted me with a kiss on the lips. Another sign, if unspoked, that I was truly loved. I most clearly understood her unspoken language.

At Pride that year, gay pride that is, I actually held a feeling of some genuine pride of my own. I could also remember back to just a few years earlier, deep in my addiction, how I'd felt shame during Pride festivities. Though, erstwhile fully taking advantage of the party atmosphere, soaking in all the sexual overflow and excess amongst and around the events that I had no money to actually attend.

Recovery brought such a change to the life I was living. Ironically, now, living a life with some actual pride, I partook in no extracurricular sexual activities happening around that year's Pride. That due to my having some scruples in which I only fucked someone willing to be around afterward.

I'd volunteered to help raise money at a beer booth, for an organization formerly known as Black and White Men Together, now known as Men of All Colors Together. The change of title sounding less provocative. I wouldn't be drinking the beer, obviously, yet the volunteering gave me a purpose to be there. Even as much as my wandering eyes and horny mind left me ogling and wanting to do such, that would have me in trouble with my recovery and doing damage to my nurtured inner pride. I noticed that day, I was actually experiencing the pride of living and being gay in the city where gay folks held power.

So, there I am hawking keg beer with the other guys when who just so happens to come up to our booth. Tom Ammiano; the openly gay member of the San Francisco City Council. At the time I thought, "I've been out for two decades," yet, standing right in front of me was an actual city council member 'queening it up'. "Honey... I remember this old drag queen once…showed me the correct way…to put on perfume." Ammiano said out; "You spray it in the air... and…walk into it." as he performed an exaggerated demonstration of the method.

I could remember back times when I had viewed such a display of femininity by a man as embarrassing, shameful, even. The times had changed. Times changed just as I witnessed changes in myself in my body and soul.

911/ It's Not the End (2001)

Some people seem to fall asleep better with a light on. Other folks find that having the television on helps put them to sleep. For moi, my sleep remedy is the radio, specifically allowing my eyelids to get heavy listening to NPR (National Public Radio) playing in the background. Somewhere along I picked up sleeping with the radio on. In my dope fiend days neighbors in the single-room hotels where I lived could have been able to tell whether I was high and tweeked. If music was playing out the radio, I was high. If I had the channel tuned to NPR, I was coming down, sleeping or sober and between dope hits. My rationale, denial, in those days went sorta like this; when high I wanted to escape from the world and its goings on therefore: music. On the other hand, when not high, I needed to be extra connected to the world outside, really know what's going on. In reality either mind state, I was still just mostly locked in a desolate flea-bag room by myself.

The morning of September 11th, I awoke bleary- eyed with the morning's headlines sinking in and out of my wakefulness while still half dreaming, as would oftentimes occur upon my waking. When I finally had fully awakened and opened my eyes and could see the sun shining outside my windows, I heard announcers telling news of jetliners having crashed and exploded into the World Trade Center Towers in New York. Listening more closely, intently, I needed to make sure if that's exactly what I'd heard. "Someone had attacked...mighty America!" is what my head said to me. Like when you see someone shout, "Yes!" using his fist and raised arm pushed out in the air as a physical exclamation point. That's my initial, first, reaction to the terrorist attack on 9/11/01.

Knowing all the history that I knew. Having had an unofficial education on when we go to war reading Studs Terkel's "The Good War" for example. News and programs on NPR, and more significantly my own official, real lived experience of a Black male descendant of slaves in this America led me to have reasons for feeling such a social and emotional reaction to that day's horrific events (My apologetic pardon to anyone who may have lost a loved one in the attack that day).

In hindsight, I had been more hopeful about the results from the nation having been attacked. Maybe, just maybe, the United States of America, the most powerful entity in the world, could and would finally learn a valuable lesson. A nation so powerful we had exercised power all over the planet to the benefit and will of our own needs. Much destruction, violence, death and harm had been committed in pursuit of all that power. Wishful thinking that morning, like a powerful bully we as a nation might have been getting some of our just due.

Coming to my senses that morning, another actual scenario became clearer to me. The attack also could be just the excuse needed for the powers that be to take over and pursue more greed, harm, destruction and death. Death of more innocents, as had happened that morning. All this rambled across my mind within that first half hour of hearing the news.

Now, I'm wide awake listening intently to all the details happening back in the East, that early Tuesday morning. All the same I'm mindful of my English 1A course due to begin at 10am at San Francisco City College. I was in the process of finishing up taking general education courses as well as studying more courses in photography.

Driving off in my black Nissan to head across the Bay Bridge into the City. Normally heavy traffic westbound on the bridge ran noticeably lighter than usual that morning. Finally, I arrived on the City College campus to discover all classes had been cancelled for the day.

I was not scheduled to be at work until 1 in the afternoon. So, I phoned Drew, now my mentor and patron of my education. I asked him if I could drop by if he wasn't doing anything too important. After driving over to Pacific Heights, I walked to his apartment building and went up the elevator. Drew greeted me in the apartment. I walked down the hall to take a seat at the kitchen table as I could see the television in the living room continuing to show wall to wall coverage of the morning's disastrous events.

Many years had since passed with Drew and I sitting across from one another at that same dining table, in his 60's style open- design kitchen, discussing politics, history, life and the general state of the world as we saw it. Yet, on that day the events going out in the bigger world upstaged any of our discussions in real time. The attack with all its worldly implications proved of no surprise to either of our viewpoints and understanding.

We both sat talking, pondering the happenings of that day. Either one of us could have summed up with a metaphorical shaking of our heads. Almost like, "we could have told you…something like this was bound to happen." Bill, Drew's roommate, a husky, gay man in his fifties came in and entered the kitchen 'roundtable'. Bill usually carried a standard mainstream opinion i.e.; White and conservative, except when matters concerned gays. One real shock that morning was hearing even Bill viewing the terror attack with resignation, as opposed to what I expected from him, just pure astonishment. Many folks I came to observe, in those beginning days, post '9/11', seemed to acknowledge some sense of inevitability and resignation. Classmates at City College very much felt so. General attitudes would come to be most in opposition to that point of view.

I arrived in time for work at the Havurah Youth Center afterschool program, a position that I had grown to rather enjoy. This particular school year our campus site was located in the naturally beautiful, yet often foggy and chilly Presidio. My hours were flexible with my school schedule and for the first time in my working life, I belonged to a union that provided health care and vacation pay. The one drawback though, I had to find other fulltime work during the summer months.

Curiously, just the day before, Monday, September 10, as the staff waited outside for our students to be picked up by parents, police had arrived to give us notice and warning that an escapee from San Quentin prison was on the loose and suspected of possibly being within the vicinity. Obviously, this information would be best kept from our students, for their safety and calm. The Presidio, a former Civil War Era military base that had since been decommissioned and turned over to the National Park Service. Our program rented space in one of the facilities there as we had construction at our main site. The vast mostly natural acres of the Presidio, was located on the San Francisco side of the Golden Gate Bridge, less than about 10 miles from the infamous prison in Marin County to the north.

That Monday, the first day of the workweek, had been scheduled for staff CPR and first aid training. A kind of foreboding atmosphere set in, after the children had all gone and we all settled back inside our building, doors checked and locked. Jeff, our office manager, a Japanese American father with a receding hairline, who always seemed to possess a kinda been there done it attitude, before the training started, went by our kitchen area. He grabbed a large butcher knife and came back to the training room with a baseball bat as well. I recall myself thinking at the time Jeff had maybe taken a noble, chivalrous stance arming himself, since most of our staff were women. More realistically, my thinking based on my minor criminal background, I more figured an escaped prisoner, on the run, was going to be looking for money or valuables and most likely have a gun himself. In other words, an escapee, desperate, with nothing to lose and might be provoked to violence by the sight of one of us wielding a big ass butcher knife and bat. Besides, what the hell was a knife, or bat going to stop against a gun and bullets. The scene was an absurd indication of middle-class, White folk's panic, even if most of us were Jewish.

I'd witness similar absurdity and panic the next day at work, the afternoon of the attack. By the time I had arrived at work, noon Pacific time, the twin World Trade Towers in New York had, by then, fallen and totally collapsed.

Some of the students in our afterschool program had arrived though most did not show up at all that day. I along with a few other staff members thought it best to forgo the usual schedule and just walk the kids over to the nearby playground the kids were familiar with. The kids took off and played that hazy afternoon under light fog and green foliage, as they usually did even though I could tell a few of them sensed something was different, something out of the ordinary. An hour or two later, after we'd given them extra outdoor play time, we returned back to the center. Keeping the rest of the day low-key we waited till parents arrived.

On returning to the building I witnessed, what I felt, the most surreal aspect of that day. A few other co-workers, Jeff included, who had remained in the building that afternoon found a portable TV to watch the news reporting on the after effects of the attack. I happened to glance in and out of our offices where the television was on, showing video footage of the towers collapsing. That destruction had already happened and taken place even before we'd taken the children to the playground. Hours later, that same exact footage of the collapsing skyscraper towers still played over and over across the TV screen. My colleagues by then had viewed the same scenes repeatedly. "What purpose did it serve…seeing that over…and over again?" I thought, "reconfirming maybe…what they knew…happened?"

Returning home to Oakland at the end of the day, somewhat mentally exhausted, I turned on the television to find that the news coverage of the attack continued on wall to wall on every station I turned the channel to. I lacked having cable so there were no other choices. Finally, in frustration I just completely turned the television off. Not until two days later did I turn the TV back on. Thank God, eventually, there was programming something besides 'terror attacks' worth watching.

By Thursday the American government in all its power, finally, knew exactly whom, what and where the source of the terrorist attack had originated. Maybe it's just me that finds it seemingly strange that only just three days before the enormous United States military-intelligence apparatus had not a clue about the largest attack ever to come to the nation. Then, just two days later knew everything. "Not all appeared…to add up…not completely,". What I am thinking.

A fellow friend in recovery had promised to let me borrow their Pentax 35mm camera for my photography studies. On Sunday, now five days after the attacks, I drove over and arrived at my friend's apartment. We greeted one another and I walked in, I noticed in the living room, on the television, she had the channel turned to watching more of that same similar footage of the jetliners crashing, and of the collapsing towers. That was too much. Man this is just insane…overkill. What else can be gained… over and over…nearly a week later?" I kept my mouth closed as my friend's eyeballs were transfixed to what was on the screen. Still, the absurdity left me astounded.

By then I regularly attended services at my church. I'd since made the decision that my recovery from drugs encompassed my mind and body as well as my spirit. In pursuit of those aims at a year clean I became a member of a gym and a church.

Following the lead of another addict friend, I took advantage of living in the Bay Area, and discovered the mostly Black and gay congregation of The City of Refuge Church. Many others of church hailed from more Southern, mostly Baptist backgrounds. Time and patience was required of me to acclimate, cause I'd been raised, religiously, starkly different in a mostly White, Midwestern, Lutheran church upbringing of my youth.

In the beginning, it always seemed off to me as if God was speaking directly to certain members in church, resulting in demonstrations of physical praise behavior. "Why did God always...be speaking... to the same members... week after week?" I'd wonder. I grew, in time, accustomed to their 'physical' praise worship. A few years later, I myself had even became overtaken by the 'Spirit" and 'fell out' myself.

The weeks right after the September 11th attacks, attendance in the folding chair pews at the City of Refuge filled up and reached almost overcapacity. Our small almost storefront congregation always welcomed new believers of the Lord and responded positively to growth. Still, I didn't think some of those recent arrivals to the 'Refuge', as we referred to our unique sanctuary, were fully aware of the difference of our spiritual element. I recall the words of the associate pastor's sermon one of those Sunday's, "Poor black folks.... especially children and young folks... face terrorism... in the 'hood' everyday! And there is still no outcry... for them!"

"Amen!...Amen." We responded.

As anyone paying attention could have seen, America, the Great, was then headed down the path on the road to war. Alas, all the new believers and the overcapacity at the City of Refuge turned out to be short lived. The weeks after Halloween, the chairs emptied back to our normal attendance. We carried on in faith, jump'in, shouting and praising and making it 'though', as we always had.

Fear, real or induced, in those days, appeared to make people behave in bizarre ways. As if God would have not have noticed that many folk's new found religious fervor carried a shelf life of about a month. "People really!"

About the Author

Juan T Salter, Born and grew up in Fort Wayne , Indiana. Came of age in Los Angeles and San Francisco, California. Earned BA in History, at Tennessee State University. Resides had taught, works, writes and is a community activist in Memphis Tennessee.

CPSIA information can be obtained
at www.ICGtesting.com
Printed in the USA
LVHW020158100723
751976LV00008B/131

9 798890 750730